A Research Agenda for Urban Tourism

Elgar Research Agendas outline the future of research in a given area. Leading scholars are given the space to explore their subject in provocative ways, and map out the potential directions of travel. They are relevant but also visionary.

Forward-looking and innovative, Elgar Research Agendas are an essential resource for PhD students, scholars and anybody who wants to be at the forefront of research.

Titles in the series include:

A Research Agenda for Political Demography
Edited by Jennifer D. Sciubba

A Research Agenda for Heritage Planning
Perspectives from Europe
Edited by Eva Stegmeijer and Loes Veldpaus

A Research Agenda for Workplace Stress and Wellbeing
Edited by E. Kevin Kelloway and Sir Cary Cooper

A Research Agenda for Social Innovation
Edited by Jürgen Howaldt Christoph Kaletka and Antonius Schröder

A Research Agenda for Multi-level Governance
Edited by Arthur Benz, Jörg Broschek and Markus Lederer

A Research Agenda for Space Policy
Edited by Kai-Uwe Schrogl, Christina Giannopapa and Ntorina Antoni

A Research Agenda for Event Impacts
Edited by Nicholas Wise and Kelly Maguire

A Research Agenda for Urban Tourism
Edited by Jan van der Borg

A Research Agenda for Urban Tourism

Edited by

JAN VAN DER BORG

Division of Geography and Tourism, KU Leuven, Belgium, and Department of Economics, University Ca'Foscari Venice, Italy

Elgar Research Agendas

Edward Elgar
PUBLISHING

Cheltenham, UK • Northampton, MA, USA

Published by
Edward Elgar Publishing Limited
The Lypiatts
15 Lansdown Road
Cheltenham
Glos GL50 2JA
UK

Edward Elgar Publishing, Inc.
William Pratt House
9 Dewey Court
Northampton
Massachusetts 01060
USA

Paperback edition 2023

A catalogue record for this book
is available from the British Library

Library of Congress Control Number: 2021949009

This book is available electronically in the **Elgar**online
Geography, Planning and Tourism subject collection
http://dx.doi.org/10.4337/9781789907407

MIX
Paper | Supporting
responsible forestry
FSC® C013604

ISBN 978 1 78990 739 1 (cased)
ISBN 978 1 78990 740 7 (eBook)
ISBN 978 1 0353 1686 1 (paperback)

Printed and bound by CPI Group (UK) Ltd, Croydon, CR0 4YY

Contents

Contributors

Dario Bertocchi is a research fellow and adjunct professor of E-tourism at Ca' Foscari University, Venice, Italy. His work focuses on understanding how tourists behave in destinations using data analysis obtained through social networks or by tracking cell phones. He lives and works in Venice where he is confronted by the impact of tourism on a daily basis.

Nicola Camatti is an assistant professor at Ca' Foscari University, Venice. He has a PhD in Urban and Regional Economics from the University of Ferrara, Italy. He has directed numerous national and international projects with tourism and urban and regional development as their central themes.

Ben Derudder is professor of City Science at KU Leuven's Public Governance Institute and associate director of the Globalization and World Cities (GaWC) research network. His main research interests are the conceptualization, analysis and governance of world city networks and the (putative) emergence of polycentric urban regions. His research has been published in leading academic journals and he co-authored the second edition of *World City Network: A Global Urban Analysis* (2016, Routledge, with Peter Taylor). He is one of the editors of Regional Studies.

Xiang Feng received her master's degree in Urban Management from the School of Economics at Erasmus University Rotterdam and her PhD in Social Science from Erasmus University Rotterdam. Xiang Feng is associate professor in the School of Environmental and Geographically Sciences, Shanghai Normal University. She is also director of the Sino-European Comparative Urban Research Center. In 2014 she was named a "National Young Tourism Expert" by the China National Tourism Administration. Her research interests include smart tourism destinations, tourism big data dashboard development and urban tourism development plans.

Tigran Haas is a tenured associate professor of Urban Planning and Urban Design at the Royal Institute of Technology, Stockholm, Sweden. He is also director of the graduate programme in Urbanism and director of the Center for the Future of Places (CFP) at the ABE School of the Royal Institute of Technology, Stockholm.

Ephrem Assefa Haile received his PhD in Business Administration from Istanbul University, Turkey. He was dean of the College of Business & Economics of Aksum University, Ethiopia and is currently affiliated with the School of Business at St. Mary's University. His research interests include tourism and hospitality innovation, tourism marketing and sustainable tourism development.

Anna-Paula Jonsson collaborates with the Stockholm Royal Institute of Technology where she works on the question how urban planning processes can impact the development of urban tourism and social sustainability in cities. She is also a project leader, part of the Urban City Research team at the Ax:son Johnson Foundation in Stockholm. Her research focuses on the inter-sections between planning, tourism, the changing character of public spaces and urban democracy.

Jeroen Klijs is a professor at Breda University of Applied Science (BUAS), the Netherlands, in Social Impacts of Tourism. He studied Regional and Urban Economics at Erasmus University Rotterdam where he worked for several years. In 2016 he obtained his PhD with research on the economic impacts of tourism at BUAS and Wageningen University and Research (WUR). He has worked on a broad range of research projects dealing with the societal impacts of tourism.

Ko Koens is professor of New Urban Tourism at Inholland University of Applied Sciences. He also works at Breda University of Applied Sciences and is a research fellow at the University of Johannesburg. His main interests are sustainable urban tourism, overtourism, destination design and governance, city hospitality and slum tourism. Ko co-authored the UNWTO Report "Overtourism? Understanding and managing urban tourism growth beyond perceptions".

Ante Mandić is an assistant professor in the Faculty of Economics, Business and Tourism at the University of Split, Croatia. His research focuses on sustainable tourism, destination management and nature-based tourism. He has wide experience in tourism-related projects and has worked as an expert on EU-funded projects, regional and local tourism destination strategies and integrated coastal zone management plans. He is a member of the IUCN World Commission on Protected Areas (WCPA), the Tourism and Protected Areas Specialist Group (TAPAS Group) and the Europarc Federation.

Bart Neuts has a PhD in Tourism and his research focuses on tourism planning and development, cultural heritage management, business strategy and innovation, and management of tourism organizations, among other things. He has worked at a policy-supporting research centre, the destination management organization of Flanders, and at universities in Belgium and abroad. His main area of expertise is in tourism externalities and sustainable development, specifically focused on social carrying capacity studies in urban environments.

Vincent Nijs is a tourism research manager in the Research and Strategy Department of VISITFLANDERS (Belgium). He acquired his master's in Sport & Leisure Sciences at KU Leuven and completed an MBA in Tourism Management at Modul University Vienna (Austria). Vincent has been working in tourism research for more than 20 years, with research projects focusing on the impact of tourism on people and places, and was part of the team that developed the new tourism vision in Flanders/Belgium.

Shirley Nieuwland works for the Department of Arts & Culture Studies at Erasmus University Rotterdam (Netherlands) within the Erasmus Initiative "Vital Cities and Citizens", where she focuses on exploring sustainable urban tourism development. Her research interest lies at the intersection of urban geography and tourism studies. It includes research topics such as new urban tourism, the sharing economy, the creative city, gentrification and just and sustainable cities.

Lidija Petrić is currently employed as a full professor in the Faculty of Economics, Business and Tourism at the University of Split, Croatia. Her scientific work focuses on different topics related to tourism economics, tourist destination management/planning and cultural tourism management. In many of the tourism-related projects she has directed she has endeavoured to employ theoretical knowledge in solving different practical problems. Lidija Petrić is also a member of the Croatian branch of the European Regional Scientists Association (ERSA), the Scientific Committee for Tourism at the Croatian Academy of Sciences and Arts and the Croatian Commission for UNESCO.

Greg Richards is professor of Placemaking and Events at the Breda University of Applied Sciences and professor of Leisure Studies at Tilburg University in the Netherlands. He is known for his research on cultural tourism and for coining the term "creative tourism".

Antonio Paolo Russo is professor in the Department of Geography at Universitat Rovira i Virgili, Tarragona, Spain. He is coordinator of the PhD programme in Tourism and Leisure in the Faculty of Tourism and Geography, and lectures in undergraduate and postgraduate courses on Destination

Management and Urban Tourism. Antonio Paolo Russo is the author of more than 50 publications in academic journals and books on research topics that range from tourism studies to cultural and urban geography. He is a member of the GRATET research group and coordinates the Special Interest Group "Space Place Mobilities in Tourism" in ATLAS.

Alessandro Scarnato studied architecture in Florence and holds a PhD from the Polytechnic University of Barcelona, where he teaches History of Architecture. He has won the competition for the reform of the largest historic square in Italy, in Prato, and has coordinated the rehabilitation project of the former Macson factory as the new headquarters of IED Barcelona. His practice is mainly focused on interior, architectural and urban refurbishment in historic contexts. His articles on heritage, tourism and gentrification have been published in scientific journals. His book *Barcelona Supermodel* won the City of Barcelona Award in 2016. He's a founding member of the think-tank "Post-Car City" and a consultant in conservation and promotion of local heritage.

Elsa Soro is post-doc researcher at the University of Turin (Italy) and is currently the Sharing Cities Taskforce – Barcelona Lead at Universitat Oberta de Catalunya (Spain). Her latest publications include "Online dating on the move. At the intersection of sexuality, tourism and space representation" in *Sex in Tourism. Exploring the Light and the Dark* (edited by Neil Carr and Liza Berdychevsky, forthcoming); and "Playful tours: digital marketing and the gamification of tourism", Semiotics and Digital Marketing, *Lexia* (2020).

Costas Spirou is the provost and vice-president for academic affairs at Georgia College & State University, where he is a professor of sociology and public administration. His most recent books include *Anchoring Innovation Districts: The Entrepreneurial University and Urban Change* (Johns Hopkins University Press, 2021), *Building the City of Spectacle: Mayor Richard M. Daley and the Remaking of Chicago* (with D. Judd) (Cornell University Press, 2016) and *Urban Tourism and Urban Change: Cities in a Global Economy* (Routledge, 2011).

Getaneh Addis Tessema is a researcher at the Division of Geography and Tourism at the KU Leuven, Belgium, and lecturer in tourism management at Bahir Dar University. His research interests include urban tourism, geotourism and sustainable tourism development.

Jan van der Borg teaches Tourism Economics and Management at KU Leuven, Belgium, and Ca' Foscari University, Venice, Italy, where he coordinates the master's degree courses in Tourism. He has a PhD in Economics from the Erasmus University Rotterdam. Building further on his dissertation on tourism development in Venice, the conditions to achieve sustainable urban tourism have been a recurring theme in most of his publications.

Egbert van der Zee works as an assistant professor in the Department of Human Geography and Planning at Utrecht University. He is involved in teaching and research related to urban tourism. His main research interests are the changing impact of tourism on cities, applying qualitative methodologies and spatial analysis of (big) data using Geographical Information Systems to study current issues such as the sharing economy and the interrelation of social media and tourism.

Ewout Versloot works as a strategist for the Netherlands Board of Tourism and Conventions (NBTC). With a background in (Urban) Sociology, he focuses on the impact visitors can have on societies, both positive and negative. He advises governments and DMOs on how they can proactively use tourism to address local challenges and maximize visitors' positive impact. Making sure tourism can again truly become a force for good is one of the main drivers behind his work at the NBTC.

Karl Wöber is full professor and founding president of Modul University Vienna. He has also been chairman of the Austrian Private University Conference since 2012 and a member of the Board of the European Union of Private Higher Education since 2018. He obtained his PhD from the Vienna University of Economics and Business. His main research contributions are in the fields of decision support systems, strategic marketing and strategic planning, particularly in the field of city tourism. Karl Wöber is the elected president of the International Academy for the study of Tourism, and has been a technical advisor to European Cities Marketing and the European Travel Commission for more than 20 years.

Bozana Zekan is an assistant professor in the Department of Tourism and Service Management at MODUL University Vienna. She holds a Master of Science degree in Service Management from the Rochester Institute of Technology, Rochester, New York, and a Doctorate in Social and Economic Sciences from the Vienna University of Economics and Business, Vienna, Austria. Bozana is a member of the International Association for Tourism Economics (IATE), European Cities Marketing (ECM), Knowledge Group Research & Statistics and the ECM Benchmarking Group. She is also a member of the editorial board of Tourism Economics. Her research interests are mainly within the field of destination management.

Sebastian Zenker holds a PhD of the University of Hamburg and is a professor (with special responsibilities) in marketing and tourism at the Copenhagen Business School, Denmark. His current research interests are mainly: crises, overtourism, place brand management with the special target group of residents and tourists. His work has been presented at various international conferences and published as book chapters and as articles in peer-reviewed journals, for example *Tourism Management, Environment and Planning A, International Journal of Research in Marketing*, and in *Psychological Science*.

Hai Xia Zhou is a Junior Researcher in the School of Environmental and Geographical Sciences, Shanghai Normal University.

Preface

When I finished my studies in Urban and Regional Economics at Erasmus University Rotterdam, Leo van den Berg, who had been one of my teachers there, asked me whether I was interested in conducting a research programme that would allow me to combine my passion for tourism research with his interest in urban development. He asked me to look into the role tourism might be playing in urban development processes and find an adequate case study. When I proposed taking Venice as a case for my research, a city where in 1986 tourism already appeared to be so overwhelmingly present that I guessed measuring the effects of it on the urban economy and Venetian society would probably be easy, Leo van den Berg put me into contact with Paolo Costa. At that time, Paolo was teaching regional economics and tourism economics at the University Ca' Foscari of Venice and it was he who introduced me to all the peculiarities of Venice and its tourism. It was under their guidance, and I will always be grateful to them for this, that my interest in urban tourism quickly grew and thus became a fundamental ingredient of my research activities until this very day.

Working in Rotterdam and Venice at the same time helped me a lot in understanding the importance of tourism for urban development. In the second half of the 1980s Rotterdam was a city with plenty of economic and social problems. Traditional economic activities were relocating or just disappearing, unemployment levels were unacceptably high and social problems were becoming unbearable. Obviously, the city's economic base needed a boost, and, also looking at the revitalization strategies of American cities such as Baltimore and Boston, tourism development was seen as an important means of achieving that goal.

With this firmly in mind, it was impossible for me to just blame tourism for everything bad that happened and still happens to Venice. It is rather easy to prove that tourism and its explosive growth until 2020 has had a devastating effect on the city of Venice. And indeed, many colleagues were so struck by what mass tourism had been doing to Venice that they unanimously condemned it and made Venice the icon of what is now called overtourism.

International, comparative research projects on tourism in heritage cities similar to Venice (see for example Costa et al., 1996) and tourism in cities very similar to Rotterdam (see for instance Van den Berg et al., 1995) led me to a different research objective: the study of the conditions under with tourism shapes urban development in a positive way and those that turn tourism into something destructive. Obviously, an adequate tourism policy is a fundamental precondition in this respect. The search for the set of conditions that guarantees *sustainable* and – a condition linked to the COVID-19 pandemic in which the world currently finds itself – *safe* development of urban tourism forms the backbone of this *Research Agenda for Urban Tourism*.

Since I started looking into the nature of urban tourism, I have had the opportunity to exchange ideas with many colleagues.

Some of them are the authors with whom I wrote the articles, book chapters and books on urban tourism that have been published over the past 30 years. Leo van den Berg and Paolo Costa have already been mentioned, but I also learned a lot from many other co-authors. Then there were the many colleagues who were themselves working on urban development issues and became sparring partners at the international meetings where I was invited to present my work. I owe a lot to the lively discussions I had on these occasions with, to mention just a few of them, Jan van der Straaten, Harry Coccosis, Paul Cheshire, Charles Leven, John Glasson, Martin Robinson, Greg Ashworth, Lidija Petric, Arrigo Cipriano and Chris Law. Moreover, I am very grateful to all the people, too many to mention, who have worked with me in Rotterdam, Venice and more recently at the KU Leuven.

A Research Agenda for Urban Tourism has therefore become a perfect occasion for bringing together a number of "pivots" of urban tourism research, such as Greg Richards, Karl Wöber and Antonio Paolo Russo, and a lot of the young, brilliant researchers I have met over the years and who share this passion for urban tourism with me and have found their place in the list of authors that can be found elsewhere. An overview of their names and short curricula can be found below. Eventually, David Graham proofread the chapters and put everything intelligently together.

I would like to use this occasion to thank all the authors who actually not only prepared the chapters I asked them for on time, but also agreed to have these papers peer reviewed by their fellow authors. The kind invitation to edit

A Research Agenda for Urban Tourism by Edward Elgar Publishers made this all possible and I am truly grateful for this. Last but not least, I would like to thank my wife Vesna and my kids Suzanne, Mia and Leo for providing me with their essential and unconditional support.

Jan van der Borg
Venice, May 2021

References

Costa, P., Gotti, G., and Van der Borg, J. (1996) Tourism in European heritage cities. *Annals of Tourism Research*, 23(2), 306–321.

Van den Berg, L., Van der Borg, J., and Van der Meer, J. (1995) *Urban Tourism.* Aldershot: Ashgate.

1 Introduction to *A Research Agenda for Urban Tourism*

Jan van der Borg

Introduction

Cities not only host more than 50% of the world's population and are supposed to generate 80% of all economic growth, they have also become important hubs for global tourism development. Although the attention of travellers on cities as the destinations of their travels already stems from the days of the Grand Tour, most cities missed the explosive growth of tourism demand that started immediately after World War II in the richest parts of the United States and of Europe. In those days, holidays were rather long, concentrated in the summer months, and the main form of transportation was the car. Furthermore, an almost absolute form of relaxation was what holidaymakers were looking for in the 1950s, 1960s and 1970s. As a consequence, the so-called *sun, sea & sand* types of holidays were booming. Cities such as London and Paris were important exceptions, as they were not only visited by business travellers, but, possessing unique museums and monuments, also attracted cultural tourists

This started to change dramatically in the 1980s. Holidays became shorter, yet more frequent. The interest in a stronger cultural component in holidays was rising exponentially and tourists became much more active during their vacations. Moreover, air transportation gradually became more accessible, also thanks to the deregulation of aviation from the second half of the 1980s on, which led to the emergence and spectacularly growing importance of low-cost airlines. This mix of changes in tourism demand and supply resulted in an increasing interest in the so-called city-trip, a short, often secondary, holiday with a city as its destination.

At the same time, many cities started to understand that the continuously expanding tourism market offered them concrete possibilities for enlarging their economic bases, which had been eroding rapidly because of deindustrialization. They were now systematically pursuing an active tourism development policy to make themselves more attractive for tourists and inhabitants alike, to develop a strong brand that reflects their uniqueness, and to offer additional tourism products, such as events, and invest in the infrastructure that helps tourists easily arrive from and return to their homes. Urban tourism thus grew to become one of the most important segments of the global tourism market.

Urban tourism became such an important segment of the tourism market that academics started studying the phenomenon intensively. Ashworth and Voogd (1990), Law (1993), Van den Berg et al. (1995), and Judd and Fainstein (1999) are some examples of the first publications that contributed to a better understanding of the opportunities that tourism offers for the economic and social development of (especially former industrial) cities. In these publications, the predominant discourse was that of urban tourism as a form of tourism able to help urban economies and societies compensate for the loss of the manufacturing sector, which was relocating to more peripheral areas in search of cheap land or to countries where labour was still cheap, in order to retain competitiveness in a global economy; and that of the population, which was moving towards the suburbs and secondary cities in search of bigger homes and amenities that could not be found in the cities, such as a cleaner environment, and where they could start reinventing themselves (see for example Van den Berg, 1987, and Cheshire and Hay, 1989). Cities such as Baltimore, Lyon, Manchester and Rotterdam were examples for other industrial and port cities to use tourism as a means of diversifying their economic base.

A much less popular discourse in those early studies on urban tourism was concentrating on what can be seen as the flipside of the success of cities in developing themselves as attractions able to capture an important share of the tourism market: overtourism. By simply applying the business model of mass tourism to urban tourism, it has become clear that tourism in cities has the potential to become a, sometimes devastating, force that could suffocate urban economies and societies. This particular discourse can already be found in studies by, among others, Van der Borg (1991), Troitiño Vinuesa (1995), and Costa et al. (1996). Most of the cases studied in this context were smaller South-European heritage cities such as Granada, Coimbra and Venice, which served as case studies to analyse the mechanisms that led to diseconomies and discontent among inhabitants.

The idea that some form of sustainable development path exists for urban destinations as much as for destinations that depend on natural wealth has now finally become mainstream in research. It seems, though, that the current and rather trendy academic attention on overtourism in cities such as Amsterdam, Barcelona, Berlin, Bruges, Dubrovnik, Prague and Venice (see for instance UNWTO, 2019) is dominating the urban research agenda, while the original idea that tourism might still be a powerful engine of economic and social development for cities tends to be neglected.

The principal objective of this book on urban tourism is, precisely by trying to find a balance between the two discourses mentioned above, to construct a research agenda that reflects the recent insights that have been gathered on the phenomenon of urban tourism and that helps cities turn tourism into a force that makes them smarter, more sustainable and safer. Twenty-six experts on urban tourism development from all over the world have contributed to this book. They will be sharing their insights in, and experience with, urban tourism from different perspectives. They embrace different disciplines and analyse urban tourism within different geographical contexts. The book thus provides readers with an overview of the issues that have proven to be essential for research in the debate on the role tourism can play in urban development processes. The resulting discourse will be relevant to discussing tourism in cities over the coming years, both from an academic and a policy point of view.

In this first chapter of the book, the phenomenon of sustainable urban tourism is defined, the principal issues regarding urban tourism discussed and the challenges that stem from these issues for research and policy presented. Particular attention will be paid to the link between theory and practice, a common theme in most of the book's chapters. It will furthermore be argued that the COVID-19 crisis – a crisis without precedents in terms of scale and duration – has had a tremendous impact on tourism, changing it permanently, but not fundamentally modifying the principles underlying urban tourism development.

The different chapters of the book are also introduced here and put in context. In the closing chapter, a tentative research agenda for urban tourism will be constructed, very much based on the various suggestions made by the authors who were invited to contribute.

This research agenda not only encapsulates their visions and their views on important research themes, but also includes suggestions for urban tourism policies. It is thus hoped that this book will not only help academics focus their investigations into urban tourism, but also help policymakers implement innovative development policies that transform tourism into an important generator of urban development.

Sustainable urban tourism development: definitions, concepts and some theory

According to the UNWTO, Urban Tourism is

> a type of tourism activity which takes place in an urban space with its inherent attributes characterized by non-agricultural based economy such as administration, manufacturing, trade and services and by being nodal points of transport. Urban/ city destinations offer a broad and heterogeneous range of cultural, architectural, technological, social and natural experiences and products for leisure and business.

This definition, which is rather broad, underlines the complex and diverse nature of urban tourism and links the phenomenon very much to the urban character of the context in which it takes place. In other words, tourism that is staged in urban space is by definition urban tourism, whatever the attractions that urban tourists use during their stay in these places and whatever the motivation that brought them there. Obviously, this territorial approach has some major limitations. It regards visitors to Rio de Janeiro who visit the city to surf, for example, as urban tourists, and makes it difficult to clearly classify excursionism – visiting a city whilst staying in the countryside, as a growing number of urban tourists seem to be doing – as urban tourism. A distinct advantage of this definition, however, is that it may facilitate the generation of straightforward statistics on urban tourism worldwide. More attention will be paid to this issue in the first, conceptual part of the book.

In order to develop a framework in which the evidence gathered through the various cases can be placed and where the innovation in urban tourism research can be presented, it is important to define the concept of sustainable tourism development.

The tourism offer of a destination is complex and composite (see for example Jansen-Verbeke, 1998, and Van den Berg et al., 1995). One of the central components of this offer are the primary tourism products, the attractions a destination offers and that have attracted the people who have decided to visit it. For any particular urban space or city, examples of primary tourism products are monuments, museums, parks and events. These primary products have two important characteristics. The first is that they are unique as they are embedded in a specific socio-economic and environmental context, as all place products tend to be. This uniqueness makes these tourism assets hardly reproducible and therefore extremely scarce. Furthermore, primary tourism products tend to be either public goods or at least goods for which it is hard to exclude specific types of users. This combination of extreme scarcity and non-excludability leads to an important challenge: how can we make the best touristic use of these assets? Moreover, and this sometimes becomes an additional complication, the content of the primary tourism products is increasingly less material and more immaterial. In fact, it is often the experience that is generated by visiting a destination that determines its overall quality and, hence, competitiveness (see for instance Pine and Gilmore, 1999, and Richards and Wilson, 2006).

Therefore, the market for primary tourism products does not provide entrepreneurs, visitors and policymakers with a clear and correct price signal embodying the extreme scarcity and the user value that characterize most of them. This absence of a market price, the traditional instrument economists refer to in the case of questions regarding the optimal allocation of assets, and the insistence on a policy that leaves much of tourism development to sheer improvisation, automatically drives destinations to either underutilizing or overutilizing their tourism assets.

In the first case, entrepreneurs, policymakers and tourists do not fully capture the potential value that the assets might have. Entrepreneurs will abstain from investing in tourism development, policymakers will not spend public money on the upgrading of these assets, and tourists will not easily put that destination on their bucket lists. The destination will miss an important part of the obvious opportunities for cultural and socioeconomic development that tourism development might generate. Hence, tourism fails to appropriately sustain the urban destination.

In the case of overutilization, the potential global demand for the destination is infinite, while the tourists only partly perceive how scarce the tourism offer of the destination is. Some tourism firms will use the rent that derives from being located in or close to that destination to premium price the services they offer without sufficiently paying for their privileged position. In addition, many visitors, especially excursionists, do not pay the full price in terms of both the collective costs their visit generates and the user value they derive from the visit. Both the firms and the visitors are freeriding on the destination's assets. This often makes the collective costs much higher than the collective benefits, and again it is easy to argue that this type of tourism development, e.g. overtourism, is not a sustainable form of tourism.

These two rather extreme forms of non-optimal use or of unsustainable tourism development are very widespread. This book will present real-world cases of both under- and overtourism in cities, and important examples of research methods that might be used and of concrete policies that might be implemented to make urban tourism development more sustainable. Getting the balance right between appreciating and protecting the tourism assets in urban destinations is far from easy. The aim of this book is to help academics, entrepreneurs and policymakers make urban tourism development more sustainable, fighting the underutilization of urban tourism assets on one hand and over utilization on the other much more effectively.

The structure and contents of this book

The central part of this book is divided into three different parts.

In the first and rather conceptual part, the market for urban tourism is described, the major tendencies in urban tourism development illustrated and quantified, and the most recent developments of research into the phenomenon are presented.

In the second chapter, by Bozana Zekan and Karl Wöber, with the title "Urban tourism: major trends", the principal characteristics of the market for urban tourism and the major market trends are analysed. They argue that tourism has become a comprehensive, highly diversified and strategically important industry that plays a strong driving role in national economic and social development. Cities have become the key nodes of world tourism development. This chapter focuses on the development of tourism in more than 100 cities in Europe and expounds upon the main trends of world tourism development as reported by European Cities Marketing and the World Tourism Cities Federation, the two leading organizations in the field of city tourism. Regarding the pattern of global tourism development, the share of the European tourism market keeps shrinking, tourism in American cities remains stable and tourism in Asia-Pacific region cities continues to expand under the influence of globalization. For Europe, the underlying causes of the changing nature of city tourism in Europe will be analysed in more detail. Greater global mobility, the information boom and increased knowledge-sharing between people in recent years have facilitated the development of urban structures and led to higher levels of city tourism demand. City tourism services are probably the most highly standardized products compared with other tourism offers and since they became available through online booking engines they are everywhere readily available for purchase. Mainly because of their easy access, cities are ideal destinations for short breaks, which perfectly match general trends in travel behaviour. Many cities have also become more attractive. Cities have constantly developed new products, upgraded their quality of services and enhanced their competitiveness. The "smart city" paradigm, which has been adopted by many cities in Europe, represents an environment where innovation and technology supplement a city's activities and services in order to provide benefits to its residents and visitors. Finally, the growth of meetings and shopping as important travel motivators has substantially supported the growth of city tourism.

The third chapter, "Urban tourism as a special type of cultural tourism", by Greg Richards, poses the question of the extent to which urban tourism can indeed be considered a special form of cultural tourism. Greg observes that Cultural Tourism has always been a key sector of the global tourism market, accounting for just under 40% of all international travel. Creative tourism is a more recent and smaller niche that has emerged both as a development of cultural tourism, and in opposition to the emergence of "mass cultural tourism". Creative tourism demand is driven by consumers who want more active and participative cultural experiences in which they can use and develop their own creativity. Creative tourism is therefore fed by the general growth in cultural tourism, but at the same time it caters to people who want more out of their cultural experiences. Europe is a well-established market for cultural tourism and cities of art in particular play an important role in all this. European travellers are increasingly interested in discovering new destinations – especially if these offer authentic activities that teach them about local culture. This makes cultural tourism a promising sector for destinations that offer flexible cultural components to appeal to both motivated and incidental cultural tourists. According to Richards, any research agenda for urban tourism should therefore be very closely linked to that for cultural tourism.

The second part of the book focuses on urban tourism in an international comparative perspective. Cases from different continents are discussed and the consequences for the analysis of urban tourism are gathered with an international, comparative perspective. The various cases discussed here are highly representative of the two principal paradigms introduced in the section above: the Croatian art cities with a focus on Split, the Flemish art cities with particular attention on Bruges, Belgium, and Venice, Italy on one hand, and Rotterdam, the Netherlands, and Stockholm, Sweden, on the other. Moreover, in this part some light will also be shone on urban tourism development and policies in African, American and Chinese cities.

In Chapter 4, entitled "Smart governance in historic urban destinations - evidence from Croatia", Lidija Petrić and Ante Mandić explore several essential smart governance elements and strategies, and the outcomes of an analysis on a sample of Croatian historic cities, both coastal and continental, with specific attention on Split, the city known for Diocletian's palace. Additionally, the focus has been made on historic cities facing specific problems related to tourism development as well as to some ecological and institutional issues, considered as contextual factors influencing smart governance. Building on an extensive literature review, an extended version of the smart governance model inaugurated by Bolivar and Meijer (2015) was suggested, to encompass the contextual factors and end with some policy measure proposals. A mixed-method approach was employed to address these issues. First, an importance–performance analysis was conducted to evaluate the cities' mayors or deputies' perception of each of the proposed smart governance categories. Subsequently, a qualitative analysis exploring the cities' strategic documents was conducted to determine progress on smart governance and their development orientation. The research results demonstrate the existence of an importance–performance gap between smart governance categories, with a few of them proving to yield significant impact.

Located in the heart of Europe, the Flemish art cities of Bruges, Antwerp, Ghent, Mechelen and Leuven have seen a steady increase in tourist arrivals and day visitors. Although absolute numbers remain below those of more popular neighbouring urban destinations, such as Amsterdam, Paris or London, growing concern has been raised about the community impact of mass tourism. In Chapter 5, "Understanding community perception through resident attitude studies: a segmentation analysis in Flemish art cities", Bart Neuts and Vincent Nijs argue that, considering the importance of local culture and lifestyle in the attractiveness of the tourism product, a healthy co-integration between resident and visitor is a prerequisite for a successful and liveable destination. In 2017, an initiative was launched to measure resident attitudes towards tourism development through a Weberian lens of formal and substantive rationality. The Resident Empowerment through Tourism Scale (RETS), as originally developed by Boley et al. (2014), was applied within the five main tourism cities, a process that was repeated in 2019. The results allow for generalization, contextualization and a limited time trend. The chapter uses confirmatory factor analysis and structural equation modelling to understand the relations between contributors and distractors for tourism support and provide insight for government actors.

In Chapter 6, Dario Bertocchi and Nicola Camatti present the case of Venice, an iconic example of overtourism, by illustrating the latest developments before the COVID-19 crisis struck its tourism system. In "Tourism in Venice: mapping overtourism and exploring solutions", the authors open their analysis stating that Venice is a tourist destination par excellence. The huge number of visitors that this unique city has hosted each year until 2020 is therefore not surprising: the most recent official estimate for 2019 is about 28 million visitors, of which only 5 million are residential tourists who, with an average duration of 2.32 nights, generate almost 12 million overnight stays in registered tourist accommodation. There have been some vicissitudes in visits to Venice in the last few decades, but, excluding 2020, the trend has definitely always been on the rise. As Bertocchi et al. (2020) have shown, it became evident that the number of people visiting Venice has become incompatible with the needs of the city as a whole and that drastic solutions to curb tourism demand are needed. Paradoxically, notwithstanding the drop in the number of visitors, the social distancing measures put in place to fight the COVID-19 pandemic have made the need to decide which share of public space and of public facilities will be dedicated to tourism only more urgent, since they reduce the tourist carrying capacity by almost two-thirds. The chapter starts by presenting updated official statistics on the Venetian tourism phenomenon, with the aim of bringing out the lesson, not yet sufficiently learned by many destinations, that the development of tourism is bound to be inevitably unsustainable if left to improvisation and short-term private interests. Reference will be made to the rather basic concept of the tragedy of the commons, to Butler's theory of the life cycle and to the model of the carrying capacity of a destination. Subsequently, a description will be provided of the development of tourism in Venice since the early 1990s, against the background of global and local changes in the tourism market. In this section the main symptoms of the "Venetianization" of a city of art will be listed and discussed, and several solutions presented to the problems of excessive tourist pressure that Venice has been experiencing for too long and their possible repeatability in other cities trampled by mass cultural tourism.

The seventh chapter, by Shirley Nieuwland, Ewout Versloot and Egbert van der Zee, entitled "The Rotterdam way: a new take on urban tourism management", looks at tourism development in Rotterdam, the Netherlands, a city better known for its port and petrochemical industry than its tourism. While most of the popular urban tourism destinations of North-Western Europe are famed for their historic city centres, a growing number of destinations, such as Rotterdam, challenge the conditionality of having a picturesque historic centre to be a successful tourist destination. Nevertheless, the city of Rotterdam is currently the second largest urban tourism destination in the Netherlands, considering nights spent by tourists. The city is witnessing a transformation from an industrial port city hosting a limited number of visitors into a visitor city with a port. As in other former industrial and port cities, the visitor economy has played an important part in the transformation of Rotterdam. While just decades ago the city was mostly shunned, present day visitors appreciate the diverse and iconic architecture, as well as the creative and vibrant atmosphere in which the roughness and edginess actually seem to work in Rotterdam's favour. In fact, Rotterdam made it into Lonely Planet's "best in travel list" of 2016 and is famed in the international media as a "must-visit destination". The city of Rotterdam and its inhabitants are happy that finally their beloved city is acknowledged by others, but at the same time there is a general consensus that the city should not be taken over by tourists. While recent developments make Rotterdam an interesting case study for illustrating how post-industrial cities can reinvent themselves on the basis of the visitor economy and simultaneously become an attractive place to live, work and visit, the present case study aims to go one step further. An important issue here is the question of how to integrate tourism proactively in the diverse landscape of contemporary urban issues and challenges and make tourism work for the city. Empowering marginal socio-economic groups, creating opportunities for local businesses and start-ups, protecting parts of the city from excessive tourism pressure, as well as dealing with the consequences of climate change are among these challenges. The rapid growth in overnight stays during the last six years has become an important reason to create a proactive (tourism) development strategy in which the challenges posed by growing tourism in combination with the broader challenges the city faces are properly addressed.

The starting point for the eighth chapter, "New urban tourism developments in a heritage area. A case study of Skeppsholmsviken 6 in Stockholm, Sweden" by Anna-Paula Jonsson and Tigran Haas, is the observation that the visitor industry is considered a primary industry for Swedish economic growth today. While the industry can bring many benefits in terms of employment opportunities and economic growth, not to mention the cultural benefits of travel, it can also bring unintended consequences of a less desirable nature for a city's population. Commonly cited reasons for increased levels of residents' aggravation vis-à-vis tourism are excessive crowds and decreased access to public space, traffic and infrastructure congestion, increased rental and living costs, crowding out of residential neighbourhoods, commercial transformations geared to target tourists rather than residents and extreme seasonality or peak intensity of visiting crowds. In Stockholm, official strategies and goals for the industry have traditionally focused mainly on quantitative aspects such as the number of arriving visitors, the number of jobs in the visiting sector or the total revenue from the same. Additionally, planners have not considered the visiting industry in their decision making to any considerable extent. It is perhaps for this reason that public strategy documents for Stockholm's tourism development have categorically framed the idea of more visitors as something leading to exclusively positive outcomes. However, as visitor numbers in Stockholm grow, and localized signs of residential discontent start appearing, it is not clear whether the large body of literature on overtourism will be able to influence the Stockholm municipality to consider a socially sustainable strategy for the visiting industry in time. By studying an ongoing conflict related to a development project that would attract more visitors to an already over-exploited area in central Stockholm, this chapter aims to explore whether there is potential in the current institutional planning environment to consider, develop and implement a socially sustainable tourist strategy when the visitor industry impacts public space. The chapter employs complementary strategies of qualitative enquiry through interviews, discourse analysis and desk-based research.

In "Urban tourism development in Africa: evidence from Addis Ababa, Ethiopia", Getaneh Addis Tessema and Ephrem Assefa Haile offer some new insights into urban tourism development in the African city of Addis Ababa. They argue that cities in general and African cities in particular offer the distinct advantage of allowing diverse tourist attractions to be visited in a specific location without the need to travel long distances. Historical sites, vibrant cultural practices, sports facilities, shopping centres and business tourism facilities, along with easy access and places to stay, have made cities the centre of attraction. Although urban tourism research dates back to the 1960s, it has disproportionately received meagre attention from scholars. The extant literature on urban tourism is quite fragmented and limited to major cities of the world. There is thus a dearth of urban tourism research in developing countries such as Ethiopia. Addis Ababa is endowed with rich cultural, historical and religious treasures and serves as a gateway for international visitors to the country. It is also the third diplomatic city after New York and Geneva, providing immense opportunity for business tourism. Notwithstanding its untapped potential, the city is not sufficiently benefiting from the tourism sector. There is a dire need for a systematic examination of urban tourism development in the city from a sustainability point of view, taking into account the multi-sectoral, multi-disciplinary and dynamic nature of tourism. The main aim of this chapter is therefore to discuss the nature, challenges and opportunities of urban tourism development in Addis Ababa. To this end, data were gathered using semi-structured interviews and document analysis (from policy documents, statistical bulletins, research outputs, etc.). They were then triangulated to verify the validity of information gathered from different sources, and subsequently coded, described and analysed thematically. The results of the study will serve as input for policymakers, researchers and practitioners in tourism and other fields such as urban planning.

In Chapter 10, titled "Municipal advancement and tourism policy in the United States: economic development and urban restructuring", Costas Spirou gives an overview of urban tourism development in the United States of

America. Tourism in North America has emerged as a central aspect of cultural policy as cities endeavour to strengthen their existing identities and/or recast new images within the pursuit of economic expansion opportunities. While today urban economic development efforts include culture, leisure and tourism as significant parts of a broader planning mix, urban tourism and related cultural forms did not fit into the schemes for growth during the 1950s and 1960s. Post-World War II urban restructuring was accompanied by a shift from a production-oriented to a consumption-oriented economy. It was within the midst of intercity competition that municipal governments aimed to construct the city of leisure, by the use of various strategies including robust private–public partnerships. The infrastructure that followed in the form of sports stadiums, conventions centres, arenas, museums, parks, concert halls and waterfront developments produced amenities that not only attracted tourists, but also reshaped the socioeconomic realities of residents. In the process, many downtowns were reformulated, giving rise to new neighbourhoods, often causing gentrification and displacement. The chapter examines cities within this broader context while also recognizing the associated complexities and dynamic nature of tourism as a driver of economic advancement and of cultural change.

Xiang Feng, Ben Derudder and Hai Xia Zhou in "Comparative study on Chinese cities as international tourism destinations" (Chapter 11) discuss the challenges that Chinese cities have recently been facing whilst striving for tourism development. The international connectivity of Chinese cities has received much policy and scholarly attention in recent years, and this research agenda is here extended by exploring the position of China's major cities as international tourism hubs. Drawing on the definition of tourism internationalization by Gorcheva (2011), their approach complements earlier research that primarily focused on understanding international tourism activities, market segmentation or spatial distributions by comparing 50 major Chinese cities' "product destination internationalization" with their "business destination internationalization". The results show that, in general, there are broad parallels between both dimensions, with a limited number of cities such as Shanghai, Guangzhou, Beijing or Shenzhen acting as key international tourism hubs in both respects. In spite of these general parallels, there are also some notable differences between some cities, which can be traced back to the often-specific tourism and city development strategies of local governments. They discuss how this study can be used as the starting point for further comparative studies on tourism internationalization in other geographical contexts.

In the third part of the book, particular attention will be paid to the urban tourism development policies that are designed to make tourism development more effective, more sustainable and safer. The idea here is to start building a toolkit of policies that seem to work, a toolkit for which innovative research forms a strong basis.

The first chapter of this particular part, Chapter 12 of the book, entitled "Overtourism: identifying the underlying causes and tensions in European tourism destinations" is a contribution by Ko Koens and Jeroen Klijs in which they analyse sustainable tourism development policies in cities. They argue that, after a period of relatively uninhibited growth, the discussions on over-tourism have again brought to the forefront the inherent tensions that exist between the ways in which local stakeholders use the city compared with tourists and day visitors. The debate on overtourism is rapidly evolving but has so far remained focused largely on single city case studies. This chapter combines research in over 25 European city destinations to provide a thorough overview of the impacts of tourism on city destinations and the extent to which they are seen to lead to overtourism. In doing so, it seeks to highlight developments within and outside tourism that have exacerbated the pressure of tourism on destinations in recent years, and which have led to the relatively sudden outburst of overtourism. It is argued that to fully understand the impacts of tourism and achieve sustainable urban development, it is necessary to better delineate the different ways in which tourism interacts with local develop-ments, be it economically, socially or environmentally. In doing so, the 12th chapter seeks to provide some more clarity on the often implicit and vague notion of sustainable urban tourism.

In their chapter "Is another tourism possible? Shifting discourses in Barcelona's tourism politics", Antonio Paolo Russo, Elsa Soro and Alessandro Scarnato start from the recent experiences gathered on Barcelona, Spain, to argue that urban regimes rely critically on consensus and the normative power of discourse. Tourism is no exception: the development and transformation of contemporary destinations must be understood in relation to discourses of competitiveness, economic buoyancy and community pride, which became hegemonic in society throughout the twentieth century. Yet we are facing a new stage in which pro-tourism discourses face increasing contestation by wider sectors of society. Critical analysis excavating the nexus between discourse, urban regimes and policy developments in the field of tourism is poorly represented in the literature, and especially so when it comes to ana-lysing shifts in the social perception of tourism. The city of Barcelona offers an exceptional context in this respect. The chapter deploys a socio-semiotics approach to reveal how discourses on tourism have been given salience by the media during the last four municipal electoral periods in the Catalan capital. The positioning of different urban actors around them and the way in which certain political forces have aligned to shifting sensibilities allow the furthering and eventually the breakdown of a pro-tourism development regime to be unpacked. In more general terms, this analysis may hint at "overtourism" bringing forward political change in cities.

In Chapter 14, Sebastian Zenker pays attention to why and how pandemics might have an impact on a research agenda for urban tourism and urban tourism policy. Unquestionable, the current COVID-19 pandemic is one of the most impactful events of the 21st century and has also had tremendous effects on urban tourism. Since urban tourism is often associated with crowding and multiple shorter trips, it is especially vulnerable to health risks and is thus logically less attractive than more social-distance-friendly rural or coastal tourism. In addition, will the crisis probably have long-term effects on urban travel demand, travel supply and urban tourism policies? Therefore, the pandemic questions some of our basic assumptions, theories and our existing tourism research as such. Obviously, not all of our knowledge and foci will become obsolete, but this chapter questions some of our assumptions and discusses the evolving realities of the urban landscape in this regard. Thereby, the chapter in question gives some guidance to how a future post-pandemic urban tourism research agenda might look.

In Chapter 15, "Towards *A Research Agenda for Urban Tourism*: a synthesis", Jan van der Borg presents a plausible trajectory for future research into forms of urban tourism. This trajectory reflects the idea that tourism development might indeed be a powerful engine of development for cities and urban areas in general and art cities in particular if the right balance is struck between appreciating and promoting urban tourism, on the one hand, and conservation of the immaterial and material cultural goods uniquely possessed by them on the other. Only by embracing a development strategy that leads to sustainable urban tourism will the assets that form the foundations of urban tourism development be used optimally, and the various stakeholders – that is the local population, local entrepreneurs and visitors themselves – truly benefit from the opportunities that tourism offers them, also in the longer run. The current COVID-19 pandemic, which has disrupted tourism probably more than any other sector in the world particularly in the bigger cities, ought to be used to accelerate the process towards a new business model for urban tourism, in which quality is preferred to quality and the local population and local entrepreneurs play a central role. In this perspective, a new research agenda may very well lay a sound foundation for constructing such a new business model and supporting an innovative and visionary development strategy for urban tourism that might help eliminate a number of recurrent paradoxes in research and in policy that Ashworth and Page have written about in 2011.

References

Ashworth, G. and Page, S. (2011) Urban tourism research: recent progress and current paradoxes, *Tourism Management*, 32(1), 1–15.

Ashworth, G. and Voogd, H. (1990) *Selling the City*, Belhaven Press, London.

Bertocchi, D., Camatti, N., Giove, S. and van der Borg, J. (2020) Venice and overtourism: simulating sustainable development scenarios through a tourism carrying capacity model, *Sustainability*, 12(2), 512.

Boley, B., McGehee, N.G., Perdue, R. and Long, P. (2014) Empowerment and resident attitudes toward tourism: strengthening the theoretical foundation through a Weberian lens, *Annals of Tourism Research*, 49, 33–50.

Bolivar, M.P.R. and Meijer, A.J. (2016) Smart governance: using a literature review and empirical analysis to build a research model, *Social Science Computer Review*, 34(6), 673–692.

Cheshire, P.C. and Hay, D.G. (1989) *Urban Problems in Western Europe, an Economic Analysis*, Taylor & Francis, London.

Costa, P., Gotti, G. and Van der Borg, J. (1996) Tourism in European heritage cities, *Annals of Tourism Research*, 23(2), 306–321.

Gorcheva, T. (2011) Measuring the internationalization of Bulgarian tourism and of 'Bulgaria' business destination, *Tourism & Management Studies*, 1(1), 80–90.

Jansen-Verbeke, M. (1998) Tourismification of historical cities, *Annals of Tourism Research*, 25(3), 739–742.

Judd, D. and Fainstein, S. (1999) *The Tourist City*, Yale University Press, New Haven.

Law, C. (1993) *Urban Tourism*, Mansell, London.

Pine, N.J. and Gilmore, J.H. (1999) *The Experience Economy*, Harvard Business Press, Harvard.

Richards, G. and Wilson, J. (2006) Developing creativity in tourist experiences: a solution to the serial reproduction of culture? *Tourism Management*, 27(6), 1209–1223.

Troitiño Vinuesa, M.A. (1995) *El Turismo en las Ciudades Históricas*, Poliginas, 49–66.

UNWTO (2019) *Overtourism? Understanding and Managing Urban Tourism Growth beyond Perceptions*, Volume 2: Case Studies. UNWTO, Madrid.

Van den Berg, L. (1987) *Urban Systems in a Dynamic Society*, Gower, Aldershot.

Van den Berg, L., Van der Borg, J. and Van der Meer, J. (1995) *Urban Tourism*, Ashgate, Aldershot.

Van der Borg, J. (1991) *Tourism and Urban Development*, Thesis Publishers, Amsterdam.

PART I

Urban tourism development

PART I

Urban tourism development

2   Urban tourism: major trends

Bozana Zekan and Karl Wöber

The main tourism trends and their impact on city tourism

Tourism is frequently the engine for the rejuvenation of cities through improving infrastructure, creating a skilled labour force, stimulating local business entrepreneurship, developing public–private partnerships, attracting other industries and services, and creating local amenities and recreation facilities (Huning and Novy, 2006). This regeneration process not only builds a quality visitor experience but also safeguards and improves the quality of life for the local community.

What makes city tourism distinct from other types of tourism is that cities have a high density of diverse cultural offerings in a relatively small area, attracting different types of tourists (Bock, 2015). Most attractions and amenities tourists are drawn to have not been primarily intended for tourists, which often leads to an interaction between tourists and citizens. In addition, cities have the potential to serve as incubators of innovation and technology (Mulas et al., 2016). But, despite the significant positioning of city tourism in the global marketplace, it is still a relatively immature field of interdisciplinary study and practical expertise. A clear understanding of city tourism and the measurement of its social, cultural, environmental and economic impacts can only progress by intensifying communication and cooperation between researchers and professionals (Mazanec and Wöber, 2009). Improving tourism data on a sub-national level, such as cities, will galvanize local action, reinforce the performance of policies and programmes, and drive investment and development projects (OECD, 2014a, 2014b).

All cities in the world are heavily impacted by the paradigm changes in production and consumption patterns and the mobility of capital, people and goods that have taken place in recent decades. It is estimated that by 2050, 70% of the world's population will be living in cities and cities will contribute over 30 trillion US dollars to the world economy by 2025 (United Nations, 2018). As the proportion of the population taking several trips per year continues to grow, there is a tendency towards an increasing number of shorter holidays rather than just one main holiday per year (Dunne et al., 2010; IPK, 2018; Tripadvisor, 2017). In some countries, city trips have already overtaken sun and beach holidays as the most popular type of holidays (Bock, 2015).

Greater global mobility, the information boom and increased knowledge-sharing between people in recent years have facilitated the development of urban structures and led to higher levels of city tourism demand. Compared with other tourism offers, city tourism is probably the most highly standardized product and since it became available through online booking engines it is everywhere readily available for purchase. Mainly because of their easy access, cities are ideal destinations for short breaks that perfectly match general trends in travel behaviour. Many cities have also become more attractive. Cities have constantly developed new products, upgraded their quality of services and enhanced their competitiveness. The "smart city" paradigm, which has been adopted by many cities in Europe, represents an environment where innovation and technology supplement a city's activities and services in order to provide benefits to its residents and visitors (Kunzmann, 2014). Finally, the growth of meetings and shopping as important travel motivators has substantially supported the development of city tourism.

The impact of globalization on tourism development in cities creates opportunities and challenges for this industry in the world. The global tourism economy has grown, and still grows, dramatically. There are many forces that shape the development of tourism in cities.

Without doubt, the global population is aging and, as a result, the silver-haired tourists, a significant tourist segment with specific desires and needs in terms of customization, service consumption, security and desired products is emerging (Vigolo, 2017). In addition, generation Y, also known as Millennials, and generation Z, known as the iGen, are likewise appearing as an influence. These are technology driven age groups, very different from one another, with specific needs for communication, consumption and tourist experience. According to Horwath HTL (2015), the increase in average income and the fall in levels of absolute poverty are resulting in a growing middle class. The middle-class population is expected to increase further, up to 5 billion by 2030, where most of the growth is expected from Asia. Their characteristics will continue to have a growing importance for and impact on the tourism sector.

New destinations are also emerging, sought after by the above segments. The emerging markets overtake developed markets in terms of international arrivals. According to Euromonitor International (2017), among the top 20 global destinations by international overnight visitors, 13 cities are in the Middle East and Asia, and many of them experienced significant growth during the last 10 years.

The technological revolution in the hotel industry is a game changer and is already dominating how the industry operates. It has greatly facilitated city tourism due to the increasing availability and penetration of internet-based services during the travel cycle. The proliferation of mobile technologies increasingly empowers consumers, in particular Millennials and iGen consumers, to create and plan further components of their trip. The speed of change is hard to keep up with and the complexity is tough to manage. Tourism is already dominated by digital channels, but the growth of social and mobile technology has caused a real revolution, which will continue disrupting the entire sector on an ongoing basis.

The technological shift in tourism is often coined as "smart tourism". Smart tourism cities take the opportunities caused by the digitalization of tourism to integrate culture and technology in new and innovative ways. Especially in Asia, but also in Europe, smart tourism has become a buzzword and a strategic priority for tourism development. Destinations such as China, Spain and South Korea are investing heavily in smart tourism-related projects. Suddenly everything becomes "smart", which raises definitional questions and calls for better conceptualization of the phenomenon. In particular, the question remains as to how smart tourism differs from the concept of technology driven tourism, for many years referred to as "e-tourism". Discussions of smart tourism have also been highly optimistic and often utopian. Robots in maintenance, guest service and room service, holograms with avatars replacing receptionists, interactive displays, smartphones and gadgets in rooms, however, are slowly becoming a reality for the hotel industry (Horwath HTL, 2015). Some parts of this technological future are expected to become an integrated part of the entire tourism sector. A critical look at challenges associated with smart tourism and smart tourism services is of course warranted.

As travel experiences become increasingly dominated by the technological changes, a change in travel behaviour can be observed in cities around the world. Loyalty within the industry, as we know it today, will decline. There will be no more complicated sign-up forms in order to collect and redeem points, and no more risk of losing them over time. Physical loyalty cards are vanishing and loyalty programmes will be integrated into the whole tourism value chain, starting from planning, accommodation, activities, experiences in a hotel and/ or in a destination, all the way to the aftermath of a travel experience. Due to the simplicity and interrelated characteristics of the product, it is very likely that this development will commence in cities. The digitalization of loyalty programmes will require an alignment of business processes and will lead to a higher level of collaboration between stakeholders.

A growing number of cities are emerging as creative forces based on the collective strength of their creative industries. Cities are focusing on the creative industries for driving new business, spurring innovation, attracting talent and investment and, in the process, accelerating urban development and improving the overall quality of life for their residents. The creative industries play a major role in generating, transforming and disseminating knowledge. They comprise many different sectors, including advertising, animation, architecture, design, film, gaming, gastronomy, music, performing arts, software and interactive games, and television and radio. They aid urban and rural regeneration and have the potential to stimulate economic growth and job creation (OECD, 2014a, 2014b).

A global urbanization trend is believed to have reinforced the trend towards city tourism as people living in cities are more likely to visit other cities (UNWTO, 2014). In addition, the increase of low cost carriers has had a major impact on the popularity of city trips, mainly due to the fact that they have made flights more affordable to the masses, but also because they have expanded and improved flight networks, thus offering more city destination options and making them more accessible from a greater number of departure points than in the past, considerably decreasing travel times. As a consequence, this development has made a wide range of cities available to tourists at lower costs (Dunne et al., 2010).

City tourism trends in Europe

European Cities Marketing (ECM) publishes its benchmarking report on an annual basis. Arguably, this report is the most elaborate overview of the trends in European city tourism, which demonstrates "... compelling evidence of the economic significance of contemporary urban tourism" (ECM, 2019a, p. III). In 2019, the fifteenth edition included 119 cities all over Europe and gave an insight into bednights along with the top nine source market developments, bed capacity, occupancy, tourism density and a comparison of city tourism to national tourism (ECM, 2019a). In more detail, a notable finding of the fifteenth edition of the report was an average growth rate of 4.2% in total bednights in 2018, which, in spite of the increase, differs substantially from 7.4% in 2017. On one hand, the high growth rate in 2017 was caused by the tourism rebound after the terrorist attacks across Europe only a year before. Yet, on the other hand, the lower growth rate in 2018 could be attributed to the general economic and political uncertainties and, thus, the impact of the decrease in bednights in London, which is repeatedly a top performing European city and a resilient tourist destination. Moreover, this average growth rate was not seen as alarming, but rather as "a healthy development" given that the focus of the ECM cities is nowadays placed on "a sustainable visitor economy" (ECM, 2019a, p. III). To support this statement, in October 2019 the Vienna Tourist Board, one of the ECM members, also presented its Vienna Visitor Economy Strategy 2025 (Vienna Tourist Board, 2019).

Furthermore, the top 15 performers in 2018 in terms of total number of bednights were as follows: London, Paris, Berlin, Rome, Istanbul, Madrid, Barcelona, Prague, Vienna, Munich, Amsterdam, Stockholm, Hamburg, Milan and Lisbon, as shown in Figure 2.1. These volumes are underestimated as they refer only to the official tourism statistics, which oftentimes do not include the volumes of Airbnb providers. This, however, is changing as an increasing number of governments have found ways to include the Airbnb statistics in their tourism statistics.

London was the only city that recorded a decrease (–8.7%), whereas Istanbul (20.3%), Munich (9.3%), and Paris (9.2%) showed substantial growth compared with 2017. Along the same lines, the analysis of the main source markets (listed in continuation according to their 2018 ranking in bednights: the US, Germany, UK, France, Spain, Italy, China, Russia and Japan) showed an increase from 1.8% (Germany) to 9.6% (China), whereas the only two markets that recorded a decrease in comparison to 2017 were France (–0.6%) and Russia (–0.1%), as illustrated in Figure 2.2 (ECM, 2019a). This type of analysis informs where tomorrow's visitors will come from.

Other notable findings include: (1) city tourism bednights again exceeding national tourism bednights, yet in 2018 only by marginal 0.1%; (2) the average growth rate of bed capacity recording an increase of 3.2% between 2017 and 2018; (3) Barcelona (78.7%), Rome (76.9%), and Helsinki (75.9%) being the top performers regarding bed occupancy in 2018, whereas the benchmark average was 51.2%; and (4) Opatija leading the rankings with the highest tourism density, irrespective of the season (ECM, 2019a).

Overall, the conclusion was derived that the main factors impacting tourism demand in European cities are "… increasing volatility within the past years, political and economic crisis, airline connectivity, and economic recovery in the long-haul markets" (ECM, 2019a, p. 5). Among other European cities,

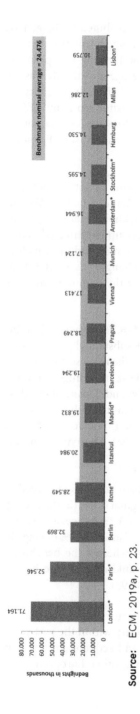

Source: ECM, 2019a, p. 23.

Figure 2.1   Top 15 cities total bednights 2018

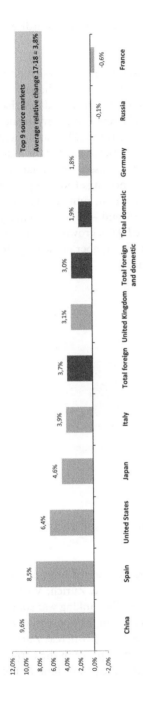

Source: ECM, 2019a, p. 47.

Figure 2.2   The main source markets 2017–2018

Istanbul was singled out with respect to airline connectivity (ForwardKeys, 2019a), which can also explain the aforementioned growth of 20.3%.

Given that various types of meetings (e.g., congresses, seminars, conferences, conventions, etc.) are important travel motivators that impact the overall tourism demand, it is necessary to highlight some of the latest findings that relate to the meetings industry in European cities. The report that investigates the meeting statistics in European cities is also published by ECM on an annual basis, yet up to now on a much smaller scale (2018: 41 cities at most in the individual analyses) when compared with the previously discussed benchmarking report. It has been noted that the total number of meetings (non-corporate and corporate combined) grew by 2.9% in 2018, whereas the number of participants and participant days both decreased, by –3.5% and –5.5%, respectively (ECM, 2019b). The non-corporate segment achieved 9.6% growth in contrast to –0.2% experienced by the corporate segment for the number of meetings in 2018 (ECM, 2019b). This is further detailed in Figure 2.3.

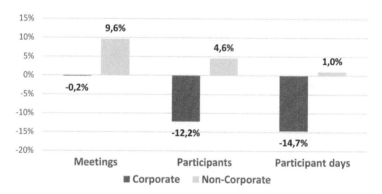

Source: ECM, 2019b, p. 31.

Figure 2.3   Development of corporate and non-corporate segments 2017–2018

Looking into the top performers in relation to the number of meetings for both corporate and non-corporate segments in 2018 alone, Zurich, Vienna, Geneva, Tallinn and Amsterdam were in the top five. The ranking was somewhat different when focusing on the number of meetings in the non-corporate segment only (Zurich, Tallinn, Bern, Vienna and Bolzano), whereas Zurich, Geneva, Antwerp, Amsterdam and Vienna were in the top five in the corporate segment. As demonstrated, some city destinations kept excelling at the number of meetings hosted, irrespective of the segment (ECM, 2019b). It does not come as a surprise that the European cities are therefore described as "... popular destinations for meetings" (ECM, 2019b, p. 3). On a relative note, European cities are also attractive shopping destinations. For instance, a study by ForwardKeys (2019b) revealed that Helsinki, Budapest and Bucharest were the top destination cities by growth in flight bookings over the 2019 Christmas period, with Christmas being described as a "peak time" for shops.

As is evident, city tourism continues to grow. Yet, this (primarily economic) growth may also come at a price, if it is not planned properly. Önder and Zekan (2020) asked whether urban tourism development in Europe is actually a double-edged sword for cities, given that the social and environmental dimensions may be at odds with the economic one, hence possibly resulting in "overtourism". This is a buzzword that has entered our vocabulary over the last few years, attracted a lot of media attention and is often associated with many European cities such as Amsterdam, Dubrovnik, Barcelona and Venice, to name a few. After the review of the status quo in the latter three cities, Önder and Zekan (2020) provided their recommendations to cities for tackling overtourism, in line with demarketing, rules and regulations, and technological solutions. In reality, overtourism should not be described as a trend within the city tourism domain; it is more appropriate to portray it as a consequence of a major growth in trends such as the aforementioned air connectivity, sharing economy (Airbnb accommodation in particular), cruise ships, etc.

A number of other research initiatives on how to deal with overtourism have been conducted over the past few years. Some noteworthy examples with hands-on suggestions include: (1) a study conducted by the Roland Berger (2018) consultancy that recommended seven measures, four proactive (short-, mid-, and long-term) and three reactive, along with a four-step plan for success that city destinations can adopt in their (anticipated) fight against overtourism; and (2) an elaborate research with 11 strategies and 68 measures for understanding and managing urban tourism growth with 19 case studies by the World Tourism Organization (UNWTO) and their collaborators: the Centre of Expertise Leisure, Tourism & Hospitality (CELTH), Breda University of Applied Sciences and the European Tourism Futures Institute (ETFI) of NHL Stenden University of Applied Sciences (UNWTO, 2018, 2019). Fifteen case studies that were analysed in their research are European cities; hence, this fact alone demonstrates the importance and actuality of this topic within European city tourism. Moreover, it was also emphasized that "successful city tourism goes hand in hand with measures to avoid overtourism", which calls for the involvement of all stakeholders and planning, thus paving the way towards "smart" rather than "mass tourism" (Roland Berger, 2018, p. 14).

Taking the above into account, it is also becoming evident that the role of city destination management organizations (DMOs) is of the utmost importance in successfully facing the challenges not only of today's tourism, but also those that the tourism of tomorrow may bring. The same goes for the need for DMOs to reinvent themselves in order to be able to address those challenges. With this goal in mind, ECM has issued its 2019–2022 strategy document, titled "Tomorrow today", intended to help the DMOs of European cities reposition themselves towards "a more sustainable tomorrow" paradigm (ECM, 2019c). The focus of their strategy is placed fully on sustainable growth and the visitor economy, which are to influence cities in a positive way. Taking no action is not an option for ECM as the risk is too high; "the risk, if we do nothing, is that tourism tomorrow will be to cities and locals what cigarettes are to personal health or plastic to the ocean – criticized and blamed for deteriorating quality of urban life" (ECM, 2019c, p. 5). Thus, European city tourism is to continue growing, but the absolute must is that it grows in a sustainable way.

Summary and outlook

City tourism has been growing for decades and will continue to grow when the COVID-19 pandemic has disappeared, alongside world prosperity and well-being. However, the industry will continue experiencing seismic changes that will increasingly create major challenges for traditional service suppliers, but also create opportunities for those who are vital enough to change and adjust. The COVID-19 pandemic is just one of these disruptive changes. Many tourist service providers have already changed their business model in order to meet the challenges arising from the trends in city tourism. Destinations, travel companies, hotel companies and other players along the value chain will have to be constantly on their toes, tracking future developments of these trends. It will continue to be a story of those who were prepared, those who were not and those who managed to adopt the change quickly enough.

As city tourism will return to growth, it is imperative to ensure its sustainability. Environmental and social conflicts are the most significant threats for the future development of city tourism (Önder et al., 2017; Lenzen et al., 2018). Crowding, congestion, waiting times in front of tourism attractions, emissions and pollution caused by mass tourism in cities are the negative effects of uncontrolled tourism development in urban regions. A major threat is that "quality tourists" avoid crowded places; the remaining tourists are masses of low-quality visitors who are more a stress than a benefit to a community. There are also obvious conflicts when cities, for instance, claim that they want to become smart or green and at the same time launch strategies to increase air transportation by building additional runways and attracting additional airlines. The relationship between tourists and citizens, or the tourism industry and the local community, is frequently compromised for environmental or social reasons. These conflicts are also the most challenging problems since they require a radical change in our current way of thinking and of planning tourism in cities.

Economic, social and environmental pillars have to be balanced in order to ensure the long-term sustainable development of tourism. Sustainable tourism development requires the participation of all relevant stakeholders as well as strong political leadership. For this purpose, city tourism worldwide needs a strong advocate for tourism affairs. Professional networks in tourism, such as European Cities Marketing (ECM) or the World Tourism Cities Federation (WTCF), must go beyond marketing and branding; they must emphasize responsible tourism, and they need to strengthen the link between the various stakeholders in their cities.

References

Bock, K. (2015). The changing nature of city tourism and its possible implications for the future of cities, *European Journal of Futures Research*, 3 (20), pp. 1–8.

Dunne, G., Flanagan, S., and Buckley, J. (2010). Towards an understanding of international city break travel, *International Journal of Travel Research*, 12, pp. 409–417.

ECM (2019a). *The European Cities Marketing Benchmarking Report*, 15th edn, ECM: Dijon.   https://www.europeancitiesmarketing.com/ecm-benchmarking-report/ [Accessed 28 September 2019].

ECM (2019b). *The European Cities Marketing Meetings Statistics Report*, 9th edn, ECM: Dijon.   https://www.europeancitiesmarketing.com/ecm-meetings-statistics-report/ [Accessed 18 January 2020].

ECM (2019c). *Tomorrow Today*, ECM: Dijon. http://www.europeancitiesmarketing .com/tomorrow-today/ [Accessed 18 January 2020].

Euromonitor International (2017). *Top 100 City Destinations Ranking – Published 2017*. https://blog.euromonitor.com/euromonitor-internationals-top-city-destinations -ranking/ [Accessed 28 September 2019].

ForwardKeys (2019a). *As European Cities Increase Air Connectivity, Istanbul Stands Out*.   https://forwardkeys.com/european-cities-increase-air-connectivity-istanbul -stands-out/ [Accessed 18 January 2020].

ForwardKeys (2019b). *Helsinki, Budapest and Bucharest Are Top of the Shops for Christmas*.   https://forwardkeys.com/helsinki-budapest-and-bucharest-are-top-of -the-shops-for-christmas/ [Accessed 18 January 2020].

Horwath HTL (2015). *Tourism Megatrends*. http://corporate.cms-horwathhtl.com/ wp-content/uploads/sites/2/2015/12/Tourism-Mega-Trends4.pdf [Accessed 28 September 2019].

Huning, S., and Novy, J. (2006). *Tourism as an Engine of Neighborhood Regeneration? Some Remarks Towards a Better Understanding of Urban Tourism beyond the 'Beaten Path'*, CMS Working Paper Series | No. 006-2006.

IPK International (2018). *ITB World Travel Trends Report 2018/19*. https://www.ipkinternational.com/en/10-news-and-events/109-itb-world-travel-trends-report-2018-2019-released [Accessed 28 September 2019].

Kunzmann, K.R. (2014). *Smart Cities: A New Paradigm of Urban Development*. https://www.academia.edu/9530213/SMART_CITIES_A_NEW_PARADIGM_OF_URBAN_DEVELOPMENT [Accessed 28th September 2019].

Lenzen, M., Sun, Y., Faturay, F., Ting, Y., Geschke, A., and Malik, A. (2018). The carbon footprint of global tourism, *Nature Climate Change*, https://doi.org/10.1038/s41558-018-0141-x.

Mazanec, J.A., and Wöber, K.W. (Eds.) (2009). *Analyzing International City Tourism*, 2nd edn, Wien-New York: Springer.

Mulas, V., Minges, M., and Applebaum, H. (2016). Boosting tech innovation ecosystems in cities: a framework for growth and sustainability of urban tech innovation ecosystems, *Innovations*, 11 (1/2), pp. 98–125.

OECD (2014a). Measuring tourism at sub-national level, centre for entrepreneurship, SMEs, and local development tourism committee, 25 September 2014. http://www.oecd.org/cfe/tourism/measuring-tourism-economic-impacts.htm [Accessed 28th September 2019].

OECD (2014b). Tourism and the creative economy, *OECD Studies on Tourism*, OECD Publishing. http://dx.doi.org/10.1787/9789264207875-en.

Önder, I., Wöber, K.W., and Zekan, B. (2017). Towards a sustainable urban tourism development in Europe. The role of benchmarking and tourism management information systems. A partial model of destination competitiveness, *Tourism Economics*, 23 (2), pp. 243–259.

Önder, I., and Zekan, B. (2020). Urban tourism development in Europe: a double-edged sword for the cities? In: A. M. Morrison and J.A. Coca-Stefaniak (Eds.), *Handbook of Tourism Cities*. Routledge.

Roland Berger (2018). *Protecting Your City from Overtourism. European City Tourism Study 2018.* https://www.rolandberger.com/en/Publications/Overtourism-in-Europe's-cities.html [Accessed 7 April 2019].

Tripadvisor (2017). *TripBarometer: Global Report 2017–2018*. https://www.tripadvisor.com/TripAdvisorInsights/w4594 [Accessed 28 September 2019].

United Nations (2018). *Department of Economic and Social Affairs, Population Division. The World's Cities in 2018—Data Booklet* (ST/ESA/ SER.A/417).

UNWTO (2014). *Global Benchmarking for City Tourism Measurement*, AM reports Vol. 10, UNWTO: Madrid. http://affiliatemembers.unwto.org/news/2014-12-15/am-reports-volume-ten-global-benchmarking-city-tourism-measurement [Accessed 28 September 2019].

UNWTO (2018). *'Overtourism'? Understanding and Managing Urban Tourism Growth beyond Perceptions. Executive Summary*. UNWTO: Madrid.

UNWTO (2019). *'Overtourism'? Understanding and Managing Urban Tourism Growth beyond Perceptions. Volume 2: Case Studies*. UNWTO: Madrid.

Vienna Tourist Board (2019). *Vienna Visitor Economy Strategy 2025*. https://b2b.wien.info/en/ strategy-brand/tourism-strategy [Accessed 18 January 2020].

Vigolo V. (2017). Population aging: challenges and opportunities for the tourism industry. In: *Older Tourist Behavior and Marketing Tools. Tourism, Hospitality & Event Management*. Cham: Springer.

3 Urban tourism as a special type of cultural tourism

Greg Richards

Introduction

Cities have always had a special role in cultural tourism. Major urban centres are places often built on a sedimentation of different cultures and their tangible heritage. The traces left by previous generations and the history of society collected in the museums and monuments often dominate urban tourism consumption. Cultural tourism, conceived of as tourists' cultural consumption, therefore plays a key role in the urban tourism economy, particularly in city centres. For example, in London, cultural tourists spend £7.3 billion a year, generating £3.2 billion in expenditure and supporting 80,000 jobs (Mayor of London, 2017).

In the past, cultural tourism was generally welcomed as a high quality, high spend form of leisure tourism (Richards, 2001). Many cities in Europe and North America built their tourism policies around the development and enhancement of cultural tourism (Smith, 2015). This policy focus was predicated on the high spend of cultural tourists, but also on a belief that the cultural tourism market was growing particularly rapidly. More recently, this very growth has become a problem, as cultural sites in many cities become increasingly overcrowded.

The growth of cultural tourism has also generated a dramatic growth in scholarship and analysis, with the production of academic papers on "cultural tourism" growing from around 100 in 1990 to almost 8000 in 2018 (Richards, 2018). There is a strong link to cities and urban tourism in the growing raft of cultural tourism publications. In 1990 about a third of publications dealt with cultural tourism in cities, but by 2018 this had risen to 43%. In spite of the frequent overlap between cultural tourism and cities, however, there is little integration of theoretical approaches to these two subjects. Tourism scholars are rarely grounded in urban studies, and urbanists only pay attention to (cultural) tourism when it impinges on what they regard as their territory.

As Novy and Colomb (2016) point out, it is becoming increasingly difficult for urban scholars or policymakers to ignore tourism in cities. The touristification of popular districts in cities such as Barcelona, Amsterdam and Berlin makes the effects of tourism more evident and many of these issues are linked to what might be termed "cultural tourism". Whereas cultural tourists were once seen as the solution, they are increasingly part of the problem. They add to overcrowding in city centres and vie with locals not just for entry to major cultural sites, but also local cafes and restaurants. The re-positioning of cultural tourism is difficult to understand without a grounded analysis of the nature of cultural tourism and how it appropriates the urban fabric.

This chapter considers the changing ways in which cultural tourism intersects with the urban. In doing so it identifies a number of key shifts in the nature of cities and cultural tourism that have caused cultural tourism to take on new roles in urban contexts. We highlight ways in which the consumption, production and intermediation of cultural tourism have been reflected in recent research on cities, and how different urban cultural tourism really is.

Changes in the objects of tourism – from high culture to everyday life

Historically, cultural tourism developed as an elite form of tourism, reflecting the fact that only the rich and well educated could afford to travel. The European Grand Tour was arranged around the cultural highlights of the continent, mainly heritage sites from antiquity or the Renaissance (Towner, 1985). As Richards (1996) describes, the extension of cultural tourism to the middle classes in the nineteenth century reinforced the primarily urban nature of cultural tourism as increasing numbers of people visited major cultural sites, delivered to city centres by the expanding railways.

This was also a period that saw a rapid increase in the development of museums, theatres and other cultural facilities, which were initially supported by wealthy patrons. This formed the basis of the early cultural democratization of cities, or "Culture 1.0", as Pier Luigi Sacco (2011) has termed it. These cultural attractions were a by-product of urban growth, in which economic surpluses were used to develop culture for the edification of the masses.

In the nineteenth and twentieth centuries, urban culture was further stimulated by the rise of the nation state. National governments invested in culture in order to boost national identity, and local authorities promoted culture as a form of civic edification and leisure consumption. These facilities also became part of the emerging urban tourism system as mass tourism grew and the economic impact of tourism spending became more evident. Public support for urban culture shifted from consumption externalities to production externalities: cultural attractions generated tourism, which supported the economy. This led, in the 1990s in particular, to a boom in cultural investment, with many cities building new museums and other cultural facilities as an engine for economic growth (Richards, 1996). The cultural sector came to be seen as an "industry", marking a shift from "Culture 1.0" to "Culture 2.0" (Sacco, 2011). The logic of culture as an intrinsically "good thing" for people became a view of culture as a generator of extrinsic value and an integral part of the economic system. Cities helped to industrialize culture with policies aimed at boosting the cultural and creative industries and creating cultural districts or quarters (Evans, 2009). Cities were seen as the leading edge of the creative industries in particular, as places that had the atmosphere to attract the mobile "creative class" (Florida, 2002). Urban culture became the source of inspiration for many new creative impulses in music, film, literature, etc., which in turn helped to attract new flows of tourists to cities (Cudny, 2011). A further shift took place as the diversification of cultural taste, the fragmentation of cultural production and access to new technologies and media challenged the monolithic production of culture. In the Culture 3.0 moment, culture also becomes seen as a means of creating identity, stimulating social cohesion and supporting creativity.

Arguably we are now entering an era of Culture 4.0, as digital culture challenges, replaces or enhances traditional forms of cultural production and consumption (Grevtsova and Sibina, 2018). Culture 4.0 integrates the internet and digital technologies to produce new forms of presentation, interaction and engagement that probe and break the boundaries of traditional institutions. Museums no longer need physical objects – they can present virtual or augmented reality instead.

Urban cultural tourism has undergone a similar trajectory as culture itself. In Culture 1.0, tourists consumed the elite culture that was deemed to be good for them. This model originally developed through the Grand Tour, when the leisured classes saw Italy as the "prize" (Towner, 1985) to be won in completing their cultural education. As the elite were joined by the expanding middle classes, and eventually also by the working class in the twentieth century, the Culture 2.0 system, with its expanded provision of museums, monuments and other cultural infrastructure, turned urban culture into an object of mass tourism: "In the past twenty years, the drive to attract more tourists and other mobile consumers has led cities to develop new cultural attractions, leading to what Ritzer (1999) termed the development of the 'new cathedrals of consumption'" (Richards, 2014a). This produced a tremendous expansion of the "real cultural capital" of cities, often adding completely new museum districts or quarters that acted as new visitor magnets.

Subsequently, Culture 3.0 (Richards, 2014b) provided a more fragmented, flexible and decentralized form of cultural tourism. "Cultural tourism" as a clearly defined market began to disappear in a welter of new niche markets, such as heritage tourism, art tourism, gastronomic tourism and creative tourism (Richards, 2014b). Richards and Russo (2016) argue that this fragmentation of the cultural market produced a new touchstone for authenticity: the local. Whereas the traditional markers of authenticity had included concepts of originality, or age or context (Wang, 1999), new notions of existential authenticity facilitated auto-generated authenticity, through the search for "local" culture. This broadened the notion of culture still further, since almost any sign of localness could be considered a cultural artefact worthy of consumption. However, the localization of cultural tourism produced a new challenge – that of coming into contact with the local. This problem was resolved by the growth of new technology and the rise of platforms that could link travellers easily with locals, such as Airbnb.

The challenge for the cultural tourist in search of the local was finding a way of connecting with local places and local people, who were not usually visible in the distribution systems of global tourism. In the past, finding the local had required devoted reading of *Lonely Planet* or engaging in time-extensive travel modes such as backpacking. From around 2014, however, platforms such as Airbnb began to grow exponentially, providing new ways of accessing the local. Airbnb developed local experiences to bring tourists directly into contact with local hosts (who were often missing from the Airbnb accommodation itself). In cultural tourism 4.0, the development of platforms for local experiences, for attraction tickets (to avoid the queues of mass cultural tourists) and transport became determinant.

In summary, we can see a number of important shifts in the relationship between tourism, culture and the city in recent decades:

- The traditional emphasis on built heritage and the physical legacy of the past in cultural tourism is gradually shifting towards "intangible heritage".
- The reframing of "culture" has created a much broader understanding of the legitimate object of cultural tourism, with vaguer boundaries between "high" and "popular" culture, with new forms of culture emerging (such as street art, for example).

- A shift from production to consumption and co-creation.
- The rise of the "local" as the arbiter of authenticity.
- The growth of platforms linking consumers and producers of culture, such as Airbnb (linking tourists and locals) and Culture Trip (linking cultural curators and tourists).

The combination of these shifts in the cultural position of cultural tourism has led to a growth in the perceived number of cultural tourists, or people travelling to consume culture. When we combine this with the general growth in city tourism in recent years (Richards and Marques, 2018), then it is clear that urban cultural tourism is a major growth area.

Changes in the distribution system. From tour operators to platforms

In the early phases of cultural tourism development in cities, the market was dominated by small scale specialist companies, often set up by entrepreneurs with a background in art. Following the logic of Bourdieu (1984), these "new cultural intermediaries" had high levels of cultural capital, but often low levels of economic capital (Richards, 2001). Producing high quality tours for generally older and wealthier tourists became an effective way of translating cultural capital into economic capital.

As tourism grew and mass market tour operators looked for new niche markets, cultural tourism was stimulated by short break holidays, often to major urban centres. Specialist travelling guides were replaced by local guides, or the tourists were left to follow the guide book, and later Google Maps, to the major cultural attractions. Cities such as Barcelona, which had previously been on the margins of the cultural tourism market, began to demand a place in the rankings through the development of new attractions and the promotion of new icons, such as Gaudí.

City trips expanded rapidly in the early years of the new millennium; major tour operators discovered city trips as a new travel segment that was also more stable than many beach destinations. Added to this was the rise of budget airlines, which often ferried tourists to smaller cultural cities, such as Girona, Dubrovnik or Oporto.

Although the early pioneers of cultural city trips, such as Studiosus in Germany or SRC Reizen in the Netherlands, are still operating, they increasingly have to differentiate themselves from mainstream tour operators with niche destinations and products and events. In this early expansion of urban cultural tourism the emphasis was on the discovery of new cities, particularly as the expansion of budget airlines made this increasingly cheap and easy. As numbers of tourists grew, however, there was increasing concentration on major sites in the centre of cities, or what Russo (2002) called the "vicious cycle" of cultural tourism.

In recent years the tour operators have come under pressure from disrupters related to the "collaborative economy" (such as Airbnb) and the rise of low-cost airlines. The new airlines not only added to the number of tourists being delivered to major city centres, but also opened up new, smaller cities to cultural tourism (Richards and Duif, 2018). In some cases, the flow of visitors to smaller secondary cities actually created new gateways to established cultural tourism destinations. This was the case in the Catalan city of Girona, for example. Initially happy with a growth in tourism from the arrival of Ryanair flights, the city increasingly saw visitors disappear in the direction of nearby Barcelona thanks to direct bus and train links.

Airbnb in particular has been responsible for a rapid increase in local accommodation in city centres, which catered to the new ideal of "living like a local" (Russo and Richards, 2016). Growth of Airbnb supply has been particularly marked in cities such as Barcelona, Amsterdam, Paris and Berlin, where the growth of "collaborative economy" accommodation supplemented an already busy cultural tourism market through the offer of Airbnb experiences (Figure 3.1). Many of these experiences are geared towards arts and culture (Figure 3.2).

Interestingly, evidence from the WYSE Travel Confederation global youth traveller survey indicates that respondents using collaborative economy accommodation were more likely to visit museums and historic monuments than other travellers. One important reason for this, however, was the longer length of stay in the destination of sharing economy accommodation users.

Changes in the cultural space of the city

Changing cultural tourism distribution systems, the arrival of low-cost carriers and greater demand for intangible culture (UNWTO, 2018) produced a shift in the nature of cultural tourism supply in cities. The previous reliance on tangible heritage began to be replaced with a mixed economy of traditional museums, new iconic structures, city tours and cultural experiences.

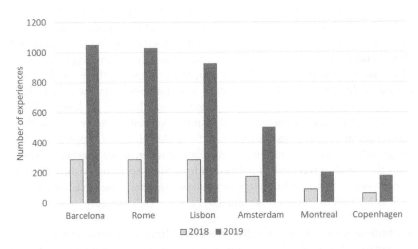

Figure 3.1   Airbnb experiences in selected cities, November 2018 and November 2019

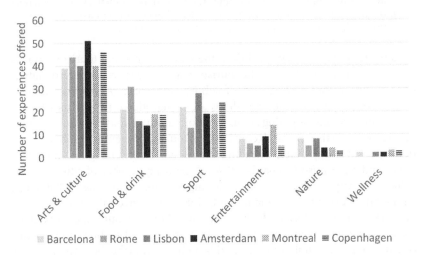

Figure 3.2   Airbnb experiences by category in selected cities, November 2019

One marked change was in the role of museums. Although museums continue to be the main type of attraction for cultural tourism consumption, the relationship of museums to the cultural tourism market has changed. Pressures to attract more visitors as a means of generating revenue have forced many museums to pay more attention to the needs of visitors in general, and tourists in particular. Museums large and small have added cafes, restaurants and gift shops; and there is a growing trend towards blockbuster touring exhibitions. These often tour between different museums, allowing them to share the considerable costs of large exhibitions. Museum buildings themselves have also become more iconic, calling on famous "starchitects" to design edifices that will attract media attention and visitors. As well as the growth of these cathedrals of consumption, Richards (2001) identified the growth of a new "postmodern" style of museums, which are smaller, more specialist institutions that tend to receive less public funding. Such specialist institutions can attract visitors to new cultural tourism hubs away from the established circuits, such as MONA in Hobart (Franklin, 2017) or the Dali Museum in Figueres.

Traditional styles of urban cultural tourism have also been supplemented by "creative tourism". Creative tourism was first defined by Richards and Raymond (2000, 18) as:

> Tourism which offers visitors the opportunity to develop their creative potential through active participation in courses and learning experiences which are characteristic of the holiday destination where they are undertaken.

Creative tourism represents a shift in the nature of cultural tourism towards more creative involvement of the tourists, with more space for interpretation of local cultures and co-creation of culture with locals. A growing number of creative experiences and workshops are being offered to tourists who are tired of just looking or gazing at buildings or paintings, and who would rather be creatively active themselves. Creative tourism programmes have been developed in many cities, including Barcelona, Recife, Bangkok, Medellín, Quito and Valparaíso (Richards, 2018). A growing number of cities are also using creativity as a means of promoting themselves on the global stage, with many seeking the designation of UNESCO Creative City. The UNESCO network includes cities of Film, Literature, Music, Crafts and Folk Arts, Design, Gastronomy and Media Arts. As Marques (2019) shows in the cases of Barcelona and Edinburgh, the UNESCO literature label becomes a means of profiling these cities globally. But such extraction and promotion of specific aspects of a city's culture may arguably be harmful: "It is too early to say, but it is perceived that the UNESCO stamp emphasizes an aspect of culture, to the detriment of urban complexity" (Ferreira and Vaz de Oliveira, 2017, 1035).

The attempts of cities to make themselves more attractive for a range of markets, including entrepreneurs, tourists, investors and students, is often based on the use of cultural assets. Romão et al. (2019) analysed the attractiveness of 40 global cities for the resident population and international tourists. They found that "cultural dynamics" (trendsetting potential, cultural resources, facilities for visitors, attractiveness to visitors and international interaction) is the major determinant for attracting new residents and tourists. The efforts of many cities to "put themselves on the map" has included the development of cultural attractions and programmes that have stimulated new flows of cultural tourism, such as the Bilbao Guggenheim (Plaza, 2006) or the Jeroen Bosch 500 programme in the Dutch city of Den Bosch (Richards and Duif, 2018). Traditional ordering of cultural tourism destinations with markers based on high culture is therefore shifting towards a new order determined by a broader mix of factors, which include intangible and everyday culture, as well as general tourist amenities.

The rise of new styles of cultural tourism also leads to new ways of "reading" the cultural tourist city. The rise of intangible culture and the emphasis on cultural events in cities produces a more rapid turnover of signifiers for cultural tourism. This also drives new selection strategies, replacing the former hegemony of the paper guidebook with new cultural intermediaries and taste leaders. One of the most prominent of these strategies is the "curation" of cultural experiences. For example, the UK company Culture Trip provides up-to-date information on cultural experiences in cities worldwide, supplied by a network of local writers, who "create stories that reveal what is unique and special about a place, its people and its culture". Culture Trip is combining big data to analyse the demand for different cultural forms, and comparing this with the supply of culture as identified by their network. For example, big data analysis indicated a growing demand for street art in major cities. A review of the available content indicated that there was already a sufficient supply of street art experiences in London, but that there was less supply in Berlin, identifying an opportunity for market development there. By matching user interest and destinations, the right content can be created to develop new cultural tourism products.

Changing modes of city use for (cultural) tourism

The growth of creative tourism and other new styles of urban tourism coincided with the rise of new platforms such as Airbnb to produce new uses of urban space. During Cultural Tourism 1.0 and 2.0, cultural consumption was concentrated in the centre of the city and most tourists stayed in hotel clusters in or near the city centre. They tended to use facilities specifically designed for tourist use (or what Edensor, 1998, called "homogenous spaces"), so there was a functional separation between tourism and everyday culture, which enabled Urry (1990) to claim that tourism was the opposite of everyday life. This opposition gradually disappeared as tourists began to penetrate the spaces of the everyday, and local residents and their everyday activities became enlisted into the cultural tourism production process.

As Richards (2017) argues, this integration of tourism and everyday life produced new possibilities for capitalist exploitation of the use value of space. For example, Airbnb enabled local residents to share their homes with tourists following the "live like a local" trend (Russo and Richards, 2016), stimulating the commodification of everyday life in the private spaces of the city. This form of "interstitial capitalism" (Richards, 2017) is supported by emotional labour from local residents, who also play a role as cultural attractions and storytellers of the city. However, Airbnb was also quickly exploited by large scale capitalists and property developers, who used Airbnb as a system for letting large numbers of apartments to tourists. The tourists paid considerably higher rents than the previous long-term residents (Cocola-Gant and Gago, 2019). The resulting displacement of local residents by tourist rentals has been one of the major criticisms of Airbnb, which has tried to sell itself as a neighbourhood friendly company, helping people pay their rent.

Such developments have stimulated debates about processes of touristification (Ollero et al., 2019) and gentrification (Cocola-Gant and Gago, 2019). One of the issues that still needs to be explored in more detail is the tendency for new cultural intermediaries, who make up a disproportionately high percentage of cultural tourists in cities (Richards, 2001), to also be the pioneers of gentrification. As more cities develop "live, work, visit, invest" promotional strategies (Richards and Duif, 2018), the idea that places that are good to live in are also good to visit for (cultural) tourism is also likely to proliferate. In such cases, the touristification of city centres (often on the basis of cultural and architectural attractiveness) is also likely to go hand in hand with gentrification, even though these processes are conceptually distinct.

One point made in the report on the European Capital of Culture in the Maltese city of Valletta in 2018 was that processes of gentrification have been going on for a relatively long time:

> We speak about gentrification nowadays, but really gentrification had already started in the 1980s, which was when my parents married. At the time, couples

getting married would look for new accommodation outside Valletta, both because it would have been more accessible and larger, and also because there was value placed on having a dwelling that was a new building. (Deguara et al., 2019, 31)

Touristification processes in major cities, on the other hand, have been relatively recently identified and analysed. Much of the recent analysis of touristification has been compounded with the concept of "overtourism", which oversimplifies complex urban economic, social and cultural processes into a function of tourism growth. However, as Jover and Díaz-Parra (2019) point out, touristification can be conceptually separated from other processes, such as gentrification and transnational gentrification. They identify dialectical processes at work, in which "The concentrated pattern of lifestyle migrants in Seville's historic district seems to respond to a general search for a better quality of life, manifested in class-based lifestyle choices, modes of consumption and cultural attractions in the city".

The movement of tourists and transnational lifestyle migrants into city centres (often stimulated by their past tourism practices) brings about changes in the property market and the structure of local services. One of the most visible changes is in the structure of retailing. Businesses orientated towards the needs of long-term residents are replaced by shops catering to passing tourists and expats. Research in Amsterdam shows that the number of ice cream shops grew by 460% between 2008 and 2014, cheese shops by 250%, souvenir shops by 80% and bike hire outlets by 130% (Richards and Marques, 2018).

The development of a retail monoculture has produced counter movements in some cities. In Lisbon, for example, the *Lojas com historia* (Shops with History) programme was launched in response to numerous closures of specialist stores and old local businesses. It seeks to conserve businesses with cultural heritage or particular local significance, by giving rent protection for five to ten years. By July 2016, 64 businesses, from restaurants to pastry shops, had received the label, and 19 additional shops were recognized in March 2017 (Richards and Marques, 2018).

Although the changes of city use are usually most evident in central districts traditionally associated with (cultural) tourism, the trend towards "living like a local" (Russo and Richards, 2016) has also driven a growth of new tourism hubs in city neighbourhoods. An expansion of cultural tourism to what Maitland has termed "New Tourist Areas", "edgy" and "cool" neighbourhoods sought after by the strategic or creative tourist (Füller and Michel, 2014). This process has been traced in detail by research on new tourism areas in London (Pappalepore et al., 2014). In areas of East London, such as Hoxton, Shoreditch and London Fields, new cultural intermediaries and creative tourists were found to be seeking authenticity in relatively untouristified areas of the inner city. Groups identified as "trendsetters", "detached fashion critics" and "cool seekers" found authenticity in areas that were slightly "run-down" or with a "bohemian" atmosphere. "judgements were made about the area's authenticity based on the nature of the crowd. For some, a crowd of creative, arty young people is seen as attractive, whereas the presence of mainstream tourists (typical of more central areas) is not".

Taken together, the shifting modes of cultural tourism consumption and production in cities are beginning to produce a new geography of urban cultural tourism. In the 1990s, it was still possible for cultural tourism to be largely connected to the "tourist-historic city" (Ashworth and Tunbridge, 2000). This was dominated by tangible, formal heritage attractions with an audience interested in high culture. In Amsterdam, Dahles (1998) also noted the cultural and spatial dichotomy between high spending, older cultural tourists focused on the city's museums and younger budget travellers seeking out the coffee shops and the Red Light District. With growing interest for intangible culture and the spread of tourism to new areas of the city, these distinctions have tended to fade, producing a new and more fragmented geography of cultural tourism. Figure 3.3 shows an idealized transition from Ashworth and Tunbridge's (2000) tourist-historic city, through Ashworth and Page's (2011) typology of urban tourism to the current landscape of Airbnb, living like a local and New Tourist Areas.

Changes in the social position of urban cultural tourism – from good to bad?

There is little doubt that cultural tourism used to enjoy a privileged position in relation to most other forms of tourism. As Richards (2001) argues, cultural tourism was long perceived as a "good" form of tourism, for example in contrast to "mass tourism". In Barcelona, for example, successive surveys of residents have shown high levels of support for the promotion of cultural tourism, even when the tourism industry as a whole was being criticized for problems related to overcrowding, noise, litter and other challenges (Richards, 2016). Slowly, however, the idea of cultural tourism as a good form of tourism has been eroding. Much of this has to do with the high levels of overcrowding experienced in many city centres, especially around major cultural sites. As must-see sites, attractions such as the Sagrada Familia in Barcelona or St Mark's Square in Venice will tend to be visited, or at least gazed at from the

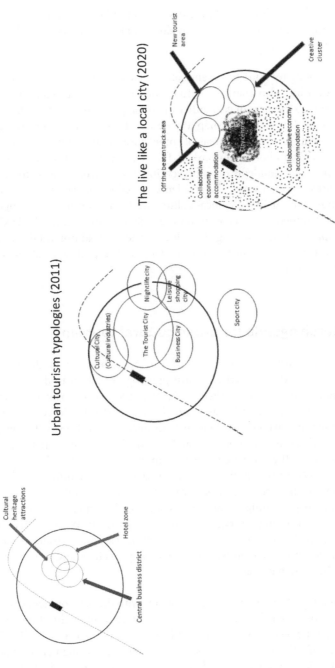

Figure 3.3   Shifting urban geographies of cultural tourism

outside, by almost all visitors to the destination. It becomes increasingly hard, under these circumstances, to see any distinction between the "good" and the "bad" tourists.

The desire of many tourists to penetrate the backstage of the city, and become part of local life, also changes attitudes of some people to cultural tourists. Tourists taking pictures of each other in public places is one thing, but traipsing over your flower bed to snap a close-up of your living room is another. Such problems have caused areas of some cultural attractions to be closed to visitors. The Begijnhof in Amsterdam, for example, now has barriers marking areas as being for residents only, preventing visitors from getting too close to their houses. In other cases, the problems caused by cultural tourists wanting to penetrate too far into the local culture are being minimized through programmes designed to increase cultural sensitivity. Advice from the UNWTO, for example, includes learning about local customs, traditions and social conditions, learning a few words of the language and respecting local dress codes (UNWTO, 2017).

A research agenda for urban cultural tourism?

A number of future research vectors can be gleaned from the foregoing analysis. One of the theoretically most pressing of these is to develop greater articulation between urban theory and the study of tourism in cities. For too long, tourism research has maintained a relatively closed silo labelled "urban tourism", which has done little to make connections with the developing strands of urban studies research. Apart from isolated attempts to link urban theory to the tourist city through multidisciplinary analysis (Judd and Fainstein, 1999) or the application of regulation theory (Hoffman et al., 2011), these remain fairly separate fields. Urbanization, for example, is a key element of urban theory (Hannigan and Richards, 2017), but in terms of tourism this remains largely limited to coastal resorts (e.g. Clavé and Wilson, 2017). There is growing evidence to suggest that cultural development strategies are also having major impacts on urbanization in a range of cities, and most notably in smaller cities (Richards and Duif, 2018).

Different types of urban regimes can coincide with the development of cultural tourism. This may be a fruitful avenue to explore in the light of the growing articulation between the creative industries and tourism (OECD, 2014). A number of cities have tried to position themselves through creative sectors such as fashion, architecture and design. Cities following such strategies not only need to attract professionals from these fields through the development of creative or cultural clusters (Evans, 2009) or knowledge-based events (Podestà and Richards, 2017), but they also need to attract creative audiences to enlarge the consumption base for these creative sectors. This is evident in cities such as Austin, where the music industry is a major driver for tourism as well as the live music industry and music-related businesses (Wynn, 2015). In such cities, creative sector development is usually supported by a favourable urban regime, which combines public and private sector interests (Stone, 2005). In these cases, the development of cultural tourism may be related to the changing fortunes of different cultural and creative sectors and their fashionability, as well as their perceived economic return. Which types of urban regimes are associated with what styles of cultural tourism development? One might surmise, for example, that a conservationist regime would be linked to an emphasis on traditional high culture and architectural preservation, whereas a development regime might push for leading sectors of the creative industries, such as fashion or digital art. A progressive regime, on the other hand, might be linked to creative tourism and other strategies designed to support the social as well as the cultural fabric.

In this vein, much value can also be gained from comparative studies of cultural tourism destinations. This is a style of research that has benefitted in the past from European Union funding, which stimulated studies of cultural tourism in different countries and cities (Richards, 1996, 2001; Van der Borg and Russo, 2005). The globalization of urban tourism and cultural tourism offers new opportunities for comparisons of different types of cities, ranging from global cities such as London and New York to cities of the global south, such as Johannesburg and Rio de Janeiro (Booyens and Rogerson, 2015). Ideas about the development of urban cultural tourism have often originated in Europe or North America, where particular trajectories of urban development have a strong influence. New studies in the global south in particular offer the possibility of responding to Storper and Scott's (2016) call for a "worlding" of urban theorizing. There is already some movement in this direction with studies of cultural tourism in the favelas of Brazil and the townships of South Africa (Ramchander, 2007), but these specific examples could be augmented with more studies of practices of cultural tourism in other major cities, such as Jakarta, Cairo, Mexico City, Hangzhou or Shenzhen.

In all cities we are seeing a growth in new forms of culture as objects for tourism. These include the rise of street art (Insch and Walters, 2017), music genres such as hip-hop (Xie et al., 2007) and cultural scenes such as Goth culture (Spracklen and Spracklen, 2014). As new cultural forms emerge, blossom and die, what impact does this have on cultural tourism in the city?

New hubs for tourism can be created by a band or a film, or even a video game. How sustainable are such cultural attractions? The pedestrian crossing used by The Beatles for the cover of Abbey Road is still a site of cultural pilgrimage, half a century after the release of the album. How many of today's artists will manage this kind of lasting impact, and how many will fade into obscurity after a few years of destination marketing hype? What impact will the new generation of virtual reality museums have on flows of visitors to and within cities? Will the ability to consume culture virtually, combined with pressures to travel less, begin to reduce levels of physical cultural tourism?

New cultural forms will also require a new class of cultural intermediaries. The tour guides of previous decades came to the fore as a result of the limited economic possibilities combined with the growth of tourism demand. Today, a host of new intermediaries is also being pushed to the fore by new cultural forms and the growth of new technologies. The ability to reach a global audience through the internet has opened up new possibilities for entrepreneurs in the cultural and creative sectors to move into the tourism industry. How will the increasing offer of "local" experiences affect the ways in which cities are represented and consumed? What effect do Airbnb and other collaborative industry platforms have on the development of cultural tourism? Many platforms are now extending their operations into the cultural content of the tourism journey as well. Will queuing for museum tickets be a thing of the past with the growing raft of "queue-jump" websites? What happens to museum marketing and management when everybody is a queue jumper?

A focus on the cultural tourists themselves would also provide interesting material for future research. Cultural tourists are arguably crucial for cities as "strategic tourists" (Wolfram and Burnill-Maier, 2013) who set trends and determine destinations for other (cultural) visitors. As social media and the internet become increasingly important as sources of information, not just on destinations, but also on how to practise tourism, the demonstration effect of such groups may well increase. What role models do contemporary cultural tourists follow? We have seen the influence of key figures before, in the shape of the Beat Generation and Tony and Maureen Wheeler as creators of the *Lonely Planet* guidebooks. These days, visits to certain websites or social media messages that go viral can have a significant influence on cultural tourism consumption. Big data offer many avenues for research, including the qualitative analysis of the texts produced by cultural tourism practitioners, and the growing information cascade that guides tourists to particular cultural sites in cities. Who are the key influencers? How big are their audiences? What curation strategies do they follow, and how do destinations try to utilize these in their marketing?

We also need to recognize that cultural tourism is political. The long tradition of countries and cities trying to promote a more favourable view of themselves by emphasizing selected elements of their culture has not gone away – it has simply moved onto CNN. Such programmes also serve to highlight conflicts over the authenticity and "ownership" of the culture sold to tourists. At a mundane level, cities dispute the origin of foods such as tiramisu, pizza, chop suey or chicken tikka masala. Higher stakes are evident in the construction of the Acropolis Museum in Athens, designed to accommodate the Elgin Marbles, once these are returned by the British Museum in London. With objects increasingly being exchanged between cultural institutions globally, how much does ownership count for? The political value of the objects of cultural tourism is clear. The protests in favour of Catalan independence in 2019 included a blockade of the Sagrada Familia. This immediately hit the cultural tourism industry, with newspaper reports of a "lost week" of rioting (Burgen, 2019).

References

Ashworth, G., & Page, S. J. (2011). Urban tourism research: Recent progress and current paradoxes. *Tourism Management*, 32(1), 1–15.

Ashworth, G. J., & Tunbridge, J. E. (2000). *The Tourist-Historic City*. Routledge.

Booyens, I., & Rogerson, C. M. (2015). Creative tourism in Cape Town: An innovation perspective. *Urban Forum*, 26, 405–424.

Bourdieu, P. (1984). *Distinction: A Social Critique of the Judgement of Taste*, trans. R. Nice, Cambridge, MA: Harvard University Press.

Burgen, S. (2019). Barcelona tourist industry counts cost of "lost week" of rioting. *Guardian*, https://www.theguardian.com/world/2019/oct/28/barcelona-tourist-industry-cost-lost-week-of-rioting?CMP=share_btn_link.

Clavé, S. A., & Wilson, J. (2017). The evolution of coastal tourism destinations: A path plasticity perspective on tourism urbanisation. *Journal of Sustainable Tourism*, 25(1), 96–112.

Cocola-Gant, A., & Gago, A. (2019). Airbnb, buy-to-let investment and tourism-driven displacement: A case study in Lisbon. *Environment and Planning A: Economy and Space*, 0308518X19869012.?>

Cudny, W. (2011). Film festivals in Łódź as a main component of urban cultural tourism. *Bulletin of Geography. Socio-economic Series*, 15, 131–141.

Dahles, H. (1998). Redefining Amsterdam as a tourist destination. *Annals of Tourism Research*, 25(1), 55–69.

Deguara, M., Bonello, M. P., & Magri, R. (2019). Community inclusion and accessibility in Valletta 2018. In *The Impacts of the European Capital of Culture: Final Research Report Valletta 2018*. Valletta: Valletta 2018.

Edensor, T. (1998). *Tourists at the Taj: Performance and Meaning at a Symbolic Site*. London: Routledge.

Evans, G. (2009). Creative cities, creative spaces and urban policy. *Urban Studies*, 46, 1003–1040.

Ferreira, V. M. S., & Vaz de Oliveira, A. M. (2017). A rede de cidades criativas da Unesco: Uma perspectiva das cidades brasileiras. *Proceedings of the V Congresso Internacional Cidades Criativas*, January 2017, Porto, Portugal, pp. 1035–1046.

Florida, R. (2002). *The Rise of the Creative Class*. New York: Basic Books.

Franklin, A. (2017). Creative exchanges between public and private: The case of MONA (the museum of old and new art) and the city of Hobart. *Proceedings of the V Congresso Internacional Cidades Criativas*, January 2017, Porto, Portugal, pp. 995–1005.

Füller, H., & Michel, B. (2014). "Stop being a tourist!" New dynamics of urban tourism in Berlin-Kreuzberg. *International Journal of Urban and Regional Research*, 38(4), 13041318. doi: 10.1111/1468-2427.12124.

Grevtsova, I., & Sibina, J. (2018). *Entre los espacios físicos y virtuales. Turismo cultural en el mundo digital*. Munich: GRIN Verlag. https://www.grin.com/document/445406.

Hannigan, J., & Richards, G. (Eds.). (2017). *The SAGE Handbook of New Urban Studies*. London: Sage.

Hoffman, L. M., Fainstein, S. S., & Judd, D. R. (Eds.). (2011). *Cities and Visitors: Regulating People, Markets and City Space* (Vol. 57). John Wiley & Sons.

Insch, A., & Walters, T. (2017). Conceptualising the role of street art in urban tourism. In Lee, C., Filep, S., Albrecht, J. N. & Coetzee, W. J. L. (Eds.). *CAUTHE 2017: Time For Big Ideas? Re-thinking The Field For Tomorrow*. Dunedin: Department of Tourism, University of Otago, pp. 512–514.

Jover, J., & Díaz-Parra, I. (2019). Gentrification, transnational gentrification and touristification in Seville, Spain. *Urban Studies*, 0042098019857585.

Judd, D. R., & Fainstein, S. S. (Eds.). (1999). *The Tourist City*. New Haven, CT: Yale University Press.

Marques, L. (2019). The making of the literary city: Edinburgh, Barcelona and Óbidos. In Jenkins, I., & Lund, K. A. (Eds.). *Literary Tourism: Theories, Practice and Case Studies Literary Tourism: Theories, Practice and Case Studies*. CAB International, pp. 57–72.

Mayor of London (2017). *Take A Closer Look: Cultural Tourism In London*. London: Mayor of London.

Novy, C., & Colomb, J. (2016). Urban tourism and its discontents. An introduction. In *Protest and Resistance in the Tourist City*. Routledge.

OECD (2014). *Tourism and the Creative Economy*. Paris: OECD.

Ollero, J. L. S., Capellán, R. U., & Pozo, A. G. (2019). The impact of cultural and urban tourism on housing. *Journal of Tourism and Heritage Research*, 2(4), 257–272.

Pappalepore, I., Maitland, R., & Smith, A. (2014). Prosuming creative urban areas. Evidence from East London. *Annals of Tourism Research*, 44, 227–240.

Plaza, B. (2006). The return on investment of the Guggenheim Museum Bilbao. *International Journal of Urban and Regional Research*, 30(2), 452–467.

Podestà, M., & Richards, G. (2017). Creating knowledge spillovers through knowledge-based festivals: the case of Mantua. *Journal of Policy Research in Tourism, Leisure and Events*, 10(1), 1–16.

Ramchander, P. (2007). Township tourism—blessing or blight? The case of Soweto in South Africa. In Richards, G. (Ed.). *Cultural Tourism: Global and Local Perspectives* (pp. 39–68). New York: Haworth.

Richards, G. (1996). *Cultural Tourism in Europe*. Wallingford: CAB International.

Richards, G. (Ed.). (2001). *Cultural Attractions and European Tourism*. Wallingford: CAB International.

Richards, G. (2014a). Cultural Tourism 3.0. The future of urban tourism in Europe? In Roberta Garibaldi (Ed.), *Il turismo culturale europeo. Città ri-visitate. Nuove idee e forme del turismo culturale*. Nilano: Franco Angeli Editore, pp. 25–38.

Richards, G. (2014b). Rethinking niche tourism in the network society. https://www .academia.edu/1868914/Rethinking_niche_tourism_in_the_network_society.

Richards, G. (2016). El turismo y la ciudad: ¿hacia nuevos modelos? *Revista CIDOB d'Afers Internacionals*, 113, 71–87.

Richards, G. (2017). Sharing the new localities of tourism. In D. Dredge and S. Gyimóthy (Eds.). *Collaborative Economy and Tourism: Perspectives, Politics, Policies and Prospects*. Springer, pp 169–184. ISBN 978-3-319-51797-1

Richards, G. (2018). Cultural tourism: a review of recent research and trends. *Journal of Hospitality and Tourism Management*, 36, 12–21.

Richards, G., & Duif, L. (2018). *Small Cities with Big Dreams: Creative Placemaking and Branding Strategies*. New York: Routledge.

Richards, G., & Marques, L. (2018). *Creating Synergies between Cultural Policy and Tourism for Permanent and Temporary Citizens*. Barcelona: UCLG/ICUB.

Richards, G., & Raymond, C. (2000). Creative tourism. *ATLAS news*, 23(8), 16–20.

Richards, G., & Russo, A. P. (2016). Synthesis and conclusions: towards a new geography of tourism. In A. P. Russo and G. Richards (Eds.). *Reinventing the Local in Tourism: Producing, Consuming and Negotiating Place*. Bristol: Channel View Publications, pp. 251–265.

Ritzer, G. (1999). *Enchanting a Disenchanted World: Revolutionizing the Means of Consumption*. Thousand Oaks, CA: Pine Forge Press, 251–65.

Romão, J., Kourtit, K., Neuts, B., & Nijkamp, P. (2019). The smart city as a common place for tourists and residents: A structural analysis of the determinants of urban attractiveness. *Cities*.

Russo, A. P. (2002). The "vicious circle" of tourism development in heritage cities. *Annals of Tourism Research*, 29, 165–182.

Russo, A. P., & Richards, G. (2016). *Reinventing the Local in Tourism: Producing, Consuming and Negotiating Place*. Bristol: Channel View Publications.

Sacco, P.-L. (2011). Culture 3.0: A New Perspective for the EU 2014–2020 Structural Funds Programming. Paper for the OMC Working Group on Cultural and Creative Industries, April 2011.

Smith, M. K. (2015). *Issues in Cultural Tourism Studies*. London: Routledge.

Spracklen, K., & Spracklen, B. (2014). The strange and spooky battle over bats and black dresses: The commodification of Whitby Goth Weekend and the loss of a subculture. *Tourist Studies*, 14(1), 86–102.

Stone, C. N. (2005). Looking back to look forward: reflections on urban regime analysis. *Urban Affairs Review*, 40(3), 309–341.

Storper, M., & Scott, A. J. (2016). Current debates in urban theory: A critical assessment. *Urban Studies*, 53(6), 1114–1136.

Towner, J. (1985). The Grand Tour: A key phase in the history of tourism. *Annals of Tourism Research*, 12(3), 297–333.

Urry, J. (1990). *The Tourist Gaze*. London: SAGE.

Van der Borg, J., & Russo, A. P. (2005). *The Impacts of Culture on the Economic Development of Cities*. Rotterdam: European Institute for Comparative Urban Research.

Wang, N. (1999). Rethinking authenticity in tourism experience. *Annals of Tourism Research*, 26(2), 349–370.

Wolfram, G., & Burnill-Maier, C. (2013). The tactical tourist. Growing self-awareness and challenging the strategists – visitor groups in Berlin. In Smith, M. & Richards, G. (Eds.). *The Routledge Handbook of Cultural Tourism*. Routledge, pp. 361–368.

Wynn, J. R. (2015). *Music/city: American Festivals and Placemaking in Austin, Nashville, and Newport*. Chicago: University of Chicago Press.

UNWTO (2017). *Tips for a Responsible Traveller*. Madrid: UNWTO.

UNWTO (2018). *Report on Tourism and Cultural Synergies*. Madrid: UNWTO.

Xie, P. F., Osumare, H., & Ibrahim, A. (2007). Gazing the hood: Hip-Hop as tourism attraction. *Tourism Management*, 28(2), 452–460.

PART II

Urban tourism in an international, comparative perspective

4 Smart governance in historic urban destinations – evidence from Croatia

Lidija Petrić and Ante Mandić

Introduction

Due to the growth of the industrial production and technical progress in the second half of the twentieth century, the world has witnessed a massive and rapid increase in both the number and size of cities. Thus, the urbanization rate grew from 30% in 1950 to 48% in 2002 (Šimunović, 2007). At present, 55% of the world's population is urban and, by 2050, this share will increase to 68% (UN, 2018). The massive concentration of people in a relatively small geographic area has set cities many challenges related to economic development, social inclusion, security, sustainability, infrastructure, transport and housing, with all of these being even more intense in cities that face extensive tourism development (García-Hernández et al., 2017; Koens et al., 2018; Seraphin et al., 2018). To address the issues posed by rapid urbanization, city authorities increasingly opt for development of the smart city concept. Among other things, this implies the development of a reliable technological infrastructure, dissemination of different kinds of information to optimize city functions, improvements in the quality of life and investments in human capital, i.e. people willing to participate in the decision-making processes (Caragliu et al., 2009).

Even with the smart city (SC) phenomenon extensively addressed in the recent research literature (Giffinger et al., 2007; Caragliu et al., 2009; Bătăgan, 2011; Batty et al., 2012; Bakici et al., 2013; Capdevila and Zarlenga, 2015; Scholl and AlAwadhi, 2016; Bolivar and Meijer, 2016; Kumar and Dahiya, 2017; Ruohomaa et al., 2019, etc.), no final consensus on either its definition or constituents has been reached. However, in their seminal work, Giffinger et al. (2007) have described a smart city framework that is widely appreciated, containing six essential elements, i.e. smart people, smart economy, smart mobility, smart environment, smart living and smart governance.

In this chapter, we focus on smart governance (SG), usually considered a crucial dimension of smart cities. City governance is an enormously complex and multi-level ecosystem of various agencies and stakeholder groups, with often-divergent interests that need to be smartly coordinated to allow knowledge transfers and facilitate decision-making to maximize cities' socioeconomic and environmental performances (Ruhlandt, 2018). Due to its complexity, the constituent categories/dimensions of SG are still blurred, which is why most researchers emphasize just one or a few. By contrast, Castelnuovo et al. (2016), Dameri and Benevolo (2016) and Bolivar and Meijer (2016) aimed to deliver a holistic approach, with the latter having systematized SG categories/dimensions into three groups, i.e. elements, outcomes and strategies.

In the related literature, smart governance was said to be influenced by different contextual factors, such as administrative cultures, political, demographic or technological factors (Ruhlandt, 2018), the degree of autonomy (Batty et al., 2012; Walravens, 2012) and different local conditions (Odendaal, 2003; Scholl and AlAwadhi, 2016). The size of a city and its location may also be understood as contextual factors affecting the way it is governed, which is why Lin (2018) strongly advocates the need to research not only big or medium-sized cities (>100,000 inhabitants) in developed Western countries, but also small cities in other parts of the world.

Given the aforementioned, this study focuses mainly on small cities located in two Croatian regions, coastal and continental. These differ from one another in terms of their history and administrative (sub)culture,[1] and the intensity of their tourism development, which may significantly affect the way the city is governed with regard to the main SG categories. The status of historic city was chosen as a common denominator for the cities in the sample, indicating the richness of cultural heritage as a valuable asset for (cultural) tourism development.

As stressed by UNESCO, there is no blueprint for a governance structure; rather, different societies and different cultures have their ideas of what proper management looks like, how it works and how different people and organizations work together. Governance solutions should undoubtedly be adapted to the local context, facilitating the generation of new smart governance categories within the existing framework. That said, this research critically reflects on recent literature and the specifics of historic urban cities oriented to the development of tourism to propose new, historic-destination-specific smart governance categories and extend the well-known Bolivar and Meijer (2016) SG model. To test their relevance, the study applies importance-performance analysis to evaluate the perception of the importance and application of smart

governance on a sample of 42 historic urban destinations in Croatia. The findings are discussed in the light of contextual factors (i.e. size – referring mostly
to the small cities; location – associated with different administrative cultures;[2]
tourism development intensity – measured by the set of intensity indicators;
the status of historic city as a specific local condition) and taking into account
the cities' key strategic documents. The conclusions facilitate further understanding of this phenomenon and shed light on the specifics of governance in
historic urban destinations within given contexts.

Smart governance. A literature review

Smart governance – the essence of the smart city concept

The term governance, understood merely as the process of governing, refers to
different aspects, i.e. public/political, economic and social, and several levels,
i.e. from business entity to state (Nzongola-Ntalaja, 2003). Although the three
aspects of governance are interdependent, public governance plays a more
important role than the other two. It provides organizational dynamics and
political and jurisdictional systems for both social and economic governance.
Moreover, it implies the state's ability to serve citizens, other actors, as well as
how public functions are carried out, public resources managed and public
regulatory powers exercised (UN, 2007). The evolution of the public governing
process began with the public administration (PA) phase in the 1950s, continued with the new public management (NPM) phase in the 1970s (Healey,
2007; Dickinson, 2016) and ended with the good governance (GG) phase at the
end of the 1980s (Gisselquist, 2012), finally supplemented by the concept of
smartness introduced by Giffinger et al. in 2007.

Smart governance does not have a unanimously accepted definition, but the
terms 'participation' and 'collaboration' are usually invoked (Castelnouvo et al.,
2016). Public participation in governance involves direct or indirect involvement through representatives of concerned stakeholders in decision-making
about policies, plans or programmes in which they have an interest (Quick
and Bryson, 2016). Active participation enhances democracy, especially on
the local level (Berntzen and Johansen, 2016), thus leading to collaborative
governance that refers to the decision-making process and that by which decisions are implemented, monitored and evaluated. Bolivar and Meijer (2016)
stress that smart urban collaboration is the perspective with the highest level
of transformation among four ideal-typical conceptualizations of smart city
governance, i.e. (1) government of a smart city; (2) smart decision-making;

(3) smart administration; and (4) smart urban collaboration. The authors also claim that smart city government does not require a transformation of governmental structures and processes. Moreover, in this conceptualization, SG is just governance of a smart city, built on urban collaboration between various stakeholders in the city and aimed at both internal and external organizations.

The *smartness* of the city governance may be enhanced by new information-communication technologies (ICTs), which force public authorities to rethink the role they have in contemporary knowledge-based society (Bolivar and Meijer, 2016). Moreover, Scholl and AlAwadhi (2016) define smart governance as the capacity of applying digital technologies and intelligent activities to the processing of information and decision-making. In doing so, governments are expected to pass through a non-linear evolutionary process, first relying on improving administrative efficiency, performance, citizen-centricity and service delivery, and ultimately developing e-government. Hence the use of ICTs evolves from supporting existing processes to facilitating new relationships (Pereira et al., 2018), thus enhancing the efficiency of interactions among stakeholders (Misuraca et al., 2011).

It is possible to conclude that citizen engagement is one of the cornerstones of smart governance, while the government remains a mechanism for collective action, acting more as "a convener and enabler rather than the first mover of civic action" (Linders, 2012). However, a city's human (intellectual) and social capital have to be adequately developed for such an achievement. In other words, smart and intelligent citizens, able to use the technology and benefit from it (Caragliu et al., 2009), are a basis for developing smart urban collaboration.

Based on a systematic review of the literature, Bolivar and Meijer (2016) have identified three constituent dimensions of smart governance, specifically: (1) *the SG defining elements*: use of ICT, external collaboration and participation, internal coordination, decision-making process, e-administration and innovation capacity; (2) *the three levels of aspired outcomes produced by SG*: efficient government organization and readiness for disaster management (government organization outcomes), citizen-centric activities, interaction with citizens and city brand (changes in the position of government vis-à-vis other urban actors), economic growth, social inclusion, ecological performance and highly educated citizens (improvements to the city); and (3) *the implemented strategies needed to realize SG*: integral vision, legislation, organizational transformations and policies for promoting smart city initiatives, and projects for strengthening innovation systems and cultural development. To address the specifics of smart governance in historic urban destinations, this model is further developed in the following section with the introduction of historic-city-specific categories within dimensions of outcomes and strategies (Figure 4.1).

Smart governance in historic cities

What makes historic city different from other cities, and which additional outcomes and strategies should accordingly be added to Bolivar and Meijer's (2016) smart governance model?

A historic city is a type of city whose continuous existence over the centuries has created a multi-layered fabric composed of a number of tangible and intangible heritage assets (Van Oers, 2010). Given its complexity, the Vienna Memorandum (UNESCO, 2005) stressed that the process of historic city management should be based on the broader regional and landscape context, thus introducing the concept of the Historic Urban Landscape (HUL). The HUL approach brings heritage conservation to a new visioning that links tradition and modernization, past, present and future, in a circular and synergistic perspective (Girard, 2013). This requires a shift towards the pursuit not only of the heritage well-being but of society as a whole, i.e. the introduction of a people-centred approach to conservation. This new paradigm, *de-secularization of heritage* (Wijesuriya, 2017), allows both goals, i.e. urban heritage conservation and social and economic development, to become equal priorities of urban development policy, including smart city development. Moreover, it brings cultural heritage into focus, finally recognizing the importance of this for tourism development (Veldpaus et al., 2013) and for urban regeneration processes (Griffiths, 1995; Van den Berg et al., 1995; Grodach and Loukaitou-Sideris, 2007; Murgoci et al., 2009; Blessi et al., 2012; Pedrana, 2013; Mikulić and Petrić, 2014, etc.)

Historic cities are increasingly becoming real tourism hubs. Moreover, in Europe, most of the urban tourism flows are concentrated in historical centres (García-Hernández et al., 2017). Increasing visitation and rapid economic and tourism development have revealed numerous flaws such as, among others, insufficient maintenance of cultural heritage and historic urban landscapes, improper rehabilitation, inappropriate new developments, traffic congestion, noise and pollution, lack of recreational and green spaces and parking places, and demolition of tangible cultural heritage and parts of the historic urban landscapes (Scheffler et al., 2009).

Given the specifics of historic cities and the challenges they face with the growth of interest in visiting them, it seems reasonable to extend Bolivar and

Meijer's (2016) original SG model with several specific (sub)categories in outcomes: *Climate mitigation system* (first level outcome), *Efficient spatial planning, Efficient traffic system, Responsible heritage use, Heritage interpretation*, and *Growth of tourism receipts* (third level outcomes) and in strategies, i.e. *Policies towards initiatives* and *projects strengthening sustainable tourism* (Figure 4.1).

The following is the logic behind introducing the specific *outcome* and *strategy* (sub)categories to Bolivar and Meijer's SG model.

Successfully implemented *spatial plans* enable a city government to optimize the use of space and make the most of it, to deal with regular space changes, to enhance urban resilience against multi-hazards and to plan for future space usage (Cartalis, 2014), for which purpose an integrated urban spatial planning methodology (Healy, 2007; Gordon et al., 2009) is used. As historic cities are under more severe threats than other cities, their governments are forced to use a variety of spatial planning tools and techniques (Runhaar et al., 2009) to cope with them efficiently.

An efficient spatial plan also integrates climate change hazards, which have recently become the focus of both scientists and practitioners. One of the potentially most dangerous hazards is rising sealevel, which directly endangers many coastal historic cities, particularly those around the Mediterranean. By implementing *mitigating systems* based on a variety of new technologies and solutions (Bulkeley and Betsill, 2003; UNFCCC, 2006; Corfee-Morlot et al., 2008; Heinrichs et al., 2011; Castan Broto and Bulkeley, 2013; Sharifia and Yamagata, 2014; Dale and Markandya, 2015; UNEP/MAP/PAP, 2016; Deng et al., 2017; Gandini et al., 2017; Moraci et al., 2018, etc.), the resilience of historic cities in the face of climate change may be enhanced.

Another challenge negatively affecting the urban economy, environment and the overall quality of life is traffic congestion (Kostakos et al., 2013; Das and Roychowdhury, 2017), especially in historic cities dependent on tourism (Riganti and Nijkamp, 2008). By making the *traffic system* more efficient, historic city authorities may also enhance visitor flow management (Gorin et al., 2015), diminish potential risks and enhance visitor satisfaction (Parahoo et al., 2014).

Due to its importance for tourism development, *cultural heritage* has to be *used responsibly and sustainably* (OECD, 2014), thus reaching new markets and stimulating sustainable growth. This goal is often addressed within smart city strategies (UNESCO, 2016; Angelidoua et al., 2017). However, the heritage will not be utilized to its full extent if not appropriately interpreted (ICOMOS, 2008). One of the principal functions of *heritage interpretation* is to enhance the visitor's sense of place and place identity (Uzell, 1996), so that empathy towards heritage, conservation, culture and landscape can be developed (Stewart et al., 1998). By supporting proper interpretation with the help of digital tools and technological appliances (Rahaman and Tan, 2011; Rahaman, 2018), smart governance helps create a *city brand*.

Finally, enhancing the development of (cultural) tourism, smart governance fosters, among other things, the *growth of tourism receipts*, thus enabling urban destinations to launch regeneration initiatives. Because of the different types of tourism-based urban regeneration strategies (Hudson, 2000; Rogerson, 2012; Mikulić and Petrić, 2014), smart local authorities are responsible for choosing such *tourism strategies and policies* that may capitalize on the city resources in a *sustainable manner* (Riganti and Nijkamp, 2008; Petrić and Crnjak-Karanović, 2016; Petrić and Pivčević, 2016; García-Hernández et al., 2017).

The original Bolivar and Meijer (2016) model has additionally been extended by the list of smart technologies/tools potentially used in managing different SG processes.

Smart governance: empirical research

Sample and framework

According to the Croatian Local and Regional Self-Government Law (Official Gazette, 123/7), city status is given to those settlements with more than 10,000 residents, are county centres or are given that status by exception (owing to some historical reasons). There are currently 127 cities in Croatia. Out of this number, 42 cities in the coastal region and 52 continental cities can be considered historic, meaning that they have a historic centre/landscape included in either the UNESCO World Heritage List (WHL) (seven cities) and/or the Croatian Cultural Goods Register.

The extended smart governance model, based on the original Bolivar and Meijer (2016) model, was used to analyse smart governance (SG) in Croatian historic cities. The initial model, comprising smart governance categories divided into elements, outcomes and strategies, has been extended to address the specifics of historic cities and to analyse the current application and use of smart

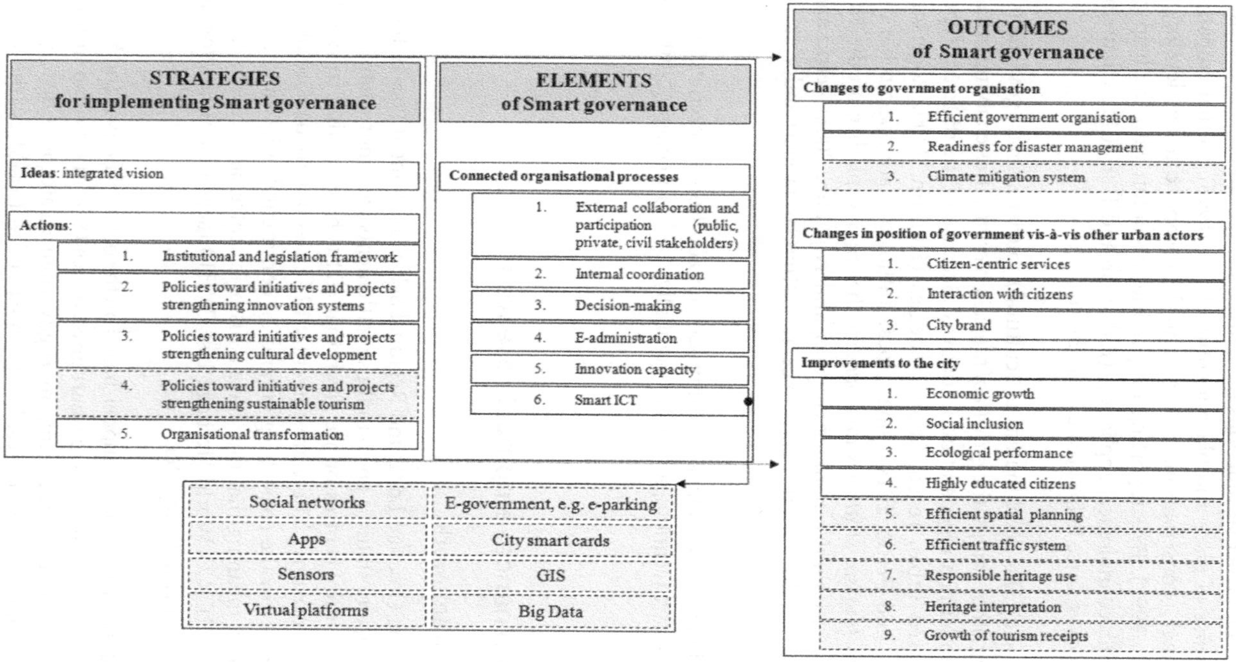

STRATEGIES for implementing Smart governance

Ideas: integrated vision

Actions:

1. Institutional and legislation framework
2. Policies toward initiatives and projects strengthening innovation systems
3. Policies toward initiatives and projects strengthening cultural development
4. Policies toward initiatives and projects strengthening sustainable tourism
5. Organisational transformation

ELEMENTS of Smart governance

Connected organisational processes

1. External collaboration and participation (public, private, civil stakeholders)
2. Internal coordination
3. Decision-making
4. E-administration
5. Innovation capacity
6. Smart ICT

Social networks
E-government, e.g. e-parking
Apps
City smart cards
Sensors
GIS
Virtual platforms
Big Data

OUTCOMES of Smart governance

Changes to government organisation

1. Efficient government organisation
2. Readiness for disaster management
3. Climate mitigation system

Changes in position of government vis-à-vis other urban actors

1. Citizen-centric services
2. Interaction with citizens
3. City brand

Improvements to the city

1. Economic growth
2. Social inclusion
3. Ecological performance
4. Highly educated citizens
5. Efficient spatial planning
6. Efficient traffic system
7. Responsible heritage use
8. Heritage interpretation
9. Growth of tourism receipts

Note: Grey shaded cells denote the sub-categories added to Bolívar and Meijer's (2016) original SG model.
Source: Adapted from Bolívar and Meijer (2016).

Figure 4.1   Historic cities' smart governance model

technologies in Croatian cities (social networks, platforms, e-government, city-smart cards, apps, geographical information systems, sensors and big data). Following the final model specification, the questionnaire containing 64 questions, rated on the 5-point Likert scale, was repeatedly sent to the mayors (or their deputies) of the historic Croatian cities using a Google form during the period September 2018 to December 2018.

Importance-performance analysis (IPA) was applied to analyse responses and deliver research results.

In addition, qualitative analysis exploring Croatian historic cities' strategic documents was performed to identify their development orientation. With this aim, the search process was run by using the following keywords: City development plan; Tourism development plan; Tourism marketing plan; Strategy/plan of cultural development; Cultural tourism development plan; Smart city strategy.

Importance-performance analysis

The importance-performance analysis is a business research technique developed as a marketing tool to examine and suggest marketing strategies (Martilla and James, 1977). It is a diagnostic decision tool that facilitates the identification of improvement prioritization, the mobilization of scarce resources and their deployment to where they are needed most and the harmonization of strategic planning efforts to enhance relative competitiveness (Azzopardi and Nash, 2013). The technique is widely used in many fields, e.g. tourism, food and beverages, education, healthcare, banking, public administration, e-business and information technologies (Sever, 2015), because of its simplicity and attractiveness in projecting results and suggesting actions. IPA allows researchers to visually identify gaps between stakeholders' perceptions of the importance of specific attributes and the actual performance (Boley et al., 2017). Moreover, researchers are able to simultaneously graph the mean importance and performance results for attributes (Sever, 2015) to indicate in which of the four quadrants the attribute falls (Azzopardi and Nash, 2013), i.e. Quadrant I: "Keep up the good work", Quadrant II: "Possible overkill", Quadrant III: "Low priority" and Quadrant IV: "Concentrate here" (Figure 4.2).

Analysis of the previous IPA studies shows that most researchers adopt a 5-point Likert-type scale, even though the 7-point scale shows more reliable results (Lai and Hitchcock, 2015). Considering there is no consensus on the scale type (Boley et al., 2017) and that a 5-point scale was used by Bolivar and

| Quadrant 2 – POSSIBLE OVERKILL
Possible overuse of attributes. Namely, they are being allocated and above average performed in the attributes that are not deemed to be exceptionally important. | Quadrant 1 – KEEP UP THE GOOD WORK
Attributes that are considered to be of above average importance and above average performance. These should be maintained to ensure they remain at this level of performance at this level. |
| Quadrant 3 – LOW PRIORITY
Lower priority attributes. Resources are not being channelled towards them as much as to the other attributes. Attributes that fall into this quadrant should remain untouched. | Quadrant 4 – CONCENTRATE HERE
Attributes which are considered as of above-average importance and yet are not being performed to the same standard. If an attribute falls within this quadrant, efforts should be made to shift it to the quadrant 1 (upper right). |

Source: Adapted from Sever (2015).

Figure 4.2   The standard IPA plot

Meijer (2016), the same approach has been applied in this paper. According to O'Neill and Palmer (2004), the performance gap is identified only when respondents' importance scores are shown to significantly differ from corresponding performance scores for a particular attribute, i.e. SG category. Moreover, Lai and Hitchcock (2015) suggest it is essential to conduct individual pair t-tests because only the attributes that show a significant difference (p-value <0.05) should be further analysed to highlight the areas of genuine concern to respondents. Therefore, the attributes with a p-value above 0.05 should be eliminated and not be plotted or discussed in the final IP mapping analysis. Table 4.1 delivers the individual paired-samples t-tests of the IP gaps for the proposed SG categories.

Regarding visual analysis, this research relies on the data-centred quadrants approach, a technique superior to direct measures of IP gaps, i.e. correlation-based measures and regression-based measures (Bacon, 2003). This technique is commonly referred to as "scale-centred", in which the cross-hairs are (1) simply placed in the middle of the 5-point Likert scale used to measure I and P (Boley et al. 2017), or the discretion of the researcher in terms of providing the greatest insight is relied on (Murdy and Pike, 2012). Following the conclusions by Bruyere et al. (2002), this research applies the grand means for placing the cross-hairs. Additionally, as this approach "suffers" from the so-called "ceiling effect" (Oh, 2001), i.e. most of the attributes often fall in the first quadrant as respondents tend to give high performance and importance ratings, research introduces an upward sloping 45° diagonal line (Azzopardi and Nash, 2013). It refers to as an Iso-priority diagonal line because it provides a visual line where all points lying along it have equal priority for improvement (I=P) (Sever, 2015). The area above the line contains attributes that have higher performance than importance ratings, while attributes below the line require improvement as the level of their performance is lower than the importance level.

Results and discussion

The analysis finally encompassed 42 historic cities (21 coastal and 21 continental/inland) out of 94 in total (Table 4.1). According to the latest census (2011), the average number of permanent residents in the coastal historic cities is 19,267. On the other hand, in the sample of continental historic cities, the average number of residents is 20,512, excluding Zagreb, the capital of Croatia (with 801,309 inhabitants). This number increases to 35,528, with Zagreb included. Hence regardless of the methodology used for grouping cities based on their size, most Croatian (historic) cities are small, except for Split (178,102 inhabitants) and Rijeka (128,624 inhabitants) in the coastal region and Zagreb and Osijek (108,048) in the continental region.

Qualitative analysis of the relevant strategic documents has shown that all the coastal historic cities, even the smallest ones, put tourism at the core of their future development efforts. Moreover, apart from general strategic documents (which all cities were obliged to deliver), where tourism development is unanimously identified as one of the strategic goals, separate tourism and/or cultural development plan has been produced by 21 coastal historic cities (out of 42 in total), with 15 of them in the sample. As for continental historic cities, 20 (out of 52) have either tourism or a cultural development strategy (with eight cities being in the sample), mostly delivered in recent years.

However, despite the richness of their cultural heritage and (declared) orientation to cultural tourism development, most coastal historic cities faced extensive "sun, sea and sand" tourism reaching its maturity phase. In contrast, while continental ones have just recently started to develop small scale tourism based mainly on cultural heritage, which is thus in its introductory life cycle phase.

Hence, considering the number of tourist arrivals and overnights recorded in 2017, the sample encompasses leading tourism destinations, mostly coastal ones, such as Dubrovnik (arrivals – 1,174,878; overnights – 3,880,065), Split (arrivals – 770,325; overnights – 2,127,350), Rovinj (arrivals – 625,665; overnights – 3,689,510), Umag (arrivals – 486,308; overnights – 2,334,171), Opatija (arrivals – 443,196; overnights – 1,361,009), etc., and a lot of smaller continental historic cities, where tourism is yet to be developed e.g. Vrlika (arrivals – 339; overnights – 1234) or Lipik (arrivals – 555; overnights – 2259). All the indicators of tourist density, especially tourist intensity rates, are highest in the coastal historic cities, namely, Umag (TIR = 6679.10), Novalja (TIR = 6600),

Opatija (TIR = 6507.40), Rovinj (TIR= 4792.2), Dubrovnik (TIR=2757.0), etc. By contrast, the tourism intensity values are low within the sample of continental historic cities.

It is worth noting that out of 94 historic cities, only ten have created a smart city strategy, six on the coast (Rijeka, Dubrovnik, Umag, Mali Lošinj, Krk and Supetar) and four inland (Zagreb, Karlovac, Jastrebarsko, Dugo Selo), all belonging to the sample.

With respect to the current application and use of smart technologies, the research results have not indicated significant differences between the coastal and continental city groups. Social networks and GIS appear to be the most used technological solutions.

The results of the analysis provide clear indications of the varied perception of the SG categories between representatives from coastal and continental historic cities. Following the suggestions made by Lai and Hitchcock (2015), the first step in this analysis was to conduct individually paired sample t-tests to see whether the identified IP gaps are significant for each of the SG categories within both of the samples. Within the sample of coastal cities, the IP gap for all smart governance categories, except for *Growth of tourism receipts*, proved significant (p-value <0.05) (Table 4.1). Furthermore, within the sample of continental cities, gaps are not significant for the following SG categories, *Sustainable use of cultural heritage* and *Interpretation of cultural heritage* (Table 4.1). Accordingly, the non-significant SG categories have been omitted from further analysis.

In both samples, the Iso-priority diagonal line proves there is a place for substantial improvement. All the SG categories with significant IP gaps in both samples are placed below the Iso-line, meaning that their performance level is significantly lower than the importance level (Figure 4.3). Although the Iso-line approach is a suitable method for identifying areas of concern, as it directly focuses on differences in IP ratings (Azzopardi and Nash, 2013), it produces less information and offers limited discriminative power compared to the IP plot with four quadrants. To deliver in-depth analysis, the data-centred quadrant approach (Oh, 2001) with actual mean data values of observed importance and performance ratings, and grand means of importance and performance for the cross-points in the IP mapping (Lai and Hitchcock, 2015), was used.

SG Elements. There are significant differences between coastal and continental cities in their perception of the importance and performance of the proposed SG categories. In the case of *coastal cities*, all the SG elements are divided

Table 4.1   Importance-performance scores on 28 smart governance categories

Historic coastal cities, n=21					Data-centred quadrants	SGC	Data-centred quadrants	Historic continental cities, n=21				
I(a)	P(b)	I – P	*t-Value	Sig. (2-tailed)				I(a)	P(b)	I – P	*t-Value	Sig. (2-tailed)
						Elements						
4.2381	3.1905	1.05	5.552	0.000	IV	1	IV	4.2857	3.3810	0.90	4.166	0.000
3.7619	2.8095	0.95	3.760	0.001	III	2	III	3.9524	3.2381	0.71	2.752	0.012
4.1429	3.0476	1.10	5.319	0.000	III	3	III	3.9048	3.2381	0.67	2.467	0.023
4.3810	2.9048	1.48	5.247	0.000	IV	4	I	4.4286	3.6667	0.76	2.961	0.008
4.3810	2.9524	1.43	4.804	0.000	IV	5	I	4.4286	3.6190	0.81	3.179	0.005
4.5238	3.0476	1.48	6.276	0.000	IV	6	I	4.5238	3.5714	0.95	4.483	0.000
4.3810	2.9524	1.43	4.564	0.000	IV	7	I	4.4286	3.5714	0.86	4.315	0.000
4.0000	2.6190	1.38	5.087	0.000	III	8	IV	4.3333	3.2857	1.05	3.740	0.001
						Outcomes						
4.5714	3.3810	1.19	5.876	0.000	I	9	I	4.7619	3.8095	0.95	4.740	0.000
4.1905	3.1429	1.05	4.690	0.000	III	10	II	4.1905	3.5238	0.67	2.751	0.012
3.8571	2.9048	0.95	3.760	0.001	III	<u>11</u>	III	3.7619	3.1429	0.62	2.914	0.009
4.2857	3.2857	1.00	4.183	0.000	I	12	IV	4.3810	3.4762	0.90	4.394	0.000
4.2857	3.1905	1.10	4.256	0.000	IV	13	I	4.4762	3.6667	0.81	3.068	0.006
4.0476	3.4286	0.62	2.540	0.020	II	14	I	4.2857	3.7143	0.57	2.828	0.010

Historic coastal cities, n=21					Data-centred quadrants	SGC	Data-centred quadrants	Historic continental cities, n=21				
I(a)	P(b)	I – P	*t-Value	Sig. (2-tailed)				I(a)	P(b)	I – P	*t-Value	Sig. (2-tailed)
4.2857	3.5714	0.71	3.627	0.002	I	15	I	4.3333	3.5238	0.81	3.302	0.004
4.1429	3.2381	0.90	4.394	0.000	II	16	II	4.0952	3.5238	0.57	2.828	0.010
4.2857	3.2381	1.05	5.215	0.000	I	17	III	4.2381	3.4286	0.81	3.442	0.003
4.4286	3.4762	0.95	3.627	0.002	I	18	I	4.4286	3.9048	0.52	2.950	0.008
4.3333	3.3333	1.00	3.873	0.001	I	19	II	4.0476	3.5238	0.52	2.329	0.030
4.5238	3.0952	1.43	6.086	0.000	IV	20	I	4.3333	3.6667	0.67	3.839	0.001
4.0952	3.4286	0.67	3.162	0.005	II	21	–	4.0476	3.6667	0.38	1.793	0.088
3.9048	3.3333	0.57	2.828	0.010	II	22	–	4.1429	3.7619	0.38	2.019	0.057
4.0000	3.7143	0.29	1.188	0.249	–	23	II	4.1905	3.6190	0.57	2.828	0.010
						Strategies						
4.0952	3.2857	0.81	3.996	0.001	II	24	III	4.1429	3.3810	0.76	3.508	0.002
4.0476	3.0952	0.95	4.740	0.000	III	25	IV	4.2857	3.4286	0.86	4.315	0.000
4.2381	3.3810	0.86	4.076	0.001	I	26	III	4.2381	3.2381	1.00	4.830	0.000
4.1905	3.3333	0.86	3.873	0.001	II	27	III	4.0952	3.1429	0.95	5.898	0.000
3.9048	3.1905	0.71	2.660	0.015	III	28	IV	4.2857	3.3333	0.95	4.074	0.001
4.1973	3.1990					Grand mean		4.2517	3.5017			

Note: *Paired Samples Test for each question:
(a) Mean value: Performance questions asked as "How well is your city doing?" on a scale with 1 – Poor and 5 – Excellent.
(b) Mean value: Importance questions asked as "How important it is following to you?" on a scale with 1 – Not at all important and 5 – Extremely important.
I Importance-Performance gaps.
(–) p-value >0.05
(_) Added Smart Governance categories.

Smart governance categories:
Elements: Q1 – (Smart external collaboration and participation of public stakeholders); Q2 – (Smart external collaboration and participation of industry); Q3 – (Smart external collaboration and participation of non-profit sector and community); Q4 – (Smart internal coordination); Q5 – (Smart decision making processes); Q6 – (Smart e-administration); Q7 – (Smart ICT); Q8 – (Innovation capacity);
Outcomes: Q9 – (Efficient internal organization); Q10 – (Readiness for disaster management); Q11 – (Climate mitigation systems); Q12 – (Citizen-centric services); Q13 – (Efficient interaction with citizens); Q14 – (City branding); Q15 – (Economic growth); Q16 – (Social inclusion – inclusion of urban residents in public services); Q17 – (Ecological performance/Environmental efficiency); Q18 – (Efficient spatial planning); Q19 – (Highly educated citizens); Q20 – (Efficient traffic system); Q21 – (Sustainable use of cultural heritage); Q22 – (Interpretation of cultural heritage); Q23 – (Growth of tourism receipts);
Strategies: Q24 – (Legislation); Q25 – (Policies towards initiatives and projects strengthening innovation systems); Q26 – (Policies towards initiatives and projects strengthening CULTURAL development); Q27 – (Policies towards initiatives and projects strengthening sustainable TOURISM); Q28 – (Collaborative governance and improvement of local government, i.e. Organizational transformation).
Coastal historic cities: Pula, Omiš, Novalja, Dubrovnik, Vodnjan, Mali Lošinj, Buzet, Rijeka, Šibenik, Zadar, Umag, Kaštela, Nin, Opatija, Rovinj, Krk, Biograd na Moru, Split, Hvar, Supetar, Skradin.
Continental historic cities: Koprivnica, Gospić, Karlovac, Donji Miholjac, Duga Resa, Jastrebarsko, Našice, Nova Gradiška, Samobor, Bjelovar, Osijek, Zagreb, Požega, Varaždin, Petrinja, Vukovar, Čakovec, Vrlika, Zlatar, Ozalj, Dugo Selo.
Source: Authors' research.

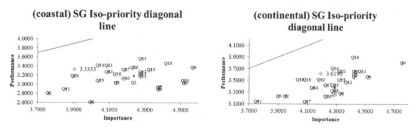

Source: Authors' research.

Figure 4.3   IP mapping for coastal and continental historic cities (Iso-priority diagonal line)

between the third, i.e. *Low priority* quadrant (III – low importance and low performance): *Smart external collaboration and participation with industry; Smart external collaboration and participation with non-profit sector and community; Smart innovation,* and the fourth, i.e. *Concentrate here* quadrant (IV – high importance, low performance): *Smart external collaboration and participation with public sector; Smart internal coordination; Smart decision making processes; Smart e-administration* (Figure 4.4). It is indicative and in line with the observation on their lower administrative culture, that coastal city representatives find external collaboration with industry, the non-profit sector and the community neither important nor well performed, while collaboration with the public sector is considered to be very important but unsatisfactory. However, they are aware that a part of the blame lies on themselves as they negatively assess internal coordination, e-administration and decision-making processes.

The IP mapping of the SG elements for the *continental cities* indicates (as expected due to their higher administrative culture) a high level of both importance and performance values for *Smart internal coordination; Smart decision-making; Smart e-administration; Smart ICT,* and have placed them in the Keep up the good work quadrant (I – high importance and high performance). Within this sample, *Smart external collaboration and participation with public stakeholders* and *Innovation capacity* are recognized as smart governance categories that should be improved (IV). Surprisingly, they, and the representatives of coastal historic cities, gave low priority to *collaboration with industry* and with *the non-profit sector and local community,* which diverges from the SG trends in big cities across Europe. The reference results of Bolivar and Meijer (2016) show that most respondents consider external collaboration and participation to be the Smart governance base.

Furthermore, representatives of both coastal and continental cities consider *collaboration with the public sector* (presumably regional and state authorities) to be extremely important but underperformed. This result is in line with Koprić's (2016) conclusion that Croatian governance requires a complete paradigm change by introducing a bottom-up instead of top-down management process.

In contrast with the continental cities, *Innovation capacity* is under-estimated in the coastal historic cities, whose authorities think it is neither well-performed nor important; likewise, the *Policies towards initiatives and projects strengthening innovation systems* (within SG Strategies). On the other hand, they stress *Smart ICT* as an important but not well performed SG element. The rationale behind this may be either a misunderstanding of the concepts or the relationship between them. *Collaborative governance and improvement of local government* (i.e. organizational transformation) (within Strategies) is also perceived as "low priority" (low importance and low performance). It is hard to find the logic for such an attitude; moreover, they negatively assess the performance of internal coordination, e-administration and decision-making processes, obviously resulting from the poor internal organization of the local governments. One of the potential explanations may lie in the fact that coastal cities have enjoyed the benefits of the growing tourism industry for which local governments take the credit and simply do not care to make any improvements (also seen in the fact that they do not consider collaboration with their stakeholders important).

SC *Outcomes*. *Coastal historic cities* in the sample mostly indicate either a high level of performance and importance (I: Q9/Q12/Q15/Q17/Q18/Q19) or a high level of performance and low importance (II: Q14/Q16/Q21/Q22). Contrary to our expectations, they placed *Readiness for disaster management* and *Climate mitigation systems* in the low priority quadrant (III – low importance and low performance). Such a result is surprising considering these two topics are currently among those most discussed by researchers, planners and developers, especially with regard to the management and planning of historic cities. Unfortunately, none of these topics has gained much attention in Croatia, thus pointing to a lack of strategic thinking that has to be seriously addressed in the near future. As an illustration, although Croatia signed the Protocol on Integrated Coastal Zone Management in the Mediterranean back in 2012, it has not yet been implemented in Croatian legislation. Moreover, coastal management plans have been implemented in only one county (Šibenik-Knin County). However, it should be noted that even in Bolivar and Meijer's research (2016), *Readiness for disaster management* scores lowest.

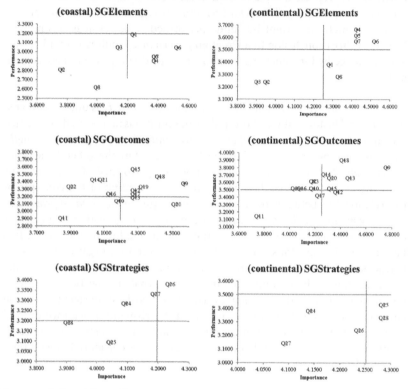

Source: Authors' research.

Figure 4.4   IP mapping for coastal and continental historic cities (data centred line)

Respondents from the *continental historic cities* indicated a high level of performance for the majority of proposed smart governance outcomes (I: Q9/Q13/Q14/Q15/Q18/Q20; II: Q10/Q16/Q19/Q23). According to them, the issue of disaster management is well performed, although not that important (II). Climate mitigation strategies are considered to be of low priority as they are probably thought to be related only to rising sea-levels and, as such, did not attract the attention of the continental city representatives. Unlike the coastal city representatives, those of the continental cities are satisfied with *Efficiency of the traffic system*, which is not so overburdened by extensive tourism demand, and stress that *Citizen-centric services* should be improved.

Coastal city authorities perceive *city branding, social inclusion of citizens, sustainable use of cultural heritage* and *interpretation of cultural heritage* to be "overestimated", i.e. not so important and above-average performed. Such attitudes suggest they are unaware of the heritage potential for city tourism and overall development or the intangible value that a city acquires if adequately branded. However, due to the growing civil sector activities, the need for the sustainable use and protection of heritage is becoming more recognized. Unfortunately, local authorities often consider these conservation efforts as an obstacle to further growth and do not consider them important. This may be one of the reasons for perceiving the *social inclusion of citizens* as "overestimated".

Furthermore, the *Sustainable use of cultural heritage* outcome is perceived as not so important while the strategy component *Policies towards initiatives and projects towards strengthening cultural development* is perceived as important; however, both of them are perceived as well performed. This may indicate a misunderstanding of the relationship between the SG outcome and a strategy for its achievement.

Finally, *Social inclusion/inclusion of citizens in public services* is claimed to be better performed than it deserves. Although citizens' participation in public processes and services is guaranteed by the Croatian Law on Spatial Planning (Official Gazette, 153/13, 65/17, 114/18, 39/19) and the Right to Information Law (Official Gazette, 25/13; 85/15), local authorities often see this requirement as an obstacle that prolongs public processes and are reluctant to be involved. Coastal city authorities consider *ecological performance* and *spatial planning* important and well performed despite the fact that there are many examples of illegal building, poor communal infrastructure, inadequate waste management and the exceeding of carrying capacities, as elaborated by Klarić et al. (2018).

Continental cities consider *ecological performance* to be of low priority (neither important nor well performed), while *spatial planning* is considered important and satisfactorily performed. However, it should not be forgotten that continental cities are not subject to extensive tourism development.

SC *Strategies*. The perception of the proposed smart governance strategies also varies. In most cases, representatives of *coastal historic cities* expressed a high level of perceived performances (I: Q26; II: Q24/27). Furthermore, they pointed out *Policies towards initiatives and projects strengthening innovation systems* and *Collaborative governance and improvement of local government* (i.e. organizational transformation) as *Low priority* strategies. On the other hand, representatives from the *continental cities* indicated these two smart governance categories as a priority, placing them in the *Concentrate here* quadrant. The rest of the strategies in the continental cities are scored as *Low priority*. According to Bolivar and Meijer's (2016) research, the highest-scoring implementation strategy is *Collaborative governance and improvement of local government*. Other strategies were also recognized as important for SG success.

One might wonder what makes the governance of historic cities specific and whether smart solutions provide feasible tools for meeting their challenges. In general, there is no unanimous answer to this question. Historic cities with outstanding cultural heritage values are often highly contested arenas of diverse and partly conflicting interests and development ideas, which challenge the safeguarding of the cultural heritage, trying to balance inherent urban structure and identity with the demands of residents, visitors and business (Ripp et al., 2011). The ultimate goal should be to capitalize on heritage and achieve the aspired residents' quality of life, visitor satisfaction, heritage conservation and socioeconomic development. To deliver these goals, Agenda 21 for culture proposes integrated (cultural) heritage management planning as a fundamental tool for managing historic urban areas. Current developments, i.e. increasing commercial competition, tourism development, global climate change, demographic changes, and new structural and technical requirements for buildings and infrastructure, present new parameters that place particular demands on all cities with historic inner-city areas (UNESCO, 2012). By addressing these parameters, historic cities are expected to improve their governance models and potentially integrate intelligent solutions. As an improved version, smart governance should encompass smart, open and agile governmental institutions and be based on stakeholder participation and collaboration at all levels of the governing process (Scholl and Scholl, 2014; Pivčević et al., 2018). It requires different needs to be coordinated and balanced. Furthermore, all the actors should contribute to delivering a balanced vision of sustainable future development in accordance with cultural heritage values. In this process, it is crucial to develop and implement proper participation plans. There is currently much excitement about using social media and other forms of ICT as a constituent element of a smart city's technological dimension to support stakeholder participation (Quick and Bryson, 2016). However, forms of e-government are highly variable (Coursey and Norris, 2008). They often serve primarily as a new mechanism to reinforce a longstanding form of government–public interaction rather than as a platform for new forms of engagement, e.g. social media (Mergel, 2013). Finally, if tourism is recognized as a historic city development option, policy measures should be focus on its sustainable development. In that process, smart governance in historic cities should seek to protect the residents; otherwise, loss of community, and thus accordingly, local identity is threatened.

Conclusions

The majority of quantitative and qualitative studies dealing with smart city governance focus on the wider European area (Ruhlandt, 2018), while only a few deliver city or country comparisons. Thus, Odendaal (2003) compares smart city initiatives in Brisbane and Durban, Giffinger et al. (2007) rank medium-sized European cities according to the smart city concept, Dimelli (2016) examines possibilities for the adaptation of global ICT practices in Greek cities and Ruohomaa et al. (2019) present three cases of smart city development in small cities in Finland, each concentrating on a different aspect.

This research supplements current literature by focusing on smart governance in 42 coastal and continental historic cities in Croatia, a southern, Mediterranean country facing extensive tourism development in its coastal region. The study identifies and elaborates on differences in perception of the three extended categories of smart governance, i.e. elements, outcomes and strategies, to address the potential of smart governance for responding to contemporary challenges in historic urban destinations.

While most of the previous studies focus on one or two categories, usually elements (components) and outcomes, only a few researchers have included contextual factors or measurements (Odendaal, 2003; Batty et al., 2012; Kourtit et al., 2014; Battarra et al., 2016; Bolivar and Meijer, 2016; Castelnuovo et al., 2016; Meijer, 2016; Marsal-Llacuna, 2016). To the best of our knowledge, this study is among the first to deliver a comprehensive analysis of SG in historic urban destinations.

The findings indicate significant differences in the perception of both the importance and performance of the proposed SG categories between historic coastal and continental cities. In both cases, all the SG categories with significant IP gaps fall under the Iso-priority diagonal line indicating that, in both samples, city representatives on average consider the importance of elements to outweigh their performance. However, comparative analysis of the two samples regarding elements, outcomes and strategies, indicates more variations between them. Though not so significant, they obviously may be related to tourism development intensity, the most important contextual factor, and different administrative cultures between coastal and continental public authorities.

To our surprise, low importance is given to the following SG outcomes: *Social inclusion, Climate mitigation* and *Readiness for disaster management*, currently the core of the research and policy agenda. We have noticed that in some cases, respondents were unfamiliar with the terms, which means that the SG agenda has not reached even highly positioned civil servants in Croatian (historic) cities. In some cases there is an ego-effect, meaning that respondents were satisfied with the performances without considering a need for any improvement. It was especially the case in the sample of coastal cities. Furthermore, although considering tourism revenues an important SG outcome, continental cities nevertheless place policies for strengthening cultural development and sustainable tourism development in the low priority quadrant. Finally, it should be noted that several SG categories are placed near the lines, i.e. cross-hair points of the grid. Considering IPA is not sensitive enough to precisely represent the data structure, we nevertheless decided to take them into account to maximize the effectiveness in the interpretation.

Despite its contribution to understanding smart governance in historic cities, two shortcomings of this research must be noted. First, although the size/smallness of the city is shown to be one of the contextual factors affecting smart governance behaviour, it may also be considered a serious constraint to even the application of most of the SG categories owing to the limited financial and human resources. It is common knowledge that the Croatian administrative-territorial structure is burdened with too many small cities/municipalities that are hardly self-sustainable (Rašić Bakarić, 2012). Second, the importance–performance analysis, as an excellent diagnostic and interpretative tool, is used in this research to indicate differences between SG in the continental and coastal cities and distinguish the importance–performance gaps to focus on. However, it may not explain in detail why certain cities perform better than others, and the rationale behind this, even though the status of historic city (richness of cultural heritage), tourism development intensity and location-related administrative culture have been used as the most relevant contextual factors. We therefore encourage any future research that would include a subsequent analysis (e.g. interviews or focus groups with city representatives), potentially contributing to an explanation of these gaps.

Notes

1   Hudson (2004, as cited by Jamil et al., 2013, 901) defines administrative culture "as general characteristics of public officials (i.e., shared values, attitude beliefs) – federal, state, and local. It is related to the broader political culture it derives, and can be further discussed in terms of sub-culture".

2   Administrative culture is often related to so-called administrative capacities that may be "measured" by a region/city (i.e. its public authorities') efficiency in attracting and using EU funds for financing different infrastructural, cultural, social, and other types of initiatives and projects. Given this, Croatian continental regions/cities are usually shown to be more efficient in this process (Croatian Chamber of Commerce/Hrvatska gospodarska komora, 2019).

References

Angelidoua, A., Karachalioua, E., Angelidoua, T. and Stylianidisa, E. (2017), Cultural Heritage in Smart City Environments. *The International Archives of the Photogrammetry, Remote Sensing and Spatial Information Sciences*, Volume XLII-2/W5, 2017, Ottawa, Canada. https://www.int-arch-photogramm-remote-sens-spatial -inf-sci.net/XLII-2-W5/27/2017/isprs-archives-XLII-2-W5-27-2017.pdf.

Azzopardi, E. and Nash, R. (2013), A Critical Evaluation of Importance-Performance Analysis. *Tourism Management*, 35, 222–233. https://doi.org/10.1016/j.tourman .2012.07.007.

Bacon, D. R. (2003), A Comparison of Approaches to Importance-Performance Analysis. *International Journal of Market Research*, 45(1), 55–71. https://doi.org/10 .1177/147078530304500101.

Bakici, T., Almirall, E. and Wareham, J. (2013), A Smart City Initiative: The Case of Barcelona. *Journal of the Knowledge Economy*, 4(2), 135–148. https://10.1007/s13132 -012-0084-9.

Bătăgan, L. (2011), Smart Cities and Sustainability Models. *Revista de Informatică Economică*, 15(3), 80–87. http://www.revistaie.ase.ro/content/59/07%20- %20Batagan.pdf.

Battarra, R., Gargiulo, C., Pappalardo, G., Boiano, D. A. and Oliva, J. S. (2016), Planning in the era of Information and Communication Technologies. Discussing the "label: Smart" in South-European cities with environmental and socio-economic chal- lenges. *Cities*, 59, 1–7. http://dx.doi.org/10.1016/j.cities.2016.05.007.

Batty, M., Axhausen, K.W., Giannotti, A., Pozdnoukhov, A., Bazzani, M., et al. (2012), Smart Cities of the Future. *The European Physical Journal Special Topics*, 214, 481–518. http://dx.doi.org/10.1140/epjst/e2012-01703-3.

Batty, M., Axhausen, K. W., Giannotti, F., Pozdnoukhov, A., Bazzani, A., Wachowicz, M., et al. (2012), Smart Cities of the Future. *European Physical Journal: Special Topics*, 214(1), 481–518. http://dx.doi.org/10.1140/epjst/e2012-01703-3.

Berntzen, L. and Johansen, M. R. (2016), The Role of Citizen Participation in Municipal Smart City Projects: Lessons Learned from Norway. In: Garcia, G., Pardo, J. R., and Nam, T. (eds), *Smarter as the New Urban Agenda*. Springer International Publishing. https://10.1007/978-3-319-17620-8.

Blessi, T. G., Trembly, D. G., Sandri, M. and Pilati, T. (2012), New Trajectories in Urban Regeneration Processes: Cultural Capital as Source of Human and Social Capital Accumulation – Evidence from the Case of Tohu in Montreal. *Cities*, 29, 397–407. http://dx.doi.org/10.1016/j.cities.2011.12.001.

Boley, B. B., McGehee, N. G. and Hammett, A. L. T. (2017), Importance-Performance Analysis (IPA) of Sustainable Tourism Initiatives: The Residents Perspective. *Tourism Management*, 58, 66–77. https://doi.org/10.1016/j.tourman.2016.10.002.

Bolivar, M. P. R. and Meijer, A. J. (2016), Smart Governance: Using a Literature Review and Empirical Analysis to Build a Research Model. *Social Science Computer Review*, 34(6), 673–692. https://doi.org/10.1177%2F0894439315611088.

Bruyere, B. B., Rodriguez, D. A. and Vaske, J. J. (2002), Enhancing Importance-Performance Analysis Through Segmentation, *Journal of Travel & Tourism Marketing*, 12(1), 81–95. https://doi.org/10.1300/J073v12n01_05.

Bulkeley, H. and Betsill, M. M. (2003), *Cities and Climate Change Urban Sustainability and Global Environmental Governance*. Routledge, London and New York.

Capdevila, I. and Zarlenga, M. I. (2015), Smart City or Smart Citizens? The Barcelona Case. *Journal of Strategy and Management*, 8(3), 266–282. https://doi.org/10.1108/JSMA-03-2015-0030.

Caragliu, A., Bo, C. D. and Nijkamp, P. (2009), Smart Cities in Europe. Proceedings of the 3rd Central European Conference in Regional Science, *Košice*, 45–59. https://inta-aivn.org/images/cc/Urbanism/background%20documents/01_03_Nijkamp.pdf.

Cartalis, C. (2014), Toward Resilient Cities – a Review of Definitions, Challenges and Prospects. *Advances in Building Energy Research* 8(2), 259–266. https://doi.org/10.1080/17512549.2014.890533.

Castan Broto, V. and Bulkeley, H. (2013), A Survey of Urban Climate Change Experiments in 100 Cities. *Global Environmental Change*, 23, 92–102. https://doi.org/10.1016/j.gloenvcha.2012.07.005.

Castelnuovo, W., Misuraca, G. and Savoldelli, A. (2016), Smart Cities Governance: The Need for a Holistic Approach to Assessing Urban Participatory Policy Making. *Social Science Computer Review*, 34(6). http://dx.doi.org/10.1177/0894439315611103.

Corfee-Morlot, J., Cochran I. and Teasdale P. J. (2008), Cities and Climate Change: Harnessing the Potential for Local Action. Competitive Cities and Climate Change, OECD conference proceedings, Milan, Italy, 78–105. http://www.oecd.org/cfe/regional-policy/50594939.pdf.

Coursey, D. and Norris, D. F. (2008), Models of E-government: Are They Correct? An Empirical Assessment. *Public Administration Review*, 68(3), 523–536. https://doi.org/10.1111/j.1540-6210.2008.00888.x.

Croatian Chamber of Commerce/Hrvatska gospodarska komora (2019), Counties and EU funds/Županije i fondovi EU. https://www.hgk.hr/documents/hgk-analiza-zupanije-i-fondovi-eu5c6d7b86886a3.pdf.

Dale, N. and Markandya, A. (2015), Local assessment of Vulnerability to Climate Variability and Change for Šibenik-Knin County coastal zone. https://climate-adapt.eea.europa.eu/metadata/case-studies/integrating-climate-change-adaptation-into-coastal-planning-in-sibenik-knin-county-croatia.

Dameri, R. P. and Benevolo, C. (2016), Governing Smart Cities: An Empirical Analysis. *Soil Science Computer Review*, 34(6), 693–707. http://dx.doi.org/10.1177/0894439315611093.

Das, S. and Roychowdhury, P. (2017), Smart Urban Traffic Management System TTEA. *Trends in Transport Engineering and Applications*, 4(1). https://www.researchgate.net/publication/317300560_Smart_Urban_Traffic_Management_System.

Deng, D., Zhao, Y. and Zhou, X. (2017), Smart City Planning Under the Climate Change Condition. IOP Conference Series: *Earth and Environmental Science*, 81. https://iopscience.iop.org/article/10.1088/1755-1315/81/1/012091/pdf.

Dickinson, H. (2016), Management to New Public Governance: The Implications for a 'New Public Service'. In: Butcher, J. and Gilchrist, D. (eds), *Three Sector Solution: Delivering Public Policy in Collaboration with Not-for-profits and Business*, ANU Press, The Australian National University, Canberra, Australia. http://press-files.anu.edu.au/downloads/press/n1949/pdf/ch03.pdf.

Dimelli, D. (2016), Can Greek Cities be Smart? *Journal of Regional Socio-Economic Issues*, 3(2), 8–22. http://www.rsijournal.eu/ARTICLES/June_2016/RSI_June_2016_VIII_(1).pdf.

Gandini, A., Garmendia, L. and San Mateos, R. (2017), Towards Sustainable Historic Cities: Mitigation Climate Change Risks. *Entrepreneurship and Sustainability Issues*, 4(3), 319–327. DOI: 10.9770/jesi.2017.4.3S(7).

García-Hernández, M., Calle-Vaquero, M. and Yubero, C. (2017), Cultural Heritage and Urban Tourism: Historic City Centres under Pressure. *Sustainability*, 9. https://doi.org/10.3390/su9081346.

Girard, L. F. (2013), Toward a Smart Sustainable Development of Port Cities/Areas: The Role of the "Historic Urban Landscape" Approach. *Sustainability*, 5(10), 4329–4348. doi:10.3390/su5104329.

Gisselquist, R. M. (2012), Good Governance as a Concept, and Why This Matters for Development Policy. United Nations University, World Institute for Development Economic Research. Working Paper No. 2012/30. https://www.wider.unu.edu/sites/default/files/wp2012-030.pdf.

Gordon, A., Simondson, D., White, M., Moilanen, A. and Bekessy, S. (2009), Integrating Conservation Planning and Land Use Planning in Urban Landscapes. *Landscape and Urban Planning*, 91(4), 183–194. https://doi.org/10.1016/j.landurbplan.2008.12.011.

Gorin, A., Gallet, J. and Bigou, L. (2015), Recent Advances of Urban Traffic Management Centers in French Cities. 22nd ITS World Congress, Bordeaux, France, 1–12. https://hal.archives-ouvertes.fr/hal-01491597/document.

Griffiths, R. (1995), Cultural Strategies and New Modes of Urban Intervention. *Cities*, 12(4), 253–265. https://doi.org/10.1016/0264-2751(95)00042-K.

Giffinger, R., Fertner, C., Kramar, H., Kalasek, R., Pichler-Milanovic, N. and Meijers, E. (2007), Smart Cities. *Ranking of European Medium-Sized Cities*. Vienna UT: Centre of Regional Science. https://www.researchgate.net/publication/228915976_Smart_cities_ranking_An_effective_instrument_for_the_positioning_of_the_cities.

Grodach, C. and Loukaitou-Sideris, A. (2007), Cultural Development Strategies and Urban Revitalization. *International Journal of Cultural Policy*, 13(4), 349–370. https://doi.org/10.1080/10286630701683235.

Healey, P. (2007), *Urban Complexity and Spatial Strategies – Towards a Relational Planning for Our Times*. London and New York: Routledge. https://www.alnap.org/system/files/content/resource/files/main/healey.pdf.

Heinrichs, D., Aggarwal, R., Barton, J., Barucha, E., Butsch, C., et al. (2011), Adapting Cities to Climate Change: Opportunities and Constraints, in Cities and Climate Change: Responding to an Urgent Agenda. In: Hoornweg, D., Freire, M., Lee, M. J., Bhada-Tata, P. and Yuen, B. (eds), *The International Bank for Reconstruction and Development/The World Bank*, 193–224. https://doi.org/10.1596/9780821384930_CH08.

Hudson, R. (2000), *Production, Places and the Environment: Changing Perspectives in Economic Geography*. Prentice Hall Person Education.

ICOMOS (2008), The ICOMOS Charter for the Interpretation and Presentation of Cultural Heritage Sites. http://icip.icomos.org/downloads/ICOMOS_Interpretation _Charter_ENG_04_10_08.pdf.

Jamil, I., Askvik, S. and Hossain, F. (2013), Understanding Administrative Culture: Some Theoretical and Methodological Remarks. *International Journal of Public Administration*, 36(13), 900–909. https://doi.org/10.1080/01900692.2013.837728.

Klarić, Z., Horak, S., Marušić, Z, Milojević, D., Tomljenović, R, Carić, H. and Knapić, L. (2018), Studija prihvatnih kapaciteta turizma na području Splitsko-dalmatinske županije (Tourism Carrying Capacity Assessment in Split Dalmatia County), Institut za turizam, Zagreb.

Koens, K., Postma, A. and Papp, B. (2018), Is Overtourism Overused? Understanding the Impact of Tourism in a City Context. *Sustainability*, 10(12), 4384. https://doi .org/10.3390/su10124384.

Koprić, I. (2016), Reforma javne uprave u Hrvatskoj: ni bolni rezovi ni postupne promjene – nužna je nova upravna paradigma. *Političke analize*, 26, 3–12. https://hrcak .srce.hr/167364.

Kostakos, V., Ojala, T. and Juntunen, T. (2013), Traffic in the Smart City Exploring City-Wide Sensing for Traffic Control Center Augmentation. *IEEE Computer Society*, 22–29.   https://people.eng.unimelb.edu.au/vkostakos/files/papers/ieeeinternet13 .pdf.

Kourtit, K., Nijkamp, P., Franklin, R. S. and Rodríguez-Pose, A. (2014), A Blueprint for Strategic Urban Research: The Urban Piazza. *The Town Planning Review*, 85(1), 97–126. DOI: http://dx.doi.org/10.3828/tpr.2014.7.

Kumar, V. T. M. and Dahyija, B. (2017), Smart Economy in Smart Cities. In: Kumar, T. M. V. (ed.), *Smart Economy in Smart Cities*. Springer Nature Singapore, 3–76.

Lai, I. K. W. and Hitchcock, M. (2015), Importance-Performance Analysis in Tourism: A framework for Researchers. *Tourism Management*, 48, 242–267. DOI: https://doi .org/10.1016/j.tourman.2014.11.008.

Lin, Y. (2018), A Comparison of Selected Western and Chinese Smart Governance: The Application of ICT in Governmental Management, Participation and Collaboration. *Telecommunications Policy*, 42(10), 800–809. DOI: https://doi.org/10.1016/j.telpol .2018.07.003.

Linders, D. (2012), From E-government to Ee-government: Defining a Typology for Citizen Coproduction in the Age of Social Media. *Government Information Quarterly*, 29(4), 446–454. DOI: https://doi.org/10.1016/j.giq.2012.06.003.

Marsal-Llacuna, M. L. (2016), City Indicators on Social Sustainability as Standardization Technologies for Smarter (Citizen-centered) Governance of Cities. *Social Indicators Research*, 128(3), 1193–1216. DOI: http://dx.doi.org/10.1007/s11205-015-1075-6.

Martilla, J. A. and James, J. C. (1977), Importance-Performance Analysis. *Journal of Marketing*, 41, 77–79. http://dx.doi.org/10.2307/1250495.

Meijer, A. (2016), *Smart City Governance: A Local Emergent Perspective. Smarter as the New Urban Agenda*. Springer International Publishing. DOI: http://dx.doi.org/10 .1007/978-3-319-17620-8_4.

Mergel, I. (2013), Social Media Adoption and Resulting Tactics in the US Federal Government. *Government Information Quarterly*, 30(2), 123–130. https://doi.org/10 .1016/j.giq.2012.12.004.

Mikulić, D. and Petrić, L. (2014), Can Culture and Tourism be the Foothold of Urban Regeneration? A Croatian Case Study. *Turizam*, 62(4), 377–395. https://hrcak.srce .hr/131934.

Misuraca, G., Reid, A. and Deakin, M. (2011), Exploring Emerging ICT-enabled Governance Models in European Cities – Analysis of the Mapping Survey to Identify the Key City Overance Policy Areas Most Impacted by ICTs. JRC Technical Notes. European Commission, Institute for Prospective Technological Studies. ftp://ftp.jrc.es/pub/EURdoc/JRC65581_TN.pdf.

Moraci F., Errigo, M. F., Fazia, C. and Burgio, G. (2018), Making Less Vulnerable Cities: Resilience as a New Paradigm of Smart Planning. *Sustainability*, 10(3), 755. DOI: https://doi.org/10.3390/su10030755.

Murdy, S. and Pike, S. (2012), Perceptions of Visitor Relationship Marketing Opportunities by Destination Marketers: An Importance-Performance Analysis. *Tourism Management*, 33(5), 1281–1285. DOI: https://doi.org/10.1016/j.tourman.2011.11.024.

Murgoci, C., Busuioc, S., Florin, M. and Ruxandra A. (2009), Urban Tourism – Form of Tourism With Real Economic Development Perspective for Cities. http://steconomiceuoradea.ro/anale/volume/2009/v2-economy-and-business-administration/27.pdf.

Nzongola-Ntalaja, G. (2003), Gouvernance et development, Conference surface a l'intention d'un groupe de politiciens Haitiens en visite d'etudes en Norvega a l'invitation du gouvemement Norvegien et de l'Institut d'Etudes International Appliquees, Oslo. http://www.undp.org/oslocentre/pub.htm.

O'Neill, M. A. and Palmer, A. (2004), Importance-Performance Analysis: A Useful Tool for Directing Continuous Quality Improvement in Higher Education. *Quality Assurance in Education*, 12(1), 39–52. https://doi.org/10.1108/09684880410517423.

Odendaal, N. (2003), Information and Communication Technology and Local Governance: Understanding the Difference Between Cities in Developed and Emerging Economies. Computers. *Environment and Urban Systems*, 27(6), 585–607. DOI: http://dx.doi.org/10.1016/S0198-9715(03)00016-4..

OECD (2014), Tourism and Creative Economy, OECD Studies on Tourism, OECD Publishing. https://dx.doi.org/10.1787/9789264207875-en.

Official Gazette (Narodne novine) (2018). 123/7, https://narodne-novine.nn.hr/search.aspx?sortiraj=4&kategorija=1&godina=2017&broj=123&rpp=200&qtype=1&pretraga=da.

Official Gazette, (Narodne novine) (2019a), 153/13, 65/17, 114/18, 39/19, https://mgipu.gov.hr/print.aspx?id=127&url=print&page=1, August.

Official Gazette, (Narodne novine) (2019b), 25/13; 85/15, https://narodne-novine.nn.hr/clanci/sluzbeni/2013_02_25_403.html, August.

Oh, H. (2001), Revisiting Importance-Performance Analysis. *Tourism Management*, 22(6), 617–627. doi:10.1016/s0261-5177(01)00036-x.

Parahoo, S. K, Radi, G. Y. and Harvey H. H. (2014), Satisfaction of Tourists with Public Transport: An Empirical Investigation in Dubai. *Journal of Travel & Tourism Marketing*, 31(8), 1004–1017. https://doi.org/10.1080/10548408.2014.890158.

Pedrana, M. (2013), Local Economic Development Policies and Tourism – an Approach to Sustainability and Culture. *Regional Science Inquiry Journal*, 5(1), 91–99. http://www.rsijournal.eu/ARTICLES/June_2013/5.pdf.

Pereira, G.V., Parycek, P., Falco, E. and Kleinhans, R. (2018), Smart Governance in the Context of Smart Cities: A Literature Review. *Information Polity*, 23(2), 143–162. https://www.researchgate.net/deref/https%3A%2F%2Fdoi.org%2F10.3233%2FIP-170067.

Petrić, L. and Crnjak-Karanović, B. (2016), Anatomy of Tourism Development Sustainability: The Case of the city of Split. Singidunum University International

Scientific Conference: Quality as a Basis for Tourism Destination Competitiveness, Belgrade, 11–16. http://sitcon.singidunum.ac.rs/2016/wp-content/uploads/sites/3/2016/11/US-SITCON-2016.pdf.

Petrić, L. and Pivčević, S. (2016), Community Based Tourism Development – Insights from Split, Croatia. Tourism & Hospitality Industry 2016, Congress Proceedings, Opatija, 294–307. https://www.researchgate.net/publication/330161967 _Community_based_tourism_development_-_insights_from_Split_Croatia.

Pivčević, S., Mandić, A. and Šalja, N. (2018), Government and Business Community Attitudes Towards Cruise Tourism Development. *Geographica Pannonica*, 22(4), 285–294. DOI: 10.5937/gp22-18750.

Quick, K. and Bryson, J. (2016), Theories of Public Participation in Governance. In: Torbing, J. and Ansell, C. (eds), *Handbook of Theories of Governance*. Edward Elgar Publishing.

Rahaman, H. (2018), Digital Heritage Interpretation: a Conceptual Framework. *Digital Creativity*, 29(2–3), 208–234. https://doi.org/10.1080/14626268.2018.1511602.

Rahaman, H. and Tan, B. (2011), Interpreting Digital Heritage: A Conceptual Model with End-Users' Perspective. *International Journal of Architectural Computing*, 9(1), 99–113. https://doi.org/10.1260%2F1478-0771.9.1.99.

Rašić Bakarić, I. (2012), A Proposal for A New Administrative-Territorial Division of the Republic of Croatia, *Economic Research-Ekonomska Istraživanja*, 25(2), 397–411. https://doi.org/10.1080/1331677X.2012.11517514.

Riganti, P. and Nijkamp, P. (2008), Congestion in Popular Tourist Areas: A Multi-Attribute Experimental Choice Analysis of Willingness-to-Wait in Amsterdam. http://degree.ubvu.vu.nl/repec/vua/wpaper/pdf/20070009.pdf.

Ripp, M., Buhler, B. and Shakhmatova, K. (eds) (2011), The Road to Success: Integrated Management of Historic Cities, Guidebook. The URBACT programme. http://urbact.eu/sites/default/files/hero_guidebook_final_01.pdf.

Rogerson, C. M. (2012), Urban Tourism, Economic Regeneration and Inclusion: Evidence from South Africa, *Local Economy*, 28(2) 1–15. DOI: https://doi.org/10.1177/0269094212463789.

Ruhlandt, R. W. S. (2018), The Governance of Smart Cities: A Systematic Literature Review. *Cities*, 81, 1–23. DOI: https://doi.org/10.1016/j.cities.2018.02.014.

Runhaar, H., Driessen, P. and Soer, L. (2009), Sustainable Urban Development and the Challenge of Policy Integration: An Assessment of Planning Tools for Integrating Spatial and Environmental Planning in the Netherlands. *Environment and Planning B: Planning and Design*, 36(3), 417–431. https://pdfs.semanticscholar.org/b5bf/ba4db40743ed4abe26d08100e1725ad931df.pdf.

Ruohomaa, H., Salminen, V. and Kunttu, I. (2019), Towards a Smart City Concept in Small Cities. *Technology Innovation Management Review*, 9(9), 5–14. http://doi.org/10.22215/timreview/1264.

Seraphin, H., Sheeran, P. and Pilato, M. (2018), Over-Tourism and the Fall of Venice as a Destination. *Journal of Destination Marketing and Management*, 9, 374–376. DOI: https://doi.org/10.1016/j.jdmm.2018.01.011.

Sever, I. (2015), Importance-Performance Analysis: A Valid Management Tool? *Tourism Management*, 48, 43–53. DOI: https://doi.org/10.1016/j.tourman.2014.10.022.

Scheffler, N., Ripp, M., and Bühler, B. (2009), Cultural Heritage Integrated Management Plans – Urbact II: HerO Project report. http://urbact.eu/sites/default/files/import/Projects/HERO/projects_media/8_GRAZ_CHIMP_Thematic_Report_2nd_edition.pdf.

Scholl, H. J. and AlAwadhi, S. (2016), Pooling and Leveraging Scarce Resources: The Smart City Governance. *Proceedings of the Annual Hawaii International Conference on System Sciences*, 2015, 2355–2365. DOI: https://doi.org/10.1109/HICSS.2015.283.

Scholl, H. J. and Scholl, M. C. (2014), Smart Governance: A Roadmap for Research and Practice. *iConference 2014 Proceedings*, 163–176. DOI: https://doi.org/10.9776/14060.

Sharifia, A. and Yamagata, Y. (2014), Resilient Urban Planning: Major Principles and Criteria. *Energy Procedia*, 61, 1491–1495. DOI: 10.1016/j.egypro.2014.12.154.

Šimunović, I. (2007), Urbana ekonomika, petnaest tema o gradu, Školska knjiga, Zagreb.

Stewart, E. J., Hayward, B. M. and Devlin, P. J. (1998), The "Place" of Interpretation: a New Approach to the Evaluation of Interpretation. *Tourism Management*, 19(3), 257–266. https://doi.org/10.1016/S0261-5177(98)00015-6.

UN (2007), Public Governance Indicators: A Literature Review. https://publicadministration.un.org/publications/content/PDFs/Elibrary%20Archives/2007%20Public%20Governance%20Indicators_a%20Literature%20Review.pdf.

UN (2018), World Urbanization Prospects 2018 Revision, https://population.un.org/wup/Publications/Files/WUP2018-KeyFacts.pdf.

UNEP/MAP/PAP (2016), Integrated Coastal Zone Management Plan of the Šibenik-Knin County, Priority Action programme, Split. https://www.msp-platform.eu/practices/coastal-plan-sibenik-knin-county.

UNESCO (2005), Vienna Memorandum on World Heritage and Contemporary Architecture – Managing the Historic urban landscape. http://whc.unesco.org/document/6814.

UNESCO (2012), Management Plan: UNESCO World Heritage Site – Old Town of Regensburg with Stadtamhof. https://whc.unesco.org/en/list/1155.

UNESCO (2016), Global Report on Culture for Sustainable Urban Development. http://www.unesco.org/culture/culture-for-sustainable-urban-development/pdf-open/global-Report_en.pdf.

UNFCCC, Secretariat for Climate Change (2006), Technologies for Adaptation to Climate Change. https://unfccc.int/resource/docs/publications/tech_for_adaptation_06.pdf.

Uzell, D. L. (1996), Creating Place Identity Through Heritage Interpretation. *The International Journal of Heritage Studies*, 1(4), 219–228. DOI: 10.1080/13527259608722151.

Van den Berg, L., Van der Borg, J. and Van der Meer, J. (1995), *Urban Tourism Performance and Strategies in Eight European Cities*. Aldershot, Hampshire, UK: Ashgate.

Van Oers, R. (2010), Managing Cities and the Historic Urban Landscape Initiative – An Introduction. In: *UNESCO, Managing Historic Cities*. UNESCO World Heritage Centre, World Heritage Papers 27. http://whc.unesco.org/documents/publi_wh_papers_27_en.pdf.

Veldpaus, L., Pereira Roders, A. R. and Colenbrander, B. J. F. (2013), Urban Heritage: Putting the Past into the Future. *The Historic Environment: Policy & Practice*, 4(1), 3–18. DOI: https://doi.org/10.1179/1756750513Z.00000000022.

Walravens, N. (2012), Mobile Business and the Smart City: Developing a Business Model Framework to Include Public Design Parameters for Mobile City Services. *Journal of Theoretical and Applied Electronic Commerce Research*, 7(3), 121–135. DOI:http://dx.doi.org/10.4067/S0718-18762012000300011.

Wijesuriya, G. (2017), Towards the De-secularisation of Heritage. International Centre for the Study of Preservation and Restoration of Cultural Property (ICCROM), Rome, Italy. Available at: http://openarchive.icomos.org/1811/1/Towards_the_De -secularisation_of_Heritag.pdf.

5 Understanding community perception through resident attitude studies: a segmentation analysis in Flemish art cities

Bart Neuts and Vincent Nijs

Introduction

Cities are multifunctional entities that support a diversity of users. Apart from a clear residential and political function, the industrial revolution introduced manufacturing, distribution and service centres to the urban core (Lampard, 1955). Since then, an increased globalized economic marketspace, coupled with changing industrial core sectors, has led to a relocation of many manufacturing firms to urban peripheries and lower wage countries, again transforming the economic base of the city with a focus on finance, business services, tourism and creative industries (Fainstein, 2008).

In the context of a changing economic landscape and increasing pressures on welfare provision, cities have increasingly moved towards an entrepreneurial mode of governance with a view to attracting capital in an interurban competitive environment (Crossa, 2009; Harvey, 1989). With tourism as a recognizable growth driver (Neuts, 2019), city marketing became an important policy field and both soft – e.g. street arts, festivals, events – and hard – e.g. flagship attractions – development strategies were pursued (Hubbard, 1995; Quilley, 2000). Nevertheless, as mentioned by Yang et al. (2013), growing tourism numbers might create tensions in the supply of local resources and, as such, create externalities for local residents. While the idea of the potential for tourism to grow to unsustainable levels is not new – and is already at the heart of Doxey's (1975) "Irridex" and Butler's (1980) "life cycle theory" – the last decade in particular has seemingly given birth to a counter-movement that criticizes the effect of tourism on urban liveability. Dissenting voices are predominantly found within European heritage cities such as Barcelona, Venice, Amsterdam, Florence and Berlin (see e.g. Henley, 2020).

Although the historic cities in Flanders (Belgium) have not yet experienced mainstream forms of significant community resistance, Visit Flanders, the destination management organization, paid close attention, within its new strategic vision for the destination, to the need for tourism to also contribute to the local community and not detract from it. Defined as a "flourishing destination", tourism is reconceptualized as a means to an end, where the main goal lies not with tourism development, but with a thriving destination community – consisting of people (both visitors, locals and others), place and profit. As mentioned in the United Nations World Tourism Organization (2018) report on "overtourism", a key strategy to prevent negative impacts from developing is communication and engagement with local stakeholders. By transparently highlighting the benefits and disadvantages of tourism to local residents and involving citizens in the decision-making processes, a more positive perception and healthier development can occur. In order to support the policy vision, Visit Flanders therefore undertook an extensive resident satisfaction study in the five main tourism cities – Bruges, Antwerp, Ghent, Leuven and Mechelen – to gauge the existing preconceptions about tourism. In this chapter we make an exception of Bruges, as this resident study was performed one year earlier (see Nijs, 2017) and did not include some questions introduced to the later surveys in Antwerp, Ghent, Leuven and Mechelen.

Encompassing cities with different spatial patterns and tourism development levels, one interesting aspect of the study is the possibility of looking at similarities and differences in attitude clusters among the various residents, specifically focusing on the sociocultural impacts of tourism. Resident segments will be compared and contrasted across four cities in order to lend validity and stability to the findings, after which the clusters will be investigated in terms of sociodemographic composition. The results will help generate a clear summarizing overview of different groups of residents and their attitude towards the benefits and disadvantages of tourism.

A historical perspective on tourism impact and resident attitude studies

The research topic of resident attitudes towards tourism is situated at the intersection of two lines of tourism research: urban tourism and tourist–resident impact studies. The former provides the spatial dimension of interest in which interactions between tourists and residents are studied, while tourist–resident impact studies traditionally focus on the externalities of such interactions in various geographical and thematic contexts.

As noted by Edwards et al. (2008) and Ashworth and Page (2011) – notwithstanding the importance of urban centres as both gateways and destinations – research on urban tourism has a relatively short history. Multiple causes can be found for the seeming dearth of urban tourism research prior to the 1980s, not least a more general disinterest in tourism and recreation research among the geographical academic community (Mitchell, 1979) and a spatial modelling history that traditionally placed tourism and recreation at the urban periphery (e.g. Christaller, 1963; Miossec, 1976; Yokeno, 1968). Another, more specific, cause relates to the inherent complexity of urban tourism, with urban tourists being integrated in a large, multifunctional entity, co-consuming urban facilities and thereby becoming largely indistinguishable from residents (Ashworth & Page, 2011). The decades following the 1980s have seen an upsurge in research attention being paid to urban tourism, partly influenced by cycles of economic restructuring and the observation that urban tourism could have urban regenerative effects (Hall & Page, 2009). The growing interest in tourism-related urban research has led to the emergence of various sub-themes (see Ashworth & Page, 2011), with tourism impact studies being foremost among them.

Pearce (1989) notes that tourism impacts are among the most documented themes in the tourism research field, dating back to the 1960s and covering a variety of disciplines due to their inherent multi-dimensional nature. Earlier work on tourism impacts originated in a non-urban context and typically focused on macro-economic effects (Deery et al., 2012), fitting the advocacy platform in tourism research (Jafari, 1989). Ideas on sustainable development, originating in the Club of Rome study (Meadows et al., 1972) and further defined by the Brundtland commission (World Commission on Environment and Development, 1987), had a significant effect on academic thinking in tourism – particularly among sociologists and environmentalists – leading to numerous studies adopting a cautionary approach to tourism (Jafari, 1974, 1989; Pizam, 1978). Rather than following any of the two polar views on tourism, a third cohort of impact studies follows an adaptancy platform, which recognizes both the positive and negative effects of tourism with a main goal of identifying more suitable forms of tourism development that protect a triple-bottom line (Hardy et al., 2002). The rationale of the adaptancy platform can be reconciled with what is defined by Saarinen (2006) as the community-based tradition in sustainability-research. In this tradition, sustainability is a social, anthropocentric construct, defined through the perspectives of local stakeholders as a limit to acceptable change.

Many of the more recent studies on resident attitudes to tourism impact have followed such a community-based approach to sustainable tourism development within an adaptancy platform. Some of these studies have a primarily descriptive purpose, attempting to create homogeneous clusters of residents based on their shared attitude to tourism development. For instance, Pavlić, et al. (2019) study local perceptions on positive and negative tourism impacts in Dubrovnik through a segmentation approach. Pérez and Nadal (2005) adopt a cluster analysis on residents in the Balearic Islands to uncover five clusters: development supporters, prudent developers, ambivalent and cautious, protectionists and alternative developers.

A second strand of research is mainly interested in uncovering causal relationships between predictor variables and resident attitudes. Examples of this can be found in Jurowski and Gursoy (2004), Ritchie and Incari (2006), Snaith and Haley (1999) and Teye et al. (2002). Common explanatory variables across studies are distance from the main tourism zone, employment within the tourism sector, level of social interaction and length of residence.

Methodology

Mirroring an earlier resident study conducted for the historic city of Bruges (Nijs, 2017), an online panel survey methodology was followed in the four Flemish cities of Antwerp, Ghent, Leuven and Mechelen. Of these four, Antwerp receives the most tourists (1,188,978 arrivals and 2,131,837 overnight stays), while also being the most populated, with the census counting 525,935 local residents in 2019. Ghent is the fourth main urban destination in Flanders – after Brussels, Bruges and Antwerp – with 625,340 arrivals and 1,160,864 overnight stays in 2018. At 262,219 residents, Ghent counts about half the population of Antwerp. Leuven and Mechelen attract fewer tourists and are comparatively less populated (101,624 citizens in Leuven, 86,616 citizens in Mechelen in 2019). According to the 2018 arrival data, Leuven received 307,600 tourist arrivals for 603,248 overnight stays, while Mechelen counted 164,150 arrivals and 279,678 tourist nights (Visit Flanders, 2019).

In order to account for differences in urban scale and the potential seasonality of tourism, monthly overnight stays are compared per 100 residents as a tourism intensity scale. In Antwerp, the average annual tourism intensity equals 1.11 tourists per 100 residents, with a maximum of 1.24 in July and a minimum of 0.85 in January. In Ghent, the average annual tourist intensity is slightly higher at 1.21 tourists per 100 residents, with a maximum of 1.50 in August and a minimum of 0.84 in January. Leuven has the highest tourist intensity on a yearly basis with 1.63 tourists per 100 residents. The highest ratio is reached in September – potentially coinciding with the start of the academic year for students at the university – at 1.95, with the lowest ratio being 1.01 in January. Finally, Mechelen has the lowest number of tourist overnights per 100 residents, at 0.88 on a yearly basis. The maximum level of 1.04 is reached in August, while again January exhibits the smallest ratio at 0.61. These numbers suggest that the higher number of visitors to Antwerp and Ghent are largely compensated by the larger scale of these cities. Furthermore, the fluctuation of the intensity-ratio between the most and least popular month of visitation is limited, indicating a limited seasonal concentration in the cities.

One final disclaimer is that these numbers regard solely commercial accommodation and do not take into account informal lodgings or day tourists, thus providing an underestimation of the real situation. For instance, in the most important art city destination in Flanders, Bruges, day tourists and leisure visitors are estimated at 6 million, significantly more than the 1,250,589 arrivals and 2,193,092 overnight stays registered officially.

The survey was conducted between 22 May and 4 July 2017. Stratified random sampling was conducted within the available panel, with representative standards for gender, education level, age and city neighbourhood. In Antwerp, only residents within the city centre were selected in order to account for the larger geographical area of Antwerp and the presence of primarily industrial zones around the harbour. A total of 4552 responses were collected across the four cities, with Ghent receiving 1476 responses, Antwerp 1620, Leuven 880 and Mechelen having the smallest sample of 576.

There was a slight majority of male respondents in Antwerp (54.1% male) and Ghent (53.6% male) while there was a higher female representation in Leuven (54.0% female) and Mechelen (55.4% female). The age groups showed a similar representation across the cities. The ≥55 age group was best represented overall (48.2% in Antwerp, 50.8% in Ghent, 41.7% in Leuven, 45.5% in Mechelen), followed by the 35–54 age group (37.7% in Antwerp, 33.5% in Ghent, 34.0% in Leuven, 33.3% in Mechelen). The comparatively smallest sample category in these cities was the youngest 18–34 age group (14.1% in Antwerp, 15.7% in Ghent, 24.3% in Leuven, 21.2% in Mechelen). In terms of education level, all four cities showed an over-representation of higher educated respondents, with around 60% or more having completed tertiary education (68.3%

in Antwerp, 58.2% in Ghent, 67.2% in Leuven, 62.2% in Mechelen). About one-fifth to a quarter of the sample had a residential address within the core tourist area of the city (27.3% in Antwerp, 21.1% in Ghent, 29.0% in Leuven and 24.0% in Mechelen). Even though the sample demographics do not perfectly resemble population statistics, for the purpose of clustering, unweighted scores will be used as clustering analysis is concerned with identifying patterns, not representative means and standard deviations. As a caveat this means that the final cluster membership percentages cannot be taken as representative for the urban population of the four cities.

The questionnaire was inspired by the Resident Empowerment through Tourism Scale (RETS) by Boley et al. (2014). The proposed model is an extension of the Social Exchange Theory, acknowledging that support is not purely a result of direct economic interest, but can also originate in socio-psychological factors. Four groups of benefits – modelled as factors of multiple measurement levels – are therefore identified as "Personal economic benefits", "Psychological empowerment", "Social empowerment" and "Political empowerment", and hypothesized to correlate with "Perceived negative impacts", "Perceived positive impacts" and "Support for tourism". The perception of impacts is particularly relevant within the scope of this study. In the research paper by Boley et al. (2014), positive impacts are measured by ten indicators while negative impacts are conceptualized through six indicators. Due to this apparent imbalance, a further six negative and one positive impact indicators were based on questions developed by the Centre of Expertise in Leisure, Tourism and Hospitality (see United Nations World Tourism Organization, 2018). All 23 impact questions were measured on a five-level Likert Scale. Table 5.1 provides an overview of the respective questions and their mean scores and standard deviation in each city.

While Table 5.1 might provide some valuable results for making an inter-city comparison, the aggregate nature of the data fails to account for individual differences within cities, as identified by the respective standard deviations. Following the research question stated in the first section, an intra-city analysis of heterogeneous resident groups is of greater policy interest.

A cluster analysis is the appropriate tool for identifying homogeneous groups within data and their respective intergroup differences on the indicators of interest. In this study, a k-means unsupervised machine learning partitioning method is adopted. As discussed by Sarstedt and Mooi (2014), the k-means cluster algorithm starts out by randomly assigning objects to a pre-specified number of clusters and consequently reassigning cases until within-cluster variation is minimized, whereas there is a low as possible inter-class similarity.

Table 5.1 Overview of impact questions and mean scores on city level

Survey question	Label	Mean (Std. Dev.)				
		Antwerp	Ghent	Leuven	Mechelen
Tourism growth will lead to friction between residents and tourists	N1	2.35 (0.95)	2.65 (1.02)	2.33 (0.90)	2.13 (0.89)
Due to tourism, the centre of ... becomes overcrowded	N2	2.63 (1.06)	2.89 (1.11)	2.52 (1.01)	2.29 (0.94)
Due to tourism, life in ... is becoming more expensive	N3	3.16 (0.95)	3.40 (0.99)	3.28 (0.95)	2.96 (0.97)
Due to tourism there is more rubbish in ...	N4	3.29 (1.04)	3.54 (1.02)	3.19 (1.00)	2.93 (1.03)
Due to tourism, there is more crime in ...	N5	2.36 (0.94)	2.40 (0.92)	2.30 (0.88)	2.16 (0.95)
Students cause more nuisance in ... than tourists	N6	3.01 (1.02)	3.59 (1.03)	3.96 (0.95)	2.88 (1.00)
Due to tourism there are more traffic problems in ...	N7	2.99 (1.10)	2.80 (1.03)	2.68 (0.99)	2.60 (1.00)
Due to tourism, the outlook of the neighbourhood, the authentic character is disappearing	N8	2.47 (0.95)	2.59 (0.97)	2.45 (0.91)	2.25 (0.89)
Due to tourism, the main streets of ... are losing diversity	N9	2.66 (1.06)	2.71 (1.02)	2.53 (0.95)	2.28 (0.88)
The attitude of tourists is a problem (e.g. arrogant, rude, dissatisfied, unfriendly, lacking respect)	N10	2.42 (0.95)	2.50 (0.97)	2.29 (0.89)	2.13 (0.88)

Survey question	Label	Mean (Std. Dev.)			
		Antwerp	Ghent	Leuven	Mechelen
The behaviour of tourists is a problem (e.g. noise, vomiting, public drunkenness)	N11	2.70 (1.05)	2.63 (1.02)	2.38 (0.94)	2.25 (0.93)
Due to the growth in tourism in ..., the attitude of other residents in relation to tourists is becoming a problem	N12	2.54 (0.85)	2.63 (0.86)	2.40 (0.83)	2.25 (0.85)
Due to touristic developments, ... is looking better	P1	3.71 (0.87)	3.65 (0.89)	3.71 (0.78)	4.01 (0.84)
Tourism stimulates new park developments in ...	P2	3.42 (0.98)	3.22 (0.97)	3.53 (0.87)	3.64 (0.88)
Due to tourism, there are more recreational opportunities for residents	P3	3.33 (0.98)	3.14 (0.99)	3.42 (0.90)	3.56 (0.91)
Tourism helps to preserve our cultural identity and to restore historical buildings	P4	4.00 (0.84)	3.92 (0.85)	3.95 (0.79)	4.10 (0.83)
Due to tourism, there are more shopping and leisure opportunities and more restaurants	P5	3.82 (0.81)	3.63 (0.87)	3.61 (0.87)	3.67 (0.87)
Tourism contributes to the income and standard of life of residents	P6	3.50 (0.94)	3.37 (0.93)	3.44 (0.92)	3.37 (0.92)
A growth in the number of tourists strengthens the local economy	P7	4.06 (0.71)	3.88 (0.77)	3.97 (0.69)	4.05 (0.74)
Touristic developments improve the quality of life in ...	P8	3.38 (0.92)	3.21 (0.92)	3.40 (0.83)	3.56 (0.90)

Survey question	Label	Mean (Std. Dev.)			
		Antwerp	Ghent	Leuven	Mechelen
Tourism offers incentives for the protection and conservation of the natural environment in ...	P9	3.37 (1.02)	3.28 (0.99)	3.53 (0.86)	3.69 (0.90)
Due to tourism, the city is more lively	P10	3.91 (0.71)	3.90 (0.74)	3.83 (0.74)	3.97 (0.74)
Due to tourism, ... gets a more international character	P11	4.17 (0.77)	4.09 (0.81)	4.04 (0.75)	4.11 (0.82)

The standard Hartigan-Wong (1979) algorithm is used, which defines the total within-cluster variation as:

$$W(C_k) = \sum_{x_i \in C_k} (x_i - \mu_k)^2$$

where x_i is an observation belonging to cluster C_k and μ_k is the mean value of the cluster C_k. After an initial random data assignment, each observation x_i is reassigned until the sum of squares distance of the observation to their respective cluster centre is minimized. The total within-cluster sum of squares, which is a measure of the compactness of the cluster, needs to be as small as possible and can be measured as:

$$total~within-cluster~SS = \sum_{k=1}^{k} W(C_k) = \sum_{k=1}^{k} \sum_{x_i \in C_k} (x_i - \mu_k)^2$$

The cluster analysis will be followed by a linear discriminant analysis. Discriminant analysis is a multivariate classification technique that separates observations into mutually exclusive groups based on predictor or independent variables. Under discriminant analysis the classification is known beforehand and a model is created to predict future observations. As such it is distinct from clustering in that the cluster assignment of observations needs to be known beforehand. Since the discriminant analysis constructs a linear combination of predictor variables to best explain differences in cluster membership, the procedure can be used to establish relevance of individual indicators on the cluster solution. In linear discriminant analysis, scores are calculated as:

$$\delta_k(X) = -\frac{1}{2} \mu_k^T \sum{}^{-1} \mu_k + \mu_k^T \sum{}^{-1} X + \ln(\pi_k)$$

with δ_k the discriminant score for cluster (or "class" in a discriminant analysis) k, X the matrix of predictor variables, μ_k a vector containing the variable means for cluster k, $\sum$ the covariance matrix of variables and π_k the prior probability that an observation belongs to cluster k. Discriminant scores are calculated for each cluster and observation and the final classification prediction for each observation is subsequently based on the largest discriminant score.

Table 5.2   Indices for optimal cluster numbers

Index	Suggested number of clusters (index value)			
	Antwerp	Ghent	Leuven	Mechelen
KL	4 (111.454)	2 (14.563)	7 (15.006)	7 (24.139)
Silhouette	2 (0.304)	2 (0.181)	2 (0.361)	2 (0.188)
SD index	2 (1.203)	3 (1.481)	2 (1.271)	5 (0.948)
SDbw	5 (0.878)	8 (0.722)	7 (0.643)	5 (0.705)
Rubin	4 (-0.865)	4 (-1.283)	4 (-1.787)	7 (-1.3224)

Results

Comparing clusters across the four Flemish art cities

Since all variables were measured on similar 5-level Likert scales, no prior standardization of variables was required and the first step of the cluster analysis was the calculation of bivariate correlations between clustering variables, in order to avoid over-representation of highly correlated variables in the final clustering solution (Sarstedt & Mooi, 2014). With all correlations falling between +0.72 and –0.44, collinearity seemed of no particular concern in the dataset and all indicators could be included. Next, the NbClust package in R was used in order to calculate a number of indices to assist in the a priori selection of cluster numbers for the k-means procedure (Charrad et al., 2014). Table 5.2 presents the results.

Since there is no general agreement across indices with regard to optimal cluster size, the final choice needs to combine statistical relevance with a subjective interpretation of the usefulness and relevance of cluster solutions. Since two clusters are of little practical use and anything above five clusters seems excessive given the number of observations and variables, solutions of three, four and five clusters were tested and compared in terms of clarity of interpretation and balance of cluster groups (i.e. no clusters with a very limited number of observations).

Table 5.3 provides an overview on cluster means by indicator and city. In Antwerp, Ghent and Leuven, a four-cluster solution was preferred while in Mechelen two clusters overlapped more significantly, leading to a preferred three-cluster solution here.

Table 5.3   K-means cluster centres

Indicator	Antwerp				Ghent				Leuven				Mechelen		
	Cl1	Cl2	Cl3	Cl4	Cl1	Cl2	Cl3	Cl4	Cl1	Cl2	Cl3	Cl4	Cl1	Cl2	Cl3
Cluster size	328	355	582	355	238	277	497	464	275	157	290	158	192	105	279
N1	3.35	1.57	2.43	2.07	3.76	2.40	2.96	1.89	1.71	3.22	2.50	2.22	1.48	2.97	2.25
N2	3.84	1.60	2.71	2.40	4.20	2.64	3.28	1.95	1.68	3.69	2.79	2.29	1.56	3.19	2.46
N3	3.89	2.47	3.32	2.93	4.33	3.23	3.62	2.78	2.70	3.90	3.59	3.10	2.29	3.74	3.13
N4	4.10	2.48	3.58	2.88	4.40	3.15	3.94	2.92	2.53	4.03	3.60	2.78	2.10	3.77	3.18
N5	3.15	1.55	2.63	1.98	3.08	2.16	2.76	1.79	1.66	3.19	2.60	2.01	1.42	3.06	2.32
N6	3.07	2.79	3.20	2.85	3.60	3.79	3.63	3.42	4.08	3.83	3.91	3.98	2.51	3.20	3.01
N7	3.89	2.06	3.31	2.57	3.82	2.41	3.17	2.11	2.00	3.73	2.94	2.37	1.79	3.45	2.83
N8	3.43	1.70	2.54	2.23	3.79	2.43	2.78	1.88	1.84	3.50	2.61	2.18	1.67	3.13	2.33
N9	3.56	1.79	2.84	2.42	3.82	2.51	2.93	2.03	1.88	3.46	2.74	2.31	1.68	3.09	2.40
N10	3.34	1.60	2.62	2.05	3.47	2.26	2.84	1.78	1.66	3.26	2.47	2.11	1.45	2.95	2.29
N11	3.70	1.78	2.99	2.21	3.59	2.32	3.04	1.88	1.60	3.43	2.69	2.11	1.54	3.14	2.41
N12	3.29	1.83	2.74	2.24	3.38	2.44	2.93	2.03	1.78	3.15	2.69	2.17	1.57	2.99	2.43
P1	3.01	4.31	3.98	3.29	2.77	3.14	3.85	4.18	4.18	3.04	3.90	3.21	4.41	3.11	4.07
P2	2.67	4.03	3.76	2.93	2.26	2.66	3.48	3.77	4.00	2.91	3.79	2.86	4.05	2.78	3.68

Indicator	Antwerp				Ghent				Leuven				Mechelen		
	CI1	CI2	CI3	CI4	CI1	CI2	CI3	CI4	CI1	CI2	CI3	CI4	CI1	CI2	CI3
P3	2.64	3.88	3.73	2.77	2.18	2.51	3.39	3.74	3.93	2.62	3.74	2.72	3.85	2.65	3.70
P4	3.41	4.54	4.24	3.61	3.14	3.52	4.05	4.43	4.40	3.24	4.12	3.56	4.48	3.16	4.18
P5	3.40	4.26	4.04	3.39	3.04	3.08	3.87	4.00	4.04	3.12	3.85	2.93	3.94	2.82	3.81
P6	2.82	4.09	3.81	3.05	2.61	2.84	3.57	3.87	3.87	2.73	3.66	3.03	3.63	2.50	3.52
P7	3.52	4.55	4.20	3.84	3.21	3.56	4.00	4.29	4.38	3.31	4.09	3.71	4.38	3.29	4.11
P8	2.45	4.20	3.67	2.95	2.11	2.74	3.37	3.90	3.97	2.55	3.58	2.94	4.03	2.50	3.63
P9	2.39	4.20	3.72	2.86	2.19	2.77	3.42	3.98	4.10	2.71	3.68	3.07	4.19	2.63	3.75
P10	3.43	4.36	4.03	3.70	3.30	3.68	3.93	4.29	4.22	3.32	3.92	3.48	4.29	3.13	4.05
P11	3.59	4.69	4.30	3.97	3.49	3.78	4.13	4.53	4.47	3.36	4.18	3.71	4.57	3.24	4.13

Figure 5.1 Provides an alternative visualization of the cluster centres for each positive and negative impact. While the table can be difficult to interpret due to the large amount of data, comparing cluster boundaries across the four cities immediately seems to uncover similarities between the identified clusters. Based on the data of Table 5.1 and the visual analysis of Figure 5.1, the different clusters will now be compared and contrasted.

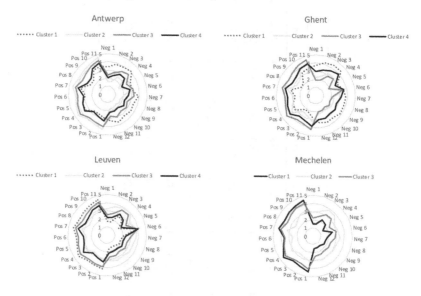

Figure 5.1   Graphical overview of clusters

A first cluster that stands out is of a predominantly negative nature. Deemed "opponents", these are found in Cluster 1 for Antwerp ($n=328$, 20.2%) and Ghent ($n=238$, 16.1%) and in Cluster 2 for Leuven ($n=157$, 17.8%) and Mechelen ($n=105$, 18.2%). Comparatively they assign the highest scores on all but one of the negative impacts (with the exception being "Students cause more nuisance than tourists", which can also be considered as a negative impact unrelated to tourism). The residents in this cluster feel that an increase in tourism will cause additional friction between tourists and residents (N1), drive negative impacts such as rising price levels (N3), littering (N4), criminality (N5) and traffic issues (N7). Furthermore, these respondents identify negative behavioural traits of tourists in terms of both attitude (N10) and behaviour (N11). While it should be noted that these "opponents" do recognize positive impacts to some extent, they assign significantly lower scores to almost all positive aspects of tourism than the other clusters. Most importantly, there is no strong agreement on the contribution of tourism to recreational opportunities (P3) or urban living standards (P6, P8). Furthermore, the benefits of tourism on park development (P2) and the general natural environment (P9) are not well considered.

At the other end of the divide are the so-called "advocates". This cluster focuses strongly on positive contributions of tourism and does not relate strong negative impacts to the presence of visitors in the city. "Advocates" can be found in Cluster 2 in Antwerp (n=355, 21.9%), Cluster 4 in Ghent (n=464, 31.4%) and Cluster 1 in Leuven (n=275, 31.3%) and Mechelen (n=192, 33.3%). In summary, respondents in these clusters do not, on average, agree with statements that tourism will increase negative effects, while they show high agreement with positive contributions to the economy and quality of life (P6, P7, P8), increased urban opportunities (P3, P5) and providing an incentive for the protection of nature and cultural heritage (P2, P4).

A third group that can be identified in all four cities is labelled "careful optimists". In Antwerp (n=582, 35.9%), Ghent (n=497, 33.7%), Leuven (n=290, 33.0%) and Mechelen (n=279, 48.4%) they are represented by Cluster 3. In all cities they represent the majority of respondents, avoiding the extremes of both "advocates" and "opponents". In terms of negative impacts, the "careful optimists" do acknowledge a range of issues. The two highest scoring negative statements in all four cities have to do with the tourist influence on rubbish (N4) and price increases (N3). In Antwerp and Ghent, traffic issues (N7) are also related to tourists, while "careful optimists" in Ghent also exhibit a concern of overcrowding (N2). Crucially, though, this group values positive impacts more highly than their negative counterparts. Particularly relevant throughout all four cities are the statements of tourism as economic driver (P7), as a contributor to the international atmosphere (P11) and an incentive to protect the cultural identity and heritage buildings (P4).

Finally, Cluster 4 in Antwerp (n=355, 21.9%) and Leuven (n=158, 18.0%), and Cluster 2 in Ghent (n=277, 18.8%), show a similar profile, which we describe as "non-opinionated". Even though the positive impacts slightly outweigh the negative ones in terms of average scoring, these groups of respondents gravitate towards the middle of the Likert scale for both positive and negative impacts with no standout opinions. Citizens belonging to this group might not have given tourism much consideration and, while not showing concerns about the developments of tourism, they also do not recognize strong positive effects that might be leveraged through tourism.

Testing the quality of the cluster solution

While the previous section helped to uncover clusters with very similar profiles across the different sample cities, a different analysis is needed if we want to be able to identify which indicators contribute most to the construction of the different clusters. This can be achieved via a discriminant analysis, which has the added benefit that it helps test the quality of the cluster solution (Madrigal, 1995). This study conducts a linear discriminant analysis, which models a best cluster membership based on a linear combination of the 23 impacts. As a general rule, there will always be one less discriminant function than there are clusters (i.e. three discriminant functions for Antwerp, Ghent and Leuven, and two discriminant functions for Mechelen). The linear combinations are generated in such a way that the first discriminant function maximizes the differences between the group averages, after which the second discriminant function does the same for the remaining variation and so forth.

Prior probabilities of groups mirror the cluster sizes discussed in the previous section. Table 5.4 gives an overview of the coefficients of each predictive variable in the construction of the respective discriminant functions. These can be interpreted as coefficients in a multivariate linear regression and indicate which indicators contribute most to the calculation of the discriminant score. The proportion of trace describes the ratio of between-class variance that is explained by each discriminant function, with, logically, the first discriminants explaining the majority of the variance.

The plots in Figure 5.2 give an overview of how well the clusters are separated according to their linear discriminant functions. Clearly, in the cases of Antwerp, Ghent and Leuven, the third discriminant function is of limited relevance, since the proportion of variance explained is already very low (see Table 5.4). The upper central frame for each city is most easily interpretable and indicates how the first discriminant function best separates "opponents" from "advocates". Particularly for Antwerp, Ghent and Leuven, the second discriminant function then serves to primarily separate "careful optimists" from "non-opinionated".

Next, the predictive accuracy of the model can be tested. In order to achieve this goal, a training set comprising 60% is randomly selected from each city sample and used in the calculation of linear discriminant functions (as in Table 5.4). These coefficients are then used on the predictive set (i.e. the remaining 40% of data) and the cluster membership prediction is compared with actual cluster membership in order to calculate the predictive error. Finally, this is repeated 100 times in order to arrive at a final mean predictive error among

Table 5.4 Coefficients of linear discriminants

Indicator	Antwerp			Ghent			Leuven			Mechelen	
	LD1	LD2	LD3	LD1	LD2	LD3	LD1	LD2	LD3	LD1	LD2
Proportion of trace	*0.787*	*0.205*	*0.008*	*0.822*	*0.168*	*0.010*	*0.808*	*0.178*	*0.014*	*0.945*	*0.055*
N1	-0.196	0.075	-0.630	-0.171	0.189	0.200	0.082	0.047	0.034	0.366	-0.126
N2	-0.308	-0.024	-0.187	-0.410	0.176	-0.432	0.402	-0.180	-0.013	0.034	0.226
N3	-0.115	0.050	0.081	-0.113	0.070	0.157	0.042	0.013	-0.585	0.178	0.186
N4	-0.165	0.212	0.186	-0.183	0.271	0.031	0.131	-0.339	-0.196	0.277	0.169
N5	-0.215	0.230	0.279	-0.100	0.135	-0.661	0.283	-0.284	0.002	0.123	0.154
N6	-0.072	0.060	0.388	-0.018	-0.057	-0.495	-0.091	0.066	0.138	0.143	0.166
N7	-0.170	0.299	0.375	-0.116	0.201	0.323	0.233	-0.087	0.243	0.273	0.189
N8	-0.165	0.033	-0.670	-0.256	0.084	0.569	0.253	-0.105	0.712	0.167	-0.247
N9	-0.238	0.172	0.389	-0.185	0.020	0.199	0.098	-0.174	-0.108	0.078	0.096
N10	-0.203	0.129	-0.235	-0.266	0.155	0.160	0.176	-0.018	0.458	0.093	0.188
N11	-0.210	0.207	-0.191	-0.078	0.208	-0.143	0.324	-0.086	-0.247	0.301	-0.142
N12	-0.106	0.131	0.285	-0.189	0.038	-0.321	0.238	-0.188	-0.549	0.218	0.343
P1	0.100	0.220	0.005	0.181	0.270	-0.137	-0.169	-0.165	0.124	-0.142	0.096
P2	0.113	0.254	-0.008	0.113	0.247	-0.360	-0.059	-0.350	0.427	-0.157	-0.128

Indicator	Antwerp			Ghent			Leuven			Mechelen	
	LD1	LD2	LD3	LD1	LD2	LD3	LD1	LD2	LD3	LD1	LD2
P3	0.108	0.305	0.229	0.171	0.332	0.097	-0.194	-0.511	-0.278	-0.065	0.301
P4	0.056	0.159	-0.127	0.123	0.224	0.123	-0.108	-0.111	-0.141	-0.203	0.150
P5	0.042	0.155	-0.557	0.018	0.207	0.163	-0.077	-0.313	0.569	-0.143	0.233
P6	0.165	0.282	0.119	0.221	0.218	0.110	-0.110	-0.120	-0.249	-0.023	0.403
P7	0.121	-0.044	-0.101	-0.007	0.096	-0.223	-0.142	0.072	-0.363	-0.064	-0.030
P8	0.210	0.294	-0.097	0.245	0.211	-0.146	-0.098	-0.227	-0.248	-0.100	0.085
P9	0.249	0.346	0.029	0.178	0.148	0.281	-0.155	-0.158	0.198	-0.273	0.139
P10	0.031	-0.066	-0.175	0.020	-0.031	-0.087	-0.097	0.014	0.354	0.002	0.515
P11	0.113	-0.013	-0.132	0.007	0.059	0.439	-0.155	-0.160	-0.266	-0.279	-0.176

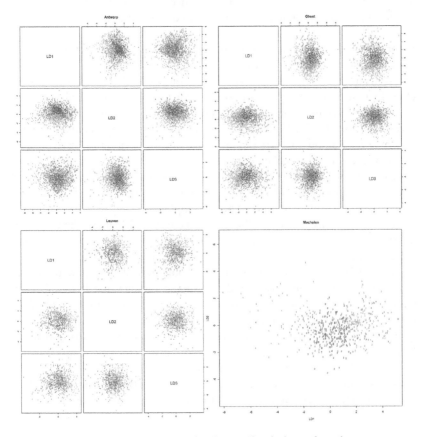

Figure 5.2   Cluster separation by linear discriminant functions

100 randomized training and predictive sets. For all four cities, the mean predictive error of classification was around 10%: 8.71% for Antwerp, 9.93% for Ghent, 9.14% for Leuven and 10.13% for Mechelen. It can therefore be concluded that for the vast majority of observations, the impact indicators provide a reliable basis for identifying homogeneous resident groups.

Sociodemographic characteristics of different clusters

Given that the cluster solutions found across the four Flemish case studies are comparable, logically valid and exhibit predictive accuracy, an additional interest lies in uncovering sociodemographic cluster profiles. Through Chi-square tests we can try to identify significant differences between clusters according to age group, residential area, education level and economic activity.

Surprisingly, area of residence did not seem to significantly affect the attitude towards tourism impacts, with the four cluster profiles rather equally spread across the inner city and the residential areas outside of the main tourist zones. Only in Ghent was a significant relationship between age groups (18–34, 35–64, ≥65) and cluster membership found, with a Chi-square of 18.085 (Df=6, p-value=0.01). Studying this relationship more closely it appears that respondents between 18 and 34 years old are more likely to belong to "careful optimists", while both groups of older respondents (35–64 and ≥65) are more likely to belong to the "opponents" cluster. The hypothesis that residents employed in tourism are more likely to be supportive of the sector could not be reliably tested due to the limited number of people employed locally within the tourism industry (85 in Antwerp, 48 in Ghent, 25 in Leuven and 20 in Mechelen). Only in Antwerp may we consider 85 to be just high enough a sample to study patterns, and here a relationship is supported (Chi-square=13.599, Df=6, p-value=0.03) between working in the local tourism field and belonging to the "advocate" cluster. The only sociodemographic variable that is significantly related to cluster membership across all four cities is education. The exhibited pattern is quite similar, with residents who have achieved at most a high school qualification being more likely to appear in the "opponents" (for Antwerp, Mechelen and Leuven) or "non-opinionated" cluster (for Ghent and Leuven) and less likely to belong to the "advocates". Comparatively, respondents with a tertiary education degree could be found more often in the "advocates" cluster, or in the case of Mechelen also the "careful optimists" cluster.

Conclusions

Destination management organizations are increasingly reconsidering their role within the tourism industry, moving from marketing tourist destinations to managing thriving local communities thanks to tourism. As such, tourism is seen as a driver instead of an objective, and community-supported goals are set to guide strategies and actions. Within this context, this chapter focused on a descriptive resident attitude analysis in four Flemish historic cities. Agreement/disagreement on 23 tourism impact statements – both positive and negative – was analysed via a k-means clustering algorithm and the predictive quality checked through a discriminant analysis.

Interestingly, even though the four cities are distinct in terms of size, population level, tourism market and tourism intensity – with Leuven having the highest tourism intensity index of 1.63 overnights per 100 residents, followed by Ghent at 1.21, Antwerp at 1.11 and Mechelen at 0.88 – the identified clusters were almost perfectly comparable in each case study, with the only minor exception being that Mechelen was represented by three instead of four clusters. The algorithm identified a broadly positive segment of residents, the "advocates", and a polar opposite of citizens who showed principal concern for negative impacts, the "opponents". Between these two extremes, we identified a cluster of "careful optimists", who showed concern for certain negative impacts but were also rather aware of the positives being brought through tourism: economic benefits, quality of life impacts, cultural heritage protection and international ambiance. A final cluster was characterized by average scores on both positive and negative impacts and seemed rather undecided or unaware, thus being labelled "non-opinionated".

Not only were the clusters constructed in a similar fashion for all four cities, it can be noted that each cluster broadly encompassed a similar proportion of the city sample. In other words, notwithstanding the fact that, for instance, Mechelen only receives about one eighth of the tourists that Antwerp does, with a lower tourism intensity rate, in both cities, the proportion of "advocates" and "opponents" is roughly the same. Based purely on our results, we might be inclined to conclude that certain attitudinal groups seem to develop irrespective of actual tourist conditions in the source city; possibly being influenced by news articles and external experiences more than by what is objectively happening in the destination. This might also be reflected by the fact that very limited significant sociodemographic differences were found across the clusters. In order to develop a better understanding of the mechanisms at play, further research should (a) perform a longitudinal cluster analysis that can observe shifts in attitudes and cluster sizes and potential underlying environmental changes, and (b) compare these results with a clustering approach in a different city where capacity problems have become more obvious. The latter might be of specific interest if we hypothesize that there is a potential natural clustering among a few attitudinal poles – primarily based on intrinsic personal characteristics – leading to rather stable groupings for destinations in balance. Under such hypothesis, a systemic shock – i.e. an unsustainable increase in tourism numbers – might then be visible in a proportional shift towards more negatively inclined clusters.

References

Ashworth, G., & Page, S.J. (2011). Urban tourism research: Recent progress and current paradoxes. *Tourism Management, 32*, 1–15.

Boley, B., McGehee, N.G., Perdue, R., & Long, P. (2014). Empowerment and resident attitudes toward tourism: Strengthening the theoretical foundation through a Weberian lens. *Annals of Tourism Research, 49*, 33–50.

Butler, R.W. (1980). The concept of a tourism area cycle of evolution: implications for management of resources. *Canadian Geographer, 24*(1), 5–12.

Charrad, M., Ghazzali, N., Boiteau, V., & Niknafs, A. (2014). NbClust: An R package for determining the relevant number of clusters in a data set. *Journal of Statistical Software, 64*(6), 1–36.

Christaller, W. (1963). Some considerations of tourism location in Europe: The peripheral regions – underdeveloped countries – recreation areas. *Papers of the Regional Science Association, 12*, 95–105.

Crossa, V. (2009). Resisting the entrepreneurial city: street vendors' struggle in Mexico City's Historic Center. *International Journal of Urban and Regional Research, 33*(1), 43–63.

Deery, M., Jago, L., & Fredline, L. (2012). Rethinking social impacts of tourism research: A new research agenda. *Tourism Management, 33*, 64–73.

Doxey, G.V. (1975). A causation theory of visitor–resident irritants. Paper presented at *The Travel Research Conference nr.6*, TTRA, San Diego, 195–198.

Edwards, D., Griffin, T., & Hayllar, B. (2008). Urban tourism research: Developing an agenda. *Annals of Tourism Research, 35*(4), 1032–1052.

Fainstein, S.S. (2008). Mega-projects in New York, London and Amsterdam. *International Journal of Urban and Regional Research, 32*(4), 768–785.

Hall, C.M., & Page, S.J. (2009). Progress in tourism management: From the geography of tourism to geographies of tourism – a review. *Tourism Management, 30*, 3–16.

Hardy, A., Beeton, R.J.S., & Pearson, L. (2002). Sustainable tourism: An overview of the concept and its position in relation to conceptualisations of tourism. *Journal of Sustainable Tourism, 10*(6), 475–496.

Hartigan, J.A., & Wong, M.A. (1979). Algorithm AS 136: A k-means clustering algorithm. *Applied Statistics, 28*, 100–108.

Harvey, D. (1989). From managerialism to entrepreneurialism: the transformation in urban governance in late capitalism. *GeografiskaAnnaler, 71*(1), 3–17.

Henley, J. (2020). Overtourism in Europe's historic cities sparks backlash. *The Guardian*, 25 January. Retrieved from https://www.theguardian.com/world/2020/jan/25/overtourism-in-europe-historic-cities-sparks-backlash

Hubbard, P. (1995). Urban design and local economic development: A case study in Birmingham. *Cities, 12*(4), 243–251.

Jafari, J. (1974). The socio-economic costs of tourism to developing countries. *Annals of Tourism Research, 1*, 227–259.

Jafari, J. (1989). Sociocultural dimensions of tourism: An English language literature review. In J. Bystrzanowski (Ed.), *Tourism as a Factor of Change: A Sociocultural Study* (pp. 17–60). Vienna, Austria: Economic Coordination Center for Research and Documentation in Social Sciences.

Jurowski, C., & Gursoy, D. (2004). Distance effects on residents' attitudes toward tourism. *Annals of Tourism Research, 31*(2), 296–312.

Lampard, E.E. (1955). The history of cities in the economically advanced areas. *Economic Development and Cultural Change, 3*(2), 81–136.

Madrigal, R. (1995). Residents' perceptions and the role of government. *Annals of Tourism Research, 22*(1), 86–102.

Meadows, D.H., Randers, J., Meadows, D.L., & Behrens, W.W. (1972). *The Limits to Growth: A Report for the Club of Rome's Project on the Predicament of Mankind,* 2nd edn. New York, NY: Universe Books.

Miossec, J.M. (1976). Un modèle de l'espace touristique. *L'Espace Géographique, 6,* 41–48.

Mitchell, L.S. (1979). The geography of tourism: An introduction. *Annals of Tourism Research, 9*(3), 235–244.

Neuts, B. (2019). Tourism and urban economic growth: A panel analysis of German cities. *Tourism Economics,* Advanced online publication.

Nijs, V. (2017). *Resident attitudes towards tourism. Testing the Resident Empowerment through Tourism Scale (RETS) in Bruges* (Unpublished master's thesis). Modul University Vienna, Vienna, Austria.

Pavlić, I, Portolan, A., & Puh, B. (2019). Segmenting local residents by perceptions of tourism impacts in an urban World Heritage Site: The case of Dubrovnik. *Journal of Heritage Tourism,* Advance online publication.

Pearce, D.C. (1989). *Tourist Development.* Essex, UK: Longman Scientific and Technical Publishers.

Pérez, E.A., & Nadal, J.R. (2005). Host community perceptions. A cluster analysis. *Annals of Tourism Research, 32*(4), 925–941.

Pizam, A. (1978). Tourism's impacts: The social costs to the destination community as perceived by its residents. *Journal of Travel Research, 16,* 8–12.

Quilley, S. (2000). Manchester first: From municipal socialism to the entrepreneurial city. *International Journal of Urban and Regional Research, 24*(3), 601–615.

Ritchie, B.W., & Incari, M. (2006). Host community attitudes toward tourism and cultural tourism development: The case of the Lewes District, southern England. *International Journal of Tourism Research, 8,* 27–44.

Saarinen, J. (2006). Traditions of sustainability in tourism studies. *Annals of Tourism Research, 33*(4), 1121–1140.

Sarstedt, M., & Mooi, E. (2014). *A Concise Guide to Market Research. The Process, Data, and Methods using IBM SPSS Statistics.* Heidelberg, Germany: Springer.

Snaith, T., & Haley, A. (1999). Residents' opinions of tourism development in the historic city of York, England. *Tourism Management, 20*(5), 595–603.

Teye, V., Sirakaya, E., & F. Sönmez, S. (2002). Residents' attitudes toward tourism development. *Annals of Tourism Research, 29*(3), 668–688.

United Nations World Tourism Organization (2018). *'Overtourism'? – Understanding and Managing Urban Tourism Growth beyond Perceptions.* Madrid, Spain: UNWTO.

Visit Flanders (2019). *Toerisme in Cijfers (gegevens verblijfstoerisme).* Retrieved 19 December 2019, from https://www.toerismevlaanderen.be/toerisme-cijfers-2018-xl

World Commission on Environment and Development (1987). *Our Common Future.* Oxford, UK: Oxford University Press.

Yang, J., Ryan, C., & Zhang, L. (2013). Social conflict in communities impacted by tourism. *Tourism Management, 35,* 82–93.

Yokeno, N. (1968). La localisation de l'industrie touristique: application de l'analyse de Thunen-Weber. *Cahiers de Tourism Série C, 9,* 1–18.

6 Tourism in Venice: mapping overtourism and exploring solutions

Dario Bertocchi and Nicola Camatti

Introduction

Because of its particular geographic and urban characteristics, as well as its cultural and tourist attractiveness, Venice has often been referred to as an emblematic case study of "hyper-tourism" (Costa & Martinotti, 2003; Minoia, 2017) and of analysis of a destination's evolution over time. Butler's (1980) life cycle model of the tourist area is provided here in order to understand the evolution of tourist destinations in terms of number of arrivals and changes in the local environment. This model shows that, like consumer products, destinations move along seven phases (exploration, involvement, development, consolidation, stagnation and decline or rejuvenation) through to the complete loss of their tourist attraction (McKercher, 2005). The approach proposed by Butler, which was further developed by McKercher, is based on the assumption that "tourism changes tourism", and this occurs in all phases of the life cycle model (McKercher, 2005). Although many argue that Venice has now reached and exceeded its carrying capacity, its attractiveness seems not to have changed and the number of tourists does not seem to show any decline even in the face of various other problems of destination management and government, as recently pointed out by Seraphin and colleagues (2018).

The physical (connected to density) and social (connected to residents' perceptions) concept of the so-called overtourism (caused by exceeding the carrying capacity) and the impossibility of moving structures and visitor flows outside, due to the geographical limits of Venice as an island surrounded by a lagoon, cause the entire destination of Venice to be considered a historical city rather than a destination with a historical centre or an area. In addition, there are many restrictions (some of which are not always respected), such as the prohibition of new buildings or limitations on the use of a structure (for example, as the only public structure), which safeguard the uniqueness of the Venetian urban structure but further reduce the space dedicated to residents and users of the city, thus leaving these areas to tourists. In addition to the continuous development of the official accommodation system (hotel and extra-hotel structures), this transformation of spaces and functions is emphasized by the growth of the activities of the shared economy linked to tourism, in particular the peer-to-peer accommodation service promoted by Airbnb (Zervas et al., 2014; Guttentag, 2015).

In recent years, this platform has ended up at the centre of the debate as the main cause of increase in tourist beds in the historical centre (see Massiani & Santoro, 2012; Schneiderman, 2014; Celata, 2017; Horn & Merante, 2017; Picascia, et al., 2017; Salerno, 2018; van der Borg, et al., 2017). Although Airbnb cannot be seen as the main cause of changes in the urban environment of Venice, thus remaining a reversible condition in contrast with the restoration of a building for the construction of a new hotel, the phenomenon of home-sharing nevertheless represents a reduction in spaces available to residents and users of the city, which in a short time has contributed to increasing the tourist accommodation offer with its advantages and disadvantages for the local economy of the historic centre and beyond. From this point of view, Airbnb seems to have further consolidated the unceasing process of "touristification", "Disneyization" (Bryman, 1999), or "McDonaldization" of Venice and its six districts (neighbourhoods). The touristification process of Venice has not only led to a change in the purposes of urban areas, but also to an economic change in all its islands: it has created a shift in other economic activities and the development of a tourist monoculture. In such an already hyper-touristic environment, tourism can take the name of "Venicefication", referring to a situation in which a destination, its inhabitants and its production sector are victims of their own success.

A "mass" of visiting tourists

To simplify the concept, overtourism occurs when there are too many visitors to a particular destination in a given period (Visentin & Bertocchi, 2019). "Too many" is a subjective term that should be defined in each destination in relation to the number of local residents, guests, entrepreneurs and even tourists with appropriate indicators. It is a concept that goes beyond mass tourism, a sort of "tourist overcrowding" (Muler Gonzalez et al., 2018; Peeters et al., 2018). In Venice, the explosion of the tourist phenomenon has contours that deserve a specific analysis in their own right, where the issue of mass tourism "should be a priority" (Russo & Sans, 2009; Seraphin et al., 2018).

From 2000 to 2017, the number of tourists coming to the historical city (arrivals) almost doubled from 1,503,913 to 3,156,000. This growth is even more surprising if associated with the number of overnight stays (presences), which went from 3,562,728 to 7,862,000 (Città di Venezia, 2017, 39). The tourist pressure is also exacerbated by the presence of day visitors and commuters. According to an estimate by Carrera (2016), commuters in Venice can be placed at around 7,500,000 every year, to which 17,500,000 day visitors are added. Considering these figures, the number of people who crowd the streets (of the historical centre) includes about 20,500 commuters and 66,800 tourists and day visitors per day.

One of the reasons for the increasing number of tourists and day visitors could be the rapid growth of low-cost aviation. According to the National Civil Aviation Authority (ENAC, 2017) report, the airports of Treviso and Verona, which host only low-cost airlines, respectively welcome an annual number of 3,015,057 (five airlines, all low-cost) and 3,099,142 passengers (19 low-cost and charter airlines). Venice airport, with its 10,371,380 passengers in 2017 (55 airlines of which about one third are low-cost) has the lion's share (for the number of low-cost airlines see the website of each airport). Obviously not all passengers are bound for Venice, but the current airport system in the north-east and beyond has made Venice more accessible to the most diverse types of tourists.

Visitors do not only come from the sky, but also from the sea. Venice is one of the most active cruise ports in Southern Europe, with almost 500 ship departures and around 1,500,000 passengers per year (Risposte Turismo, 2018). The image of one of the many cruise ships that cross the Giudecca Canal in front of Piazza San Marco has become an(other) symbol of overtourism. The ongoing debate on limiting/prohibiting, containing and managing the phenomenon of large ships in the lagoon, which has been magnified by recent accidents (June and July 2019), will have to be managed from several perspectives, ranging from tourism to the environment.

In 1991, Canestrelli and Costa estimated the level and optimum composition of arrivals compatible with the full functionality of the different subsystems used by citizens and tourists (e.g. transport, waste collection, access to cultural institutions, etc.), i.e. socioeconomic carrying capacity, and indicated that Venice could absorb a maximum total number of approximately 22,500 daily arrivals, of which no more than 10,700 are day visitors. These limits have been largely overcome since then, "nonostante i tentativi di attenuare i picchi attraverso la regolamentazione e la pianificazione" ("despite attempts to mitigate peaks through regulation and planning", *our translation*) (Russo, 2002, 173).

The city administration has only recently started experimenting with new solutions and plans to control the number of visitors. In 2018, a "segregation" system was tested, by which access to popular sites such as Rialto and Piazza San Marco is controlled in case of need due to overcrowding, diverting tourists to alternative routes (City of Venice 229/2018 Ordinance). The Municipality of Venice itself acknowledges the phenomenon of overtourism and the continuous excessive flow, by means of a tourist tax for the high season from February to December, 11 months a year.

In 1996, Van der Borg et al, (1996, 314) defined Venice as "...the city that most clearly represents what the term touristification means for an urban area". Venice is now one of the most cited case studies to describe the growing global problem of mass tourism. One of the key issues that has characterized the debate on overtourism associated with the city is the sharp decline of the Venetian population – a real depopulation, a phenomenon described by researchers, directors (such as the docufilm "La Sindrome di Venezia", 2012) and by the residents themselves through protests and demonstrations (Quinn, 2007; Cavallo, 2016; Minoia, 2017; Visentin & Bertocchi, 2019). For example, in 2008, when the population dropped below 60,000, a group of residents staged a fake "funeral" for the city. Before the funeral, in Campo San Bortolomio, a stone's throw from the Rialto Bridge, there was a luminous sign in the window of the Morelli pharmacy, which indicated in real time the number of residents in the historical centre of Venice. The digital residents counter was inaugurated on 21 March 2008, the date on which the LED screen indicated 60,699. At the beginning of 2019 the figure was 52,966.

The equation that best seems to represent Venice is therefore the following: more tourists and less inhabitants.

Overtourism (almost) by default

According to Zanetto (1986) and Davis et al. (2004), tourism has been a central part of Venetian culture and society since at least the eighteenth century. Today, however, there is ample evidence that tourism has taken control of the historical city of Venice. To highlight these impacts, we here present a small account of the change in tourism subsystems over the past 10 years (see Table 6.1).

According to Russo and Van der Borg (2002), a tourist destination structure can be divided into two different systems that make up the "tourist product".

Table 6.1   2007-2017 trend of tourist subsystems and residents in the historical centre of Venice

	2007	2017	VAR %
Residents	60,755	53,835	-9.96%
Arrivals	2,165,656	3,156,000	33%
Stays	5,875,370	7,862,000	20%
Hotels	249	274	9%
Hotel beds	16,015	18,384	13%
Complementary structures	1408	5535	129%
Beds in complementary structures	9218	25,301	74%
Public businesses	395	370	-6%
Commercial facilities	2605	2035	-22%

The first system represents the primary resources of a destination (consisting of its internal assets – e.g. attractions, tourist image and attractiveness); the second is outlined by the external environment (such as the local administration and the tourism industry in general). It is essential to illustrate and study the subsystem of secondary tourism products, i.e. tourist structures (accommodation facilities, restaurants and shops) to better understand the city's infrastructure and outline a tourist trend in the districts of Venice. The situation of the tourist subsystems in Venice at the beginning of 2018 is described by the following categories:

- *Hospitality sector*: hotels, complementary structures (B&B, hostel, etc.) and Airbnb (capable of representing the phenomenon of holiday homes). The complementary sector consists of the total number of lodgings governed by regional law no. 33 (Veneto Region), with the addition of holiday homes legally registered by the municipality; in this case, however, it is appropriate to isolate these dimensions to study the local impacts of the complementary structures and holiday homes represented by Airbnb. The impacts on the destination's districts are described and illustrated below.
- *Catering services (public businesses)*: These are widespread in the largest and most populous districts of the historical city, in the Cannaregio, Castello and Dorsoduro districts (see Figure 6.2).
- *Commercial facilities (shops)*: Shops include three categories: food, non-food and mixed. The commercial structure of Venice has already been well illustrated by Zanini et al. (2008), who analysed and defined the various (almost 80) types of retail outlets, based on the goods displayed in

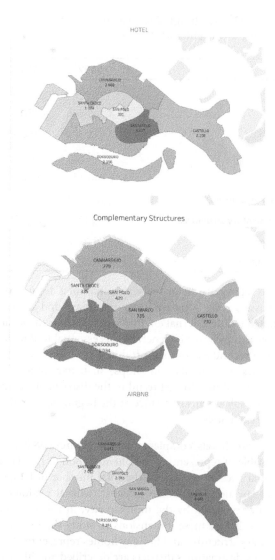

Figure 6.1   Distribution of hospitality sector by single Venetian district.
A darker colour represents a higher number of facilities
– 2018

the windows. Aggregation in a single category allows the strong impact of the commercial sector in the city's most tourist and "touristified" districts (based on the number of hotel beds) to be underlined (Figure 6.3). By breaking down the product types, the prevalence of non-food shops can be seen, almost representing a district dedicated to visiting, shopping and tourist accommodation.

The three types of accommodation affect different places in the historical centre (Figure 6.1). The hotels are concentrated in the San Marco district, in the most touristic area of the destination, whereas the complementary sector is fairly well distributed with a greater impact on the Dordosuro district (which also includes Giudecca island). Airbnb develops rather more in the larger (in terms of area) and historically more populated districts. In fact, the Cannaregio and Castello districts are the most popular with multiple houses, where Airbnb is more likely to spread and convert the use of housing into tourist locations. Overall, it seems that the island is balanced as regards accommodation and that there are few non-tourist areas in the city.

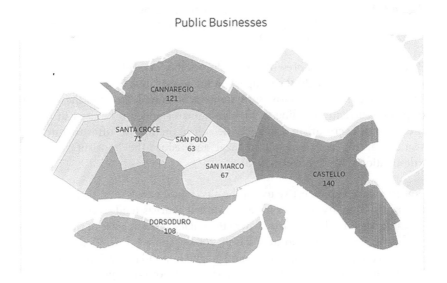

Public Businesses

Figure 6.2   Distribution of public businesses by single Venetian district. A darker colour represents a higher number of facilities – 2018

Commercial Establishments

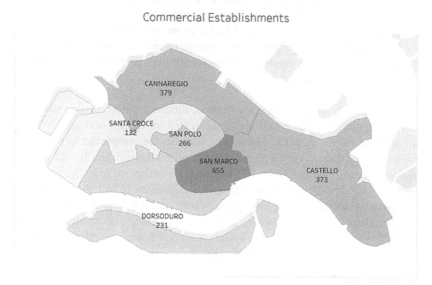

Figure 6.3   Distribution of commercial facilities by single Venetian district. A darker colour represents a higher number of facilities – 2018

By comparing the data presented with the number of residents in the districts, it is possible to highlight their impact on the social fabric by means of indices. These indices have the tourist subsystems as a denominator and the number of people currently residing in the denominator and can be used to report situations of overtourism due to the default of the tourist infrastructure, but also as warning signs to avoid, manage and reduce the "touristification" of a destination (Ma & Hassink, 2013).

Tourists make very selective use of the city. Studies analysing spatial patterns of tourism mobility in cities have shown that tourists tend to concentrate in specific areas of urban centres, where they make intensive use of the facilities and services available (Shoval & Raveh, 2004). Figure 6.4 shows the relationship between tourist infrastructure and inhabitants and the various imbalances between neighbourhoods. By studying the results of this report, it is possible to underline the strong impact of tourism on the San Marco district. This area hosts the main attractions of Venice (Piazza San Marco, the Rialto Bridge, Palazzo Ducale). In this district, which is more devoted to tourists and therefore less populated (3632 inhabitants at the beginning of 2019), tourists can visit the main tourist attractions, do some shopping and stay in hotels (where one third of the hotel rooms in the entire historical centre are located). On the other hand, residents try to avoid this overcrowded and poorly served area (in terms of facilities for the inhabitants).

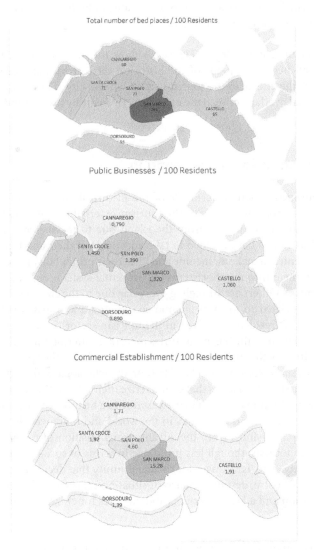

Figure 6.4   Tourist sub-systems by number of residents in the historical centre of Venice

Although the impact of the accommodation facilities ratio per 100 inhabitants is extremely unbalanced with respect to a rather tourist-centred San Marco (241 beds per 100 residents), the situation is even worse in the other areas of the city, which demonstrate a ratio that is always higher than 50%, with one bed for tourists every two inhabitants.

The correlations illustrated in Figure 6.4 show the indices of tourism subsystems on all neighbourhoods of the historical city, providing a geographical analysis of the effects of the tourism sector on the city. These effects lead to a widespread overlap between the use of the city made by tourists and residents.

A Venetian resident's perception

In the outlined situation, residents of the historical city of Venice seem to play different roles to deal with the tourism externalities. As shown before, some have decided to move from the island due to the increase in the cost of daily life, others have decided to take advantage of their apartments in the historical centre to make an income and raise their profitability by selling them or putting them into the short-term tourist rental system (e.g. Airbnb as discussed above). Others are struggling every day due to the changes and impacts on the city related to tourism phenomena in a gain and loss situation, with one part of the residents involved in the tourism sector (in this monoculture situation, tourism is the biggest business in Venice, offering the majority of job opportunities) with tangible economic benefits, and the other part involved in different business sectors not related to tourism, who apparently suffer more of the overtourism externalities that characterize their city. In the current picture, the win-win situation occurred in the past due to a hedonic cost of living in one of the more attractive destinations in the world and moreover the possibility of setting up a business from the advantageous position of owning a flat to be rented to tourists, though less profitable in terms of social capital and residents' society. This is stronger for the community that decided to still live in the historical centre, despite the current situation represented by a prominent tourism vision and a lack of services and facilities for citizens (Martín Martín et al. 2018).

In this research we also wanted to investigate the raised the voices of Venetians, not only those represented by associations and cultural groups, such as "no grandi navi" against big cruise ships in the lagoon, "Venezia non è Disneyland – Venice is not Disneyland" against impolite visitors and touristification, "Gruppo 25 Aprile", unfriendly with the destination management actions of the last years, "OCio – Osservatorio Civico sulla casa e sulla residenza", which focuses on the situation of public residential housing and tourist rentals, but also that of ordinary people living in the city. On the basis of the UNWTO global survey[1] carried out during 2018 and 2019 involving around 12,000 residents in 15 countries to better understand the residents' attitudes to overtourism (other recent research on this topic is that by Kuščer and Mihalič of 2019), which identified what residents consider to be the best ways of managing rising numbers of tourists, we tried to interview and listen to Venetian residents on the same topic through an online questionnaire[2] spread by social networks (Facebook and Instagram), messaging apps (WhatsApp groups) and local newspapers. In particular, we took the same structure of UNWTO questions regarding the need perceived by residents to develop measures to better manage tourism in their city (possible yes or no answer) and about which measures they think are best suited to dealing with the increase in the number of tourists to their city (we decided to leave an open answer, while the UNWTO fixed the possible answers, in order of importance, as: (1) Improve infrastructures and facilities; (2) Create experiences and attractions that benefit residents as well as visitors; (3) Ensure local communities benefit from tourism; (4) Communicate with and engage local communities; (5) Communicate with and engage visitors; (6) Promote tourism to other type of visitors; (7) Promote dispersal of visitors throughout the year; (8) Set up a system to measure and monitor tourism; (9) Promote the dispersal of visitors within the city and beyond; (10) Limit the number of tourism establishments; (11) Limit the number of visitors; (12) Stop tourism promotion).

The sample of the 2018 survey on Venetians' perception of overtourism was made up of 7381 current residents in the historical centre, almost 14% of the total population. The majority of the respondents agree with the need to have new policies and new management strategies for tourism flows and regulation for tourism facilities, 73% consider the introduction of a visitor fee useful to control, monitor and manage tourism flows (responses 4 and 5), but less than half (48.6%) have a solution for overtourism problems. Residents who suggest actions, policies and strategy that the city and the community need to deal with massive tourism flows and with the hospitality and tourism increase rate showed before, are grouped in three main clusters: (1) Limits; (2) Facilitations and (3) Actions and measures.

Limits

Residents' solutions to overtourism problems and to the negative externalities due to tourism raise the necessity to put different limits on visiting the destination and the growth of tourist facilities. Almost 20% of those interviewed suggested placing limits on the number of tourists visiting the city every day, followed by 9% who suggest limits on the ways of reaching Venice (cruises, low-cost flights, tourist boats, tourist coaches), and moreover limits on the accommodation sector, with 8% regarding the need for a limitation of vacation rentals in the city (e.g. Airbnb) and another 8% who want to limit the official hospitality systems to hotels and B&Bs. Only 3% suggest placing a limit on tourist facilities in general, such as restaurants and bars.

Facilitations

The facilitations most suggested by Venetian residents are those regarding renting a house without a transitory or temporary contract (8%), but in the form of a long-term contract (3+2 years or 4+4 years) aimed at residents. The other facilitations proposed by Venetians regard other services not related to tourism but more to daily life in the city, such as public and private facilities (6%). Another interesting point raised by the community concerns some facilitations (mainly tax reductions) for those wishing to set up a new business on the island not related to tourism (3%). Finally, another aspect regarding living in Venice is the need to invest in the renovation of empty and abandoned houses and apartments (1%).

Actions and policies

To the Venetians answering this survey, the most important action (9% of the sample) for regulating tourism in their city is a booking system for visiting Venice and/or the Marciana area (Saint Mark's Square). Another 8% are in favour of introducing entry tickets to Venice (e.g. visitor fee) while other residents focus more on promotion of the destination that underlines the need to promote not-tourism activities (5%), stimulate diversification of the tourism offer by visiting less famous parts of the city or other neighbouring destinations (3%), and lastly promoting Venice as a high-quality destination (2%). Another point Venetians raised in this survey is related to the need to adopt a better tourism management system of the destination (3%), improve the mobility plan of the city (2%) regarding the entry points to the destination, public transport reserved for residents and other lines dedicated to tourists or the quality and typology of the shops and commercial systems (1.5% suggested regulating souvenir shops). Other interesting actions suggested by Venetians are more concerned with the city's history and tradition, which should be preserved (1%) and more education for tourists and visitors (1%) about how to behave in the city and what is or is not allowed (e.g. swimming in the canals and cycling are prohibited in Venice). Lastly, Venetians suggest better managing the seasonality of the destination also in terms of a sustainable number of people and different price rates (1%) and raising tourist taxes and prices in general (1.5%).

The city council's strategy

Other or similar measures have been drafted by the local administration in the management and governance tourism plan of 2016.[3] The main points of this document, as the local administrators illustrated, are based on the principle that "Venice can innovate itself through sustainable tourism to enhance its urban dimension, respecting its authenticity and uniqueness, sharing it with the world as a World Heritage Site" (Città di Venezia, 2016). The project and operational proposal is based on the need to "Regulate tourist flows to make them compatible with the daily life of residents, remodulate, also by contrasting evasion, the tourist tax and organize services and transport to avoid congestion, creating new routes" (Città di Venezia, 2016), identifying four general macro objectives in turn enabled specific objectives to be studied – see Table 6.2.

An alternative approach: carrying capacity, reservation system and entry fee

The analysis of the spread of tourist infrastructure in the historical city of Venice highlights the important transformations that have affected some neighbourhoods. These transformations tend to attract more and more tourists who find infrastructure dedicated to them within the island, thus making the environment more hospitable to tourists than to residents.

By using some of the subsystems illustrated and analysing them with a linear programming method, it is possible to develop a model capable of processing a number (or range) of users that is sustainable for the destination (Canestrelli & Costa, 1991). According to various surveys on visitors to Venice conducted by the Department of Economics at the University of Venice, it is possible to measure the average expenditure of each individual profile: hotel tourists spend €210 per day, tourists in the complementary sector spend an average of €180 per day while each day visitor spends €60 in the city. The results of the model see a maximum daily capacity of around 19,000 hotel tourists, 25,000 tourists from the complementary sector and a few thousand day visitors, almost equalling the number of current residents. The city would thus see

Table 6.2   Measures for Venice – management and governance plan of the destination of Venice, 2016

Macro Objectives	Specific measures
(A) Managing the resource	Smart Control Room: an integrated system for the control and management of mobility and road safety
	Monitoring and control of access and mobility within the city through the installation of people-counting systems, use of big data, monitoring of pedestrian flows, agreements with managers of accommodation reservation systems, agreements with transport carriers.
	Coordination of the functions of control and security aimed at combating the phenomena of abuse, degradation and protection of urban and behavioural decorum.
	New strategies of urban and metropolitan mobility for the appreciation of Venice and its mainland: this action includes the Venezia Metropolitana 24 (a single ticket for public transport valid for the entire municipality) and diversification of the landing points of the Gran Turismo launches.
	Experimentation of access reservation systems for the Marciana area, starting from 2017
	Booking systems and tourist maps
	Interventions in support of the exercise of the professions of tourist guide in Venice in order to enhance the cultural offer
(B) Residential protection	Revision of town planning rules in favour of residence.
	Limitations of the so-called "take away activities".
	Reorganization of the so-called plans and concession areas for commercial activities.
	Accessibility and overcoming architectural barriers
	Selective waste collection and measures aimed at containing the load of waste produced in the city to protect public hygiene and urban decorum

Macro Objectives	Specific measures
(C) Balancing extra costs to favour the appreciation and development of the City	Application of tariff class 8 of the TARI non-household users to all those who pay the tourist tax as substitutes
	Application of the tourist tax to tourist leases in proportion to the price of the overnight stay
D) Innovate information. Educating for responsible and eco-sustainable tourism	Strengthening of the #Detourism communication project
	Introduction of special posters and information totems
	The forecast of interventions of cultural relevance in the mainland (also in the light of the emerging M9 museum)
	Launch of the "Forti in rete" project
	Identification of refreshment areas, mapping of the City's gardens and parks and an increase in public toilets
	Introduction of a behavioural decalogue for the visitor and the launch of an international awareness-raising campaign (#EnjoyRespectVenice)

a distribution of 45% of residents, 38% of tourists and day visitors and 17% of city users (commuters and students, according to estimates in Carrera, 2016). This division is possible given the diffusion of the accommodation sector seen previously. A less widespread and/or controlled sector, especially as regards the complement related to Airbnb, could significantly decrease the results of the calculation model and reduce the impact of tourists on the city.

Another strategic solution, which is included in future development plans but postponed pending further technical and regulatory assessments for its full application, is the imposition of a contribution to the management of Venice attributable to users classifiable as day visitors i.e. the supposed landing tax that the Municipality of Venice is planning to introduce in this period. This model, in addition to monitoring arrivals and allowing a more precise estimate of the real number of visitors, can be used to find new economic resources for the improvement of tourist services, the modernization of the tourist offer as well as the protection of the city and even financial incentives for residency and the resident population.

Stopping the process of further "Venetianization" of Venice is not some sort of snobbish desire of a Venetian elite to curb the number of mass tourists, keeping Venice to themselves. It is a fundamental ingredient of a deliberate urban strategy to economically and socially revitalize the city so that it can become strong enough to be proudly preserved, as well as being beneficial for people who want to both live in and visit this world heritage site in the future. Without a tourism policy, not only aiming to control and manage but also to revitalize the commercial sectors and services to residents (non-tourist leases), the path to decline is clearly marked.

A key factor: the resilience of residents and local activities

The term resilience applied to a society and to a human group means "the ability of groups or communities to cope with external stresses and disturbances, while maintaining their functional characteristics and defined identity" (Biggs et al., 2012). In the last decades this resilience of the Venetian community was not as strong as has emerged in recent years. In the past, Venetians almost preferred to escape from a city shaped for tourism activities and tourist purposes. Living Venice made the transition we described above, becoming an urban place more dedicated to tourists than inhabitants. In addition, some residents took advantage of this change, selling their houses located in the historical city or making additional income by using Airbnb or holiday rental websites for the tourism market. Some signals of Venetian community resilience have, slowly, and sometimes not well coordinated (mostly due to fragmentation and constellation), emerged in the last years, through the creation of cultural associations and local movements related to inhabitants and city needs that have not been listened to for various reasons for various periods of time. In addition to cases related to major issues such as cruises and large ships (NOGrandiNavi), Venice has seen the birth of movements related to residence (OCio), the protection of local traditions (VeneziaAutentica, Ass. Batipai), the protection of the environment and the lagoon ecosystem (VeniceCalls) and the preservation of public property (Ass. LaVida, ExGasometri Committee). Resilience is the capacity of a community not only to adapt after a shock (which could here be the effects of overtourism and the extreme growth of tourism facilities), but also to develop new growth pathways. As shown by the results of the community consultation, the new growth actions could take an extreme shape, able to overturn the priorities defined by the UNWTO as a result of the global survey. In fact, Venetians express the need to have different limits, from one related to the daily number of tourists and visitors in the city, to one connected to the expansion of the accommodation sector. Citizens raised their voices to obtain stronger and more marked actions to solve or mitigate the negative externalities of the changing urban structure and dynamics. In addition, residents underlined the importance of alleviating the city tourism pressure of tourist facilities, hotels and holiday rentals by activating facilitations and policy actions able to regulate tourism flows (e.g. entry tickets), but also to motivate new residents and the opening of new, non-tourism activities with measures addressed at housing availability and the residential accommodation.

Although the Venetians' resilience and desire for change have become more tangible, the municipal administration has not yet been able to give concrete and immediate solutions, especially by activating an effective strategy to protect housing, open new activities and increase non-tourism job creation, fighting the unsustainable growth that this iconic destination of urban tourism has suffered.

Notes

1   See   https://webunwto.s3-eu-west-1.amazonaws.com/imported_images/51637/unwtoispsosglobalsurveysummary.pdf.
2   We would like to thank dott.ssa Cecilia Scarpa and Professor Silvio Giove for the questionnaire used, and also for the master's thesis entitled: "Venezia e l'over-tourism: Problematiche e possibili soluzioni legate alla sostenibilità sociale" and local newspaper promoting it as https://ricerca.gelocal.it/nuovavenezia/archivio/nuovavenezia/2019/05/05/venezia-un-questionario-cittadino-sull-affollamento-turistico-02.html and https://www.ilgazzettino.it/pay/venezia_pay/la_tesi_di_cecilia_test_social_sul_boom_dei_turisti_in_citta-4470824.html.
3   See   https://live.comune.venezia.it/sites/live.comune.venezia.it/files/articoli/allegati/Prog.governance%20terr.%20turismo_13_luglio.pdf.

References

Biggs, R., Schlüter, M., Biggs, D., Bohensky, E.L., BurnSilver, S., Cundill, G., ... & Leitch, A. M. (2012) Toward principles for enhancing the resilience of ecosystem services. *Annual Review of Environment and Resources*, 37, 421–448.
Bryman, A. (1999) The Disneyization of society. *The Sociological Review*, 47(1), 25–47.
Butler, R.W. (1980) The concept of a tourist area cycle of evolution: Implications for management of resources. *Canadian Geographer*, 24(1), 5–12.
Canestrelli, E., & Costa, P. (1991) Tourist carrying capacity: A fuzzy approach. *Annals of Tourism Research*, 18, 295–311.
Carrera, F. (2016) Soluzioni 'made in Venice' per un Turismo Sostenibile. Presentation at the Venice Municipality, 5 December 2016. Available at: https://docs.google.com/document/d/1Nk_cf08Qjsa20S-GcPds2cqv4-tuD-qgetxWAC00t9o/edit (last accessed 19 July 2018).

Cavallo, F. (2016) La Laguna di Venezia, dispute territoriali e movimenti sociali. *Rivista Geografica Italiana*, 123(2), 125–140.
Celata, F. (2017). La "Airbnbificazione" delle città: gli effetti a Roma tra centro e periferia. Report Università di Roma La Sapienza, Dipartimento MEMOTEF. Available at: https://www.memotef.uniroma1.it/sites/dipartimento/files/Celata _Airbnbificazione_Roma.pdf (last accessed 23 June 2018).
Città di Venezia (2016) *Progetto di governance territoriale del turismo a Venezia.* *Assessorato al turismo.* Available at: https://live.comune.venezia.it/sites/live.comune .venezia.it/files/articoli/allegati/Prog.governance%20terr.%20turismo_13_luglio .pdf.
Città di Venezia (2017) *Annuario del turismo 2017.* *Assessorato al turismo.* Centro Produzione Multimediale, Venice.
Costa, N., & Martinotti, G. (2003). Sociological theories of tourism and regulation theory. *Cities and Visitors: Regulating People, Markets, and City Space*, 53–71.
Davis, R.C., Marvin, G., & Garry, M.R. (2004) *Venice, the Tourist Maze: A Cultural Critique of the World's Most Touristed City.* University of California Press.
ENAC (2017) Dati di traffico 2017. Available at: www.enac.gov.it/info13355240029 .html (last accessed 20 July 2018).
Guttentag, D. (2015) Airbnb: Disruptive innovation and the rise of an informal tourism accommodation sector. *Current Issues in Tourism*, 18(12), 1192–1217.
Horn, K., & Merante, M. (2017) Is home sharing driving up rents? Evidence from Airbnb in Boston. *Journal of Housing Economics*, 38, 14–24.
Ma, M., & Hassink, R. (2013) An evolutionary perspective on tourism area development. *Annals of Tourism Research*, 41, 89–109.
Martín Martín, J., Guaita Martínez, J., & Salinas Fernández, J. (2018) An analysis of the factors behind the citizen's attitude of rejection towards tourism in a context of over-tourism and economic dependence on this activity. *Sustainability*, 10(8), 2851–2869 10.3390/su10082851
Massiani, J., & Santoro, G. (2012) The relevance of the concept of capacity for the management of a tourist destination: Theory and application to tourism management in Venice. *Rivista Italiana di Economia Demografia e Statistica*, 66(2), 141–156.
McKercher, B. (2005) Destinations as products? A reflection on butler's life cycle. *Tourism Recreation Research*, 30(3), 97–102.
Minoia, P. (2017) Venice reshaped? Tourist gentrification and sense of place. In: Bellini, N. & Pasquinelli, C. (Eds.), *Tourism in the City: Towards an Integrative Agenda on Urban Tourism.* Springer International Publishing, New York, pp. 261–274.
Muler Gonzalez, V., Coromina, L., & Galí, N. (2018) Overtourism: residents' perceptions of tourism impact as an indicator of resident social carrying capacity-case study of a Spanish heritage town. *Tourism Review*, 10.1108/TR-08-2017-0138
Ordinanza 229/2018 Città di Venezia (2018) Misure urgenti per garantire l'incolumità pubblica, la sicurezza e la vivibilità nella città storica di Venezia in occasione del ponte della festività del 1° maggio 2018. Available at: https://www.comune.venezia .it/it/content/2292018 (last accessed 27 November 2018).
Peeters, P. M., Gössling, S., Klijs, J., Milano, C., Novelli, M., Dijkmans, C.H.S., ... & Mitas, O. (2018) Research for TRAN Committee-Overtourism: impact and possible policy responses. European Parliament, Directorate General for Internal Policies, Policy Department B: Structural and Cohesion Policies, Transport and Tourism.
Picascia, S., Romano, A., & Teobaldi, M. (2017) The airification of cities: Making sense of the impact of peer to peer short term letting on urban functions and economy.

In: *Proceedings of the Annual Congress of the Association of European Schools of Planning*. Lisbon, pp. 11–14.

Quinn, B. (2007) Performing tourism in Venice: Local residents in focus. *Annals of Tourism Research*, 34(2), 458–476.

Risposte Turismo (2018) Il traffico crocieristico in Italia nel 2017 e le previsioni per il 2018. Available at: http://www.risposteturismo.it/Public/RisposteTurismo(2018)_SpecialeCrociere.pdf (last accessed 11 August 2018).

Russo, A.P. (2002) The 'vicious circle' of tourism development in heritage cities. *Annals of Tourism Research*, 29(1), 165–182.

Russo, A., & Sans, A.A. (2009). Student communities and landscapes of creativity: How Venice—'the world's most touristed city'—is changing. *European Urban and Regional Studies*, 16(2), 161–175.

Russo, P., & Van der Borg, J. (2002) Planning considerations for cultural tourism: A case study of four European cities. *Tourism Management*, 23, 631–637.

Salerno, G.M. (2018) Estrattivismo contro il comune. Venezia e l'economia turistica. *ACME: An International E-Journal for Critical Geographies*, 17(2).

Schneiderman, E.T. (2014) Airbnb in the city. *New York State Office of the Attorney General. New York*. Available at: https://ag.ny.gov/pdfs/AIRBNB%20REPORT.pdf (last accessed 16 July 2018).

Seraphin, H., Sheeran, P., & Pilato, M. (2018) Over-tourism and the fall of Venice as a destination. *Journal of Destination Marketing & Management*, 9, 374–376.

Shoval, N., & Raveh, A. (2004) Categorization of tourist attractions and the modeling of tourist cities: Based on the co-plot method of multivariate analysis. *Tourism Management*, 25(6), 741–750.

Van der Borg J., Costa, P., & Gotti, G. (1996) Tourism in European heritage cities. *Annals of Tourism Research*, 23(2), 306–321.

Van der Borg, J., Camatti, N., Bertocchi, D., & Albarea, A. (2017) *The Rise of the Sharing Economy in Tourism: Exploring Airbnb Attributes for the Veneto Region*, Venezia, Working Paper Working Paper Economics Department Ca' Foscari Venezia. Available at: https://econpapers.repec.org/paper/venwpaper/2017_3a05.htm (last accessed 27 July 2018).

Visentin, F., & Bertocchi, D. (2019) Venice: An analysis of tourism excesses in an overtourism icon. *Overtourism: Excesses, Discontents and Measures in Travel and Tourism*, 18–38.

Zanetto, G. (1986) Une ville touristique et ses habitants: le cas de Venise. *Loisir et Société/Leisure and Society*, 9, 117–124.

Zanini, F., Lando, F., & Bellio, M. (2008) *Effects of Tourism on Venice: Commercial Changes over 30 Years*. Venezia, Working Paper Economics Department, Ca' Foscari Venezia. Research Paper Series No. 33/WP/2007. Available at: http://www.unive.it/media/allegato/DIP/Economia/Working_papers/Working_papers_2008/WP_DSE_zanini_lando_bellio_33_08.pdf (last accessed 11 July 2018).

Zervas, G., Proserpio, D., & Byers, J.W. (2014) The rise of the sharing economy: Estimating the impact of Airbnb on the hotel industry. *Journal of Marketing Research*, 54(5), 687–705.

7

The Rotterdam way: a new take on urban tourism management

Shirley Nieuwland, Ewout Versloot and Egbert van der Zee

Introduction

While most of the popular urban tourism destinations of North-Western Europe are famed for their historic city centres, a growing number of destinations, such as Rotterdam, challenge the conditionality of having a picturesque historic centre for being a successful tourist destination. The city of Rotterdam, which is shaped by its industrial past as well as a significant scar left by carpet bombings during World War II, is currently witnessing an urban revival. While just decades ago the city was mostly shunned because it was described as rough, edgy and even boring (Kasteleijn & Maas, 1995), present day visitors appreciate the diverse and iconic modern architecture, as well as the creative and vibrant atmosphere in which the roughness and edginess actually seem to work in Rotterdam's favour (Richards & Wilson, 2004). In this light, the city is acclaimed by the international media as a must-visit destination, with Rotterdam featuring in Lonely Planet's "best in travel list" of 2016, describing it as a "metropolitan jewel of the Netherlands riding a wave of urban development, redevelopment and regeneration" (Lonely Planet, 2016).

The effects of this redevelopment and regeneration can be seen in the recent rise of the city's popularity as a tourist destination. Rotterdam is currently the second largest urban tourism destination in the Netherlands, considering nights spent by tourists (CBS, 2019a). The growing influx of tourists follows three decades of developments aimed at shifting the city's economy from a predominance of port-related industrial production and services towards a more diverse economic system with a strong focus on culture and consumption (Van Tuijl & van den Berg, 2016). As in other former industrial cities, an economic transition aimed at cultural-driven regeneration has played an important part in this transformation (Richards & Wilson, 2004; Russo & van der Borg, 2010; Zukin, 1995).

While several indicators highlight the rapid expansion of tourism in Rotterdam, the question of the extent to which this development can be considered beneficial for the city needs to be posed. Post-industrial cities such as Rotterdam face myriad challenges while working towards an economically, socially and environmentally sustainable urban future (Judd & Fainstein, 1999; van Tuijl & van den Berg, 2016). Empowering marginal socio-economic groups, creating opportunities for local businesses and start-ups, and dealing with the consequences of climate change are among these challenges. Additionally, the rising awareness of the adverse effects tourism can have on local living conditions has set a new challenge for cities (Colomb & Novy, 2016; but see also Van der Borg et al., 1996); the praised solution of the past decades, using cultural regeneration and the visitor economy to reinvent cities, seems to be turning into a problem in cities such as Barcelona, Berlin and Amsterdam (Colomb & Novy, 2016; Füller & Michel, 2014; Pinkster & Boterman, 2017). Even though Rotterdam is not experiencing anything like the level of tourism in the cities focused on in this debate, the rapid growth in overnight stays during the past six years, the changing consumption landscape and economic make-up of the city, and the increasing attention given by print and online media fuel the need to create a proactive strategy in which the challenges posed by growing tourism in combination with the broader ones faced by the post-industrial city are addressed.

While recent developments make Rotterdam an interesting case study for illustrating how post-industrial cities can reinvent themselves based on the visitor economy by becoming attractive places to live, work and visit, the present case study aims to go one step further. Even though Rotterdam has come a long way, a relatively large part of the population is still in a vulnerable socio-economic position and inequality in the city is growing due to gentrification processes as a result of Rotterdam's popularity (Doucet & Koenders, 2018; Hochstenbach & Musterd, 2018). In addition, like many other cities, Rotterdam is increasingly confronted with issues related to climate change and aims, for example, to halve all greenhouse gas emissions by 2030 (Hölscher et al., 2019; Rotterdamse Klimaat Alliantie, 2019). In this chapter we consider how tourism can be integrated into the wider urban policy agenda by making it achieve broader goals rather than simply pursuing its growth by making the city attractive to visitors. At the same time, we aim to contribute to ideas about sustainable urban tourism development based on the observation made by Ashworth and Page (2011) a decade ago that often, in urban tourism policy, "the local is explored and exploited in search of the unique global competitive advantage by a tourism industry that is itself global with a strong tendency towards a risk-averse replication of products and their delivery". This shows that a balance should be sought between the expansion of the visitor economy for the better, and the extent to which tourism policy allows the "city to be sold". This chapter is thus intended to indicate how and to what extent Rotterdam manages to integrate tourism proactively in the diverse landscape of contemporary urban issues and challenges and to make it work for the city.

The chapter will subsequently discuss the history and transformation of the city from an industrial port city into a diverse city with a port, industrial roots and an increasingly important visitor economy, position the city in the light of contemporary and future challenges, and provide an insight into the way urban tourism is currently being integrated in the wider policy landscape. Through the latter topic, critical examination of the development and organization of urban tourism in Rotterdam can provide insights into the discussion on what could help urban tourism contribute to a sustainable urban future and give colourful insights for academics and policymakers dealing with this topic in transforming industrial cities.

Introduction of the case of Rotterdam

Although the real story of Rotterdam is one of centuries rather than mere decades, the story of modern day Rotterdam often starts with the devastation of the city centre during World War II. On 14 May 1940, the German Luftwaffe dropped bombs on the city to support their troops and to break Dutch resistance in order to force surrender. The explosions and subsequent fires killed almost 900 civilians and made another 85,000 Rotterdammers homeless (van der Pauw, 2006). These events colour Rotterdam to this day, providing the groundwork for a story about resilience and working together to get things done. The current city marketing slogan, "Rotterdam. Make it Happen" connects directly to the "can-do mentality" that Rotterdammers are still known for, just like shortly after the war. The current perspective towards promoting the city reaches beyond storytelling as it is rooted in the modern history of the city. The bombing and subsequent rebuilding of the city centre according to a modernist planning approach had a major effect on the development of the city itself, ensuring that the new city looks nothing like other typical Dutch cities (Rooijendijk, 2005). The current image of the city as related to modern architecture, as well as the presence of a well-developed cultural infrastructure and the present-day mentality, all have their origin in the need to rebuild the city after World War II (Hitters, 2000).

Rotterdam was long seen as the ugly duckling of Dutch cities, being famed for many things a typical city does not want to be known for. A touristic image study comparing 18 Dutch cities conducted in 2010 ranked Rotterdam as the most unsafe and unfriendliest city and ranked it second-to-last for cleanliness and beauty (LAgroup, 2010). Next to the touristic image, Rotterdam suffers from high crime levels, high unemployment and low education levels compared with other Dutch cities (Snel & Engbersen, 2009). Over the last few years, however, the city seems to have found its second youth, becoming more popular nationally and internationally, leading to an increase in inhabitants (CBS, 2019b), expats (Rotterdam Partners, 2019a) and a general growth of the economy (Gemeente Rotterdam, 2019a). In addition, the city has become increasingly attractive in recent years, also from a tourism perspective.

Rotterdam is currently the second most-visited city of the Netherlands. Although Amsterdam hosts considerably more tourists, Rotterdam's tourism statistics are striking because of the constant and significant growth the city has witnessed since the global recession and subsequent Eurozone financial crisis, with a staggering 68% growth in nights spent between 2012 and 2018 leading to over 2 million nights in the city's official accommodation (CBS, 2019a), and an estimated additional 350,000 nights in the informal accommodation sector (van der Zee & Krist, 2019). Also, compared with Amsterdam and The Hague, the first and third cities ranked according to number of nights spent there by tourists, and in the Netherlands in general, Rotterdam shows a remarkably strong growth rate. Since 2012, this has reached between 4% and 16% more nights spent per annum, which is faster than the Dutch average growth or the growth in any other Dutch city (Figure 7.1). While the demand-side thus shows significant growth patterns, the tourism industry has been expanding rapidly as well. Between 2012 and 2018 the number of hotel beds rose by 37% (CBS, 2019c) and, between 2013 and 2018 the number of restaurants grew by 34% (van Vliet, 2018), indicating the visitor economy is increasing in both absolute and relative terms. The presence of an impressive number of one-off and repetitive events, such as the European Capital of Culture in 2001, the Grand Depart of the Tour de France in 2010, the postponed (due to Covid-19) 2020 Eurovision Song Contest, the annual International Film Festival and World Port Days, along with the ongoing addition of hallmark architecture such as "de markthal" also illustrate this development.

These developments, however, have not remained unquestioned. The growing popularity of the city as a place to live, work and visit also leads to an increasing pressure on the city, its housing prices, access to public space and liveability, leading to debates concerning the city's accessibility for lower and medium income groups (Doucet et al., 2011; Hochstenbach & Musterd, 2018; Stouten,

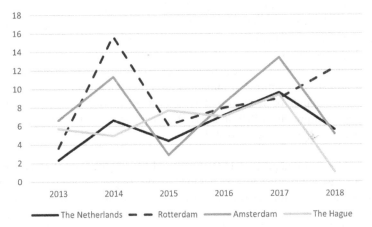

Source: CBS, 2019a.

Figure 7.1   Relative development (in %) of the change of nights spent in hotels per year compared with the previous year (2013–2018)

2017). As a result, in 2017, a large-scale study on the prospects of the city's development over the next 20 years was conducted with 9000 residents, certified by the city administration (Het verhaal van de stad, 2017). Tourism was one of the six main themes derived from the study, showing both support for and hesitation about the city's newfound popularity. Its inhabitants feel a sense of pride because the city is also acknowledged by visitors, they appreciate the positive impact visitors can have on the economy and also like how their direct environment has become more lively. At the same time, people are wary of the negative effects the increasing numbers of visitors might have. In the report, the general sentiment has been voiced that "Tourists are beneficial for the economy, but we have to steer clear of the situation in Amsterdam, where tourists have taken possession of the city. The city must remain ours!" (Het verhaal van de stad, 2017, 44, translated by the authors).

With the absence of a historic city centre, an important part of the touristic attractiveness of Rotterdam is embedded in its living culture, which is set in a landscape determined by modern and, in some cases, iconic architecture. In this sense, "tourism is a 'local' industry characterised by grassroots cultural production, spatial fixity of the tourism commodity and localised consumption of place" (Gotham, 2005, 1102). Even though global forces have a strong influence on the development of tourism, it can be argued that the recent success of tourism development in Rotterdam can, to an important extent, be attributed to "the local" (Massey, 2005). This makes finding the balance between further tourism development and safeguarding local living conditions while also protecting the local economic and cultural sector of prime importance, but precarious (Ananian et al., 2018; Gotham, 2005; Novy & Colomb, 2019). However, while an increasing number of cities are struggling to find this balance and strive for more sustainable tourism development, "most tourism policies have to date been conceived as stand-alone marketing and promotion strategies" (Pasquinelli & Bellini, 2017, 4) rather than as part of broader urban policymaking (Novy & Colomb, 2019).

Urban tourism management is thus in need of practical proof-of-concepts that showcase alternative approaches able to inspire policymakers. In the case of Rotterdam, the rapid growth of visitor numbers, along with the changing sentiment among the city's inhabitants on the recent development of tourism, prompted the municipality and Rotterdam Partners, the local Destination Management Organization, to take steps towards creating a new vision on tourism for the city of Rotterdam. The remainder of the chapter will shed light on how Rotterdam Partners and the Municipality have been working on creating a shared vision that is supported by a broad range of stakeholders. After going into this collaborative process, the expected level of government intervention in developing more sustainable models of tourism is discussed.

Towards a shared and supported vision on urban tourism

This process towards a new vision consisted of three phases. First, the municipality laid out its ambitions for tourism in the city. Local stakeholders were then asked to reflect on these ambitions and give their input. Lastly, an International Advisory Board (IAB) was formed to give an outsider perspective on the questions asked and advise the municipality on different aspects of the new vision (Gemeente Rotterdam, 2019b). The last two elements of these processes were outsourced to the local DMO, Rotterdam Partners. The findings are bundled in *The Rotterdam Way* (Rotterdam Partners, 2019b).

As worded by the tourism spokesman in a letter to the City Council on 26 March 2019 (Gemeente Rotterdam, 2019b), the municipality wanted to guide the conversation with stakeholders in the city by laying out its own ambitions for tourism in the city. In the letter, the spokesman mentions the need for a different way of thinking, meaning that tourism is no longer seen as a goal in itself, but as a means of achieving municipal ambitions. These are described as (1) work and income for local Rotterdammers; (2) supporting a more sustainable city; (3) lively and liveable neighbourhoods; and (4) a hospitable and proud city (Gemeente Rotterdam, 2019b, 2). These ambitions were then used to start the conversation with stakeholders from within and outside the city with the aim of developing broadly supported and well-informed advice. As reported by Rotterdam Partners (2019b, 15), the stakeholders involved represented a wide range of parties, divided into four groups: Off the beaten track ("hidden" gems such as local and original hotels, city guides and art institutions), Travel (institutions that facilitate a stay for visitors in Rotterdam such as Airbnb, Booking.com), National Experts (tourism experts from the field and academia) and Well-known & Well-liked (famous attractions, hotels, catering, shops, transport companies, festival organisers). In total, approximately 50 different stakeholders participated in focus groups or were consulted during this process.

Rotterdam is a forerunner when it comes to collaborative governance, in which the importance of including many stakeholders is part of effective policymaking and place making (Kavaratzis, 2017; Koens et al., 2019). The aims of such collaborative processes and place making are to address community impact and achieve sustainable tourism development (Bramwell & Lane, 2011; Hardy et al., 2002), while also creating a liveable and lively place for residents that is closely aligned with their identity and that of the city (Braun et al., 2013). The destination in this way becomes attractive without decreasing the quality of life in the city (Colomb & Kalandides, 2010; Marques & Borba, 2017; Markusen & Gadwa, 2010). In the process of forming a tourism vision for Rotterdam, however, residents are not consulted, even though they could be considered important stakeholders in the tourism network (Klidas & Papageorgiou, 2018; Rodríguez-Díaz & Espino-Rodríguez, 2008; Tham et al., 2015). The absence of residents as stakeholders in Rotterdam is interesting to note as community well-being and balanced tourism for city residents are an important factor in the city's tourism development strategy. Part of the explanation for this is that, in practice, involving a large number of stakeholders can be complicated as opinions are often diverse, which makes it difficult to come to a shared vision (Kasabov, 2015; Koens et al., 2019; van der Zee et al., 2017).

In the case of Rotterdam, it might thus come as no surprise that the different stakeholders consulted in this process had many overlapping views about the future of tourism, as most of them work closely with the tourist industry. First, it was noted by the stakeholders that they feel Rotterdam still has room to grow but that tourism should not engulf the city. According to them this could be done by promoting the right kind of growth, meaning visitors are well distributed throughout the year and tourism is well aligned with Rotterdam's identity. A second point the different stakeholders agreed on was that the whole city should be able to benefit from tourism and not only certain (central) parts. As a consequence, tourism could be developed in different parts of the city that are not yet noticed by tourists. An UNWTO report (2019) noted that dispersing tourists across time and space has indeed been identified as a potential measure to achieve a more balanced form of tourism. However, effectively achieving this can be difficult in practice (Koens et al., 2019; van der Zee et al., 2020).

Furthermore, stakeholders agreed that the "Rotterdam Way" should remain central in all tourism development activities. This means that only certain types of tourist profiles that match the city's ambitions should be approached through promotion strategies. Finally, there is a general consensus that the municipality should play a major role in the development of tourism in the city by adopting a clear vision and working towards a specific goal, and thus also excluding certain things that do not fit with this vision and goal. In short, these mostly commercially oriented stakeholders would like to see growth, but seem to support a coherent and strong governmental approach that guides this growth towards a more balanced and sustainable form of urban tourism.

To clarify the direction Rotterdam should or should not take, related to the development of tourism, all stakeholders were asked to collaboratively form doom and dream scenarios for tourism development. Stakeholders also held similar views on the worst-case scenarios for the future of tourism in Rotterdam. According to them, one of the worst things that could happen is for the city to resemble a touristic theme park in which big international chains predominate and Rotterdam loses its authentic identity, a perception that is quite common in more mature tourist destinations in Europe (Cócola Gant, 2015; Gotham, 2005). Local entrepreneurship would then slowly disappear and with that the city would take on a generic nature (Russo, 2002). According to recent contributions in the literature, this process of tourism-driven gentrification is a clear and imminent threat, especially in post-industrial cities (Sequera & Nofre, 2018). An opposing scenario is for the city to become unattractive and unpopular again, as it was for many years in the past. These two doom-scenarios already clearly indicate that there is a strong need for a governance strategy in which a balance between the two is maintained. Other negative scenarios described relate to attracting "the wrong kind of tourist", such as drug tourists and hen and stag parties that mostly lead to disturbance for local inhabitants. Furthermore, city life becoming too expensive and the feeling of alienation from the city because of its changed character are described as doom scenarios. Finally, stakeholders describe a scenario in which the municipality is not prepared for tourism that would lead to an imbalance between residential city life and tourism, which again shows that there is a clear need for a strategy that safeguards balanced urban tourism activities.

The dream scenarios described are mostly the opposite of the doom scenarios. Stakeholders dream of balanced tourism, evenly spread over the city in space and time while causing little disturbance to local residents. Furthermore, in the dream scenarios, Rotterdam attracts young and curious visitors that contribute to the city's positive development, not just by spending money but also by sharing cultural and social capital with residents and entrepreneurs. The city constantly innovates and looks towards the future by continuously renewing its offer. Another important aspect of the dream scenarios is that residents form an essential part of the development of both tourism and the city. In addition, local residents would be proud of this growing industry and understand that it is an important economic sector and a socio-cultural enrichment for the city.

Even though the stakeholders all work in or with the tourist industry, it is still interesting to note that big international stakeholders, hotels and small local entrepreneurs all hold similar views about tourism development in Rotterdam. This is partly due to the fact that the sessions were designed in such a way that they would lead to a broad shared vision rather than working out all the details in which opinions might differ more from one another. This also shows that a balanced and more sustainable form of tourism in which residential and city life are preserved might be beneficial to all kinds of stakeholders in the long run and is broadly embraced

Level of government intervention

As a final step in looking at the ways and extent to which the government should take part in Rotterdam's tourism development, an international advisory board was invited to the city to reflect on the outcomes of the stakeholder groups and provide the city with recommendations. This International Advisory Board (IAB) consisted of seven experts in the fields of tourism, city branding and urban development, with backgrounds in, for example, public policy, consultancy and academia. The IAB gave a series of recommendations to the city supported by several suggestions, examples and possible steps the city should take. For the purpose of clarity, we will only discuss the overarching themes of the IAB's advice. These themes can be characterized as (1) overarching principles, (2) the need for better and transparent data, and (3) the need for a bottom-up approach in conjunction with (4) clear top-down policies.

The principles the IAB describes in the first recommendation are notions around identity and inclusivity while adopting a holistic approach in which long-term benefits are safeguarded. The complexity of what it calls the visitor economy and the impact this has on the city are mentioned here as an important factor to be considered. According to the IAB, this means that the visitor economy should take these impacts into account, but also that other aspects of city development need to take note of the visitor economy. It is thus clear that tourism is no longer confined to the boundaries of the traditional touristic sector and policymaking has to include many other areas as well (Koens et al., 2018; Sequera & Nofre, 2018).

The next recommendation focuses on the need for better and more transparent research into the visitor economy. The IAB notes how current research often only expresses the impact of the visitor economy in financial and economic terms but pays little attention to the impact in other areas. This is a commonly heard critique in the assessment of tourism impact, as made a decade ago by Ashworth and Page (2011) and reflected in various recent publications on sustainable urban tourism development (Wise, 2016). They recommend measuring the environmental, social and cultural effects as well, for example with regard to cruises, hotels and tour operators. Simultaneously, the IAB advises monitoring how local residents feel about the visitor economy as well as the interests of the tourism industry. Monitoring the effects of tourism, both positive and negative, on a broad range of stakeholders is thus an important part of the advice.

In the third recommendation, the IAB mentions the need for an inclusive bottom-up approach to building a tourism vision and strategy. This includes having a conversation with local communities about their needs, but also helping them understand the possible value of the visitor economy and the choices they might have in developing the visitor economy in their neighbourhood. This is something relatively new as many destinations do not yet consider residents one of their primary stakeholders, but is strongly encouraged for those cities seeking to develop more balanced forms of tourism (Koens et al., 2018; Timur & Getz, 2008; UNWTO, 2019). It is, however, important to note that while the IAB focuses on the needs and ambitions of local citizens and entrepreneurs, it primarily sees a leading role for the municipality.

This brings us to the final recommendation in which the IAB outlines the importance of a top-down approach, which in this case would be complementary rather than contrary to community initiatives. In this sense there could be clear top-down policy guidelines that ensure positive outcomes for the city and its residents as a whole. This top-down approach consists, for example, of defining what constitutes a healthy visitor economy and the implementation of a hotel and home rental policy (Nieuwland & van Melik, 2018). These policies can be implemented proactively to avoid potential undesirable impacts in the future.

Based on these recommendations it seems that, within a framework of general guidelines and policies in the development of tourism, the city should at best have space for citizen engagement and community initiatives. A healthy balance between top-down governance with room for bottom-up initiatives seems to be thought of as most effective. The importance of a collaborative process of developing tourism is thus a strong part of this advice and is in line with many other recommendations from the academic world on more sustainable city and tourism development (for example, Koens et al., 2018; Timur & Getz, 2008; van der Zee et al., 2017; Volgger & Pechlaner, 2014).

Conclusion and discussion

In summary, we can say that in terms of government intervention there is a clear role for the municipality to steer Rotterdam towards more sustainable forms of tourism that take into account the balance between the potential positive and negative impacts the visitor economy can have on the city. In order to come to those balanced forms of tourism it is the municipality's role, in association with the local DMO, to integrate tourism into broader policymaking, monitor the impact of tourism on multiple stakeholder groups and include them in the development process, while at the same time creating a broader regulatory framework within which there is room for bottom-up initiatives from the diverse groups of stakeholders. Previous research into the effects tourism can have on urban livelihoods suggests there is a delicate balance between becoming increasingly attractive for tourists and safeguarding local livelihoods (Ananian et al., 2018; Cócola Gant, 2015; Gotham, 2005), which is specifically the case in post-industrial cities (Sequera & Nofre, 2018). The IAB report concluded that in order to be sustainable, urban tourism development needs both continuous impact monitoring that goes beyond solely economic indicators as well as stakeholder and community involvement. In this sense, tourism development is both urged and forced to pay respect to the living culture that forms the core of the attractiveness of a regenerating post-industrial city such as Rotterdam (Ashworth & Page, 2011; Massey, 2005).

Returning to the ambitions of Rotterdam's tourism spokesman, we can now draw connections between the dream and doom scenarios from stakeholders and the recommendations of the IAB report and see how they can contribute to more sustainable tourism development in Rotterdam. By following the recommendations of the IAB report and having a better idea of the impact of tourism on the city not only in economic terms, but also taking into account socio-cultural and environmental aspects (Wise, 2016), Rotterdam can adopt data and research driven policies that respect the needs and wishes of multiple stakeholder groups. Taking a holistic approach to tourism and making it part of city-wide policymaking ensures that it will result in long-lasting benefits and values for all residents. Moreover, by opening up more space for bottom-up initiatives with an inclusive approach, the city allows many citizens to benefit from tourism while at the same time working on projects that are closely aligned with the city's identity and so create a diverse and lively city. A scenario such as this would be very much in line with the dream scenario of the different stakeholders, in which balanced tourism growth that stays close to the identity of the city and in which residents have a prominent role are key to the tourism development of Rotterdam. An important side note must be made here, however. Even though the process of forming a new tourism vision for Rotterdam was aimed at including a broad representation of stakeholders directly related to the city's tourism sector, as well as external experts, the local residents were not actively included in this process. Our recommendation is that future vision-forming or policymaking activities should also aim to involve local residents in order to be truly inclusive.

The outcomes of the collaborative approach for forming a new tourism vision in Rotterdam have resulted in a widely accepted structure aimed at a new policy approach to developing urban tourism in such a way that it actually works towards achieving the ambitions of the city as laid out by the spokesman, and as explained at the beginning of this chapter: employment and income for all citizens, a more sustainable city, dynamic and liveable residential areas, and staying true to the city's identity. In this sense, our main recommendation for future urban tourism policymaking is that tourism should not be seen as an outcome but as a means of improving the city for its residents and users in which the growth of tourism numbers is not the main goal. What is clear is that strong and bold leadership from the municipality and active participation of the local communities are required for this. In Rotterdam, the municipality has already taken various important first steps, for example by being the first major Dutch city to increase the legitimacy of tourism as an integrated element of urban policy by nominating a city council spokesman for tourism. The formation of the tourism vision by the IAB together with local and national stakeholders and experts can be seen as the starting point for creating a comprehensive and contemporary approach to sustainable urban tourism development that is supported and complemented by the various local stakeholders at the core of what makes Rotterdam an attractive tourism destination. The next step would be to follow up on this vision, and further develop "the Rotterdam way" into a guiding example for the wide selection of regenerating and developing post-industrial cities exploring how to make tourism work for the city and its inhabitants.

Acknowledgements

We would like to thank Professor Leo van den Berg for his valuable guidance and feedback. We would also like to thank Rotterdam Partners and the participants in the stakeholder consultations that led to the IAB report and were used as input for this chapter.

References

Ananian, P., Perras, A., & Borde, M. A. (2018). Living in Old Montreal: Residents' perceptions of the effects of urban development and tourism development on local amenities. *The Canadian Geographer/Le Géographe Canadien, 62*(4), 535–550.

Ashworth, G., & Page, S. J. (2011). Urban tourism research: Recent progress and current paradoxes. *Tourism Management, 32*(1), 1–15.

Bramwell, B., & Lane, B. (2011). Critical research on the governance of tourism and sustainability. *Journal of Sustainable Tourism, 19*(4–5), 411–421.

Braun, E., Kavaratzis, M., & Zenker, S. (2013). My city–my brand: The different roles of residents in place branding. *Journal of Place Management and Development, 6*(1), 18–28.

CBS (2019a). Central Bureau for Statistics Open Data. Dataset: Gasten en overnachtingen in hotels, motels, pensions, jeugdaccommodaties en b&b naar woonland (herkomst) gast per regio. Available online: https://opendata.cbs.nl/statline/portal.html ?_la=nl&_catalog=CBS&tableId=82061NED&_theme=428 (accessed 19 January 2020).

CBS (2019b). Central Bureau for Statistics Open Data. Dataset: Bevolking; ontwikkeling in gemeenten met 100 000 of meer inwoners. Available online: https://opendata.cbs .nl/statline/#/CBS/nl/dataset/70748NED/table?fromstatweb (accessed 19 January 2020).

CBS (2019c). Central Bureau for Statistics Open Data. Dataset: Logiesaccommodaties; capaciteit, accommodaties, bedden, regio. Available online: https://opendata.cbs.nl/ statline/#/CBS/nl/dataset/82062NED/table?fromstatweb (accessed 19 January 2020).

Cócola Gant, A. (2015). Tourism and commercial gentrification. Paper presented at the RC21 International Conference *The Ideal City: Between Myth and Reality. Representations, Policies, Contradictions and Challenges for Tomorrow's Urban Life*, 27–29.

Colomb, C., & Kalandides, A. (2010). The 'be Berlin' campaign: Old wine in new bottles or innovative form of participatory place branding? In G. Ashworth, & M. Kavaratzis (Eds.), *Towards Effective Place Brand Management*. Cheltenham, UK & Northampton, MA, USA: Edward Elgar Publishing.

Colomb, C., & Novy, J. (2016). *Protest and Resistance in the Tourist City*. London: Routledge.

Doucet, B., & Koenders, D. (2018). 'At least it's not a ghetto anymore': Experiencing gentrification and 'false choice urbanism' in Rotterdam's Afrikaanderwijk. *Urban Studies*, 55(16), 3631–3649.

Doucet, B., van Kempen, R., & van Weesep, J. (2011). 'We're a rich city with poor people': Municipal strategies of new-build gentrification in Rotterdam and Glasgow. *Environment and Planning A*, 43(6), 1438–1454.

Füller, H., & Michel, B. (2014). 'Stop being a tourist!' New dynamics of urban tourism in Berlin-Kreuzberg. *International Journal of Urban and Regional Research*, 38(4), 1304–1318.

Gemeente Rotterdam (2019a). Economische Verkenningen Rotterdam. https://evr010 .nl/highcharts/ (accessed 19 January 2020).

Gemeente Rotterdam (2019b). Raadsinformatiebrief 'Stand van zaken visie toerisme'. https://rotterdam.raadsinformatie.nl/document/7460170/1.

Gotham, K. F. (2005). Tourism gentrification: The case of New Orleans' *vieux carre* (French Quarter). *Urban Studies*, 42(7), 1099–1121.

Hardy, A., Beeton, R. J., & Pearson, L. (2002). Sustainable tourism: An overview of the concept and its position in relation to conceptualisations of tourism. *Journal of Sustainable Tourism*, 10(6), 475–496.

Het verhaal van de stad (2017). Het verhaal van de stad: hoe ziet Rotterdam er uit in 2037? Rotterdam, Roos & van de Werk. Available online: www.hetverhaalvandestad .nl

Hitters, E. (2000). The social and political construction of a European cultural capital: Rotterdam 2001. *International Journal of Cultural Policy*, 6(2), 183–199.

Hochstenbach, C., & Musterd, S. (2018). Gentrification and the suburbanization of poverty: Changing urban geographies through boom and bust periods. *Urban Geography*, 39(1), 26–53.

Hölscher, K., Frantzeskaki, N., & Loorbach, D. (2019). Steering transformations under climate change: Capacities for transformative climate governance and the case of Rotterdam, the Netherlands. *Regional Environmental Change*, 19(3), 791–805.

Judd, D. R., & Fainstein, S. S. (1999). *The Tourist City*. London: Yale University Press.

Kasabov, E. (2015). Managing the unmanageable: Stakeholder involvement in creating and managing places and their brands. In F. Go, A. Lemmetyinen & U. Hakala (Eds.), *Harnessing Place Branding through Cultural Entrepreneurship* (pp. 65–78). Springer.

Kasteleijn, D. & Maas, R. (1995). Rotterdam heeft architectuurtoerist veel te bieden. *Agora Magazine*, 11(3), 10–11.

Kavaratzis, M. (2017). The participatory place branding process for tourism: Linking visitors and residents through the city brand. *Tourism in the City* (pp. 93–107). Berlin: Springer.

Klidas, A., & Papageorgiou, G. (2018). Ecosystem alliances as drivers of tourism destination dynamics in Western Peloponnese, Greece. Paper presented at the ATLAS Annual Conference, Aalborg University Copenhagen.

Koens, K., Melissen, F., Mayer, I., & Aall, C. (2019). The smart city hospitality framework: Creating a foundation for collaborative reflections on overtourism that support destination design. *Journal of Destination Marketing & Management*, 100376.

Koens, K., Postma, A., & Papp, B. (2018). Is overtourism overused? Understanding the impact of tourism in a city context. *Sustainability*, *10*(12), 4384

LAgroup (2010). Toeristisch imago-onderzoek 2010. Available online: https://app4 .nijmegen.nl/rapportenzoeker/Docs/Toeristisch_Imago_Onderzoek_2010_jul2010 .pdf

Lonely Planet (2016). Rotterdam in top 10 Lonely Planet's Best in Travel 2016. Available online: https://en.rotterdam.info/about-rotterdam/rotterdam-in-top-10 -lonely-planet-s-best-in-travel-2016/.

Markusen, A., & Gadwa, A. (2010). *Creative Placemaking*. Washington, DC: National Endowment for the Arts.

Marques, L., & Borba, C. (2017). Co-creating the city: Digital technology and creative tourism. *Tourism Management Perspectives*, *24*, 86–93.

Massey, D. (2005). *For Space*. Sage.

Nieuwland, S., & van Melik, R. (2018). Regulating Airbnb: How cities deal with perceived negative externalities of short-term rentals. *Current Issues in Tourism*, 1–15.

Novy, J., & Colomb, C. (2019). Urban tourism as a source of contention and social mobilisations: A critical review. *Tourism Planning & Development*, *16*(4), 358–375.

Pasquinelli, C., & Bellini, N. (2017). Global context, policies and practices in urban tourism: An introduction. In *Tourism in the City* (pp. 1–25). Springer, Cham.

Pinkster, F. M., & Boterman, W. R. (2017). When the spell is broken: Gentrification, urban tourism and privileged discontent in the Amsterdam canal district. *Cultural Geographies*, *24*(3), 457–472.

Richards, G., & Wilson, J. (2004). The impact of cultural events on city image: Rotterdam, cultural capital of Europe 2001. *Urban Studies*, *41*(10), 1931–1951.

Rodríguez-Díaz, M., & Espino-Rodríguez, T. F. (2008). A model of strategic evaluation of a tourism destination based on internal and relational capabilities. *Journal of Travel Research*, *46*(4), 368–380.

Rooijendijk, C. (2005). Urban ideal images in post-war Rotterdam. *Planning Perspectives*, *20*(2), 177–209.

Rotterdam Partners (2019a). Groeiend aantal banen dankzij buitenlandse bedrijven. Available online: https://rotterdampartners.nl/persberichten/groeiend-aantal-banen -dankzij-buitenlandse-bedrijven/

Rotterdam Partners (2019b). The Rotterdam way. Available online: https://en .rotterdampartners.nl/wp-content/uploads//2019/09/IAB-Final-Report-PDF.pdf

Rotterdamse Klimaat Alliantie (2019). Rotterdam Klimaat Akkoord. Retrieved from: https://www.persberichtenrotterdam.nl/uploads/Rotterdams_Klimaatakkoord.pdf

Russo, A. P. (2002). The "vicious circle" of tourism development in heritage cities. *Annals of Tourism Research*, *29*(1), 165–182.

Russo, A. P., & Van der Borg, J. (2010). An urban policy framework for culture-oriented economic development: Lessons from the Netherlands. *Urban Geography*, *31*(5), 668–690.

Sequera, J., & Nofre, J. (2018). Shaken, not stirred: New debates on touristification and the limits of gentrification. *City*, 1–13.

Snel, E, & Engbersen, G.B.M. (2009). Social reconquest as a new policy paradigm. Changing urban policies in the city of Rotterdam. In: K. de Boyser, C. Dewilde, D. Dierickx & J. Friedrichs (Eds.), *Between the Social and the Spatial. Exploring the Multiple Dimensions of Poverty and Social Exclusion* (pp. 149–166). Farnham, UK: Ashgate.

Stouten, P. (2017). Gentrification and urban design in the urban fabric of Rotterdam. *Journal of Urban Regeneration & Renewal, 11*(1), 92–103.

Tham, A., Ogulin, R., Selen, W., & Sharma, B. (2015). From tourism supply chains to tourism value ecology. *The Journal of New Business Ideas & Trends, 13*(1), 47.

Timur, S., & Getz, D. (2008). A network perspective on managing stakeholders for sustainable urban tourism. *International Journal of Contemporary Hospitality Management, 20*(4), 445–461.

UNWTO (2019). *'Overtourism'? Understanding and managing urban tourism growth beyond perceptions volume 2: Case studies.* Retrieved from https://www.e-unwto.org/doi/book/10.18111/9789284420629

van der Borg, J., Costa, P., & Gotti, G. (1996). Tourism in European heritage cities. *Annals of Tourism Research, 23*(2), 306–321.

van der Pauw, J. L. (2006). *Rotterdam in de Tweede Wereldoorlog.* Meppel: Boom, Rotterdam: Gemeentearchief Rotterdam.

van der Zee, E., Bertocchi, D., & Vanneste, D. (2020). Distribution of tourists within urban heritage destinations: A hot spot/cold spot analysis of TripAdvisor data as support for destination management. *Current Issues in Tourism, 23*(2), 175–196.

Van der Zee, E., Gerrets, A. M., & Vanneste, D. (2017). Complexity in the governance of tourism networks: Balancing between external pressure and internal expectations. *Journal of Destination Marketing & Management, 6*(4), 296–308.

van der Zee, E. L., & Krist, J. D. (2019). *Airbnb Monitor Utrecht: Editie 4–de ontwikkeling van Airbnb in de gemeente Utrecht tot april 2019.* Utrecht: Utrecht University

Van Tuijl, E., & Van den Berg, L. (2016). Annual city festivals as tools for sustainable competitiveness: The World Port Days Rotterdam. *Economies, 4*(2), 11.

Van Vliet, D. (2018). Explosieve groei Rotterdamse horeca: Dit gaat een keer mis. Algemeen Dagblad. Available online: https://www.ad.nl/rotterdam/explosieve-groei-rotterdamse-horeca-dit-gaat-een-keer-mis~a6df8a45/

Volgger, M., & Pechlaner, H. (2014). Requirements for destination management organizations in destination governance: Understanding DMO success. *Tourism Management, 41*, 64–75.

Wise, N. (2016). Outlining triple bottom line contexts in urban tourism regeneration. *Cities, 53*, 30–34.

Zukin, S. (1995). *The Cultures of Cities* (Vol. 150). Oxford: Blackwell.

8 New urban developments in a heritage area. A case study of Skeppsholmsviken 6 in Stockholm, Sweden

Anna-Paula Jonsson and Tigran Haas

Introduction

Residents in a given location have several reasons to celebrate a strong and growing visitor industry. The very reason for visitors to go somewhere is typically a seal of approval of a location. Visitors, whether international or local tourists, choose their destination based on some kind of expectation. When tourists come to Stockholm, for example, they often want to see the quaint and historical neighbourhood of *Gamla Stan* (Old Town). Another top destination is *Djurgården* (Stockholm's Royal National City Park). In fact, Djurgården has been called "Scandinavia's #1 attraction" (Royal Djurgården, 2020). Both places are the result of hundreds of years of history and careful development; such places cannot easily be replaced or "fast-tracked" into being. In other words, there is an imperative to manage them well to preserve the high quality of urban public space that characterizes them.

While both Gamla Stan and Djurgården are examples of public space where people like spending time, they are not particularly similar in morphology and content. Hence, what can be understood as good public space does not have a clear prescription for form or substance, and the built developments that create – frame, if you like – our urban public spaces can come in many different shapes and sizes. As such, appreciated public spaces of high-quality may change in the specific way and shape of how they accommodate different groups of people over time – they remain fluid and contextual (Carmona et al., 2010).

This lack of definition can arguably pose a challenge for urban planners in charge of developing places that, due to their high-quality environment, attract the attention and interest of many distinct stakeholders. Almost inevitably, this leads to conflicting interests with regards to how such places should develop. While residents are likely to want to ensure their own life quality and permanence in their neighbourhoods and homes, corporate actors might be looking to exploit places for profit, Destination Management Organizations (DMOs) might be looking to grow visitor numbers and local visitor industry actors might be keen to attract a certain type of visitor. If pushed to its limits, opposing interests can generate fierce conflict leading all the way to the agenda of political campaigns (Russo & Scarnato, 2018).

As a response to the growing conflicts of this nature in European heritage cities, there is a plethora of tourism research describing and investigating phenomena such as *overcrowding*, the growth of Airbnb, social sustainability and the "Disneyfication" of local economies, to name a few (Doxey, 1975; Butler, 1980, 1999; Van Der Borg et al., 1996; Goodwin, 2017; Alvarez-Sousa, 2018). The resulting body of academic articles, reports and books on tourism management offers plenty of suggestions for how to manage, or even avoid, such phenomena. These range from introducing an "entry fee" for Venice to further restrictions on Airbnb rentals in a number of cities and new models for more "inclusive" and "sustainable" forms of tourism (Lagrave, 2018; UNWTO, 2018, 2019; Milano et al., 2019).

With conflicting interests at hand, it becomes relevant to look at the political regimes and planning processes that, by democratic legitimacy, are endowed with the institutional power to oversee the processes that might contribute to such phenomena. However, the aspect of *why* urban governance often seems to fail to preview and/or manage the process leading to overtourism, and consequential impact – which may then lead to conflict – remains relatively unexplored. With that said, the idea that tourism-related conflicts could be better managed, or even avoided altogether, if political and planning processes managed tourism as "integral to wider processes of economic and political development processes and even constitutive of everyday life" in cities, has been discussed before (Lew, 2007; Hannam et al., 2014, 172).

With the intent of building on this school of thought to gain a better understanding of how the visitor industry and urban planning processes work in synergy, or not, this case study goes beyond the traditional tourism research and tourism management literature to investigate the conflict around a new urban development in the Djurgården in Stockholm. The theoretical framework used for this chapter is therefore focused more on the processes of urban planning and "the politics" of urban development, than urban tourism management per se.

The conflict studied revolves around a new urban development in Stockholm, located in one of the most visited spots in the National City Park. The plan for the new development has been criticized by residents and experts on heritage and urban planning for not considering the needs of residents suffering from loud noise levels and overcrowding during summer months, or respecting the heritage environment where the development is planned to take place. According to critical voices, the new planned development is inappropriate owing to its perceived excessive impact on the Royal National City Park's visual, cultural and spatial environment. These same voices claim that the design of the new urban development is informed mainly by the interests of the private developer behind it. Some of the critics go as far as to question the democratic legitimacy of the politicians and institutions developing the plan and "whose side they are on". As a result, the case illustrates how complex and inherently conflict filled the processes of urban planning in heritage areas can be. Finally, the case study provides some suggestions with regards to how the planning process could develop to support new urban developments in areas of high potential for exploration, with less contention.

Urban planning theory, contemporary research and conflict management

The outcome of urban planning decisions has an immense impact on people's lives through shaping the physical world in which they live, socialize and work (Gehl, 2010; Carmona et al., 2010). One could therefore argue that "getting planning right" is the essence of social well-being and sustainability in urban contexts. And here we find ourselves in a bit of a pickle, because the definition of "getting it right" is conditional on one's moral underpinnings and on which qualities and spatial features are considered "right" and desirable in the first place. That said, it becomes relevant to study the outcomes of alternative planning regimes, both in today's urban development context and over time, to be able to compare the results and motivations of different alternatives.

The problem of urban planning

It is not difficult to see that planning outcomes are very seldom win-win solutions for all parties concerned. Determining what the outcome of urban planning should be is hence a so-called *wicked problem*

Nonetheless, and maybe as a necessary consequence, many attempts are made to state normative claims about what planning should accomplish. For example, many planning theorists consider planning to be an ethical activity, one that should be concerned with values such as social justice, equity and environmental sustainability (Carmona et al., 2010). If this sounds like a reasonable goal, there is an argument to be made for the follow up question of *How?* In the book *Public Places Urban Spaces*, Mathew Carmona et al. (2010) express their view that: "Rather than what urban design is or should be, the focus is *how* decisions become outcomes ('ends'), and the processes ('means') by which this happens" (Carmona et al., 2010, viii).

What emerges then, when working with research related to public space and urban planning, are complex questions such as: Who is entitled to design and define public spaces? Who is to say what such design and definitions should be? Is the idea of public and openly accessible public spaces for both residents and visitors ideologically motivated and, if so, to what end? (Carmona et al., 2010). And herein lies the complexity of urban design and planning. Ultimately, urban planning is a political arena in as far as the outcome of how our cities are designed and built are the outcome of often fierce political battles for influence, decision-making power and profits (I. Johansson, 1991).

Planning practices in Stockholm

Like many of its European neighbours, Sweden has also been considerably influenced by Social Democratic ideologies when it comes to planning practices. Through the practices and policies of the welfare state, the idea of interventionist planning – and indeed the existence of institutions that govern interventionist planning processes – have been embedded and, over time, gained legitimacy (Allmendinger & Haughton, 2012; Zakhour & Metzger, 2018; Davoudi et al., 2019).

Some elements of these institutions include the *Municipal planning monopoly* (planmonopol) and the procedural transparency of developing *Detail Plans* (Detaljplan). The Municipal planning monopoly gives the municipality the last word on what should be built, when and where, in the form of veto-right (Blücher, 2006). Furthermore, the technical description and details of what is allowed to be built on a given plot of land must be made public during the development phase, to allow for citizens to make comments (through so-called *samråd*) (Blücher & Graninger, 2006, 17). Throughout these examples of "checks and balances", the planning process has been designed with the aim of making it democratically legitimate vis-à-vis the electorate and as such in the best wider interest of a city's citizens through the municipality's active steering role (Zakhour & Metzger, 2018).

Nonetheless, in light of a number of new urban developments that have received criticism by civil society groups as well as some Swedish celebrities and journalists (E. Andersson, 2016, 2020; Britton et al., 2016; Britton, 2020; L. A. Johansson, 2020), reports (Ingo et al., 2018) and research (Caesar, 2016; Zakhour & Metzger, 2018) investigating planning processes in Stockholm are emerging. The story told by critics and the research from this school of thought includes variations of related narratives. General findings point to a sense that those in charge of the planning process engage with public opinion and recommendations from traditional referral bodies (specialized in architecture and planning) because it is a procedural requirement from them, rather than ensuring optimal outcomes for new urban developments. To illustrate this, some studies describe cases where Stockholm's City Planning Office (Stockholm's Stadsbyggnadskontor) takes on more of an administrative role vis-à-vis developers, to facilitate a process where *exchange-value* steers planning decisions, rather than an active steering role conditioning new urban developments to the *use-value* of a place (Ingo et al., 2018).

One piece of academic research from Stockholm's Royal Institute of Technology (KTH) has coined this observation a transition from what is called a "Planning-Led Regime" to a "Development-Led Regime" (Zakhour & Metzger, 2018). According to the study, which draws on empirical research on the organization of Stockholm's urban development process from 2006 onwards, as well as historical accounts, it is argued that the essential outlines of final regulatory plans for new urban developments (e.g. Detail Plans) have increasingly come to reflect agreements between developers and planning offices. Qualitative research illustrates how these agreements are, in turn, based on dialogues predominantly informed by developers and development engineers before the formal (public) planning-stage of development is initiated (Ingo et al., 2018; Zakhour & Metzger, 2018, 52).

The authors of the study, Sherif Zakhour and Jonathan Metzger, build on the work of researchers such as Patsy Healey (1992a, 1992b) and Kerstin Bodström (1994, 1997) in their description of the shift as a "handing over of the urban development initiative to market actors", which in turn would have resulted in a "drastic reduction in the capacity of plans, plan-making and planners to actively influence land use in Stockholm" (Zakhour & Metzger, 2018, 48). Similar observations have been made by other studies, bringing researchers to refer to the planning stages that were designed for accountability and dialogue as mere "exercises of window dressing" (Ingo et al., 2018, 47).

The peril, authors of such findings say, is that when formal processes are followed, without the democratic influence on quality and legitimacy they were designed for, the desired outcome (i.e. a legitimate one) is jeopardized. In other words, when a planning system ceases to be the space it was designed to be, i.e. a space for debating wide-ranging social alternatives for new urban development, it becomes a system that gives a superficial appearance of engagement and legitimacy. In reality, it may be delivering pre-meditated outcomes from processes where conflicting views have in fact not been given a meaningful hearing and debate (Allmendinger & Haughton, 2012, 90).

The value of the political in planning

Based on the classification of planning as a wicked problem then, the quality of the outcome of a planning process can be understood as subjective, depending on specific stakeholder interests (Johansson, 1991; Hall & du Gay, 1996; Davoudi et al., 2019). Defining "good planning", on the other hand, has to do with navigating a wider context of urban politics, where different definitions of "good outcomes" are (hypothetically) voiced by different political actors. As a result, the way urban planning is carried out, and how conflict is managed, says a lot about values, ideology and the political order of the day (Davoudi et al., 2019).

The antagonistic nature of conflicting political standpoints does not have to be a bad thing according to Chantal Mouffe. In *On the Political* (2005), Mouffe calls for the admission of antagonism in politics, arguing that it is an absolute necessity for effective democracy (Mouffe, 2005). By antagonism, the idea is "the political" or "...the space of power, conflict and antagonism within human societies, ..." (Allmendinger & Haughton, 2012, 91), and "the very way in which society is instituted" (Mouffe, 2005, 9). "Politics", on the other hand, she says, is "...the set of practices and institutions through which an order is created, organizing human coexistence in the context of conflictuality provided by the political" (Mouffe, 2005, 9). According to Mouffe:

> Instead of trying to design the institutions which, through supposedly 'impartial' procedures, would reconcile all conflicting interests and values, the task for democratic theorists and politicians should be to envisage the creation of a vibrant 'agonistic' public sphere of contestation where different hegemonic political projects can be confronted. This is, in my view, the sine qua non for an effective exercise of democracy. There is much talk today of 'dialogue' and 'deliberation' but what is the meaning of such words in the political field, if no real choice is at hand and if the participants in the discussion are not able to decide between clearly differentiated alternatives? (Mouffe, 2005, 3)

A practical example of the absence of "clearly differentiated alternatives" is, for example, when a strategy for new urban development is claimed to be based on "sustainable development" or "smart growth". Making such a statement is not to present the electorate with a strategy among several alternative ones, or to be straightforward about the ideological underpinnings of what one hopes such a strategy will accomplish. Few people would advocate "unsustainable development" or "dumb growth". Such use of so called "fuzzy" terms encourages consensus politics and elimination of apparent conflict in the planning process, because there is simply nothing to disagree with in the governing discourse (Allmendinger & Haughton, 2012, 94). According to Mouffe, such a "quest for consensus politics" undermines democracy when a debate about possible alternatives is substituted by a consensus culture where the electorate is deprived of the possibility to debate for and choose from differentiated democratic positions and alternatives (Mouffe, 2005).

Let us summarize the theoretical section and bring the focus back to the planning practices of Stockholm and the outlook for planning in heritage environments for social sustainability and attractive places for visitors. Three main contributions make up the theoretical framework for the case observations: Matthew Carmona's argument for why planning theory should be more about processes than outcomes; Mouffe's critique of a post-political way of doing politics – encouraging vibrant antagonistic spheres of debate for retaining faith in democracy; and Zakhour and Metzger's observation that Stockholm has moved to a Development-led planning regime – one that has resulted in a "drastic reduction in the capacity of plans, plan-making and planners to actively influence land use in Stockholm" (Zakhour & Metzger, 2018, 48).

The studied case: a conflict about a new urban development in a heritage area in Stockholm

The case study investigates a conflict that emerged over a new Detail Plan for a plot called *Skeppsholmsviken 6*. The plot is located in Stockholm's urban archipelago and the conflict concerned the content of the so-called Detail Plan for how the developer is allowed to make use of the plot. The stakeholders opposing the plan were a group of residential activists and a number of civil society organizations and referral bodies[1] specialized in heritage, urban planning and architecture.

The owner and developer of the discussed site is *Parks and Resorts*, the owner of a number of Swedish theme parks, including Gröna Lund, which was to be expanded with the new Detail Plan. Skeppsholmsviken 6, the site being developed, is adjacent to Gröna Lund's current grounds. The development hence concerns an extension of the theme park's existing area. The existing area is currently populated with a number of rollercoasters, joy-rides and infrastructure for theme park activities, including concerts and performances.

The object of conflict, the Detail Plan, is developed by Stockholm's City Planning Office in collaboration with the developer. Representatives from the governing coalition in Stockholm's Planning Committee (Stadsbyggnadsnämnd) exercise oversight of the process from start to finish, and it is the full body of representatives from the Planning Committee that ultimately vote to approve or reject the Detail Plan. At the time of the vote, the Planning Committee consisted of 13 appointed and politically partisan members. The majority consisted of a coalition of Kristdemokraterna (1), Moderaterna (3), Centerpartiet (1), Liberalerna (1) and Miljöpartiet (1). The opposition parties were made up of Sverigedemokraterna (1), Socialdemokraterna (3), Vänsterpartiet (2), and Feministiskt Initiativ (0).

The main hot points of the Detail Plan that generated conflict concerned the proposed maximum height of the ride attractions, privatization of the shore line, expected deterioration of noise pollution for neighbouring residents, expectations of increased numbers of visitors to the park during already over-crowded times, and lack of suggestions for how to use the existing or new area to develop suitable accommodation of arriving and leaving visitors in large numbers.

About the location to be developed

The site known as Skeppsholmsviken 6 is located in the small dotted circle on Djurgården (Figure 8.1), which is outlined by the large dotted circle. Djurgården is located on the South side of the Royal National City Park and the peak season for visitors is during the summer months. Historically, Djurgården was part of the Swedish King's hunting grounds, and today it hosts a number of popular museums (most of them located along the dotted line in Figure 8.1) and scenic places in the park.

The Royal National City Park is classified as a national interest area due to its history and unique green space in the centre of the city's urban archipelago. Due to its classification as an area of national interest, the park comes with a distinct legal framework, written to protect the space and its heritage (Sporrong, 2018).

Gröna Lund has been a part of Stockholm since 1883. Until 2006, when it was acquired by Parks and Resorts, it was managed as a family firm. Since then, the

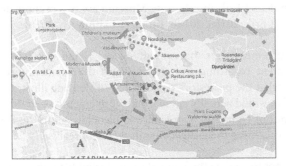

Figure 8.1   Map over Stockholm urban archipelago and part of Djurgården

pace of densification of rides and the construction of new rollercoasters and other attractions (currently 30 in total) increased and about two-thirds of the area has been rebuilt. An earlier detail plan was developed to expand Gröna Lund on this same site in 1999, but was abandoned in 2015. The current Detail Plan process was initiated in 2016 (Kulturförvaltningen, 2018).

The park is host to an intense entertainment schedule during the summer months when around 70 evening concerts are held in the theme park. Some events attract close to 20,000 visitors a night. At these times, those travelling to or from Gröna Lund make up large crowds of pedestrians and contribute to traffic jams and delays for overcrowded public transport. During 2018 the amusement park received 1.7 million guests, of which a majority come during evenings and weekends to go for rollercoaster rides and attend concerts. During the winter months the amusement park is mostly closed.

The unfolding of the conflict in more detail

The conflict regarding how the site should be developed took its current proportions in late 2018. It was around September/October when residents in the neighbouring area of Gröna Lund took note of the Detail Plan for the site and its contents, and that it had reached its final stages of public review before political approval.

Aware of the advanced stage of the Detail Plan, the residents' group formed an association called *Friends of Djurgården*, with the intent of changing the technical content of the plan. They also engaged with and gained support from a number of local neighbourhood societies and organizations specialized in urban planning and heritage. It should be noted that some of these organizations had already expressed critical views of the proposed Detail

Plan. Samfundet S:t Erik and the City Museum are two of these organizations (Samfundet S:t Erik, 2018a, 2018b; Kulturförvaltningen, 2018).

Besides disagreement over the contents of the Detail Plan, there was additional discontent regarding the Detail Plan's development process, which consisted of what the protestors perceived as misleading illustrations of what the Detail Plan would actually entail if fully implemented and developed. This led the Friends of Djurgården and allies to file a lawsuit to the Parliamentary Ombudsman claiming the visual contents were not realistic.

In their attempt to change the content of the Detail Plan, the residential association also made an effort to meet with the City Planning Office, as many politicians from the Planning Committee as possible, representatives from the County Administrative Board (Länsstyrelsen) and representatives from the Royal Administration for Djurgården. A Facebook page was initiated to raise awareness of the cause. Formal expressions of opinion during a later public review period were also made by all the opposing organizations involved. Broadly, with some smaller variations, these expressions of opinion contained the above-described issues and argumentation for why the Detail Plan should be redesigned.

Perhaps as a result of these efforts, or partly thereof, the Detail Plan was withdrawn from public review and returned to development with the City Planning Office, again in autumn 2019, rather than proceeding to approval by the Planning Committee as scheduled. Once reassessed, the plan was once again made public for feedback. The opposing organizations noted little change to the detail plan; the main change was a lowering of the highest height, to 45 m instead of 60 m.

In early 2020, the Detail Plan was accepted by voting in the Planning Committee. All political representatives participated, with the exception of the Chairman and Vice-chairman who abstained from the vote. The only vote against the Detail Plan was cast by Sverigedemokraterna.

Following the sequential approval of the Detail Plan by the Stockholm Council (Kommunfullmäktige) in April 2020, several of the opposing organizations appealed the Detail Plan through the Land and Environment Court (Mark- och Miljödomstolen). The verdict from the Land and Environment Court was still pending when this case study was written.

Results and analysis

A few lines on methodology

Shortly after the residents' association was created, one of the authors was invited to participate in informative meetings about the development of the Detail Plan. This invitation resulted from previous engagements by the author on matters of heritage and urban planning in Stockholm. Ideologically and stylistically, it would therefore be correct to say that the authors sympathized with the critique of the Detail Plan.

It was after a few months of accompanying the conflict and participating in meetings that the idea of writing a case study emerged. The desire to have a closer look at the conflict emerged from the apparently intricate, and somewhat unclear, reasons why the planning process was unable to produce a Detail Plan that all parties could accept. Interest in this new urban development on Djurgården – a well-known tourist destination – also emerged naturally, given one of the author's research areas being tourism research. When later developing a methodology for the case study, this potential partiality was given careful consideration.

To develop an understanding of planning practices with regards to new urban development in places of heritage in Stockholm, a methodology was developed to collect information through interviews and desk-based research. The structure of the interviews was along the lines of Czarniawska (2014) for semi-structured qualitative interviews. These were complemented by desk-based research of official documents, newspaper articles and reports, as well as participatory observations in meetings and seminars. All interviews were carried out in Swedish, but the quotations presented in this paper have been translated into English by the authors. When possible and deemed necessary, information from the interviewees' accounts has been verified via official documents or other reliable sources, such as official governmental reports and planning documents.

The issue of perceived partiality on behalf of one of the authors was considered in order to limit influence over interview content (observer bias) as much as possible. Importance was therefore given to establishing a sense of trust between the interviewer and interviewees, for example through transparency by clearly communicating the separation of intent of the interviews and the study on the one hand, and personal opinions about the Detail Plan on the other. Assurance of anonymity with regards to information shared in the interviews was also communicated to all those interviewed.

The research collected for the case study is intended to shed light on how the conflict between corporate interests, those of residents and of other opposing groups, was managed through the municipal planning process. The chosen method for the study was exploratory empirical research in line with that of Bent Flyvberg, and hence conducted similarly (Flyvbjerg, 1998). The investigation was open-ended rather than based on a hypothesis put forward in advance of the research being collected (Hansson, 2007, 62). Ultimately, it is hoped that the case study will contribute to how opposing interests can be reconciled or at least coexist in more productive ways for better planning processes, and consequently also improvements in outcome for new urban developments.

The qualitative interviews were carried out during 2019 with six public servants and elected representatives in the City of Stockholm who carry varying degrees of responsibility over Stockholm's urban development. These included one public servant from the City Planning Office and five politicians from the City's Planning Committee. Furthermore, one political adviser, two officials from Stockholm's DMO Visit Stockholm, four representatives from different organizations with relations to the visitor industry in Stockholm and one representative from Parks and Resorts were also interviewed. Finally, four resident activists, and three representatives from the group of heritage organizations were interviewed as well. Neither the Commissioner (Head) nor the Vice Commissioner of the Planning Committee agreed to be interviewed.

The content presented in the next two sections is a result of this chosen method for research.

A justifiable vision for Skeppsholmsviken 6?

A surprising finding from the grand majority of interviews was the general consensus around how people idealized the final result of the Detail Plan. With a few exceptions, answers to the question "If this was up to you, what would you like to see on Skeppsholmsviken 6 at the end of this process?" were very similar. Representatives from civil society agreed more green space was at the top of their wish list, and general consensus was the tall ride attractions should in all cases be left out to give space to lower rides only (maximum height 12 m). Enabling a more family-friendly environment was brought up several times, as was the interest to see a space that could stay open all year around for more even visitor flows to the location.

Political representatives from the Planning Committee gravitated towards some kind of urban park as the final outcome of the planning process. Here again, green space, lower construction, and access to the shore line with improved access for boats (both public transport and privately owned leisure boats) featured as desirable outcomes among the interviewees. Some mentioned the potential of staying open all year round and being open to the public (with a business model based on other incomes than entry fees). No one interviewed was in favour of the tall rides on the new site, and the alternative to concentrate all tall rides in the existing park area was brought up a few times.

As per the description of the final Detail Plan, these views rather surprisingly reflect disagreement with the final vote. Interviews also disclosed that several members from the Planning Committee were made aware of the more detailed aspects envisioned by the plan when the Detail Plan was already well developed:

> From our party's perspective we didn't see any problems about this planned development. We thought it was great that Gröna Lund wanted to develop the parking lot into something else. Back then we didn't really realise the development plans included more problematic aspects as well.

The developer had no intention of keeping the new development of the park open all year around, and the new area showed no signs of being geared towards smaller children and families in any particular way. The goals were rather clear, namely to extend the existing model of a successful business into more of the same. In the words of a representative from the Parks and Resorts:

> Most of our visitors want to go on rides that require at least 1.20 m in height [of the person riding] and we want to build an area that caters to the majority… we want to be able to build anything from roller coasters to gaming facilities … we will fight for it for as long as we can.

That the developer and critics, including residents, might differ in their opinion of how the plot should develop is perhaps not a revelation. A private corporate actor is not surprisingly guided by the exchange-value of a location, in line with the profit driven rationale most private enterprises are rightfully guided and influenced by. Residents (and those appreciating a place in its own right) on the other hand, would reasonably be more informed by their interests in the use-value of a place, seeing as they live there or occasionally spend time there. But in the case of the conflict between critics and the City Planning Office, the answer of why there should be disagreement over the content of the Detail Plan may not be as intuitive. Impressions from the interviews suggest that the conflict may be related to what Phil Allmendinger and Graham Haughton (2012, 94) refer to as the use of "fuzzy" terms.

The "fuzziness" that Allmendinger and Haughton theorize refers to expressions of choice and goals – in contexts of politics and policy – that don't necessarily reveal "more concrete policy implications and objectives" (Allmendinger & Haughton, 2012, 89). To compare this understanding with the language used by the representative from the City Planning Office, it is helpful to reiterate how the ideal outcome for the Detail Plan was expressed more in terms of goals than specific features for design. For example, the representative expressed hopes that:

> ...the proposal would be good for Stockholm, a nice addition to the visual character of Stockholm, that Gröna Lund can continue with its business, that those who have had opinions on the Detail Plan feel they have in some way been heard, and finally that the politicians can feel safe with the final decision.

While the goals expressed by the interviewee would certainly be shared by all the stakeholders involved, the "fuzziness" of how they were expressed allows a plethora of possible scenarios for the Detail Plan. The use of "fuzzy" language then, seems to produce expressions of intent that no one disagrees with, but that paradoxically allow for numerous subjective interpretations that could cause just as many conflicts over disagreement.

This subjectivity with regards to interpreting how the said goals should materialize was something that also appeared in the City Planning Office representative's own understanding of the planning process. The representative from the City Planning Office explained how their development of the Detail Plan was based on interpretation of the formal guidelines for how and where Gröna Lund should be able to expand. Consequently, according to the judgement of the City Planning Office and the supporting curator (antikvarie), the Detail Plan posed no threat to cultural heritage or the national interest.

This might explain why, after conferring with referral bodies that perceived the contents of the Detail Plan as undesirable, the contents remained unchanged and were seen as legitimate in the eyes of the City Planning Office. Two such referral bodies that were cited by the representative from the City Planning Office were the *City Museum* (Stadsmuseet) and the *Stockholm Beauty Council* (Rådet till skydd för Stockholms skönhet). In early 2018, the City Museum expressed their opinion as follows:

> In the impact assessment carried out by Tyrens AB, 2017-10-30, the technical proposal is illustrated with only two towers, which is in itself a misleading element of the document when the detail plan permits the construction of four towers. The City Museum notes that even two towers would negatively impact views and outlooks from the water, as well as compete with church towers and other landmarks for attention. All in all it is considered to impact the national interest and the National City Park negatively. From the point of view of cultural heritage the City Museums

would prefer to see nothing but lower heights of rides on the new site to be developed. (Kulturförvaltningen, 2018)

This conflict of subjective interpretations for the new urban development on Skeppsholmsviken 6 was not perceived as something that indicated flaws in the effectiveness of the planning process by the representative from the City Planning Office:

> The way I see it this whole plan process serves this very purpose, that is that you put a development proposal out there to be tried, and you give the public and referral bodies the right to make statements. All of this is designed to enable these items of conflict to surface.

The question that then arises is what one does with the surfaced items of conflict. The City Planning Office does respond to points of controversy in a so-called Review report (Granskningsutlåtande), which reiterates what the purpose and objective of the Detail Plan is, summarizes the main points of critique and how the City Planning Office justifies its contents vis-à-vis these conflicting opinions. Over 1400 expressions and comments were received by the City Planning Office on the Detail Plan. However, it is not clear how many expressed approval and how many expressed (complete or partial) disapproval with the proposed contents (Stadsbyggnadskontoret, 2019, 2).

According to the report, the plan aims to ensure that buildings, objects and public spaces are designed with care and that they adapt in scale and character to the heritage milieu that Djurgården consists of, which is also part of the national interest as Stockholm's central area has Djurgården and the National City Park. Furthermore, the report states that the plan aims to create a new and appealing silhouette with rides sticking up in a few places (Stadsbyggnadskontoret, 2019, 2). In the aftermath of the public review period 21 November 2018 to 19 December 2018, some changes were made to the Detail Plan, among them a lowering of maximum heights from 60 m to between 30 and 45 m. As a result, the author of the report claims that the negative impact on the city's silhouette has been reduced to "moderate" (Stadsbyggnadskontoret, 2019, 11).

It is clear that a main argument in the report motivating the expansion of Gröna Lund is that it is considered to be part of the national interest in nature and in shape. Less clear is the motivation for the height of the rides, an aspect that seems to have become the main point of attrition in this conflict. Considering that the City Planning Office expresses the Detail Plan will result in a "moderate" negative impact on an area defined as one of national interest and cultural heritage, the picture that emerges is that of a Detail Plan that is the result of a compromise between the developer and requirements for quality:

> A great deal of the planning process is about a tight collaboration [with the developer] to arrive at something that the City can back and that the developer feels it can realistically build. (Representative from the City Planning Office in interview)

This is essential information, because in a place of heritage, this MO clashes with what the critics expect from the City Planning Office. And hence the conflict shows clear signs of a being a matter of failed expectations. To them, the City Planning Office should not merely act as an enabler for as many private actors' plans that can be interpreted as *possible* within the frameworks of guiding and legal documents. In an area of heritage such as Djurgården, those opposing the Detail Plan expected agency with regard to stylistic aspects, to develop something that is *desirable*, and more: something without any substantial negative impact given its unique location.

The critics did not perceive that the City Planning Office had embodied such agency. And as a result of how the city planning office engaged with those stakeholders who consider themselves to be experts on the subject matter, the critics failed to see how the City Planning Office represented, or responded to, the arguments from the electorate who they (the City Planning Office) are seen to represent, as representatives of Stockholm's democratic planning institutions.

The scenario created a sense among critics that the City Planning Office was serving the interests of private corporate actors rather than public interests. The context is further reinforced by the statement of a politician who, during a meeting, expressed helplessness at what he could do by exclaiming, "it is their private property, we can't tell them what to build there!". The politician's expressed helplessness can only be said to be half justified, given that the Plan Monopoly does at least empower the city to say what developers can*not* build.

Another example of what was perceived as want of active steering of what is developed was the declaration by a prominent politician in Stockholm, who said that Stockholm is growing and, as a result, Gröna Lund had to be allowed to expand as well. The statement was delivered as a given fact that was undebatable, irking those of a different opinion. Statements that claimed that something "must" be allowed to happen, or that something will be "good" for Stockholm, without providing arguments in the form of "because…" or "or else…", to express trade-offs and alternative scenarios, caused great frustration among critics on several occasions.

Perhaps this is one of the reasons why the City Planning Office is experiencing a perceived increase in engagement from citizens:

> Yes a lot of expressions of opinion have been received [for the Detail Plan suggestions for Skeppsholmsviken 6], but there seems to be some kind of trend because several cases [lately] are receiving more and more expressions of opinion.

A process of politics and the political

While the final version of the Detail Plan would certainly be reason enough for contention between the stakeholders, the interviews disclosed that aspects of the planning process itself seem to have been perceived as just as much, if not more, cause for grief amongst the critics. Many of those interviewed cited different kinds of failure in communication as an explanation for this. For example, some politicians expressed surprise that conflict erupted so late in the process, and wondered why residents raised concerns as late as the end of 2018. However, it should be noted that when residents became aware of the Detail Plan and began formulating their critique, more or less similar feedback had been made by referral bodies at least about a year earlier. A statement from one of Stockholm's traditional referral bodies, *Samfundet S:t Erik*, reiterates their understanding of how the plot should develop after the referral period 21 November 2018–19 December 2018 (Samfundet S:t Erik, 2018b, 1)

> Samfundet made a statement regarding the development plan of Skeppsholmsviken 6 on 26 January 2018. When the detail plan now comes out for public review again Samfundet can conclude that none of the recommendations made have been applied. A summary of these suggestions follows:
>
> (a)   The 60m high rides should be excluded;
> (b)   The waterborne bridges 20 metres from the shore line should be excluded;…

Another form of communication drawback relates to the early dialogues between the developer and referral bodies. These dialogues seem to have started out as constructive dialogue, only to transition to a perceived sense of "having been naïve":

> The first thing we were shown was the picturesque housing facing Falkenbergsgatan, we thought that perhaps they should be a bit lower and designed with some modification here and there, and that's great and all … but we were never informed of what was meant to be built behind … My own interpretation is that we were pretty naïve, and I must say that Gröna Lund has always been a place where people go to have fun and what's wrong with that? But when I was informed of the Detail Plan of what was to be built I felt pretty silly, I admit that, I had no idea what they [Gröna Lund] were planning to build. And I think it was a legitimate feeling to have, and

to ask ourselves – what now? How to relate to all these things, privatizing the shore line, the tall rides, and what the added noise levels will mean for all the neighbours...

Hence, interview content seems to support the claim that a lot of the conflict was due to flaws in how communication was carried out during the planning process. This was also supported by a member of the Planning Committee, who gave the following explanation for the conflict:

> ... one hasn't been seen or heard, this is the most classic reason for discontent, and I think it applies here as well, one has a feeling of having been informed too late, and that one's opinions haven't been heard, and taken seriously, one experiences the process as one that is not serious, and most of all that the outcome feels very unsure. It is very common that this is the case.

These are certainly issues that deserve attention, whether the perceptions described are true or not. However, imperfect communication seems to have been only part of the story. First, the mass of critical actors included many of the referral bodies that were consulted early on in the process. Furthermore, numerous meetings were held between the conflicting stakeholders, providing an opportunity to correct faulty communication. Instead, the lack of progress to influence the contents of the Detail Plan, despite repeated efforts for dialogue and discussion of alternatives, worsened the conflict that turned out to be part of a wider context of dissatisfaction.

The plot thickens

The Detail Plan was developing in the midst of a pre-existing source of aggravation regarding over-crowding. Residents and visitors of Djurgården feared the problem would deteriorate further with the new Detail Plan. The fear was that even larger crowds would now spill out onto streets, pavements and green areas in a way that severely obstructs passage for children, pedestrians, people on bicycles, public transport and motorized vehicles, including taxis. The risk of a terrorist attack in the form of a vehicle driving into a crowd of people is also mentioned by those critical of the crowds that congregate in the summer. In the words of a resident:

> There is a desire to constantly increase the number of visitors to Djurgården, from 10, 15 and now 20 million people a year. And how when in this little part of Djurgården there is no intention to solve or do anything about the crowds that ensue or how to even arrive at Djurgården with public transport [during peak hours]. Djurgården is a fantastic place for people in Stockholm. Djurgården is unique, and this little part of Djurgården doesn't need to be exploited any further. ... the current conflict consists of an understanding of Gröna Lund as a commercial venture that places its own commercial interests above all else, which means they are willing to

create a really bad environment for those living here... Ten years ago there were 15, 20, maybe 25 concerts each summer,[2] now there are 75... and they [Gröna Lund] show no active signs of wanting to solve the traffic chaos this causes ... huge crowds flock there [to the park] and they [the visitors] don't care about quality like the residents do. And this type of visitor also shapes the type of commercial activity we see around the park. How could you have for example restaurants of quality in a place which is closed nine months of the year? ... It's just chaos in the summer. Too much traffic. Too much noise.

This picture was also described by stakeholders from organizations that have accompanied the Detail Plan, many of which have been engaged with the preservation of the Royal National Park for many years. They confirmed the perception that the area surrounding Gröna Lund is undergoing a process of "popularizing" and mainstreaming, rather than a process of safeguarding the heritage and local identity of the place while also allowing for new developments.

As a result, those opposing the plan again called for agency, arguing that the City Planning Office should ensure the new Detail Plan addresses some of these issues, rather than enabling a worsening of them by enabling more people to visit the park with an enlarged park area. The City Planning Office, however, did not define these complications within the scope of their mandate:

> We investigate the possibility of reaching a given destination by public transport. But then, we probably look more at how a given project impacts traffic from a broader perspective. We've seen that there is worry around the development of the traffic situation ... but that is sort of not within the scope of this Detail Plan, which needs to be resolved through a different agreement by different actors.

The growing frustration towards the city's planning processes and perceived lack of engagement from politicians appear to have come to a sort of *coup de coeur* with the Detail Plan for Skeppsholmsviken 6. The elements of the illustrations perceived as misleading in particular were detrimental to trust in the legitimacy of planning processes. As a result, those who signed the lawsuit did so as much as a legal request to what was perceived as compliance with the technical requirements of the Detail Plan process, as an act of principle to correct what has been perceived as an issue of failing morality in a broader sense. One of the interviewees commented on the case in the following way:

> No, I mean, that lawsuit was important because it highlights the city's lack of honesty. ... To submit misleading illustrations, what one as a citizen immediately suspects, is that the politicians go hand in hand with the interests of the private sector...

Whether the illustrations were intentionally misleading, as per the belief of the critics, is beyond the scope of this case study to comment upon. But interviews with both critics and politicians from the Planning Committee suggest it might be a systematic weak spot in the process. One Planning Committee member's description of the role of illustrations:

> ... one has, being in politics, got used to not really taking illustrations seriously. ... It shouldn't be that way ... but one could probably have been more precise in showing what was intended by Gröna Lund.

Considering the importance of illustrations – given the politicians' often limited ability and time to review the technical content of Detail Plans – this points to weaknesses in the due diligence carried out by the politicians before voting on a plan.

Additionally, as part of a longer trend of reporting on perceived lack of trust in the motivations of the City Planning Office, material emerged in a Swedish newspaper, in January 2020, describing accusations of conflict of interests and suspicions of corruption and illegal construction projects involving Parks and Resorts (E. Andersson, 2016; E. Andersson, 2020). The relation between the City Planning Office, the Planning Committee and critics hence seemed to be gravitating towards a point where trust in the democratic effectiveness of the planning process was severely damaged. It also tells the story of critics, often part of referral bodies traditionally considered to be experts on the subject matter, opposing a string of new urban developments without a sense of real representation in the politics of urban planning.

In line with the idea of the "Development-led regime", a possible interpretation of such a scenario is that the political regulation for planning may have lost some of its intended function and impact. Laws and administrative procedures, such as plan monopoly and planning processes, formalized to ensure transparency and accountability vis-à-vis the general public through democratic debate, may be less efficient than intended due to more recently developed customs and practices that make them ineffective.

To further contextualize our case in the theory discussion from the second section, Mouffe's theory invites a comparison with what she defines as "the effective exercise of democracy" with the "Development-led" planning regime. In a scenario where the planning process in Stockholm is perceived to have become depoliticized by locking in the main outlines of new urban developments *outside* of the public realm, and where debate is a procedural requirement rather than an effective element of the process, those who oppose the outcomes of such processes find themselves in a difficult environment (Ingo et al., 2018). If this is so, the removal of conflict from open debate in a political arena could imply a process where the creative process leading to new urban developments has become depoliticized and if so ineffective (Mouffe, 2005).

An additional risk with an electorate that loses faith in the ability of *politics* to manage *the political* is when those expressing antagonistic opinions consider themselves forced to seek alternative avenues beyond the democratic channels of the planning institutions. One such avenue is judicial review, which then becomes an outlet for frustrations at not being heard in a planning process. When judicial review becomes an option, the conflict is merely dislocated, not debated. Furthermore, judicial review can be a costly process; it requires know-how and resources, and often both time and money (Allmendinger & Haughton, 2012). For these reasons it is a long way from the democratic conflict resolution mechanism that the planning process is designed to be.

Discussion

The attentive reader will have noticed that one inconsistency in the narrative remains absent from the analysis. This regards the question of why so many politicians from the Planning Committee expressed a vision for the Detail Plan similar to that of critics, and then voted for a Detail Plan that represented something else. One answer could simply be that they changed their minds. Another answer, perhaps more likely, is that the committee members did not vote according to personal preferences, but according to negotiated positions resulting from political bargaining processes, a not uncommon way to enable decision-making across party lines (March, 1994, 195). Nevertheless, the answer would ultimately require further research and investigation to be properly hypothesized.

Based on the findings and analysis from this study, this section will focus on the potential for future research areas that might contribute to less contentious planning processes and socially sustainable urban governance for places of heritage.

Managing the market?

The exploratory research for this study looked at a conflict involving criticism of the content of a Detail Plan for a new urban development in a heritage area. The somewhat justified view among critics seems to have been that the City

Planning Office's work reflected the preferences of private market interests rather than a concern to safeguard the heritage environment of the place. This irked the critics as their expectations of the City Planning Office was that it should develop a Detail Plan that resonated with the needs and preferences of residents and their allies as well.

There are arguments for believing that the market does not necessarily self-regulate to produce places that correspond to the needs and preferences of citizens when left to its own devices (Russo & Scarnato, 2018). Nonetheless, that should not be confused with a statement against markets and beneficial environments for private corporate actors, on the contrary. To borrow a page out of Patsy Healy's theory on types and roles of urban planning, the issue with so-called Development-led regimes relates to what Healy describes as the type of planning where development plans are informed primarily by the market:

> This approach thus focusses on 'investor' rather than 'user' interests. It takes a 'short-term' view, lacks any 'vision' of 'quality of space' beyond the project, and is likely to privilege those with good contacts with planning authorities. It has little capacity to transform the qualities of areas, and thus contributes little to urban regeneration strategies.

In such cases, the needs of people, communities and residents at large, which are not manifested through market demands, tend to be ignored for those features that do manifest in market demands (Healey, 1992b, 17). As a preferable option to such a planning regime, Healey proposes a regime that "manages markets" instead.

Healey's argument for why there is merit to a pro-active planning system is that it comes with a higher "market awareness". She argues that if the private sector is to be the main provider of development, then the planning system in land-use has to be a pro-active in regulating the development process. This of course raises questions of what "managing markets" means in the context of Stockholm and development in places of heritage.

A discussion of the benefits and drawbacks of regulation in planning and governance is one that could never end as our urban environments and shaping forces are constantly changing. To cite Jaques Rancière (2007, 42):

> There is never such a thing as a good regime, in fact, only regimes of-course engaged in perpetual work of self-correction – one might say of self-dissimulation.

Learning from similar cases is always useful, for example Hyde Park in London. Hyde Park is a top destination for both residents and visitors. To ensure the sustainable use of the park by some 13 million visitors each year, the space is highly regulated when it comes to traffic, commercial activity and what sort of development is allowed (Land Use Consultants, 2006, 13; The Royal Parks, n.d.).

Furthermore, there is plenty of empirical evidence of cities arriving at the conclusion that social and economic impact from the visitor industry is best developed with oversight, strategies and management. San Francisco is an example of a city where regulations concerning the shape and content of commercial establishments are in place to protect the location's character (San Francisco Planning Department, 2014). Much further research could be done with regards to how regulation could be designed to ensure creativity in new urban developments while still acknowledging interest of a less market-driven rationale.

Managing dissent for democratic effectiveness

Despite the merits of regulation, there is a limit when rules and laws cease to protect, and become stifling to economic growth and creativity instead. The reality is probably that some ambiguity will always remain in the guiding documents of planning regulation. In any other case, the planning process would become rather anaemic, empty of the innovation and originality that make places change and develop in a meaningful way. Due to each city's political context and the goals of its respective advocates, suitability of the outline and limits of regulation then necessarily becomes contextually determined.

While the level of ambiguity of the guiding principles for new urban development on Djurgården may have contributed to the conflict by leaving space for subjective interpretations, the qualitative descriptions of the conflict do not suggest that ambiguity itself was the heart of the issue. Rather, the conflict seems to be located closer to how critics perceived the City Planning Office to misuse the ambiguity to enable the developers' vision.

The "political" that the critics represented was perceived not to be heard, considered or even argued against. Such a scenario resonates somewhat with Jaques Rancière's writings on the nature of politics and the inherent incentive of each political actor to deliver their own view as the sole option to be considered (Rancière, 2007, 19 and 11):

> Depoliticization is the oldest task of politics, the one which achieves its fulfilment at the brink of the abyss

because

> politics is the art of suppressing the political.

Our interpretation of what Rancière calls "the abyss" can be likened to Mouffe's idea of failed democratic effectiveness. Mouffe argues that unless antagonisms meet in open confrontation, democratic institutions cannot remain effective in fulfilling their role, and as a result they lose their legitimacy as a place for *all* viewpoints to be channelled and debated. The phenomenon of constraining accepted topics for debate in politics has in later years been used to explain the emergence of political actors seen as illegitimate, often associated with populism. The risk of planning failing to engage with the consequences of over-tourism, for example, was mentioned as a potentially politically divisive issue on the agenda of populists. The interviewee in this case, a political adviser, used the word "hyper tolerant" when describing a general attitude among politicians and planners towards some behaviours, changes or developments that a considerable number of citizens oppose:

> ... I definitely think this issue [overtourism] could be a potential issue for populists to explore as part of a larger narrative of 'us and them'. They [populists] explore all simmering issues where there is a critical number of people taking issue in some way, of course we could see that happening. 'We need to clean up our streets and get back our streets', it's a spot-on narrative for them [populists] to use.

One way to interpret Mouffe and Rancière would be for a suggestion that Stockholm's spaces of planning demonstrate signs of the need for re-politicization to restore popular faith in democratic institutions (Rancière, 2007, 106):

> What we must do instead is repoliticize conflicts so that they can be addressed, restore names to the people and give politics back its former visibility in the handling of problems and resources.

How then – in an imagined antagonistic space that conforms to the requirements of Mouffe's "effective democracy" – should conflict over wicked planning problems be processed? According to Amy Guttman and Dennis Thompson (1996), to carry legitimacy, political outcomes that result from conflicting viewpoints must carry some minimum level of legitimacy if they impact the collective. To have faith in the democratic institutions, such outcomes should be perceived as justifiable. To achieve this, in an environment where conflicts about fundamental values take place, such as in planning for example, they offer a theory called *deliberative democracy*. In their book called *Democracy and Disagreement* (1996), they make the argument that, in the absence of foundational knowledge of what is right and wrong about what is being decided upon, there is a need to understand political deliberation so that decisions can be justified in a way acceptable to all members of the electorate (acceptable, not necessarily appreciated by – author's remark).

An important piece of the puzzle to foster this sort of justification of the decision-making in democratic institutions is what Guttman and Thompson call the land of *middle democracy*. That is, spaces that are lower in the institutional hierarchy than, say supreme courts. Forums of middle democracy are rather spaces where citizens meet to debate and reach collective decisions or perceptions about public issues. Such forums include administrative hearings on all levels of government as well as shareholder meetings and citizens' committees. One could probably imagine the Swedish process of *samråd* as part of middle democracy.

However, politics is not, as Perry Andersson argues, an exchange of opinions but very much a contest for power (Anderson, 1994, 43). Hence deliberative democracy would depend on an institutional framework that conditions and channels conflict in such a way that outcomes are seen as democratically legitimate among opposing stakeholders. The pursuit of a political context for planning, with features of deliberate democracy, then begs the question of how to transition. Examples and theory of transition management would be useful to understand how less contentious and more sustainable urban development processes could be developed. Planning processes that enable and ensure "the political" to play out its course in our urban politics are also likely to benefit effective institutions and processes for governance of the visiting industry.

Planning for a sustainable visitor industry

Finally, a planning process that takes a growing visitor industry into account is well-positioned to help Stockholm maximize the benefits of this economic segment, one that has an important role to play in Europe's urban economies today. In a post-industrial age where the number of jobs in traditional industries is decreasing in parallel with growing numbers of urban residents, the visitor industry can add considerable economic value, particularly in the form of job creation and investments. Stockholm is doing well on this front. Overnight stays in the capital region are increasing steadily, from just over 9.3 million year in 2008, to almost 15 million in 2018 (Tillväxtverket, 2019).

The trend for growth can be expected to continue given the above 5% growth of non-European tourism to Sweden during the last few years, and the global growth of tourism, expected to stay at approximately 3% per annum reaching 1.8 billion by 2030 (UNWTO, 2011). While these numbers are likely to have been adjusted since the Covid-19 epidemic engulfed the tourism industry in 2020, travel patterns are likely to return to previous levels unless societies are paralysed over the long-term.

One potentially limiting factor of such growth is that cultural heritage cannot be exploited and leveraged for economic gains *ad infinitum*. The concept of limitations to how many visitors a location can support before overtourism occurs is often known as the carrying capacity of a place (Van Der Borg et al., 1996). This opens up the realization that tourism must be expected to grow beyond the city centre of our cities, or authentic residential environments risk being lost to over-crowdedness and its impacts (Goodwin, 2017; Koens et al., 2018; Seraphin et al., 2018; UNWTO, 2018, 2019; Milano et al., 2019).

The implication of the research this study suggests is the need for the planning process to engage with the vision for what constitutes "a good city" in areas that are impacted, or with potential to be impacted by the visitor industry through new urban developments. Kreg Lindberg and colleagues (Lindberg et al., 1997) write about how dealing with the impacts of a developing visitor industry begins with agreeing what social conditions one desires in a city or its neighbourhoods. It is on the back of a joint understanding of what a municipality aims to achieve in social terms that effective indicators of success can be developed.

Indicators, and agreement around what the desirable standards and conditions are for them, make up a framework against which a cost-benefit analysis can be performed and economic growth aimed for. An increased number of overnight stays in Stockholm, for example, is just one indicator, and it should feature among many more to achieve a desired social outcome whose own indicators need to be evaluated (Lindberg et al., 1997). To know where the sweet spot is for the concentration of visitors in Stockholm or in a specific area, an understanding of a location's carrying capacity, or if preferred, "Levels of Acceptable Change" (LAC), are concepts to consider (McCool & Lime, 2001).

A more integrated approach to sustainable tourism, which involves the planning institutions, also calls for one factor that is mentioned by the great majority of professionals in the tourism industry and tourism research: data. Overtourism is by most accounts a locational and seasonal phenomenon. The managerial toolkit that policymakers require would therefore benefit from the capacity to conduct more granular analysis of hot pockets of overtourism by tracking the ratio of visitors vis-à-vis residents on a neighbourhood and local visitor streams within the Stockholm destination (G. Andersson, 2017).

Fortunately then, the quality of a location's local heritage can be managed, and new places can be created where, in the words of Alan L. Lew "people want to live, work, play, shop, learn, and visit" (Wyckoff et al., 2015, vi). Respect for historic structures and monuments, where they exist, can also enhance the interesting aspects of a place (Lew, 2017). A good example of such a contemporary development is the place making project development for Guldbergsgade in Copenhagen in 2012. Notwithstanding its recent success as a modern meeting point for Danish urbanites, many who consider it one of the coolest areas in the Danish capital, the real achievement of the project lies in how it leveraged the industrial heritage that was already in place to connect contemporary residents and visitors to a story with its past (Holland, 2017; Briq, 2020).

The good news is that actors from the visiting industry (including organizations such as *Visita AB*, *Royal Djurgården* and *Swedish Trade* (Svensk Handel)) who participated in interviews, showed high levels of engagement and interest towards more integrated approaches to urban planning. The following citations give a taste of how representatives from this segment reasoned:

> Successful public space is a big puzzle. You can't plan for infrastructure in one part of the municipality, housing in a second, and then look at what type of transport arrangement you need when it's all practically done. Planning needs to be much more holistic, including actors from all relevant sectors at the earliest stages of urban development projects. Collaboration can't just be operative, it needs to be strategic as well. Of course a real estate developer has a vision; it's a numbers vision to maximize profit margins. It says nothing of whether people will want to live in those houses, or merchants will want to open stores there.

> But the Municipality needs to be able to lead this process. It is through its tools of regulation (for example Plan Monopoly) and capacity to plan that it must lead the way for how all the other actors must fit in and what they are able to do. What business wants to operate in a Municipality that doesn't have a vision and clear leadership outlining the rules? Politicians need to be more courageous in their decision making, ensuring all departments work together and that the vision that leads it all is a better city. Politicians and their staff might know the theory, but they must work together with those who understand the practical side of things as well.

> … but unfortunately I think the way it works in most cities is that you have one organization dealing with the visitors and talking about that with the politicians, and another organization dealing with the inhabitants and talking about that with the politicians, but to me they are talking about the exact same thing because they are talking about public space, the development of public space and if you would just join these two sides it would become so much more clearer for the politicians to understand that what needs to be developed are attractive places, and then in the end you'll simply have two different groups [residents and visitors] using them.

and finally

> ... I mean they [residents and visitors] want the same thing, but more importantly, step one is ensuring your residents are happy, and as a cherry on top of the cake the visitors will follow as a given number 2 if you achieve that.

Research in this area could perhaps investigate what a more integrated governance structure would look like. Barcelona presents options for new urban management where urban planning and tourism management go hand in hand, for example (Municipality, 2020).

Conclusion

Hopefully, the case of Skeppsholmsviken 6 has provided insights about the challenges for how to manage, plan for and develop spaces of heritage. Contrary to first impressions, the conflict is not a NIMBY (Not In My Backyard) situation. Instead, it is a story of the particular needs and considerations that apply to new urban developments in places of heritage, when the needs of an actor from the visitor industry opposes the needs and interests of residents.

Places of heritage hold a special place in the hearts of those who live there. In some cases, several generations have unfolded their family stories in the same streets, watching the gradual changes of time evolve and shape the buildings and public spaces of the place. There is value in preserving these places for the lives that provide its residential character and atmosphere. And additional gains stand to be made. The preservation and socially sustainable development of heritage also attract eligible tourists looking for a unique and authentic experience.

In Stockholm, the distinctive morphology in the shape of watersides, its built structure and traditions provide an identity framework for visitors and residents alike (Glasson et al., 1995; UNESCO, 2013). The local framework of Stockholm is one that could be explored more by the municipality when overseeing the design for contemporary architecture and public spaces. For therein lies the identity of Stockholm that residents love and that tourists come to experience. Anecdotally, even seemingly banal things about Swedish life fascinate tourists, such as looking at dads with strollers, known as "Latte pappor". Most visitors, local or national, have interest in accessing heritage and the 'local', in some way (Glasson et al., 1995).

In a globalized world, where many new urban developments have a place-less character to them that offers an urban environment that could be experienced anywhere, the search for authenticity becomes a documented urban phenomenon (D'Eramo, 2021). Edward Relph (1976) provides a useful definition of the idea of place and identity:

> While place meanings are rooted in the physical setting and its activities, they are not a property of them but a property of human interaction and experiences of those places. (Relph, 1976, 47)

There are numerous cases of excellent developments in Stockholm that could serve as inspiration for new destinations and be explored by tourists for their uniqueness and charm, take for example the Old Town with its medieval architecture; Östermalm with its classical architecture; Röda Bergen, Lärkstaden and Hornstull with their neo-classical (Swedish grace) style; or the Meatpacking District (*Slakthusområdet*) with its industrial structures that come to life at night as one of the city's most popular scenes for night life.

Managed in a sustainable manner, historical landscapes can leverage tourism and the service sector to increase welfare for its residents. It is therefore a fair claim to say that to attract a sustainable and desirable visitor industry, while validating those who call it home, carefully protecting and managing the identity of a place becomes an imperative (Ashworth & Voogd, 1990; UNESCO, 2011). It follows that to deliver heritage and an attractive local culture to visitors, a destination might need to consider trade-offs in immediate and localized economic growth in some locations, and for some stakeholders.

The aim of this study was to develop insights into how research on planning for more socially sustainable cities can look, from the perspective of long-term growth of the tourism industry, as well as the well-being of residents. The hopes are that this will inform inclusive, interesting, economically thriving and socially sustainable new urban developments. In other words, places worth being in and worth visiting.

Notes

1   For example Stockholm Beauty Council, Samfundet S:t Erik, Djurgårdens Hembyggdsförening, Urban City Research, Förbundet för Ekoparken, Stockholms sjögård, Stiftelsen Djurgårdsskolan, Kungliga Djurgårdens Arrendeförening, Konsthallen 14, Djurgårdens vänner.

2   In 2008, after complaints about the noise caused by shows at Gröna Lund, the Environment and Health Administrations (Miljöförvaltningen) suggested limiting the numbers of concerts to 15 per year ("Grannar stoppar konserter på Grönan | Aftonbladet", n.d.).

References

Allmendinger, P., & Haughton, G. (2012). Post-political spatial planning in England: A crisis of consensus? *Transactions of the Institute of British Geographers, 37*(1), 89–103. https://doi.org/10.1111/j.1475-5661.2011.00468.x

Alvarez-Sousa, A. (2018). The problems of tourist sustainability in cultural cities: Socio-political perceptions and interests management. *Sustainability, 10*(2), 503. https://doi.org/10.3390/su10020503

Anderson, P. (1994). Power, politics and the enlightenment. In D. Miliband (Ed.), *Reinventing the left* (p. 43). Retrieved from https://books.google.se/books/about/Reinventing_the_Left.html?id=5ollQgAACAAJ&redir_esc=y

Andersson, E. (2016). Maktspelet bakom exploateringen av Stockholm | SvD. Retrieved 30 May 2019, from https://www.svd.se/maktspelet-bakom-exploateringen-av-stockholm

Andersson, E. (2020). Bjudfester, svartbygge och skatteupplägg – så har Gröna Lund expanderat. *Svenska Dagbladet*. Retrieved from https://www.svd.se/bjudfester-svartbygge-och-brevladeforetag--sa-expanderar-grona-lund

Andersson, G. (2017). *Visitor streams in city destinations* (pp. 147–161). Springer International.

Ashworth, G. J., & Voogd, H. (1990). *Selling the city: marketing approaches in public sector urban planning*. Retrieved from https://books.google.se/books/about/Selling_the_City.html?id=5q1PAAAAMAAJ&redir_esc=y

Blücher, G. (2006). 1900-talet: Det kommunala planmonopolets århundrade. In G. In Blücher & G. Graninger (Eds), *Planering med nya för- utsättningar: ny lagstiftning, nya värderingar* (pp. 133–156). Vadstena: Stiftelsen Vadstena forum för samhällsbyggande.

Blücher, G., & Graninger, G. (Eds) (2006). *Planering med nya förutsättningar: ny lagstiftning, nya värderingar*. Vadstena: Stiftelsen Vadstena Forum för samhällsbyggande.

Bodström, K. (1994). *Marken, makten och bostäderna: markanvisning inom mark-och bostadspolitiken i Stockholm/Land, political influence and housing (English)* (Stockholm University, Faculty of Social Sciences). Retrieved from http://www.diva-portal.org/smash/record.jsf?pid=diva2%3A1208971&dswid=3638

Bodström, K. (1997). Stockholm: ett mönster av välfärd. In K.-O. Arnstberg & T. Lundén (Eds), *Stockholm – den planerade staden*. Retrieved from https://biblioteket.stockholm.se/titel/457989

Briq (2020). Guldbergsgade – BRIQ. Retrieved 16 January 2020, from https://briqgroup.com/work/guldbergsgade/

Britton, C. (2020). Claes Britton blir chockad av guldbron vid Slussen. *Dagens Nyheter*. Retrieved from https://www.dn.se/kultur-noje/claes-britton-mycket-kravs-for-att-chocka-i-dag-men-nya-guldbron-lyckas/

Britton, C., Andersson, K., August, P., Endre, L., Geijerstam, E. af, Kihlgård, P., ... Östergren, K. (2016, November 20). Ska skövlingen av Klara återupprepas på

Stureplan? *Svenska Dagbladet*. Retrieved from https://www.svd.se/ska-skovlingen
-av-klara-aterupprepas-pa-stureplan

Butler, R. W. (1980). The concept of a tourist area cycle of evolution: implications for management of resources. *The Canadian Geographer/Le Géographe Canadien, 24*(1), 5–12. https://doi.org/10.1111/j.1541-0064.1980.tb00970.x

Butler, R. W. (1999). Sustainable tourism: A state-of-the-art review. *Tourism Geographies: An International Journal of Tourism Space, Place and Environment, 1*(1), 7–25. https://doi.org/10.1080/14616689908721291

Caesar, C. (2016). Municipal land allocations: Integrating planning and selection of developers while transferring public land for housing in Sweden. *Journal of Housing and the Built Environment, 31*(2), 257–275. https://doi.org/10.1007/s10901-015 -9457-2

Carmona, M., Heath, T., Oc, T., & Tiesdell, S. (2010). *Public places urban spaces: the dimensions of urban design* (2nd ed.). Routledge.

Czarniawska, B. (2014). Why I think shadowing is the best field technique in management and organization studies. *Qualitative Research in Organizations and Management, 9*(1), 90–93.

Davoudi, S., Galland, D., & Stead, D. (2019). Reinventing planning and planners: Ideological decontestations and rhetorical appeals. *Planning Theory, 1960*, 1–28. https://doi.org/10.1177/1473095219869386

D'Eramo, M. (2021). *The world in a selfie*. Retrieved from https://www .penguinrandomhouse.com/books/646948/the-world-in-a-selfie-by-marco -deramo/

Doxey, G. (1975). *Sixth Annual Conference Proceedings of the Travel Research Association, San Diego*. Retrieved from http://www.economics-ejournal.org/ economics/journalarticles/2012-40/references/Doxey1975

Flyvbjerg, B. (1998). *Rationality and power: democracy in practice*. https://doi.org/10 .2307/3005579

Gehl, J. (2010). Cities for people. Retrieved 8 May 2019, from Island Press website: https://www.adlibris.com/se/bok/cities-for-people-9781597265737

Glasson, J., Godfrey, K., & Goodey, B. (1995). Towards visitor impact management: Visitor impacts, carrying capacity, and management responses in Europe's historic towns and cities. In *Urban and regional planning and development*. Avebury.

Goodwin, H. (2017). *The challenge of overtourism*. Retrieved from https://haroldgoodwin .info/pubs/RTP'WP4Overtourism01'2017.pdf

Grannar stoppar konserter på Grönan | Aftonbladet. (n.d.). Retrieved 30 September 2019, from https://www.aftonbladet.se/nyheter/a/kaveXL/grannar-stoppar -konserter-pa-gronan

Guttman, A. & Thompson, D. (1996). *Democracy and disagreement*. Cambridge, MA: Harvard University Press.

Hall, S., & du Gay, P. (1996). *Questions of cultural identity*. https://doi.org/http://dx.doi .org/10.4135/9781446221907

Hannam, K., Butler, G., & Paris, C. M. (2014). Developments and key issues in tourism mobilities. *Annals of Tourism Research, 44*, 171–185.

Hansson, S. O. (2007). *The Art of Doing Science, 1*(90), 61.

Healey, P. (1992a). An institutional model of the development process. *Journal of Property Research, 9*(1), 33–44. https://doi.org/10.1080/09599919208724049

Healey, P. (1992b). Development plans and markets. *Planning Practice & Research, 7*(2), 13–20. https://doi.org/10.1080/02697459208722842

Holland, M. (2017). Why Guldbergsgade is Copenhagen's best street - Condé Nast Traveler. Retrieved 16 January 2020, from https://www.cntraveler.com/story/why -you-should-spend-a-whole-day-in-copenhagen-on-one-street?fbclid=IwAR 2dEbzPgFD6JSj2rfhMz4fZySvmElGO-jzTHlu9G8xTadZOwt35CZvt0Lo

Ingo, S., Berglund, K., & Pemer, A. (2018). *Hur kundet det bli så här?*

Johansson, I. (1991). *StorStockholms bebyggelsehistoria: markpolitik, planering och byggande under sju sekler.* Retrieved from https://stockholmskallan.stockholm.se/ post/952

Johansson, L. A. (2020). Kampen om staden. *Byggnadskultur*, 15–20.

Koens, K., Postma, A., & Papp, B. (2018). Is overtourism overused? Understanding the impact of tourism in a city context. *Sustainability*, *10*(12). https://doi.org/10.3390/ su10124384

Kulturförvaltningen. (2018). *Remissvar stadsmuseiavdelningen.*

Lagrave, K. (2018). 13 places cracking down on Airbnb. *Conde Nast.* Retrieved from https://www.cntraveler.com/galleries/2016-06-22/places-with-strict-airbnb-laws

Land Use Consultants (2006). *Hyde Park Management Plan.*

Lew, A. A. (2007). Invited commentary: Tourism planning and traditional urban planning theory—the planner as an agent of social change. *Leisure/Loisir*, *31*(2), 383–391. https://doi.org/10.1080/14927713.2007.9651387

Lew, A. A. (2017). Tourism planning and place making: Place-making or placemaking? *Tourism Geographies*, *19*(3), 448–466. https://doi.org/10.1080/14616688.2017 .1282007

Lindberg, K., McCool, S., & Stankey, G. (1997). Rethinking carrying capacity. *Annals of Tourism Research*, *24*(2), 461–465. https://doi.org/10.1016/S0160-7383(97)80018-7

March, J. G. (1994). *A primer on decision making: how decisions happen.* Free Press.

McCool, S. F., & Lime, D. W. (2001). Tourism carrying capacity: Tempting fantasy or useful reality? *Journal of Sustainable Tourism*, *9*(5), 372–388. https://doi.org/10 .1080/09669580108667409

Milano, C., Novelli, M., & Cheer, J. M. (2019). Overtourism and tourismphobia: A journey through four decades of tourism development, planning and local concerns. *Tourism Planning and Development*, *16*(4), 353–357, https://doi.org/10.1080/ 21568316.2019.1599604

Mouffe, C. (2005). *On the political.* Retrieved from https://www.adlibris.com/se/ bok/on-the-political-9780415305211?gclid=CjwKCAjwltH3BRB6EiwAhj0IUP9xsm 1g2WYtdOse87j7TNmGjJiOyOF91WFy_JbVUSRZOVDe-1upjBoCGagQAvD _BwE

Municipality, B. (2020). Tourism in Barcelona | Tourism | Barcelona City Council. Retrieved 16 January 2020, from https://ajuntament.barcelona.cat/turisme/en/home

Rancière, J. (2007). *On the shores of politics.* Retrieved from https://www.amazon.com/ Shores-Politics-Radical-Thinkers/dp/1844675777/ref=sr_1_1?crid=QJ3H62S2HFLI &dchild=1&keywords=on+the+shores+of+politics&qid=1595948874&sprefix=on+ the+shores+of+po%2Caps%2C236&sr=8-1

Relph, E. C. (1976). *Place and placelessness.* Retrieved from https://openlibrary.org/ books/OL4954978M/Place_and_placelessness

Rittel J., H. W., & Webber, M. M. (1973). Dilemmas in a general theory of planning. *Policy Sciences*, *4*, 155–169. https://doi.org/10.1080/01636609209550084

Royal Djurgården. (2020). Homepage. Retrieved 20 June 2020, from https:// royaldjurgarden.se/

Russo, A. P., & Scarnato, A. (2018). "Barcelona in common": A new urban regime for the 21st-century tourist city? *Journal of Urban Affairs*, *40*(4), 455–474. https://doi .org/10.1080/07352166.2017.1373023

Samfundet S:t Erik. (2018a). *Gröna Lund Skeppsholmsviken 6 m fl S-Dp 2016-06685. pdf 2018.01.26*. Retrieved 14 July 2020, from https://drive.google.com/file/d/ 1zDMWEeIvGn4qCRbKlT_XivaWWIlv25VE/view

Samfundet S:t Erik. (2018b). *Gröna Lund Skeppsholmsviken 6 m fl S-Dp 2016-06685.pdf 2018.12.11*. Available upon request.

San Francisco Planning Department. (2014). *Commission guide for formula retail: determining locational appropriateness and performance-based design guidelines.* Retrieved from http://default.sfplanning.org/publications_reports/Formula_Retail _Commission_Guide.pdf

Seraphin, H., Sheeran, P., & Pilato, M. (2018). Over-tourism and the fall of Venice as a destination. *Journal of Destination Marketing and Management, 9*. https://doi.org/ 10.1016/j.jdmm.2018.01.011

Sporrong, U. (Ed.). (2018). *Platsens kulturella betydelse, juridiken kring nationalstadsparken.*

Stadsbyggnadskontoret (2019). *Granskningsutlåtande Detaljplan för Skeppsholmsviken 6 i stadsdelen Djurgården i Stockholm Dp 2016-06685.* Stockholm.

The Royal Parks (n.d.). Park regulations, legislation and policies. Retrieved 31 July 2020, from https://www.royalparks.org.uk/managing-the-parks/park-regulations -legislation-and-policies#carparking

Tillväxtverket (2019). Gästnätter 2018. Retrieved 31 May 2019, from https://tillvaxtverket .se/statistik/vara-undersokningar/resultat-fran-turismundersokningar/2019-02-07 -gastnatter-2018.html

UNESCO (2011). *Rekommendation om det historiska urbana landskapet.* Retrieved from www.unesco.se

UNESCO (2013). *The historic urban landscape approach explained New life for historic cities United Nations Educational, Scientific and Cultural Organization.* Retrieved from https://whc.unesco.org/uploads/news/documents/news-1026-1.pdf

UNWTO (2011). International tourists to hit 1.8 billion by 2030 | Communications. Retrieved 27 May 2019, from http://media.unwto.org/en/press-release/2011-10-11/ international-tourists-hit-18-billion-2030

UNWTO (2018). 'Overtourism'? – Understanding and managing urban tourism growth beyond perceptions, Executive Summary. In *'Overtourism'? – Understanding and Managing Urban Tourism Growth beyond Perceptions, Executive Summary.* https://doi.org/10.18111/9789284420070

UNWTO (2019). 'Overtourism'? Understanding and managing urban tourism growth beyond perceptions Volume 2: Case studies. In *'Overtourism'? Understanding and Managing Urban Tourism Growth beyond Perceptions Volume 2: Case Studies.* https://doi.org/10.18111/9789284420643

Van Der Borg, J., Costa, P., & Gotti, G. (1996). Tourism in European heritage cities. *Annals of Tourism Research.* https://doi.org/10.1016/0160-7383(95)00065-8

Wyckoff, M. A., Neumann, B., Pape, G., & Schindler, K. (2015). *Placemaking as and economic development tool: a placemaking guide.* East Lansing, MI: Michigan State University Press.

Zakhour, S., & Metzger, J. (2018). From a "planning-led regime" to a "development-led regime" (and back again?): the role of municipal planning in the urban governance of Stockholm. *Disp – The Planning Review, 54*(4), 46–58. https://doi.org/10.1080/ 02513625.2018.1562797

9 Urban tourism development in Africa: evidence from Addis Ababa, Ethiopia

Getaneh Addis Tessema and Ephrem Assefa Haile

Introduction

Urban tourism is an important segment of the tourism industry. In the last decade, urban tourism demand has increased by about 50% worldwide (UNWTO and WTC, 2018). According to UNWTO and WTC data, cities currently host above 50% of the world's population and generate more than 60% of gross domestic product. They state that as urban population is projected to increase in the years to come, it is essential to monitor urban tourism performance.

Urban tourism studies of the 1960s were sporadic and had limited scope, only emerging as an important field of study in the 1990s (Pearce, 2001). There is an accusation that tourism studies of the past had a rural bias (Ashworth and Page, 2011). The increased attention to urban tourism is partly attributed to the growth of tourism in cities and the resulting policy implications (Pearce, 2001). Bădiţă (2013, p. 65) asserts that "cities have become centres of culture and leisure, with tourists spending their time in public spaces located especially in the centre".

Cities have a paramount importance for urban tourism development, which is a driving force for creating economic, social and spatial dynamics for transforming the urban landscape through the rejuvenation of public space, public infrastructure and connectivity and development of local amenities and recreational facilities as well as stimulating business entrepreneurship, developing public–private partnerships, attracting other industries and services and building citizen awareness on cultural and natural protection. (UNWTO and WTC, 2018).

Although most urban tourism research in Africa has concentrated on South Africa, it is now emerging in other cities as well, with a focus on tourism and the urban economy, slum and pro-poor tourism, business tourism and the informal tourism sector (Rogerson and Visser, 2014). However, they admit that, in general, there is a lack of comprehensive study on urban tourism in Africa.

As Ashworth and Page (2011) have pointed out, cities that are highly connected with transport infrastructure and linked to other world cities provide a major nucleus for business travel. They also argue that business tourism has now emerged as a key driver of urban tourism in Africa, and the most economically vibrant cities are the major foci for business tourists. The expansion of intra-Africa tourism, the establishment of meeting and exhibition facilities and the construction of high standard hotels have stimulated a rapid increase in business tourism on the continent (Rogerson and Visser, 2014). They also point out that business tourism is critically important for (urban) tourism development in Africa, and cities such as Accra, Addis Ababa, Nairobi, Cape Town, Johannesburg and Durban are considered to be important business tourism destinations.

King (2004) has stated that one of the issues to be addressed by future studies is "how do cities in less developed countries perform as urban tourism destinations relative to their equivalents in the developed world and how can we assess the adequacy of the infrastructure that they provide?" Most urban tourism research in Africa is concentrated in South Africa (e.g. Rogerson, 2002, 2004, 2008, 2011, 2013; Rogerson and Rogerson, 2014; Rogerson and Visser, 2005, 2007, 2011), with limited studies in Kenya (e.g. Okech, 2009; Wambalaba and Wambalaba, 2009) and Egypt (e.g. Nasser, 2007; Al-Saad and Ababneh, 2017). Hence, urban tourism study in the other African cities is limited.

Addis Ababa could be an interesting case for studying urban tourism development in Africa as it represents other African Cities in many aspects. This is mainly because it is the seat of the African Union (AU), the United Nations Economic Commission for Africa (UNECA), and a regional office for many international organizations such as the UNDP, UNESCO and the European Economic Commission (Wubneh, 2013), which support development in Africa. In addition, like other African cities, it is expanding rapidly.

Despite the city's huge potential, it is not generating the required benefit from its tourism industry. The city even lags behind some African cities in terms of generating tourism revenues. For instance, in 2014, African cities such as Lagos, Cairo and Johannesburg received 1.33 million, 1.35 million and 4.25 million international visitors respectively (MasterCard, 2014). In the same year, Addis Ababa received only 681,249 international visitors (United Nations Economic Commission for Africa, 2015). The nature of urban tourism development in Addis Ababa has not yet been comprehensively investigated. The main aim of this study is to explore urban tourism development in Addis Ababa, the results of which can provide evidence on urban tourism development in Africa. The study assesses the state of the art of urban tourism development in the city, with a focus on supply, demand, destination organization and stakeholder collaboration frameworks.

Tourism development in Addis Ababa

Addis Ababa is located at the heart of Ethiopia (Figure 9.1). The city is administratively divided into 10 sub-cities. According to the 2007 census, Addis Ababa has a population of 2,739,551 (Central Statistical Agency, 2007), and hosts 30% of the country's urban population (Kassahun and Tiwari, 2014). At an average elevation of about 2355 metres above sea level, Addis Ababa is the fifth highest capital in the world (*The Telegraph*, 2018).

Addis Ababa is endowed with several colourful festivals, creative arts and cultural heritage (see Figure 9.1 for their location in the greater Addis Ababa area). It is also the diplomatic capital of Africa and home to several international and regional organizations, as discussed above. It is also the city with the third highest number of diplomatic missions in the world (UNECA, 2015). Its central location, being about three to five hours flight from Europe, the Middle East and many African cities, provides an important advantage for tourism development in the city. Furthermore, fed by the three times best airline award winner in Africa, Ethiopian Airlines, Addis Ababa is well connected to the rest of the world. From its hub in Addis Ababa, Ethiopian Airlines serves hundreds of international destinations.

Methodology

This is a descriptive type of research intended to unlock the nature of urban tourism development in Africa with more emphasis given to Addis Ababa, Ethiopia. Primary data were gathered using a semi-structured interview from 10 December 2019 to 15 January 2020. As shown in Table 9.1, interviews were conducted with 14 key informants working in private and public tourism entities. Each interview lasted an average of about 50 minutes. Key informants were chosen based on a purposive sampling method – due to their appro-

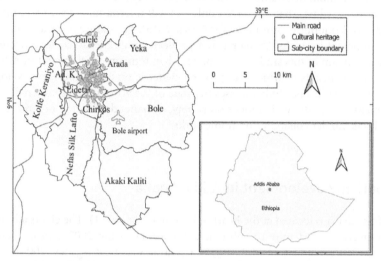

Note: The cultural heritages were mapped based on data from Addis Ababa Culture and Tourism Bureau.

Figure 9.1 Location map of Addis Ababa, its ten sub-cities and the cultural heritages

priateness in offering the required information. Tour operation managers were selected on the recommendation of the Ethiopian Tour Operators' Association. Primary data were supplemented with secondary data gathered from documents such as tourism policies, development plans, directives, regulations, statistical bulletins, books, manuscripts and websites.

Data gathered from multiple sources were triangulated to verify their validity. In this study, thematic analysis was used to analyze qualitative data. Qualitative data collected from different sources were coded, grouped, described and analysed. This analysis method was supplemented by content analysis as it enables inferences to be made about a given issue by systemically examining trends and patterns in relevant documents or texts. It involves the coding and categorizing of data.

Table 9.1   Profile of the interview participants

Name of institution	Position	No. of key informants	Code
Addis Ababa Culture and Tourism Bureau	Tourism promotion expert	1	K1
Addis Ababa Culture and Tourism Bureau	Heritage Protection & Conservation Director	1	K2
Addis Ababa Culture and Tourism Bureau	MICE Tourism expert	1	K3
Addis Ababa Culture and Tourism Bureau	Tourism product development expert	1	K4
Tourism Ethiopia (TE)	Tourism marketing expert	1	K5
Tourism Ethiopia (TE)	Tourism product development expert	1	K6
Ethiopian Hotel Owners' Association	Head of the association	1	K7
Ethiopian Hotel Professionals' Association	Head of the association	1	K8
Ethiopian Tour Operators' Association	Head of the association	1	K9
Tour operators	Tour operation manager	1	K10
	Tour operation manager	1	K11
	Tour operation manager	1	K12
	Tour operation manager	1	K13
	Tour operation manager	1	K14

Results and discussion

In this study, the drivers for urban tourism development are clustered into three broad categories, namely supply, demand, and destination organization and collaboration related factors. These factors are discussed taking into account Addis Ababa as a case study, vis-à-vis other African cities.

Supply-related factors

Supply-related factors are destination-related drivers that determine the development of urban tourism in a given area. These include core supply factors (such as attractions, accommodation establishments, food and beverage outlets, transportation facilities and travel arrangements), support facilities and services (such as tourist information, safety and security, facilitation systems) and general infrastructure (such as roads, water supply, electricity and telecom services). These factors will be discussed taking Addis Ababa (Ethiopia) as a case in point vis-à-vis some competing African cities.

Attractions

The country is often dubbed as a mosaic of peoples and cultures and is home to more than 80 nations. Addis Ababa is endowed with a rich historical, religious, cultural and natural heritage. According to the Addis Ababa Culture and Tourism Bureau report (2019), there are 12 museums, 13 monuments, four historic palaces and many churches, mosques and traditional market places. The sites of the city's main tangible heritage, which are worth visiting and are often included in tour operators' packages, include museums (the National Museum, the Ethnographic Museum, the Red Terror Museum, the Zoological Museum and the Addis Ababa Museum); the Holy Trinity cathedral church and museum, Entoto St Mary's church and museum, St Raguel's church (Entoto) and the Elfign Palace; historical monuments (such as the Emperor Menelik monument, the Abune Petros monument, the Martyr's monument, the Victory monument, the Sebastopol monument, the *Tiglachen* monument, etc.); the Merkato (an open-air market), St George's cathedral church and museum, the Patriarchate museum and library, and the Entoto Mountains (the city's only major natural heritage). In addition to these, there are historical houses and places of tourist interest such as Meskel Square, Amsale Genet Palace (currently housing Addis Ababa University's Faculty of Law), the Sheik Hojele Palace and the residence of the World Laureate Maître Artist Afework Tekle. The newly opened Unity Park (by the current prime minister of the country, Dr Abiy Ahmed), which is located inside the Grand Palace, houses a wide mix of attractions such as historical buildings including the Elfign palace, the "egg" house, the coronation house, the black lion's zoo (though under construction at the time of publication), the nine regions' pavilion and a green area. A total of 168 tangible cultural heritage sites with a potential for tourism development are identified and registered in Addis Ababa by the city's Culture and Tourism Bureau, the great majority of which are located in Arada sub-city (Figure 9.1).

The country in general and the city in particular are also endowed with intangible cultural heritages. So far four examples of intangible cultural heritages in the country have been registered by UNESCO, namely the *Meskel* festival – celebrated in commemoration of the Finding of the True Holy Cross of Jesus Christ (registered in 2013); the *Fiche Cahmbaalalla* – New Year festival of the Sidama people (registered in 2015); the Geda system – an indigenous democratic socio-political system of the Oromo people (registered in 2016) and the newly added *Timket* or Ethiopian Epiphany religious festival (registered in 2019). *Meskel* and *Timket* are colourfully celebrated in Addis Ababa and are attended by thousands of tourists ever year. Cinema, theatre, traditional music and dance (in *Azmari Bet*) are other examples of the city's intangible cultural heritage that are a source of attraction for tourists.

According to an inventory conducted by the Addis Ababa Culture and Tourism Bureau two decades ago, more than 440 immovable sites of cultural heritage were identified in the city. However, these are currently suffering from many problems. According to the interviews conducted with heritage experts in the aforementioned bureau, the major challenges facing the cultural heritage include its age, urban development works, a poor conservation system and a lack of organizations to carry out the required maintenance. In relation to the first factor, most sites are old and so suffer from existential problems. Huge urban development works such as roads and buildings are also being carried out in the city, often with no regard for their possible detrimental impact on heritage. Moreover, the owners of the heritage sites (private individuals, religious institutions and government) have a poor conservation system. The budget allocated for heritage maintenance works is quite small and hence insufficient to cover conservation-related costs. In addition, there are very few heritage conservation and maintenance organizations in the country and they have capacity-related problems. These are further aggravated by the nature of heritage ownership in the city. Heritage experts from the bureau have also pointed out that most heritage sites (such as Sheik Hojele) are still in the hands of private citizens. This has certainly hampered the government's efforts to conduct heritage protection and conservation efforts. Heritage sites, including museums, also suffer from poor lighting and sanitation problems, such as untidy toilet facilities. Weak promotional efforts have also further heightened the problem. Although the country has ratified research and conservation of heritage proclamation No 209/2000, there are serious challenges when it comes to implementation. The Authority for Research and Conservation of Cultural Heritage (ARCCH) is mandated by the proclamation to identify, inventory, safeguard and promote the country's tangible and intangible cultural heritage. However, conservation of the heritage sites is still a serious challenge.

In order to develop, protect and promote the city's cultural heritages, mainly historical buildings and royal houses, the Addis Ababa Culture and Tourism Bureau has developed a document to transfer heritage sites owned by the government and private individuals to a third party on a contractual basis. Under this arrangement, the heritage transferee (a third party on a contractual basis, often individuals) is responsible for developing, conserving and promoting the heritage site. The heritage transferor (the Addis Ababa Culture and Tourism Bureau together with the Authority for Research and Conservation of Cultural Heritage), is responsible for providing professional and technical support to maintain and protect the heritage sites and ensure they are used for the intended purpose as clearly stipulated in the heritage proclamation. Under this scheme, so far, the bureau has transferred some historical buildings such as Dejazmach Ayalew Biru's residence building, Kachik Bogosian's residence building and Biteweded Haile Giorgis's residence building. Overall, this arrangement has helped to free some of the heritage buildings that were once inhabited by locals. Some of these buildings are currently serving as art galleries and the households previously living in them have now been relocated to other areas such as condominiums.

Diversified tourism products enhance the quality of the visitor experience, extend visitors' length of stay, increase tourism receipts and, as a result, influence destination competitiveness. Addis Ababa is a metropolitan city and the third diplomatic capital in the world next to Geneva and New York. Being the seat of the AU, the ECA, other international and regional organizations and a renowned airline company (Ethiopian Airlines); an entrance to and exit from the country, striving to become a regional hub and with a good climate, the city can be a magnet for Africans and other tourists. Despite this truth, the city is not tapping the required benefits from the tourism sector. One of the major impediments to urban tourism development in the city – as key informants (K4, K6, K9, K10 and K11) have clearly pointed out – is the lack of diversified tourism products that would attract the attention of visitors. Tourism in the city depends highly on limited resources and, as a result, most tour operators tend to organize homogeneous tour programmes. The city is often considered as a gateway to and from the country rather than a destination *per se*. Due to this, tourists stay for a brief period often not exceeding one or two nights. As key informants have indicated, more has to be done to expand the city's extant tourism product base by developing potential tourism offers such as culinary tours, mountain trekking and stopover tourism.

There are several recently started projects in Addis Ababa which, on completion, could be a source of attraction for the city. These include the Entoto Park project and beautification of the city's rivers. The government's "beautification of Addis Ababa" project is promising for the city's future urban tourism development. One of the target markets for these attraction developments is that of international transit passengers traveling via Bole International Airport to various parts of the world. Ethiopian Airlines is planning to promote Addis Ababa to its transit passengers so that they spend some time visiting the city.

Table 9.2   MICE tourism arrivals and growth rate in Ethiopia

Year	MICE Tourism market segments		Total	Growth rate (%)
	Business	Conference		
2014	143,949	69,808	213,757	10.3
2015	161,845	79,114	240,959	12.7
2016	98,789	55,650	154,439	-35.9
2017	54,899	16,909	71,808	-53.5
2018	134,318	62,077	196,395	173.5
2019*	93,521	44,925	138,444	**

Note: *Data only compiled for the first three quarters (1st, 2nd and 3rd quarter).
** Growth rate not calculated due to incomplete data.
Source: Ministry of Culture and Tourism (2016, 2019).

As Spirou (2011) has mentioned, arts, festivals, urban parks and urban beauti-fication help support urban tourism development.

As mentioned, Addis Ababa is the headquarter for many international and regional organizations such as the African Union, the United Nations Economic Commission for Africa, the European Commission for Africa and the seat of more than 100 embassies. Despite this mammoth potential, the city has not that much benefited from the MICE (meeting, incentives, con-ventions and exhibitions) tourism sector. As shown in Table 9.2, the MICE tourism figure has shown an inconsistent growth rate over the last five years (2014–2019). According to the MoCT, the country accommodated 213,757 MICE visitors in 2014. This figure increased by 12.7% (240,959) in 2015. However, in subsequent years, this figure declined by 35.9% (154,439 arrivals in 2016) and 53.5% (71,808 arrivals in 2017). Among other things, the political unrest in the country, which forced the government to declare a state of emer-gency, contributed to the poor performance in the stated period. However, in 2018, there were 196,395 arrivals, showing an increase of 173.5% compared with the preceding year. Although incomplete, based on the three quarters data compiled by the MoCT, the country received 138,444 MICE visitors in 2019.

Data from the Addis Ababa Chamber of Commerce and Sectoral Association showed that there are 56 event organizers in Addis Ababa. According to an interview conducted with a MICE tourism expert from the Addis Ababa Culture and Tourism Bureau, although the city has tremendous MICE tourism potential, it is not benefiting sufficiently due to a multitude of reasons, such as a lack of awareness about (MICE) tourism, a shortfall in the budget allocated

Table 9.3   Number of international association meetings per city: African and Global rank of selected African cities.

S. No.	City name	No of international association meetings		African rank		Global rank	
		2017	2018	2017	2018	2017	2018
1	Cape Town	53	42	1	1	44	63
2	Johannesburg	23	16	2	6	113	180
3	Kigali	21	26	3	2	130	103
4	Marrakech	20	24	4	3	133	115
5	**Addis Ababa**	**17**	**13**	**5**	**7**	**156**	**214**
6	Nairobi	13	22	6	4	206	129
7	Durban	12	12	7	8	228	225
8	Cairo	11	20	8	5	248	143
9	Accra	10	–	9	–	266	272
10	Kampala	10	–	9	–	266	302
11	Dakar	–	12	–	8	325	225
12	Abuja	–	11	–	10	–	241

Source: International Congress and Convention Association (2017, 2018).

to marketing MICE tourism, an absence of stakeholder coordination and a lack of qualified and skilled manpower in the MICE Tourism sector. Furthermore, although the number of star rated hotels is increasing, there are only 49 hotels with a 3-star rating or above in a city striving to respond to the ever changing needs of the affluent business tourism market.

An international association meeting is one of the segments of the meetings industry. As shown in Table 9.3, the number of international association meetings held in African cities in the years 2017 and 2018 was 361 and 415 respectively (International Congress and Convention Association, 2017, 2018). Addis Ababa is in the top ten list for Africa in terms of the number of international association meetings it hosted in the years 2017 and 2018.

With regard to the institutional framework, the government has very recently established the Ethiopian Convention Bureau with the aim of developing, organizing, marketing and leading the MICE tourism industry. However, more is said than done to coordinate and lead the MICE sector in a sustainable manner. Moreover, MICE tourism is an international business sector and hence demands strong collaboration with different international institutions such as the International Congress and Convention Association. The country very recently (2019) developed its first MICE Tourism Strategy, but its impacts are not yet evident. The strategy is intended to make Addis Ababa one of the top five MICE tourism destinations in Africa. Tourism Ethiopia (a national government tourism body mainly working on tourism destination development, marketing and management), has created a unit called the Tourism Ethiopia Convention Bureau to implement the MICE tourism strategy. However, its impacts are to be seen in the future.

Hosting (mega) events helps develop urban tourism (Spirou, 2011). A number of events are held in Addis Ababa attracting both international and domestic visitors. These include the Hotel Show Africa – an annual event held in June every year that focuses on the hospitality industry, the Great Ethiopian Run, the Ethiopian New Year/*Enkutatash*/, Christmas and Easter expos in Addis Ababa Exhibition centre, etc. Ethiopia is known for its great long distance runners, most of whom live in Addis Ababa. About 44,000 people (from different parts of the country and from abroad) took part in the annual Great Ethiopian Run of 2017.

Accommodation establishments

It is quite difficult to cite the total number of accommodation establishments (standard and substandard) in Ethiopia in general and Addis Ababa in particular. So far there is no study that exclusively uncovers hotel-related data in the country. However, the current study relies on hotel statistics recently developed by the Ethiopian Ministry of Culture and Tourism (hereafter MoCT), which is responsible for administering the country's tourism sector. According to MoCT (2018) data, there are 165 star-rated hotels in Ethiopia. Seventy-nine of these (47%) are concentrated in the capital city, Addis Ababa. At an aggregate level, there are more 2- and 3-star hotels in Addis Ababa than in the country as a whole. Moreover, there is a disproportionately small number of top end hotels (four and five star hotels) in the country. In fact, there are eight 5-star hotels in Ethiopia and seven of these are in Addis Ababa. Likewise, half of the 3- and 4-star hotels in the country are found in the city. This is due to Addis Ababa's position as a political, business and diplomatic city not only for Ethiopia but also for Africa and the rest of the world.

Some of the star rated hotels in Addis Ababa are internationally managed chain hotels. These have received their fair share of popularity. Addis Ababa has seen a large influx of hotel investment in recent years. According to a study conducted by Knight Frank Research (2018), region-wise, North, South and East Africa took the lion's share in terms of hosting chain hotels in Africa while West and Central Africa have an insignificant share of branded hotels on the continent. The share of chain hotels in the North, South and East Africa regions is 38%, 30% and 21% respectively. The same study shows that in terms of ongoing hotel development projects, East Africa is topped by the North and West Africa regions. The new hotel projects in Africa are concentrated in the West, North and East Africa regions with their respective share of 35%, 29% and 27%.

According to Knight Frank Research (2018), countries such as South Africa, Egypt, Morocco, and Tunisia have the highest number of chain hotels in Africa. South Africa alone accounted for 30% (430) of the chain hotels in Africa, followed by Egypt (300 hotels), Morocco (153 hotels) and Tunisia (103). Across Africa, more than half of the continent's capital cities each have fewer than five chain hotels. The same research indicates that the major chain hotels operating in Africa are Marriott International (149/20), Accor Hotels (116/20), Tsogo Sun (96/7), City Lodge (58/4) and the Radisson Hotel Group (42/20). The figures inside the brackets show the total number of hotel branches and the number of African countries in which they operate, respectively. According to MoCT data (2019), there are only nine chain hotels in Addis Ababa (as well as in Ethiopia). These are the Ramada Addis, the Marriot, the Radisson Blu, the Sheraton Addis, the Hilton Addis, the Golden Tulip, the Tulip Inn, the Hayat Regency Hotel and the Best Western.

As far as occupancy rate and average daily rate (ADR) are concerned, the sub-Saharan region has outperformed other parts of the continent. According to Smith Travel Research (STR) Global data (2017), region wise, sub-Saharan Africa registered the highest hotel room occupancy rate (60%), which is even slightly above the continent's average, i.e., 58%. As shown in Figure 9.2, the room occupancy rate in North Africa (55%) is below the continent's and the sub-Saharan average. The top five countries in terms of room occupancy rate are Mauritius (80%), Seychelles (73%), Senegal (71%), Cape Verde (68%) and South Africa (64%). Although Ethiopia has a relatively moderate occupancy rate (54%), it has one of the highest average daily room rates in Africa ($192) next to Seychelles ($368) and Mauritius ($211). This is also above the continent's average daily room rate ($107). Likewise, in terms of revenue per available room (REVPAR), Ethiopia is ranked third ($104) after Seychelles ($270) and Mauritius ($168).

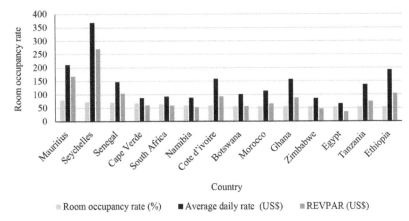

Country

■ Room occupancy rate (%)   ■ Average daily rate (US$)   ■ REVPAR (US$)

Note: REVAPR is calculated by dividing the total room revenue in a given period by the total number of available rooms during that period.
Source: STR Global data, 2017.

Figure 9.2   Room occupancy rate, average daily rate and REVPAR in Africa

However, the city's hospitality industry is facing many challenges. According to the interview conducted with the head of the Addis Ababa Hotel Owners' Association, there are a number of challenges facing hospitality businesses in the city. One of these is the lack of skilled and qualified manpower that can respond to the dynamic customer preferences. As a result there are customer handling problems. This is in line with the study conducted by Aschale (2013), who stated that a lack of professional services is one of the major challenges facing hotel businesses in Addis Ababa. The other problem is the shortage of hard currency, which limits the ability of hospitality firms to import in a timely fashion the necessary equipment and join the market. Due to this problem, the completion rate of hotel projects is quite slow. Furthermore, at a macro level, the country is lagging in terms of marketing and attracting international tourists.

Travel trade business

Travel intermediaries such as travel agencies and tour operators play a crucial role in the development of urban tourism. Among other things, travel inter-mediaries trigger the motivation of visitors via their promotional campaigns and arrange tours to different attractions. Travel intermediaries also play a key

Table 9.4   Travel agency and tour operation companies in Ethiopia

Region	Ownership		
	Local	Foreign	Total
Addis Ababa	337	111	448
Oromia	5	1	6
Amhara	5	0	5
SNNP	0	0	0
Tigray	5	0	6
Dire Dawa	1	0	1
Harari	0	0	0
Somali	1	0	1
Afar	1	0	1
Ethiopia	355	112	467

Source: Ministry of Culture and Tourism (2018).

role in terms of building destination image by meeting visitors' expectations. Since the propensity to travel to urban destinations such as Addis Ababa is partially shaped by promotional campaigns, it is quite important to assess the current status of travel intermediaries in terms of the size, quality and variety of services offered to visitors. According to the MoCT (2018), there are 467 travel agencies and tour operation companies in Ethiopia (Table 9.4). Among these, 355 (76%) are locally owned while the remaining 112 (24%) are foreign owned. Travel intermediaries are unevenly distributed in the country. More specifically, 448 (96%) travel companies operating in the county are concentrated in the capital, Addis Ababa.

The itineraries of ten purposefully selected tour operators in Addis Ababa that organize city tours were reviewed (Figure 9.3). The results showed that most tour operators allocate a one-day tour programme for Addis Ababa. Tour operators even arrange half-day city tour programmes depending on visitors' interest. The tour programmes are not only short in duration but also quite similar in nature, often focusing on museums and historical places. The top four most frequently mentioned attractions in the tour operators' itineraries are the National Museum, the Entoto Mountains, the Ethnographic Museum and the Merkato. This indicates that, despite its huge potential for urban tourism development, the city is not yet well developed and promoted as a tourist destination on its own.

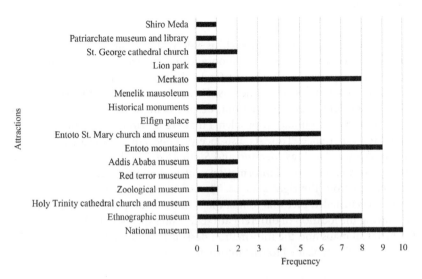

Figure 9.3   Number of times major attractions of Addis Ababa are mentioned in the itineraries of ten tour operators

The major issues relating to the travel trade in Addis Ababa include a failure to properly use modern technology to promote and sell tours for visitors. Most of the tour operators are small scale, family-owned businesses and could not use modern technology to market Addis Ababa or the other destinations in the country. Furthermore, the results of the interviews conducted with the head of the Ethiopian Tour Operators' Association, with tour operators and the review of secondary sources reveal that most tour operators tend to offer undifferentiated services to tourists. In other words, with few exceptions, most tour operators are tempted to arrange all types of tours rather than specializing in specific tours (for instance, historic, cultural or nature-based tours) and market segments such as business or leisure tourists. As a result, there is high duplication of tour programmes and the services offered often lack variety. Moreover, due to the lack of tourism acts or legal frameworks used to guide the tour operation business, there is an escalation in entrance fees by destination managers and in service prices by local tourism businesses such as hotels, even after reservations made by tour operators. There are also capacity problems, including the ability to use digital technology to reach different visitor markets, promote their products and compete with foreign tour operators. Furthermore, the field vehicles being used by most tour operators are not modern and hence reduce the overall visitor experience.

Support services and facilities

Support services and facilities such as safety and security systems, tourist information centres, travel facilitation and manpower are crucial for urban tourism development. Visitors are attracted by destinations that are clean and free from hassle and safety concerns. However, as key informants (K1, K8, K9, K10 and K11) have pointed out, despite being a diplomatic city, Addis Ababa has serious sanitation problems that are detrimental to the quality of the visitor experience. Tourists also face pickpocketing problems, especially in marketplaces (such as *Merkato* and *Shiro Meda*) in the city. However, the presence of well-organized information centres does help visitors get accurate information from the right sources. The Addis Ababa Culture and Tourism Bureau has installed pictorial tourist maps in the main parts of the city aimed at showing the location of different attraction sites for tourists. But apart from the pictorial maps and the information desk at Bole international airport, the city lacks well-established tourist information centres.

In order to reap the economic benefits of international tourists, it is necessary to work on a travel facilitation system (such as visas, travel regulations and immigration offices). To this end, the government of Ethiopia has recently launched "visa-on-arrival" and electronic visa schemes. The "visa-on-arrival" measure is mainly aimed at attracting tourists from African countries. The government also issues a transit visa for up to 72 hours on arrival at Bole International Airport with the aim of attracting transit passengers. Although these facilitation measures help to induce international tourist flows to Addis Ababa, there are still complaints about the lengthy security checks at the airport.

Human capital is the engine of any development activity. Tourism as a service industry depends on skilled and qualified manpower, both quality and quantity wise. Most of the private colleges offering training in tourism and hospitality programmes in Ethiopia are found in Addis Ababa. There are ten private colleges providing education in the field of tourism and hospitality, some up to the level of a bachelor's degree. In addition, there are ten government-owned Technical and Vocational Education Training centres and one university in Addis Ababa, the latter offering a master's degree in Tourism Development and Management. A bachelor's degree course in tourism and/or hospitality fields is offered by 24 universities in Ethiopia, some of which also offer a master's degree in either tourism or hotel management. All these educational institutions contribute to the (urban) tourism industry in Addis Ababa by supplying the necessary manpower. However, these educational institutions are criticized for not producing the necessary qualified manpower that the dynamic tourism industry requires. The major areas criticized by graduates are those of language skills and the use of new/modern technologies.

General infrastructure

General infrastructure such as roads, water supply, electricity and telecom facilities are crucial supply side components of urban tourism development. These facilities not only serve the general public but also visitors. As a result, they influence the overall visitor experience and destination competitiveness. However, as key informants (K3, K9, K10, K11 and K14) have pointed out, a limited water supply, power cuts, poor internet connections, substandard roads and traffic congestion are the major infrastructure-related problems that diminish the quality of visitor experience in the city.

Demand-related factors

Demand-related factors include tourist arrivals, receipts and purpose of visit. Although the number of tourist arrivals in Ethiopia has shown an increase from time to time, it still remains below 1 million. In 2012, the country recorded 596,340 tourist arrivals and five years later (2017) this figure had increased to 933,343. In 2018 it declined by 9% (to 849,122) from the preceding year mainly due to political instability in the country. It is assumed that 95% of visitors to the country pass through Addis Ababa (Gobena and Gudeta, 2013; LIA, 2017). On this basis, tourist arrivals in the city have increased from 566,340 in 2012 to 806,666 in 2018. As a result of Bole International Airport, Addis Ababa serves as the main gateway for tourists planning to visit various parts of Ethiopia (LIA, 2017).

As far as purpose of visit to the country is concerned, from 2012–2019 the majority were leisure and holiday visitors. The relatively higher number of VFR tourists in 2017 might be attributed to the then political change in the country, which enabled many diasporas to travel to Ethiopia. As compared with other tourism motives (for instance leisure and holidays), travel for business purposes (i.e., business tourism) is less seasonal and involves higher average spending per visitor.

Although data about how many of the business and professional visitors stayed in Addis Ababa are absent, it is believed that the vast majority of these visitors who came to Ethiopia stayed in Addis Ababa as the city is the seat of many international organizations, the political, cultural and economic capital of the country and also due to its relative abundance of conference facilities.

Based on data from the MoCT (2013), the average length of stay of tourists in Ethiopia was 16.5 nights. In terms of travel motives, there is a disparity among different travel market segments, where the VFR segment (19.4 nights) has a longer duration than those of business (17.5 nights), leisure and holiday (16.1 nights) and conference attendance (9.8 nights). The ministry also stated that the average length of stay of tourists in the country is estimated to be 16 days. However, there is a lack of clear information showing the length of stay of tourists in different destinations, including Addis Ababa. As some scholars (e.g. Van den Berg et al., 1995) argue, the duration of stay of tourists in popular urban destinations does not exceed two days. The case in Addis Ababa will not be far from this figure as the city is considered a crossroads to other tourist attractions in the country rather than a destination per se.

Tourist arrivals to Ethiopia are still below one million (Figure 9.4). It is assumed that Addis Ababa hosts about 95% of international tourist arrivals in Ethiopia (Gobena and Gudeta, 2013; LIA, 2017). The decrease in tourist arrivals in 2018 is probably due to the political instability in the country that particular year.

The major source markets for inbound tourism to Ethiopia are Europe, Africa and America (Figure 9.5). Africa accounts for about 30% of international business tourists to Ethiopia, followed by Europe, which accounts for 29%. Africa's higher share as a source market for business tourists is no surprise as Addis Ababa is the "diplomatic capital" of Africa. On the other hand, about 31% of leisure and holiday visitors to Ethiopia are European visitors, while about 29% are Africans. The numbers of transit passengers from Europe and Africa are almost equal, each representing about 30% of all international transit visitors to Ethiopia. One of the major targets of urban tourism development in Addis Ababa is to encourage transit passengers to spend some time in the city.

The contribution of tourism to GDP in Ethiopia is much lower than in other African countries. For example, in 2017, tourism's total contribution to GDP in South Africa, Egypt and Morocco was respectively 31 billion USD, 21 billion USD and 20 billion USD (WTTC, 2018). In the same year, the contribution of tourism to Ethiopia's GDP was about 5 billion USD. On the other hand, in terms of contribution to employment, Ethiopia and South Africa had almost equal figures: 1,537,800 and 1,530,300 jobs, respectively. As mentioned above, about 95% of international visitors travelling to Ethiopia stay in Addis Ababa.

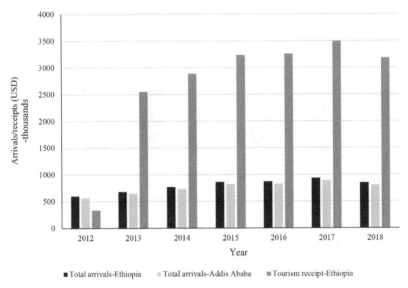

Source: Ministry of Culture and Tourism (2016, 2019).

Figure 9.4   Annual international tourist arrivals to Ethiopia and Addis Ababa, and annual tourist receipts from international visitors in Ethiopia

The city is therefore expected to get higher economic benefits from tourism than other destinations in the country.

Destination organization and stakeholder collaboration

In order to properly guide urban tourism development, there should be a policy framework, strategies and guidelines. So far, the country has ratified different policies, proclamations and strategies aimed at bringing cultural and tourism development. These macro interventions can serve as a building block to develop tourism in the country in general and Addis Ababa in particular. Such actions include ratification of the Ethiopian Culture Policy (in 1997), the Cultural Heritage Proclamation No. 206/2000 (in 2000) and the Tourism Development Policy (in 2009). The government has also established different tourism organs such as the Ethiopian Tourism Transformation Council, Tourism Ethiopia (formerly known as the Ethiopian Tourism Organization/ETO) and the Tourism Board. Tourism Ethiopia, the former ETO, is man-

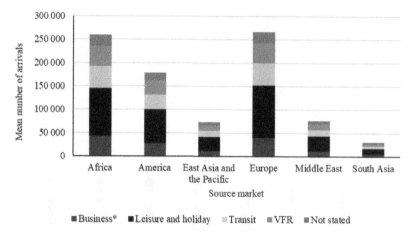

Note: Business includes professional and conference visitors.
Source: Ministry of Culture and Tourism (2019).

Figure 9.5   Average number of international tourist arrivals in Ethiopia based on purpose of visit and source market from 2016 to 2018

dated to develop tourist destinations, coordinate the operations of different stakeholders and promote the tourism sector. This specialized destination management organization (DMO) is responsible for integrating the activities of different tourism stakeholders in the country. The government has also launched visa-on-arrival and e-visa schemes aimed at easing the facilitation system and boosting international tourist arrivals to the country, especially from African countries.

Although the above efforts show the government's active involvement in the tourism sector, there are limitations when it comes to proper implementation. According to the interview conducted with different tourism stakeholders (K1, K2, K4, K9 and K10), the major problem facing the city's tourism industry is the absence of an integrated stakeholders' participation framework. The partnerships are not strategic and hence of a short-term nature. The loose, fragmented and uncoordinated operations by tourism stakeholders have limited the impact of tourism on the various socio-cultural, economic and environmental dimensions of sustainable development in the city. Due to the absence of a teamwork culture among tourism stakeholders, the city has not benefited from the collective efforts of different key actors.

Furthermore, the interview conducted with the Addis Ababa Culture and Tourism Bureau marketing and promotion experts indicates that the bureau is currently promoting the city's tourism mainly for the domestic tourism market via radio and television programmes. However, the bureau is facing problems including an insufficient budget for promoting the city using international media networks, lack of professionals and limited capacity to conduct digital marketing; while minimal attention is paid by the city administration to promoting tourism. Furthermore, as pointed out by marketing experts in Tourism Ethiopia, there is a lack of any clear strategic tourism marketing plan for the country, and the city in particular does not have its own distinct tourism brand. This in turn has shadowed proper positioning and market development efforts.

Conclusion and recommendations

Urban tourism is one of the mushrooming areas of research, especially in African tourism scholarship. Despite its tremendous contribution to reviving the urban economy, revitalizing culture and pooling technological developments, it has received disproportionately little attention. This study was conducted with the aim of exploring urban tourism development in Addis Ababa vis-à-vis other African cities.

The research findings indicated that Addis Ababa has tremendous potential for urban tourism development for a multitude of reasons including its strategic location (being the headquarters of the AU and the ECA), associated opportunities for becoming a strong MICE Tourism destination in Africa and its unique endowment of historical, religious and cultural heritages. In addition, the formulation of policies and proclamations related to culture and tourism, easing travel to Ethiopia by relaxing the visa rules, and the establishment of a number of new government organs could also facilitate urban tourism development in the country in general and in Addis Ababa in particular.

Despite these opportunities, the tourism industry in Addis Ababa is challenged by many factors. The major supply-related factors include a lack of professional service offered by accommodation establishments, the hospitality sector being dominated by substandard hotels that fail to meet the ever-changing customer demand; limited attention and insufficient budget allocated to protecting and conserving the city's heritage and also to developing new tourism products; weak promotional campaigns, the absence of digital marketing practices and lack of qualified tourism and hospitality professionals. These problems are further exacerbated by the absence of stakeholder collaboration frameworks, leading to a duplication of activities, the loss of priceless heritage and, in general, a weakening of synergy effects. Furthermore, despite the growing number of tourist arrivals from time to time, due to the aforementioned problems, this figure is still low compared with other African countries such as Morocco, Egypt, South Africa and Kenya. Therefore, there should be a concerted effort by the government and the private sector to solve the above problems.

The following are some of the possible solutions for the sustainable development of urban tourism in Addis Ababa: the use of modern technology in marketing, paying due attention to heritage conservation and management, the development of new tourism products and packages (such as gastronomic tours, transit tourism, etc.), which consider the changing needs of the urban tourist, the allocation of sufficient budget to enhance the capacity of destination management organizations such as "Tourism Ethiopia", and stakeholder collaboration and integration, the training of well-versed and tech-savvy tourism professionals, the establishment of well-organized tourist information centres and a special task force – commonly called *tourism police* – to protect the safety of tourists, and improvements in the quality and accessibility of the general infrastructure such as roads, electricity supply and telecom services so as to serve the changing demands of the general public and of tourists.

This study was mainly conducted based on secondary data supplemented by information gathered from key informant interviews with private and public sector stakeholders. There was some difficulty in getting supply and demand related data for Addis Ababa (such as tourist arrivals and receipts, length of stay and average daily expenditure) and, as a result, national figures are sometimes used in our study. In addition, making comparisons of urban tourism in Addis Ababa with that in other African cities was quite hard due to the difficulty to getting data about urban tourism in the latter.

References

Al-Saad, S. A., & Ababneh, A. (2017). Concept, opportunities and challenges of urban tourism in the Arab world: Case studies of Dubai, Cairo and Amman. *Turizam: međunarodni znanstveno-stručni časopis*, 65(3), 361–375

Aschale, A. (2013). *Critical Research on the Major Challenges of the Hospitality Industry in Addis Ababa*. Catering and Tourism Training Institute (CTTI).

Ashworth, G., & Page, S. J. (2011). Urban tourism research: Recent progress and current paradoxes. *Tourism Management*, 32(1), 1–15.

Bădiță, A. (2013). Approaches to the analysis and evaluation of urban tourism system within urban destinations. *Revista de turism-studii si cercetari in turism*, 16, 58–66.

Central Statistical Agency (2007). *Addis_Ababa_Statistical*. Accessed 23 January 2020 from http://www.csa.gov.et/census-report/complete-report/census-2007.

Gobena, E. C., & Gudeta, A. H. (2013). Hotel sector investment in Ethiopia. *Journal of Business Management*, 1(2), 35–54; Ref 0520130801. GTP plan, 2010; volume I.

International Congress and Convention Association (2017). *ICCA Statistics Report Country & City Rankings*. Public Abstract.

International Congress and Convention Association (2018). *ICCA Statistics Report 2018: Country & City Rankings*. Public Abstract.

Kassahun, S. and Tiwari, A. (2012). Urban development in Ethiopia: Challenges and policy responses. *The IUP Journal of Governance and Public Policy*, 7(1), 60–75.

King, B. (2004). Book review of managing urban tourism by SJ Page and CM Hall. *Tourism Management*, 25(2), 290–291.

Knight Frank Research (2018). *Hotels Africa: Accommodating Growth in Africa*. Knight Frank Research.

LIA (2017). Addis Ababa City Structure Plan: draft final summary report (2017–2027). Addis Ababa, Ethiopia: Addis Ababa City Administration.

MasterCard (2014). *Global Destination Cities Index*. MasterCard.

Ministry of Culture & Tourism (2016). *Tourism Statistics Bulletin 2012–2015*. No. 11.

Ministry of Culture & Tourism (2019). Unpublished official document about tourism statistics.

Ministry of Culture & Tourism (Various years). *Tourism Statistics Bulletin 2012–2018*. Nos 10–19.

Nasser, N. (2007). A historiography of tourism in Cairo: A spatial perspective. In R. F. Daher (Ed.), *Tourism in the Middle East: Continuity, Change and Transformation*. Multilingual Matters. pp. 70–94.

Okech, R. N. (2009). Developing urban eco-tourism in Kenyan cities: A sustainable approach. *Journal of Ecology and Natural Environment*, 1(1), 1–6.

Pearce, D. G. (2001). An integrative framework for urban tourism research. *Annals of Tourism Research*, 28(4), 926–946.

Rogerson, C. M. (2002). Urban tourism in the developing world: The case of Johannesburg. *Development Southern Africa*, 19(1), 169–190.

Rogerson, C. M. (2004). Urban tourism and small tourism enterprise development in Johannesburg: The case of township tourism. *GeoJournal*, 60(3), 249–257.

Rogerson, C. M. (2008). Shared growth in urban tourism: Evidence from Soweto, South Africa. *Urban Forum*, 19(4), 395–411.

Rogerson, C. M. (2011). Urban tourism and regional tourists: Shopping in Johannesburg, South Africa. *Tijdschrift voor economische en sociale geografie*, 102(3), 316–330.

Rogerson, C. M. (2013). Urban tourism, economic regeneration and inclusion: Evidence from South Africa. *Local Economy*, 28(2), 188–202.

Rogerson, C. M., & Rogerson, J. M. (2014). Urban tourism destinations in South Africa: Divergent trajectories 2001–2012. *Urbani izziv*, 25, S189–S203.

Rogerson, C. M., & Visser, G. (2005). Tourism in urban Africa: The South African experience. *Urban Forum*, 16(2–3), 63–87.

Rogerson, C. M., & Visser, G. (Eds.). (2007). *Urban Tourism in the Developing World: The South African Experience*. Transaction Publishers.

Rogerson, C. M., & Visser, G. (2011). Rethinking South African urban tourism research. *Tourism Review International*, 15(1–2), 77–90.

Rogerson, C. M., & Visser, G. (2014). A decade of progress in African urban tourism scholarship. *Urban Forum*, 25(4), 407–417.

Spirou, C. (2011). *Urban Tourism and Urban Change: Cities in a Global Economy*. Routledge.

STR Global data (2017). https://str.com.

The Telegraph (2018). Cities in the sky: The world's 15 highest capitals. Retrieved from https://www.telegraph.co.uk/travel/lists/capital-cities-with-highest-altitude/addis -ababa/.

United Nations Economic Commission for Africa (UNECA) (2015). *Sustainable Tourism Master Plan of Ethiopia 2015–2025*. UNECA.

UNWTO and WTC (2018). *City Tourism Performance Research*. Retrieved from http:// cf.cdn.unwto.org/sites/all/files/docpdf/9789284419616.pdf.

Van den Berg, L., Van der Borg, J., and Van der Meer, J. (1995). *Urban Tourism*. Aldershot: Ashgate.

Wambalaba, F., and Wambalaba, A. (2009). Conceptualizing structures for urban tourism in Kenya: A strategy for enhancing entrepreneurship. *Journal of Language Technology and Entrepreneurship in Africa*, 1(2), 36–45.

World Travel and Tourism Council (WTTC) (2018). *Travel & Tourism Economic Impact, Ethiopia*. WTTC.

Wubneh, M. (2013). Addis Ababa, Ethiopia – Africa's diplomatic capital. *Cities*, 35, 255–269. https://doi.org/10.1016/j.cities.2013.08.002.

10 Municipal advancement and tourism policy in the United States: economic development and urban restructuring

Costas Spirou

Introduction

The devastating effects of economic restructuring connected to globalization, de-industrialization and decentralization following World War II forced urban centres across the United States to search for policies to remedy the negative consequences of these structural forces. The implications became more pronounced and evident during the 1970s and 1980s with prevalent signs of decay and social dislocation. Within a mix of possible policy tools, urban tourism has emerged as a viable option, and its advancement and promotion through the use of cultural planning tools is now a commonly used strategy by municipal leaders and economic development professionals. Cities now-adays pursue the creation and maintenance of comprehensive approaches to assess current resources, induce the rebirth of existing cultural assets, develop new ones, invest in physical infrastructure and commit to related policies; all actions occurring within complex social, political and economic milieus that are reshaping metropolitan areas.

Scholarship in the United States has explored the unique issues surrounding the development and impact of tourism, including on the built environment (Ioannides and Debbage, 1998; Judd and Fainstein, 1999; Judd, 2003; Hoffman et al., 2004; Füller and Michel, 2014; Miller et al., 2015; Wise, 2016; Otgaar et al., 2016; Spirou et al., 2017; Evans, 2019). In fact, tourism activities have evolved into multi-billion-dollar enterprises, causing local governments to view them more favourably than ever before. In addition, the growth of this sector has brought about extensive reorganization of the urban landscape. Scholars have argued that an outcome of this development has been the incredible growth observed in major mega-projects in downtown areas (Judd, 2002; Nelson, 2014; Lim et al., 2019). In the end, the goal becomes to accommodate the needs of visitors whose spending increasingly becomes a major fiscal source of city budgets. This reliance by even small municipalities is causing a recalibration of past economic development approaches which rarely considered the positive contributions of this sector.

The introduction of substantial infrastructural facilities, in the form of museums, parks, stadiums, convention centres, etc., has not only expanded the availability of services; it has also strengthened existing amenities and introduced new ones. This broad direction has also encouraged inter-city competition, forcing cities to engage in a differentiation of entertainment possibilities. As a result, Las Vegas has pursued strengthening one type of tourist strategy, which has varied from the one employed by New York, Chicago and Los Angeles.

This chapter considers a number of elements that have made possible the rise of tourism as a factor in metropolitan development within the American context of urban change. Specifically, I begin by assessing the search for alternative development strategies as part of a wider scheme of urban competition. Then, I discuss the role of private–public partnerships in urban tourism, as well as the building and financing of the tourist city. The chapter concludes by examining the associated infrastructure, including stadiums and convention centre development initiatives.

The postwar fiscal stress and urban decline

While today urban economic development efforts include culture, leisure and tourism as a significant part of the broader planning mix of tools employed, tourism and related cultural forms did not fit the agenda of growth practices in the 1950s and 1960s. At best they were viewed as an inconsequential element of financial activity. But the post-World War II urban restructuring caused chronic fiscal stress, most visible during the 1970s. As a result, local governments were forced to search for new sources of economic growth. Furthermore, the production-oriented economy began to be replaced by a consumption-oriented one.

Many cities responded to these trends by divorcing themselves from their manufacturing dependency, searching to diversify and strengthen the various economic sectors. It is within this framework that urban tourism becomes an appealing alternative, one that slowly gained the favour of officials and civic boosters as a viable development tool. As a result, we begin to see the emergence of public investments and private-sector activity in the form of infrastructure and programming geared toward the advancement of the tourism industry. These sectors were eventually to work together as urban centres sought to enhance their spaces and rushed to take advantage of this new growth potential. However, a number of challenges arose, mainly in the areas of urban identity and urban competition. Specifically, how can a city with a formerly strong and nationally/internationally identifiable manufacturing economy convert itself into a tourist destination? Most importantly, how does it convince potential visitors of its new services and sense of "attractiveness"? It is through the interplay between structure and agency that we are able to gain insights on the transformation of urban centres into tourist cities. Local leaders must respond to structural conditions and urban processes that are beyond their control. Their vision though, including its execution, becomes part of the quest to achieve this new status.

The rise of urban tourism required an entrepreneurial and business-like approach. In that context, the city is not different from the corporation which must engage in image-building activities, promote its products and be prepared to deal with change if it wants to maintain its competitive edge and grow its market share. Given this new economic outlook, it is apparent that the financial stakes are very high (Kotler et al., 1993). As a result, we observe the re-making of local policymakers from service providers to active participants in local economic affairs. Private–public partnerships, neo-liberalist policies and aggressive marketing strategies and campaigns reorganized the urban space to include new infrastructure and specialized districts. This in turn reshaped the socio-economic characteristics of the residents, giving rise to new neighbourhoods, often the outcome of gentrification and displacement.

Tourism development and the amenities infrastructure

Developing an urban tourist economy meant financing a different type of city. By the late 1980s and early 1990s an extraordinary construction programme unfolded, spanning across downtowns and also focusing on the creation of services necessary to attract and retain visitors. Convention centres, theme parks, stadiums, casinos, waterfront developments and riverboat gambling complexes reshaped the physical landscape and helped restructure hundreds of urban cores.

A central aspect of tourism as a regeneration strategy is the development of an amenities infrastructure. Recent research documents the physical restructuring of large areas as the outcome of developing an urban tourist economy (Spirou, 2011; Dieterich-Ward, 2017; Edgell and Swanson, 2018). A vast array of major construction programmes in downtown areas focus on engaging and retaining visitors. Since the competition is fierce, the introduction of new attractions on a continuous pace is critical. These trends are not only visible in large cities, but also in smaller and medium-sized municipalities that try to re-brand themselves to ensure that they can capture as much of the visitor's disposable spending as possible.

Entertainment and gaming districts in US cities, such as those in Seattle, New Orleans and San Diego, have been spruced up with the aim of capturing the discretionary spending of local residents and tourists. Waterfront areas and their associated recreational facilities have received great attention in the revitalization efforts of Miami, San Francisco, New York City and Philadelphia. In Atlanta, Chicago, Milwaukee, Minneapolis and Pasadena, enclosed shopping malls have anchored downtown redevelopment plans. Finally, new or expanded convention centres in Chicago, New York, Kansas City and Orlando seek to tap the wellspring of large-scale trade shows and business gatherings. These projects, in turn, count on spin-off hotel, restaurant and entertainment expenditures to stimulate their cities' economies. The financing of these rapidly advancing urban infrastructures has been primarily driven by a combination of private and public sources. The privatization of funding and the willingness of local governments to integrate this sector have resulted in the development of urban tourism. Some centres have utilized tax increment financing techniques to support construction projects which, directly or indirectly, promote tourism growth. This was closely tied to the considerable growth of the United States economy during the 1990s.

There are many factors that contributed to this direction. For example, the introduction of new technologies in the latter part of the 1980s brought new consumer electronics and telecommunications to the consumer market. The computer industry grew rapidly and the internet not only entered American households, but also helped businesses function more effectively and provided numerous growth opportunities and new markets. The end of the conflict between the US and the former Soviet Union also provided trade opportunities in Eastern European countries, which rushed to grow their economies. Additionally, the federal government's reduction of expenditure on military development furthered the good economic climate. Low inflation and low rates of unemployment dominated the 1990s. The stock market increased and tax revenues grew rapidly, giving local governments considerable resources at their disposal. The economic expansion of the 1990s also translated to urban growth. It is within this broader framework of economic and urban growth of the 1990s that cities aggressively pursue the construction of a significant tourist infrastructure.

While the finance mechanisms employed by cities to advance the tourism and entertainment infrastructure vary, it is clear that local authorities tend to generally pursue similar approaches. Property taxes and bonds have been the most common methods employed to finance public investments in stadium development, but motel/hotel taxes, rental car surcharges, sports lottery revenues and ticket taxes have also been used to provide the needed revenue stream. The economically regressive impact of sales tax collections means that the poor and underprivileged pay more than their fair share of the stadium development costs. There are three specific categories. Primary facilities and services, which include historic, cultural and/or entertainment districts, convention centres, stadiums and performing arts centres. Secondary tourist facilities and services, which entail the availability of accommodation/hotels, restaurants, major convention hotels, as well as travel and tour services. Finally, tertiary tourist facilities and services, aimed at providing needed support which typically extends to additional sectors beyond tourism. For example, financial and personal services and safety and emergency care services would be part of this category.

A number of common themes can be observed when assessing the building and financing of the tourist city. Special purpose authorities have become common, increasingly playing a leading role, and have emerged as the most common approach to developing and operating these structures. Additionally, the private sector has become more and more involved, playing a greater role in the advancement of the urban sector. Finally, the localized nature of this strategy has placed offices of mayors centre stage, which has helped further intensify the competition between cities.

The role of private–public partnerships in constructing the city of play

With limited resources to recondition and retool, the needed tourist infrastructure necessitated the advancement of new models, which required an increased role to be played by the private sector. Specifically, the building and operating of an economy related to culture, leisure and entertainment provide us with an opportunity to witness the "privatizing discourse of public infrastructure" in urban tourism. Increasingly, we can observe that private sector participation entails investment, ownership and/or management in the building of the city. An expanded and deeper connection between state and capital has emerged as the prevailing force in the creation of the tourist infrastructure (Perry, 2003; Ascher and Krupp, 2010).

This intersection has given rise to special and discretionary purpose authorities and special districts. These have become popular with local governments, which utilized their institutionalization to meet various goals. Community development, transportation, economic development, parks and recreation, medical and health, environment and criminal justice are some of the areas within which we see the presence of these government forms. Subsequently, the use of private–public partnerships in the development of urban tourism and the building of the city of leisure has become a very common sought-after strategy. The logic behind these practices is the notion that growth is central to urban well-being and this form of tourism is simply another means of achieving that standing. The purpose of public subsidies then is to induce private investment and entice commerce ventures. That commitment by business creates jobs and a healthy tax base, which is then utilized by the municipality to improve basic services as well as maintain and expand infrastructure. This then results in prosperity and a good business climate which in turn can encourage additional private investment. The outcome of this strategy is the rise of local growth coalitions and regimes that aggressively pursue tactics focusing on attracting and retaining corporate investment. Within this scheme, tourism, culture, leisure and entertainment are similar to the status that manufacturing held within the economy of cities during the early part of the twentieth century (Gibson, 2003; Clark, 2011; Cowan, 2016).

Many American cities pursue their commitment to the advancement of urban tourism through the creation of focused organizational entities. These typically entail connecting economic development and tourism while also considering the advancement of culture. The main objectives of these offices relate to furthering approaches to strengthen the tourism sector, promoting and supporting new investment while responding to the needs of local tourism sector businesses. At the same time, officials provide advice and encouragement to help businesses and operators attract the tourist market and create packages and other forms of cooperative ventures while supporting measures creating a "tourist-friendly" environment. The primary engagements of these units relate to forging strong partnerships with other levels of government, agencies and the private sector, and with helping new tourism sector entrepreneurs and investors access the information needed to find sites and locate in their city. Broadly, helping businesses identify new markets in the tourism sector is the overarching vision that guides these rapidly developing organizations. In the end, this direction clearly denotes that role of the local government and its desire to closely partner with the private sector in advancing this industry.

In recent decades there are numerous examples of public–private partnerships in the United States, from infrastructure development to marketing tourism. *Visit Florida*, an $80 million a year, public–private tourism agency is responsible for promoting the state as Florida's official source for travel planning. In San Diego, the city pays about $1.2 million a year for eight business groups charged with its promotion. The San Francisco Convention & Visitors Bureau, the city's promotion agency, was funded by a combination of public and private resources (Strasburg, 2004). In 2017, states averaged about $20 million annually in executing tourism development campaigns.

The promotion of tourism and the cities that host their various attractions has emerged as a key aspect of the urban development strategy. Cities and states will invest millions in transforming their past images and perceptions in an effort to forge new urban identities that will draw visitors. It is also within this framework that we can observe the intersection of the public and private sectors. Cities expect businesses to invest by creating jobs and expanding their tax base, while, in exchange, the commercial sector relies on the government to promote and introduce amenities that will help maximize their profit.

Stadium construction as a contributor to the urban tourist strategy

Sports and stadium development is a key area associated with the urban tourism development strategy. In recent decades, cities across the United States have invested large sums of public money to build sports stadiums and arenas. There are primarily two rationales that have driven these policy considerations: economic benefits and social considerations. By employing economic impact studies and multiplier calculations, advocates note the positive direct and indirect economic outcomes. At the same time, many have cited community-building and cultural identification functions of sporting events. But with the emerging corporatization of sport and its maturation as a culture industry, there remains considerable uncertainty concerning the utility of these construction projects as tools for economic development and urban regeneration (Podair, 2017; Scherer et al., 2019).

The economics of upscale sports viewing in the United States has also produced a new type of sports arena. The expectation of private viewing environments and the infrastructure requisites for delivering an array of foods, beverages and other commodities have dictated various design innovations. The current trend in stadiums favours single-purpose facilities that make room for restaurants and taverns, gift shops, and, in some cases, overnight accommodation. Given the presumed economic and civic benefits derived from the hosting of sports franchises, municipal sponsorship of stadium projects is easily rationalized as a powerful economic development tool. The drive to attract teams is consistent with, indeed integral to, the municipal growth ideology.

Cities thus compete with each other to attract existing clubs or to win the honour of hosting an expansion team. The justification for subsidies to often profitable professional teams grows from the perception that public funding constitutes a form of capital investment and, as such, is akin to other urban redevelopment outlays. Furthermore, project proponents also outline adjacent entertainment districts with retail shops, outdoor music in the summer and additional recreational opportunities. One of the key trends has been the recent construction of new stadiums in downtown areas. More than half of the 32 NFL teams have downtown or urban stadiums. A similar trend can be observed in Major League Baseball.

As sports slowly became part of the tourism development strategy, stadium development proved a critical means of retaining or attracting professional franchises. From 1970 to 1990 we can observe an increase in the proportion of publicly owned facilities used by professional sports teams, from 70% to 80% (Quirk and Fort, 1992). From 1993 to 1996, more than $7 billion was spent on the construction and renovation of major league facilities. The public sector provided 80% of these funds, resulting in the introduction of 50 new stadiums across the various US professional leagues (Solomon, 2004). Even smaller cities have aggressively pursued minor league sports franchises by offering stadiums to team owners (Johnson, 1993).

This development craze has persisted in the last two decades. For example, from 2000 to 2008, 11 new stadiums were developed in the National Football League (NFL) at a cost of $4.43 billion (average of $402 million per project). New homes for the Dallas Cowboys and the New York Yankees opened in 2009 for $1.3 billion and $1.6 billion respectively. More recently, new stadiums for the Minnesota Vikings (2016, cost $1.1 billion), and for the Atlanta Falcons (2017, cost $1.6 billion) revealed that spending will continue. In fact, in 2020, the Las Vegas Raiders began play at a brand new $1.9 billion domed stadium. Eclipsing all of these projects, the new SoFi Stadium in Inglewood, California was unveiled in 2020 to house the Los Angeles Rams and the Los Angeles Chargers. The construction cost of the complex was a staggering $5 billion.

At the same time, these initiatives are controversial since many question the public value of these practices. Arguing that local governments often go too far in their efforts to attract investment, opponents charge that these strategies are pursued at the expense of taxpayers. The construction of stadiums in cities across the country through the use of public funding has stalled in some cities through referendums. Local newspaper editorials and community groups typically lead the anti-approval efforts by referencing these practices as examples of corporate welfare. Notably, in 2007, the Cincinnati Reds (Major League Baseball) saw the voters of Sarasota, Florida reject a taxpayer-supported stadium project. The team sought $16 million to help pay for a $45 million renovation (Hackett, 2008). But in what may be the most surprising turn of events, in 2006, Seattle voters approved a ballot initiative that restricted taxpayer subsidies for professional sports teams. This action hampered plans for the construction of a $500 million arena complex requested by the SuperSonics, Seattle's professional basketball team. This eventually led the team, which had been in Seattle since its founding in 1967, to relocate to Oklahoma City during the 2008–2009 season (Balko, 2008). In 2013, taxpayers in Houston rejected the authorization to expend $217 million to turn the Astrodome into a giant convention and event centre. Interestingly, when constructed in 1965, the facility was referenced as the "eighth wonder of the world" (Hennessy-Fiske, 2013). One of the NBA's original franchises, the Golden State Warriors decided to relocate from Oakland back to San Francisco in 2012 in search of a larger market. Without public dollars available, the team self-financed their $1.4 billion sports venue. The facility opened in 2019 (Davis, 2019).

Cities and states have created agencies responsible for the development of stadium projects. For example, in Chicago, the Illinois Sports Facilities Authority was responsible for the construction of New Comiskey Park (now Guaranteed Rate Field for the Chicago White Sox) and Soldier Field (Chicago Bears). In Washington, the District of Columbia government created an independent agency, the DC Sports and Entertainment Commission, which oversaw the construction of Nationals Park for $611 million in 2008 (Washington Nationals) and is responsible for the management and operation of the Robert F. Kennedy Memorial Stadium (Washington Redskins).

The pursuit of the convention centre strategy

American cities organized themselves to advance business tourism as far back as the early part of the twentieth century. In 1907, the Chicago Association of Commerce identified a subcommittee to work on attracting convention meetings to the city. Like Chicago, many others formed formal agencies out of loosely defined civic or business groups whose agendas centred on promoting and attracting tourism and related businesses to their respective locales. Convention and visitor bureaus were created across the country in San Francisco (1909), St. Louis (1909), Atlanta (1913), Kansas City (1918), Minneapolis (1927), Washington (1931), Cleveland (1934), New York (1935), Philadelphia (1941), Las Vegas (1960), New Orleans (1960), Anaheim, CA (1961), Orlando (1984) and Miami (1985). The Chicago Convention and Visitors Bureau (CCVB) was founded in 1943 and eventually expanded in 1970 to include the Tourism Council of Greater Chicago, forming the Chicago Convention and Tourism Bureau. The management and operation of Chicago's McCormick Place was added to the CCVB's responsibilities in 1980.

The rationale that drives the construction of stadiums has also fuelled public investment into convention centres. Since governments have embraced the urban tourism and leisure industries as contributors to local economies, huge expenditures in this area are evident, especially among cities ailing from de-industrialization. When examining convention centres, three tiers of convention cities can be identified. The first includes the most success-ful cities, such as Las Vegas, Orlando and Chicago. The second-tier cities, notably San Francisco, San Diego, Anaheim, Atlanta and Washington, DC, have also focused on developing their economies by investing heavily in their convention centres. Finally, third-tier cities have been most aggressive in their convention development; they include Seattle, Reno, Nashville and Portland. This last set of cities aims to strip convention market share from the tier-one and tier-two urban centres.

An examination of the top convention cities in the United States reveals the intensity of the competition. In 1980 the top cities hosting meetings with exhibits included New York, Chicago, and Atlanta (Las Vegas ranked fourth and Orlando ranked 27th). A decade later, in 1992, the three top convention cities included Chicago, Orlando (from fifth in 1991), and Dallas (Las Vegas ranked 13th that year). In 2004, 12th-ranked San Antonio, 17th Tampa-St Petersburg-Clearwater, FL, 18th Austin-San Marcos, TX, 20th Seattle (metro area), and 23rd-ranked Riverside-San Bernardino, CA had not even made the top list ten years earlier. Securing conventions, especially the 200 largest trade shows (Tradeshow 200), has direct and indirect economic ramifications for the local economy. In 2012, the three top convention cities included Las Vegas, Orlando and Chicago. In recent years, Atlanta and Washington have also entered that coveted list behind dominant Las Vegas and Orlando. But ranking cities in this area is a difficult proposition since the guidelines can include physical size, attendance, attractiveness of the given city, proximity to amenities and many other factors.

As part of a growth ideology, these policies sometimes run the risk of becoming unfocused, often lost in the haze of intense inter-city competition for visitor expenditures. A construction explosion started during the 1990s and continued in the 2000s. In 2007 alone, 93 new or expanded convention centres were introduced across the country. The total amount of exhibit space from 1990 to 2003 rose 51% from 40.4 million to 60.9 million square feet, doubling the public spending on infrastructure to more than $2 billion annually. Cities in this intensely competitive environment have been forced to reduce their rental pricing resulting in numerous convention centres operating at a loss. In the first part of 2009, city officials announced the grand openings of 15 new, expanded or renovated venues (Zerlin, 2008).

The latter part of the 2010s revealed that the United States is in a new era of convention centre expansion. Philadelphia completed a $787 million Pennsylvania Convention Center (PCC) expansion in 2011, aiming to rank in the top 20 convention centres in the country. In 2013, the Orlando Convention Center celebrated its 30th anniversary and embarked on a five-year, $187 million capital improvement project. More recently, in 2019, the Austin City Council approved a $1.2 billion convention centre expansion (Findell, 2019). That same year, Texas Arlington, Texas, announced a massive $810 million hotel and convention centre (DiFurio, 2019) and in 2020 Fort Worth, TX, embarked on a $500 million expansion of the Fort Worth Convention Center which includes plans to demolish an arena on the site (Ranker and Dorsey, 2020). Finally, in 2020, New Orleans announced a massive transformation of the city's lakefront that is expected to include a revamped Convention Centre with a new Convention Centre hotel and adjacent pedestrian parks (Bridges, 2020). Similarly, Las Vegas ($980 million), Orlando ($605 million), Denver ($250 million) and many others are either completing or considering expansions. In many of these cases cities are pursuing the development of Convention districts.

Projected job creation, increased tax revenues and direct and indirect opportunities for economic growth rationalized the convention centre building boom. At the same time, it has left municipalities wondering if the benefits outweigh the extensive renovations, maintenance and unfavourable lease agreements. But adding convention space does not guarantee success. During the first decade of the 2000s, Chicago's McCormick Place's woes – diminishing shows, attendees and square feet of utilized space were heightened by the loss of the National Association of Realtors' 100th-anniversary convention to Las Vegas in 2007. Like other cities, Chicago has also experienced competition from nearby smaller cities. Rosemont, IL, which in 2006 ranked ninth in total exhibit space, and the opening of the Renaissance Schaumburg Convention Center that year with 100,000 square feet of exhibit space continuously aim to erode Chicago's tourist dollars dominance. Other smaller cities are pursuing the convention centre strategy, hoping to take away market share from the most dominant counterparts (Holdman, 2019).

Tourism, cultural amenities and downtown residential development

One of the outcomes for cities focusing on urban tourism since the 1990s has been the growth of residential development in downtown areas. Substantial investment in tourism infrastructure not only expanded the availability of services to visitors, but also to locals. In the process it has strengthened existing amenities and introduced new ones. As a result, central business districts experienced considerable transformation in the last 30 years with new downtown neighbourhoods re-emerging in both smaller and larger cities. These new communities have been carved out of existing commercial and industrial properties via loft conversions and built anew by residential developers.

The result is a notable shift in the population make-up of downtowns. An analysis of downtown household and income trends of 44 cities from 1970 to 2000 revealed that during the 1990s, downtown population increased by 10%. During that same period, the number of downtown households increased between 8% and 13% and the homeownership rates more than doubled, reaching 22% in 2000. Other related observations include the fact that, in 2000, 25 to 34 year olds represented nearly a quarter of the downtown population – up from 13% in 1970. Only four of 22 downtowns with a population of at least 10,000 residents experienced population decline from 1990 to 2000. From 1970 to 1980, 16 of these recorded population decreases (Birch, 2005).

The trend continued as the 2010 census data showed that many cities continued to see population increases in their downtowns. Between 2000 and 2010, Boston's core experienced a 46.4% jump, the highest population growth rate. This helped the area reach an all time, decade-long high of 16,298 residents (Rocheleau, 2011). Downtown Minneapolis' population grew by 32% during that same timeframe and nearby St. Paul by 18% (Rao, 2012). To the west, data compiled by the Downtown Phoenix Partnership indicated that the population growth in the downtown was 30.5% (within one mile of the core);

13.1% (within two miles of the core) and 8.4% (within three miles of the core) (Downtown Phoenix Partnership, 2011). Denver's downtown also recorded a staggering 61% residential growth between 2000 and 2010 (Downtown Denver Partnership, 2011).

The case of downtown Miami aptly captures the qualitative characteristics of these residents. From 2000 to 2010, the population in this less than four square mile area rose by 68%. The number of households also increased by an impressive 93%. These are year-round residents with the majority (57%) between 20 and 44 years of age. Over 65% of downtown residents worked as professionals, with 20% as managers and executives in financial services. The income of these residents is also 38% higher than citywide Miami (Goodkin and Werley, 2011). It is expected that the 2020 US census will reveal a continuation of these trends (Garvin, 2019).

Cities suffering from the effects of deindustrialization looked to connect new amenities to residential development. Detroit, Michigan, for example, introduced an aggressive greater downtown residential development plan which added almost 2500 condominium units from 2000 to 2006. The use of incentives as a result of the creation of enterprise zones accelerated the rapid pace of construction. The survey findings of community residents conducted in 2006 concluded that "convenience to dining and entertainment" and "proximity to arts and cultural institutions" proved to be the most influential factors that motivated these individuals to move downtown (Beebe and Associates, 2006). This part of the city has experienced an astonishing rebirth, which accelerated in the last few years (Kickert, 2019).

Residential developers took advantage of the opportunities presented as local officials pushed for the rebuilding of their once dilapidated and abandoned downtowns. The leisure and amenities-based infrastructure meant that in addition to visitors seeking entertainment opportunities, existing and new residents were drawn in by the improved quality of life experiences offered by these same attractions. However, this resulted in increased gentrification and displacement. Many existing residents found it difficult to afford increased property taxes and decided to move out of their neighbourhoods. An expanded tourism economy and accompanying residential development alone are not guaranteed to turn around ailing districts. Nonetheless, this planning strategy aggressively embraced by civic leaders and local boosters during the last few decades proved to fundamentally alter the postwar decline of the 1970s and 1980s. In the process, it helped craft a new direction regarding the function of these historically significant urban spaces.

Conclusion

The above observations reveal the considerable complexities evident when examining the nature and effect of the tourism industry on urban centres in the United States. The competition for the revenue generated by visitors through expansive infrastructure raises a number of questions and issues in this arena. Furthermore, the evolving condition of American cities and their ever-growing reliance on this industry makes inquiry on this subject highly important. Equally critical is research on understanding the processes and forces responsible for shaping urban tourism; from urban politics/power, corporate interests, pro-growth and image building rationales to the role of civic groups and the importance of quality of life attitudes and considerations within a new global economy of information technology and entertainment.

It is apparent that structural changes have impacted cities in the United States over the last five decades. De-industrialization, population decentralization and globalization have played a critical role, leaving the urban core subjected to disinvestment, decline and widespread social problems in housing and education amongst others. Within this rapidly evolving socio-economic environment, and fiscally strained to provide needed social services to their residents, cities increasingly identified urban tourism and its potential revenue capability as a viable approach and a key economic development strategy.

There are a number of themes that can be observed regarding the infrastructure finance of urban tourism. First, special authorities have become central to this policy implementation and are increasingly playing a critical role. Second, the private sector proved key to the advancement of this city building effort. Third, given the localized nature of this strategy, the competition between cities has intensified as major construction projects commonly include convention centres, amusement parks, casinos, riverboat gambling complexes, shopping centres and waterfront development, all of which are part of producing an entertainment city that aims to attract and retain visitors. Finally, the revitalization of the urban core brought new residents but also caused gentrification and displacement.

In the last 30 years, American cities have made a deliberate effort to physically reorganize their locales and embrace the advancement of urban tourism as an economic development tool. However, the success of this strategy hinges on a continuously concerted effort to maintain the needed organizational capacity in marketing and image building, while balancing that against the competitive desires of other cities that have also intensified their efforts to attract visitors to their locales. That will likely determine, both quantitatively and qualitatively, how the social force of urban tourism will unfold in the coming years.

References

Ascher, W., and Krupp, C. (2010). *Physical Infrastructure Development: Balancing the Growth, Equity, and Environmental Imperatives*. New York: Palgrave.

Balko, R. (2008). So long, Seattle: Stadium welfare schemes. *Reason*, May 1.

Beebe, K., and Associates. (2006). Downtown residential market study. Report prepared for the Lower Woodward Housing Fund. September 23.

Birch, E. (2005). *Who Lives Downtown*. The Brookings Institution, Living Cities Census Series.

Bridges, T. (2020). Inside plans to 'turbocharge' New Orleans' riverfront: New parks, hotels, housing, more underway, February 19. https://www.nola.com/news/business/article_15375634-4778-11ea-99ff-47850086841c.html.

Clark, T. N. (Ed) (2011). The city as an entertainment machine. *Research in Urban Policy*, (Vol. 9). Boston, MA: Elsevier/JAI.

Cowan, A. (2016). *A Nice Place to Visit: Tourism and Urban Revitalization in the Postwar Rustbelt*. Philadelphia: Temple University Press.

Davis, S. (2019). Warriors President Rick Welts explains why their new $1.4 billion self-financed stadium was a one-of-a-kind situation other teams can't replicate. *Business Insider*, March 28.

Dieterich-Ward, A. (2017). *Beyond Rust: Metropolitan Pittsburgh and the Fate of Industrial America*. Philadelphia: University of Pennsylvania Press.

DiFurio, D. (2019). Arlington gives go-ahead to ambitious $810 million hotel, convention center. *The Dallas Morning News*. December 17.

Downtown Denver Partnership, Inc. (2011). *Downtown: State of Denver*. July.

Downtown Phoenix Partnership. (2011). *Phoenix Demographic Summary Report*. April.

Edgell, D. and Swanson, J. (2018). *Tourism Policy and Planning: Yesterday, Today, and Tomorrow*. London: Routledge.

Evans, G. (2019). *Mega-Events: Placemaking, Regeneration and City-Regional Development*. London: Routledge.

Findell, E. (2019). City Council says yes to $1.2 billion convention center expansion. *The Statesman*. May 23.

Füller, H. and Michel, B. (2014). 'Stop being a tourist!' New dynamics of urban tourism in Berlin-Kreuzberg. *International Journal of Urban and Regional Research*, 38(4), 1304–1318.

Garvin, A. (2019). How and why downtown America is changing. In: *The Heart of the City*. Washington, DC: Island Press.

Gibson, T. (2003). *Securing the Spectacular City: The Politics of Revitalization and Homelessness in Downtown Seattle*. New York: Lexington.

Goodkin, L. and Werley, C. (2011). Miami DDA – Population & Demographic Profile. Report prepared for the Downtown Development Authority (September).

Hackett, K. (2008). Stadium strike-out: after a last inning defeat, is the game really over for the Reds and their supporters? *Sarasota Magazine*, February 1.

Hennessy-Fiske, M. (2013). Houston voters skip nostalgia, reject measure to save Astrodome. *Los Angeles Times*, November 6.

Hoffman, L., Fainstein, S. S., and Judd, D. R. (2004). *Cities and Visitors: Regulating Cities, Market, and City Space*. New York: Blackwell.

Holdman, J. (2019). Columbia wants to expand SC's smallest convention center. Is it worth the price? *The Post and Carrier*, September 1.

Ioannides, D. and Debbage, K. (Eds). (1998). *The Economic Geography of the Tourist Industry: A Supply-side Analysis*. London: Routledge.

Johnson, A. T. (1993). *Minor League Baseball and Local Economic Development*. Champaign: University of Illinois Press.

Judd, D. (2002). *The Infrastructure of Play*. New York: Routledge

Judd, D. R. (2003). *The Infrastructure of Play: Building the Tourist City*. Armonk: M. E. Sharpe.

Judd, D. R. and Fainstein, S. S. (1999). *The Tourist City*. New Haven, Yale University Press.

Kickert, C. (2019). *Dream City: Creation, Destruction, and Reinvention in Downtown Detroit*. Cambridge: MIT University Press.

Kotler, P., Haider, D. H., and Rein, I. (1993). *Marketing Places: Attracting Investment, Industry, and Tourism to Cities, States and Nations*. New York: Free Press.

Lim, C., Zhu, L. and Koo, T. (2019). Urban redevelopment and tourism growth: Relationship between tourism infrastructure and international visitor flows. *International Journal of Tourism Research*, 21(2), 187–196.

Miller, D., Merrilees, B., and Coghlan, A. (2015). Sustainable urban tourism: Understanding and developing visitor pro-environmental behaviors. *Journal of Sustainable Tourism*, 23(1), 26–46.

Nelson, R. (2014). *Developing a Successful Infrastructure for Convention and Event Tourism*. New York: Routledge.

Otgaar, A., Van Den Berg, L., and Feng, R. (2016). *Industrial Tourism: Opportunities for City and Enterprise*. New York: Routledge.

Perry, D. (2003). Urban tourism and the privatizing discourses of public infrastructure. In D. R. Judd (Ed.), *The Infrastructure of Play: Building the Tourist City* (pp. 19–49). Armonk: M.E. Sharpe.

Podair, J. (2017). *City of Dreams: Dodger Stadium and the Birth of Modern Los Angeles*. Princeton: Princeton University Press.

Quirk, J. and Fort, R. (1992). *Pay Dirt: The Business of Professional Team Sports*. Princeton: Princeton University Press.

Ranker, L. and Dorsey, M. (2020). Fort Worth plans up to $500 million expansion of downtown convention center. *Fort Worth Star Telegram*, January 16.

Rao, M. (2012). Downtown Minneapolis is seen as drowning in a sea of parking lots. *Start Tribune*, July 25.

Rocheleau, M. (2011). Census data: Downtown population soared 46 percent. *Boston Globe*, April 6.

Scherer, J., Mills, D., and McCulloch, L. (2019). *Power Play: Professional Hockey and the Politics of Urban Development*. Edmonton: University of Alberta Press.

Solomon, J. (2004). Public wises up, bulks at paying for new stadiums. *USA TODAY*, April 1.

Spirou, C. (2011). *Urban Tourism and Urban Change: Cities in a Global Economy*. New York: Routledge.

Spirou, C., Miller, C., and Baker, B. (2017). Urban coalitions and the production of Atlanta's downtown. In N. Wise (Ed.), *Sport, Events, Tourism and Regeneration* (pp. 118–135). London: Routledge.

Strasburg, J. (2004). Will they visit S.F.?: Budget battle pits funding for tourism bureau vs. social services. *San Francisco Chronicle*, December 11.

Wise, N. (2016). Outlining triple bottom line contexts in urban tourism regeneration. *Cities*, 53, 30–34.

Zerlin, K. (2008). 15 Convention center openings slated. *Tradeshow Week*, September 15.

11 Comparative study on Chinese cities as international tourism destinations

Xiang Feng, Ben Derudder and Hai Xia Zhou

Introduction

It is now widely accepted that the Chinese tourism industry has evolved into a critical economic sector that is fast expanding and has further significant growth potential (Xiao, 2006). Tourism in China has been developing in a specific context due to the country's unique political, economic and cultural background. It is increasingly establishing itself as a major economic sector with an increasingly international outlook (Feng, 2011). China's economic growth and the international dimension of that growth have a decidedly urban focus (Taylor et al., 2014). Because many key tourist facilities and infrastructures as well as major historical and new attractions tend to be located in or near to cities, it is obvious that China's major cities have come to play a key role in the development of its tourism industry (Feng, 2011). This urban focus is even more pronounced in the international tourism industry because of the accessibility offered by major airports and a range of implicit facilitating factors such as the level of English in tourism services (see Zhang et al., 2011; Deng et al., 2017).

The objective of this chapter can be cast in two different forms, one methodological and the other empirical. The methodological purpose is to explore ways to differentiate cities' roles as international tourism hubs. The empirical purpose is to illustrate the practical implementation of this methodology by focusing on the case of China. In its narrowest sense, the term "internationalization" can simply be used to describe processes of increasing involvement in international operations (Welch & Luostarinen, 1988). Following Gorcheva (2011), this chapter proposes that tourism internationalization entails (1) the production of services to be consumed by international tourists, while also (2) seeking out and creating business environments for organizing and disseminating these services. This chapter argues that although both dimensions – captured by Product Destination Internationalization (PDI) and Business Environment Internationalization (BEI) – are indeed two pertinent themes for tourism research, their parallels and differences have not been specifically broached in the scientific literature. Furthermore, we follow previous research (e.g., Sun, 2007; Cui & Ryan, 2011; Zhang et al., 2011; Wang & Bramwell, 2012; Ma & Hassink, 2013; Liang & Hui, 2016; Liu, Nijkamp & Lin, 2017; Su et al., 2017; Peng & Xiao, 2018; Valadkhani & Omahony, 2018) and indicate PDI as a combination of (1) the number of international arrivals and (2) the length of stay of international visitors in a destination in a certain year. And we follow Derudder et al. (2013) to concern BEI as tourism firms' presence and performance in a "foreign" destination.

Data sources and operationalization

Selection of cities and PDI data

The first step in the construction of our dataset is the choice of cities. Our analysis focuses on the 50 cities in mainland China that were identified in the China National Tourism Statistics as the country's major international tourism hubs in 2017 (Table 11.1).

Measuring BEI

To operationalize BEI, firms were chosen based on their ranking in lists of the largest international tourism firms for each of the different categories. These rankings were the most recently available at the planning of the research in 2018, and tended to be based on 2017 data. For the international restaurant, supermarket and insurance sectors, we included the top firms by cross-checking two indices, i.e. the Forbes 2000 (http://www.forbes.com/) and the Fortune 500 rankings (http://fortune.com/). A total of 13 restaurant, 10 retail and 42 insurance groups were identified as having a presence in (some of) the 50 Chinese cities. For the international hotel sector, 85 global hotel companies from the "Hotel 325" list (www.marketingandtechnology.com/) were identified as having at least one presence in China. For international travel agencies, we reviewed the list of international travel agencies that are allowed to operate in China by the Chinese government (www.qualitytourism .cn/). For international theme parks, we reviewed the top ten theme park groups worldwide from the global attractions attendance report of the Themed Entertainment Association (TEA) (http://www.teaconnect.org/) and identi-

Table 11.1   Fifty most important Chinese cities in terms of PDI

Ranking	City	Abbreviation	International arrivals (IA) (in thousands and rounded)	Length of stay (LS), days	Product destination internationalization (in thousands and rounded)
1	Shenzhen	SHZ	11,700	2.35	27,500
2	Guangzhou	GZ	8,600	3.11	26,800
3	Shanghai	SH	6,900	3.21	22,200
4	Beijing	BJ	4,200	4.30	17,900
5	Xiamen	XM	2,300	4.98	11,500
6	Chongqing	CQ	1,800	5.30	9,600
7	Suzhou	SZ	1,600	4.19	6,800
8	Quanzhou	QZ	1,300	5.06	6,300
9	Wuhan	WH	2,200	2.80	6,300
10	Fuzhou	FZ	1,100	5.85	6,200
11	Zhuhai	ZH	3,200	1.79	5,700
12	Chengdu	CD	2,700	1.93	5,200
13	Guilin	GL	2,300	2.24	5,200
14	Hangzhou	HZ	1,600	2.60	4,100
15	Xi'an	XA	1,300	2.92	3,900
16	Qingdao	QD	900	3.65	3,400
17	Huangshan	HS	1,500	1.86	2,800
18	Tianjin*	TJ	800	2.95*	2,400
19	Dalian	DL	1,000	2.10	2,200
20	Nanjing	NJ	600	3.51	2,200
21	Shenyang	SY	700	3.19	2,200
22	Zhangzhou	ZAZ	600	3.89	2,200
23	Kunming	KM	1,200	1.67	2,100
24	Ningbo	NB	800	2.18	1,800
25	Yantai	YT	400	4.14	1,700
26	Zhongshan	ZS	600	2.66	1,700
27	Changchun	CC	500	3.40	1,500
28	Yanbian	YB	700	2.08	1,500

Ranking	City	Abbreviation	International arrivals (IA) (in thousands and rounded)	Length of stay (LS), days	Product destination internationalization (in thousands and rounded)
29	Wuxi	WX	400	3.09	1,400
30	Sanya	SY	400	2.61	1,200
31	Wenzhou	WZ	500	2.34	1,200
32	Nanning	NN	600	1.99	1,100
33	Qinhuangdao	QHD	100	7.23	1,100
34	Urumqi	URU	300	3.45	1,100
35	Weihai	WEH	300	3.01	1,000
36	Zhengzhou	ZZ	400	2.48	1,000
37	Changsha	CS	600	1.53	900
38	Hefei	HF	300	2.94	800
39	Jinan	JN	300	3.16	800
40	Chengde	CDE	200	2.40	600
41	Jiujiang	JJ	300	2.12	600
42	Lhasa	LS	200	3.00	600
43	Luoyang	LY	300	1.80	600
44	Harbin	HRB	200	2.23	500
45	Nanchang	NC	200	2.03	500
46	Nantong	NT	200	2.82	500
47	Shantou	ST	200	2.04	500
48	Guiyang	GY	200	2.00	400
49	Taiyuan	TY	200	2.67	400
50	Zhanjiang	ZJ	400	0.81	300

Note: *The length of stay data for Tianjin city was replaced with the average across the 49 other cities because of a data error in the *Yearbook of China Tourism Statistics*.

Source: *Yearbook of China Tourism Statistics* (2017).

fied two theme parks operating in China. For international NGOs, we identified seven organizations affiliated with the UNWTO and WTTC and having offices in China. By crawling the data on international hospitals in China provided by the Allianz international medical insurance group, we identified ten international hospital groups that have branches, joint ventures or cooperation agreements in China. Taken together, this resulted in a list of 205 international firms with a direct or indirect tourism component that have set up some sort of presence across 50 major Chinese cities.

The total number of branches or offices of international tourist companies in a city is our measure of the city's BEI. Linking firms with a city was done based on the information available on each firm's website. Typically, the website provides an option that allows "location" to be selected, giving the addresses of the offices, and often with a world map of their distribution to emphasize their presence. We used the websites to "scavenge" all possible relevant available information, firm by firm (cf. Derudder et al., 2013). When tourism firms exist as groups, they were treated as a single network in our research and allocated to their core sector.

Recurring patterns of Chinese cities being international tourism hubs

Table 11.3 shows the transformed PDI and BEI values across the 50 Chinese cities. Figure 11.1 reflects the results obtained in Table 11.3.

When taking a closer look at the standardized residual in Figures 11.2 and 11.3 with 0.35 as the natural breaks (Jenks), the relative balance of BEI and PDI for each individual city is easily seen. Except for the 14 cities with relatively similar positions in BEI (i.e., attractiveness for international tourism business) and PEI (i.e., attracting international tourists), when comparing with 49 other cities across China, 21 cities show relatively higher positions in BEI and 15 cities perform adversely.

When specific cities are concerned, five cities' individual standardized residual exceeds 1, which means they attract relatively more international tourism firms. Among these, Shanghai, Wuxi and Hangzhou are located in the Yangtze River Delta region, arguably one of the three leading regions in China in terms of both economic development and internationalization (Liu et al., 2015). Shanghai is not abundant in tourism resources (Feng, 2011). Compared with its tourism development, this global city's business achievements have been extensively documented in the literature (e.g., Yusuf & Wu, 2002; Gaubatz, 2005; Wu, 2011; Derudder et al., 2013; Taylor et al., 2014; Arkaraprasertkul, 2016). As China's largest and most urbanized city, it has seen unprecedented growth in foreign investment and foreign trade since the adoption of the opening up policy in 1978. The influence of globalization does not lie in the quantity of foreign investment but in the catalytic effect brought by foreign

Table 11.2   Fifty most important Chinese cities in terms of BEI

ID	City	BEI
1	Shenzhen	951
2	Guangzhou	1516
3	Shanghai	4449
4	Beijing	2045
5	Xiamen	214
6	Chongqing	622
7	Suzhou	1042
8	Quanzhou	124
9	Wuhan	672
10	Fuzhou	213
11	Zhuhai	115
12	Chengdu	637
13	Guilin	47
14	Hangzhou	856
15	Xi'an	321
16	Qingdao	333
17	Huangshan	12
18	Tianjin*	719
19	Dalian	375
20	Nanjing	480
21	Shenyang	285
22	Zhangzhou	29
23	Kunming	156
24	Ningbo	348
25	Yantai	104
26	Zhongshan	128
27	Changchun	144
28	Yanbian	18

ID	City	BEI
29	Wuxi	387
30	Sanya	98
31	Wenzhou	125
32	Nanning	112
33	Qinhuangdao	37
34	Urumqi	33
35	Weihai	37
36	Zhengzhou	188
37	Changsha	232
38	Hefei	180
39	Jinan	175
40	Chengde	16
41	Jiujiang	32
42	Lhasa	10
43	Luoyang	38
44	Harbin	198
45	Nanchang	120
46	Nantong	151
47	Shantou	68
48	Guiyang	78
49	Taiyuan	106
50	Zhanjiang	49

Note: *The length of stay data for Tianjin city was replaced with the average across the 49 other cities because of a data error in the *Yearbook of China Tourism Statistics*.
Source: *Yearbook of China Tourism Statistics* (2017).

investment and foreign trade (Wu, 2003). Hangzhou city shows another modality that a city's business environment, residents' living habits and consumer behaviour can be important factors in attracting international companies to settle there. As the core city in the Yangtze River Delta region, Hangzhou relies on its highly developed e-commerce (Alibaba's hometown and headquarters location) and internet industries to attract a large number of international tourism firms (Wang et al., 2018). The city of Wuxi is different again. It is not

Table 11.3   Logged and normalized degree of PDI and BEI of 50 Chinese cities

ID	City	PDI		BEI	
		Logarithmic degree	Normalized degree	Logarithmic degree	Normalized degree
1	Shenzhen	17.131	1.000	6.858	0.747
2	Guangzhou	17.104	0.994	7.324	0.823
3	Shanghai	16.914	0.952	8.400	1.000
4	Beijing	16.701	0.905	7.623	0.873
5	Xiamen	16.260	0.807	5.366	0.502
6	Chongqing	16.076	0.767	6.433	0.677
7	Suzhou	15.726	0.689	6.949	0.762
8	Quanzhou	15.661	0.675	4.820	0.413
9	Wuhan	15.656	0.674	6.510	0.690
10	Fuzhou	15.647	0.672	5.361	0.502
11	Zhuhai	15.552	0.651	4.745	0.401
12	Guilin	15.469	0.632	3.850	0.254
13	Chengdu	15.459	0.630	6.457	0.681
14	Hangzhou	15.229	0.579	6.752	0.730
15	Xi'an	15.180	0.568	5.771	0.569
16	Qingdao	15.036	0.536	5.808	0.575
17	Huangshan	14.849	0.495	2.485	0.030
18	Tianjin	14.705	0.463	6.578	0.701
19	Nanjing	14.621	0.445	6.174	0.635
20	Dalian	14.601	0.440	5.927	0.594
21	Shenyang	14.591	0.438	5.652	0.549
22	Zhangzhou	14.585	0.437	3.367	0.175
23	Kunming	14.539	0.427	5.050	0.451
24	Ningbo	14.407	0.397	5.852	0.582
25	Yantai	14.341	0.383	4.644	0.384
26	Zhongshan	14.318	0.378	4.852	0.418
27	Changchun	14.245	0.362	4.970	0.437
28	Yanbian	14.212	0.354	2.890	0.096

ID	City	PDI		BEI	
		Logarithmic degree	Normalized degree	Logarithmic degree	Normalized degree
29	Wuxi	14.121	0.334	5.958	0.600
30	Wenzhou	14.033	0.315	4.828	0.414
31	Sanya	13.974	0.301	4.585	0.374
32	Nanning	13.916	0.289	4.718	0.396
33	Urumqi	13.907	0.287	3.497	0.196
34	Qinhuangdao	13.868	0.278	3.611	0.215
35	Zhengzhou	13.846	0.273	5.236	0.481
36	Weihai	13.810	0.265	3.611	0.215
37	Changsha	13.697	0.240	5.447	0.516
38	Jinan	13.592	0.217	5.165	0.469
39	Hefei	13.533	0.204	5.193	0.474
40	Lhasa	13.304	0.153	2.303	0.000
41	Luoyang	13.302	0.153	3.638	0.219
42	Jiujiang	13.280	0.148	3.466	0.191
43	Chengde	13.234	0.138	2.773	0.077
44	Nantong	13.138	0.117	5.017	0.445
45	Shantou	13.117	0.112	4.220	0.314
46	Harbin	13.092	0.106	5.288	0.490
47	Nanchang	13.044	0.096	4.787	0.408
48	Taiyuan	12.924	0.069	4.663	0.387
49	Guiyang	12.814	0.045	4.357	0.337
50	Zhanjiang	12.612	0.000	3.892	0.261
	Standard deviation	1.165	0.258	1.337	0.219
	Mean	14.499	0.418	5.074	0.455

Note: PDI and BEI values range from 0 to 1, with 1 indicating most internationalization and 0 least internationalization. For example, Zhanjiang has a total absolute value of PDI 300,000 and Lhasa's BEI value is 10. Because they both position at the bottom among 50 cities, the normalized measure for both cities is 0 for PDI and BEI, respectively.

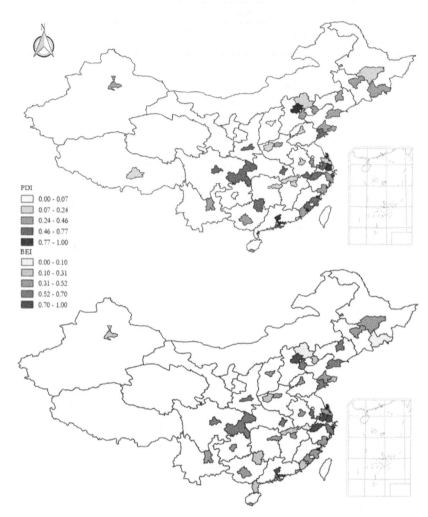

Figure 11.1   Maps of logged and normalized degree of PDI and BEI of 50
Chinese cities

that rich in natural and cultural resources (Zhang et al., 2005), but the city has
been designated by the central government as a micro-electronics industrial
base since 1983 and has shared the economic spillover impacts of Shanghai to
become the main preferred city for international tourism enterprises to settle
in (Chou et al., 2014). The city of Harbin was the first city established after
the liberation of China, featuring the largest land area and highest latitude of

all Chinese cities (Xie et al., 2016). The city is famous for its ice, snow and ski travel in winter, attracting millions of visitors every year (Wang et al., 2013). However, compared with its tourism achievements, which have been attracting more attention recently, Harbin, as the cradle of heavy industry in China, has been suffering during the transition to a market economy. For the last ten years, the transition is painfully challenged by the strong socialist legacies of SOEs. The new initiatives of Harbin, based on local endowments, cold climate and geolocation, demonstrate fast revitalization in its international business environment (Xie et al., 2016), which in time could benefit the initiatives for attracting international tourism business to the city of Harbin.

Furthermore, Huangshan, Guilin and Lhasa's individual standardized residual is below –1.8, which means they attract many more international tourists compared with their embeddedness in the networks of international tourist firms. The internationalization of tourists in these cities is significantly better than its commercial internationalization. Guilin and Huangshan are famous international tourist destinations in China and attract a large number of international tourists every year (Ma and Hassink, 2014; Qian et al., 2016). Both cities have similar tourism development policies that are designed to support the development of local small and medium-sized tourism enterprises instead of giving market opportunities to international tourism companies. In addition, domestic tourism development in both cities is regarded as more important to local economic development than international tourism and enjoys a higher profile in both the local and provincial level of policy development (Xu, 1999; Polsa & Fan, 2011). In this sense, both cities are far from being favoured by international tourist firms. It is also worth mentioning that the city of Lhasa, with unique heritage sites, religious sites, traditional Tibetan yards, daily life and customs, and Tibetan medicines, is very popular for domestic and international tourists (Wu & Pearce, 2014). However, the procedures for international companies to locate in Lhasa are far more complex (Chen et al., 2018), so the number of international tourist companies in Lhasa is the lowest among the 50 Chinese cities.

Although there are diverse reasons why cities are international, some recurring patterns of Chinese cities as international tourism hubs can still be seen. In order to gauge these variations among cities, a typology is presented based on the degree of PDI and BEI of different cities. Table 11.4 compares individual cities' PDI and BEI. Individual cities are plotted with their scores on the tourism internationalization measures as coordinates. By centring on the point with natural-break values of PDI and BEI, Figure 11.4 is divided into four clusters (see also Table 11.5).

Table 11.4 Standardized residuals of PDI and BEL of 50 Chinese cities

City	Standardized residual	Value range
Shanghai	1.553	st.r ≥0.35
Tianjin	1.319	st.r ≥0.35
Harbin	1.258	st.r ≥0.35
Wuxi	1.143	st.r ≥0.35
Hangzhou	1.111	st.r ≥0.35
Nanjing	0.985	st.r ≥0.35
Changsha	0.956	st.r ≥0.35
Nantong	0.954	st.r ≥0.35
Suzhou	0.945	st.r ≥0.35
Beijing	0.914	st.r ≥0.35
Hefei	0.829	st.r ≥0.35
Ningbo	0.828	st.r ≥0.35
Nanchang	0.798	st.r ≥0.35
Taiyuan	0.766	st.r ≥0.35
Dalian	0.759	st.r ≥0.35
Jinan	0.757	st.r ≥0.35
Chengdu	0.653	st.r ≥0.35
Zhengzhou	0.639	st.r ≥0.35
Wuhan	0.563	st.r ≥0.35
Guiyang	0.544	st.r ≥0.35
Shenyang	0.498	st.r ≥0.35
Qingdao	0.325	st.r ∈ (−0.35,0.35)
Guangzhou	0.308	st.r ∈ (−0.35,0.35)
Zhanjiang	0.232	st.r ∈ (−0.35,0.35)
Xi'an	0.184	st.r ∈ (−0.35,0.35)
Shantou	0.179	st.r ∈ (−0.35,0.35)
Chongqing	0.177	st.r ∈ (−0.35,0.35)
Wenzhou	0.101	st.r ∈ (−0.35,0.35)

City	Standardized residual	Value range
Changchun	0.084	st.r $\in$ (-0.35,0.35)
Nanning	0.080	st.r $\in$ (-0.35,0.35)
Kunming	-0.053	st.r $\in$ (-0.35,0.35)
Zhongshan	-0.085	st.r $\in$ (-0.35,0.35)
Sanya	-0.094	st.r $\in$ (-0.35,0.35)
Shenzhen	-0.194	st.r $\in$ (-0.35,0.35)
Yantai	-0.304	st.r $\in$ (-0.35,0.35)
Luoyang	-0.533	st.r $\leq$ -0.35
Fuzhou	-0.565	st.r $\leq$ -0.35
Jiujiang	-0.688	st.r $\leq$ -0.35
Weihai	-0.929	st.r $\leq$ -0.35
Qinhuangdao	-0.971	st.r $\leq$ -0.35
Xiamen	-1.028	st.r $\leq$ -0.35
Zhuhai	-1.102	st.r $\leq$ -0.35
Quanzhou	-1.110	st.r $\leq$ -0.35
Urumqi	-1.112	st.r $\leq$ -0.35
Chengde	-1.340	st.r $\leq$ -0.35
Zhangzhou	-1.731	st.r $\leq$ -0.35
Lhasa	-1.854	st.r $\leq$ -0.35
Guilin	-1.921	st.r $\leq$ -0.35
Yanbian	-1.926	st.r $\leq$ -0.35
Huangshan	-2.790	st.r $\leq$ -0.35

Cluster 1

The formation of this cluster can primarily be understood within the context of regional economic disparities within China. Five coastal cities (Shanghai, Beijing, Guangzhou, Shenzhen and Suzhou) and one city in central China (Chongqing) have large values for both BEI and PDI. Although these cities differ considerably in terms of the structure of their economies, urban governance structures and natural endowments, they share a common performance in tourism internationalization. These similarities can be summarized as follows.

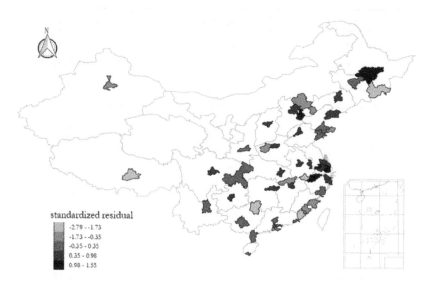

Figure 11.2   Map of standardized residuals of PDI and BEL of 50 Chinese
cities

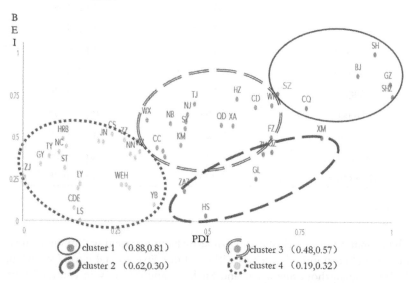

Note: The position of a Chinese city reflects the city's PDI (x-axis) and BEI (y-axis).

Figure 11.3   Clustering of 50 Chinese cities in terms of PDI and BEI
degree

Table 11.5   Clusters of 50 Chinese cities in terms of PDI and BEI degree

cluster	City
1	Shanghai, Beijing, Guangzhou, Shenzhen, Chongqing, Suzhou
2	Guilin, Huangshan, Quanzhou, Xiamen, Zhangzhou, Zhuhai
3	Changchun, Chengdu, Dalian, Fuzhou, Hangzhou, Kunming, Nanjing, Ningbo, Qingdao, Shenyang, Tianjin, Wuhan, Wuxi, Xi'an, Zhongshan, Yantai
4	Sanya, Changsha, Chengde, Guiyang, Harbin, Hefei, Jinan, Jiujiang, Lhasa, Luoyang, Nanchang, Nanning, Nantong, Qinhuangdao, Shantou, Taiyuan, Urumqi, Weihai, Wenzhou, Yanbian, Zhanjiang, Zhengzhou

According to data on total passenger traffic from the Civil Aviation Administration of China (CAAC), Beijing, Shanghai and Guangzhou were the top three major international airports in China in 2018. International airports in Shenzhen and Chongqing are also among the top 10 in China (ranked 5th and 9th, respectively). At the same time, the global network connectivity (GNC) of the advanced producer service (APS) industry of these cities is also ranked higher across Chinese cities (nationwide, Beijing ranked 2nd, Shanghai 3rd, Guangzhou 5th, Shenzhen 6th, Chongqing 12th and Suzhou 13th). In addition, most cities are either provincial-cities or provincial capitals. Shenzhen and Suzhou are beyond those groups, although they are still the second largest cities in their respective provinces. They both attract many international tourists and tourism enterprises because of their benefits from the spillover impacts of the great Shanghai region to a large extent.

Cluster 2

Urban regions in this cluster are associated with comparatively higher international tourist connections but lower business connections. Six southern located cities fall into this cluster. It is argued that the main process underlying this tourism internationalization profile is that of local international tourism policies and plans. Tourism is a major industry in most cities in this category. These cities have different responses to the rapidly developing international tourism market.

Some local governments' economic interests are more conservative. While attracting international tourists, they focus more on speeding up the development of local tourism enterprises, especially small and medium-sized ones. Examples are Guilin and Huangshan. Local authorities would not necessarily aim at attracting international tourism giants to participate in local tourism market competition and could well benefit the strategic significance of the dominance of local tourism enterprises (Xu, 1999; Polsa & Fan, 2011; Ma & Hassink, 2013). In some cities the international business environment is relatively poor and the local government has no energy or initiatives to improve the overall international business environment. They do not attach enough importance to international tourism enterprises in their policies. Xiamen and Quanzhou are good examples. Both cities have remarkable advantages in attracting international tourists because of their abundant coastal tourism resources and geographical locations adjacent to Taiwan (Xiao, 1997; Chen, 2010). Consequently, both city governments have weighed heavily on policies attracting international tourists. In comparison, there are few local strategies for improving the city's overall international business environment and overall level of internationalization (such as English penetration rate, etc.) (Yin et al., 2010; Li et al., 2016). Zhuhai city is another case. Located in the fast growing Pearl River Delta (PRD) region, it was one of the first four Special Economic Zones in China for economic-reform experiments set up in early 1980 (Sheng & Tang, 2013). National reform and opening up policies have brought a large number of foreign enterprises to the city. However, because its location is too close to the larger metropolitan city of Guangzhou, especially after the establishment of the Guangzhou–Zhuhai direct railway in recent years, it is much less likely to have advantages in attracting international tourism enterprises (Xu & Yeh, 2013).

Cluster 3

Cities in this group are associated with average BEI and PDI values. It is argued that the main process underlying this political profile is the political hierarchy of a city. Sixteen cities in this cluster are mainly coastal and central cities. Although the cities in this cluster are diversified in terms of economy, society and culture, they do share some common tourism internationalization dimensions. On the one hand, they are basically provincial capitals or sub provincial-cities (such as Changchun, Chengdu, Dalian, Fuzhou, Hangzhou, Kunming, Nanjing, Ningbo, Qingdao, Shenyang, Tianjin, Wuhan, Wuxi and Xi'an). On the other, in the process of tourism development, these cities, like other major cities in China, still focus on attracting domestic tourists. In turn, they encounter various challenges in attracting international tourists, such as the low English service level and low international traffic convenience. However, these cities have started trying to attract international tourists so their PDI performance has improved in recent years (Xu and Zhang, 2016). On the other hand, cities in this cluster are not the first cities to open up to the outside world (Howell, 1993), but, with the expansion of China's opening-up process, they are becoming the main cities attracting foreign investment after Beijing, Shanghai and Guangzhou. The central and provincial governments have given a lot of policy and financial support to these cities in this regard (Wei & Li, 2002). For example, since the 2000s, Chengdu's new political position as the largest international shipping centre in Western China makes the city stand out in attracting international tourist firms to settle there (Taylor et al., 2015). Nanjing is the capital city of Jiangsu province. In recent years, developing Nanjing into an outstanding global city has become a city-wide consensus (Yuan et al., 2016).

Cluster 4

There are 22 cities in this cluster, the most of all four clusters. The cities in the less developed western part of China and some of the less important cities in central China fall into this cluster, characterized by low levels of PDI and BEI indicators. Changsha, Hefei, Jinan, Luoyang, Nanchang, Taiyuan and Zhengzhou fall into this cluster. The level of tourism development in these cities is at the primary stage. The cities are more likely to benefit from new economic opportunities, such as the relocation of advanced manufacturing jobs from the east coast or state-initiated large-scale investment (Zhou, 2001; Mao & Yu, 2009; Zhang et al., 2010; Li, 2011; Liu, et al., 2015; Liu, Tian, Chen, & Guo, 2017). This would leave less growth potential for the tourism industry in these cities, giving rise to a more manufacturing-oriented economic pattern.

Conclusions

This chapter has introduced a new and more refined way of evaluating the tourism internationalization of a city. It has contributed to the current literature by calling for an acknowledgement that cities where key firms active in international tourism locate are co-driving the position of cities as international destinations. Our study clearly has its limitations, which at the same time leads to possible future avenues for research. This is a cross-sectional analysis, and an obvious extension of the research presented here would be a longitudinal analysis to gauge how internationalization of urban tourism in China changes over time. The study is nonetheless based on the Chinese context, which may limit its application outside China. Importantly, however, this does not imply that the generalization and application of the research is problematic in itself. There are countries with similar "historical stories" and

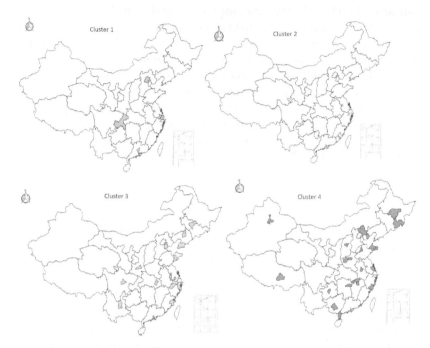

Figure 11.4   Maps of clusters of 50 Chinese cities in terms of PDI and BEI
degree

tourism development patterns, for instance in Central and Eastern Europe. The generalization and application of this research to differentiating business destination internationalization and product destination internationalization in those countries might be feasible. Furthermore, the research framework is not rigidly confined to the tourism sector. We expect that our study will also be applicable to other sectors featuring export orientation.

References

Arkaraprasertkul, N. (2016). *Locating Shanghai: Globalization, Heritage Industry, and the Political Economy of Urban Space in a Chinese Metropolis* (Doctoral dissertation).

Chen, C. M. (2010). Role of tourism in connecting Taiwan and China: Assessing tourists' perceptions of the Kinmen–Xiamen links. *Tourism Management, 31*(3), 421–424.

Chen, T., Lang, W., Chan, E., & Philipp, C. H. (2018). Lhasa: Urbanising China in the frontier regions. *Cities, 74*, 343–353.

Chou, T. L., Chang, J. Y., & Li, T. C. (2014). Government support, FDI clustering and semiconductor sustainability in China: Case studies of Shanghai, Suzhou and Wuxi in the Yangtze delta. *Sustainability*, 6(9), 5655–5681.

Cui, X. M., & Ryan, C. (2011). Perceptions of place, modernity and the impacts of tourism-differences among rural and urban residents of Ankang, China: A likelihood ratio analysis. *Tourism Management*, 32(3), 604–615.

Deng, T., Li, X., & Ma, M. (2017). Evaluating impact of air pollution on China's inbound tourism industry: A spatial econometric approach. *Asia Pacific Journal of Tourism Research*, 22(7), 771–780.

Derudder, B., Taylor, P. J., Hoyler, M., Ni, P., Liu, X., Zhao, M., & Witlox, F. (2013). Measurement and interpretation of connectivity of Chinese cities in world city network, 2010. *Chinese Geographical Science*, 23(3), 261–273.

Feng, X. (2011). *Regional Tourism Cooperation: Factors Influencing the Performance of Regional Tourism Cooperation in China*. Maastricht: Shaker Publishing.

Gaubatz, P. (2005). Globalization and the development of new central business districts in Beijing, Shanghai and Guangzhou. *Restructuring the Chinese City: Changing Society, Economy and Space*, 98–121.

Gorcheva, T. (2011). Measuring the internationalization of Bulgarian tourism and of "Bulgaria" business destination. *Tourism & Management Studies*, 1(1), 80–90.

Howell, J. (1993). *China Opens its Doors: The Politics of Economic Transition*. Lynne Rienner Publishers.

Li, R., Wang, Q., & Cheong, K. C. (2016). Quanzhou: Reclaiming a glorious past. *Cities*, 50, 168–179.

Li, X. (2011). The analysis on the factors of developing Zhengzhou city into a regional center of international logistics. In *International Conference on Advances in Education and Management* (pp. 586–591). Berlin, Heidelberg: Springer.

Liang, Z., & Hui, T. (2016). Residents' quality of life and attitudes toward tourism development in China. *Tourism Management*, 56–67.

Liu, J., Nijkamp, P., & Lin, D. (2017). Urban–rural imbalance and tourism-led growth in China. *Annals of Tourism Research*, 24–36.

Liu, W., Tian, J., Chen, L., & Guo, Y. (2017). Temporal and spatial characteristics of lead emissions from the lead-acid battery manufacturing industry in China. *Environmental Pollution*, 220, 696–703.

Liu, X., Derudder, B., & Wu, K. (2015). Measuring polycentric urban development in China: An intercity transportation network perspective. *Regional Studies*, 50(8), 1302–1315.

Ma, M., & Hassink, R. (2013). Path dependence and tourism area development: The case of Guilin, China. *Tourism Geographies*, 16(4), 580–597.

Mao, M., & Yu, X. (2009). The construction of the Chengdu-Chongqing logistics corridor and its characteristics analysis. In *Logistics: The Emerging Frontiers of Transportation and Development in China* (pp. 813–820). Reston, VA: American Society of Civil Engineers.

Peng, J., & Xiao, H. (2018). How does smog influence domestic tourism in China? A case study of Beijing. *Asia Pacific Journal of Tourism Research*, 23(12), 1115–1128.

Polsa, P., & Fan, X. (2011). Globalization of local retailing: Threat or opportunity? The case of food retailing in Guilin, China. *Journal of Macromarketing*, 31(3), 291–311.

Qian, C., Sasaki, N., Shivakoti, G., & Zhang, Y. (2016). Effective governance in tourism development – An analysis of local perception in the Huangshan mountain area. *Tourism Management Perspectives*, 20, 112–123.

Sheng, N., & Tang, U. W. (2013). Zhuhai. *Cities*, 32, 70–79.

Su, R., Bramwell, B., & Whalley, P. (2017). Cultural political economy and urban heritage tourism. *Annals of Tourism Research*, 30–40.

Sun, Y. (2007). Marginal economic impacts of inbound tourism to Taiwan and policy evaluation. *Asia Pacific Journal of Tourism Research*, 10(3), 309–327.

Taylor, P., Derudder, B., Hoyler, M., Ni, P., & Witlox, F. (2014). City-dyad analyses of China's integration into the world city network. *Urban Studies*, 51(5), 868–882.

Taylor, P., Ni, P., & Liu, K. (2015). *Global Research of Cities: A Case of Chengdu.* Springer.

Valadkhani, A., & Omahony, B. (2018). Identifying structural changes and regime switching in growing and declining inbound tourism markets in Australia. *Current Issues in Tourism*, 21(3), 277–300.

Wang, J., Huang, P., Zhao, H., Zhang, Z., Zhao, B., & Lee, D. L. (2018). Billion-scale commodity embedding for e-commerce recommendation in Alibaba. In *Proceedings of the 24th ACM SIGKDD International Conference on Knowledge Discovery & Data Mining* (pp. 839–848).

Wang, Y., & Bramwell, B. (2012). Heritage protection and tourism development priorities in Hangzhou, China: A political economy and governance perspective. *Tourism Management*, 33(4), 988–998.

Wang, Y., Li, G., & Bai, X. (2013). A residential survey on urban tourism impacts in Harbin. In *Urban Tourism in China* (pp. 87–100). Routledge.

Wei, Y. D., & Li, W. (2002). Reforms, globalization, and urban growth in China: The case of Hangzhou. *Eurasian Geography and Economics*, 43(6), 459–475.

Welch, L. S., & Luostarinen, R. (1988). Internationalization: Evolution of a concept. *Journal of General Management*, 14(2), 34–55.

Wu, F. (2003). Globalization, place promotion and urban development in Shanghai. *Journal of Urban Affairs*, 25(1), 55–78.

Wu, J. (2011). Globalization and emerging office and commercial landscapes in Shanghai. *Urban Geography*, 32(4), 511–530.

Wu, M. Y., & Pearce, P. L. (2014). Asset-based community development as applied to tourism in Tibet. *Tourism Geographies*, 16(3), 438–456.

Xiao, H. (1997). Tourism and leisure in China: A tale of two cities. *Annals of Tourism Research*, 24(2), 357–370.

Xiao, H. (2006). The discourse of power: Deng Xiaoping and tourism development in China. *Tourism Management*, 27(5), 803–814.

Xie, L., Yang, Z., Cai, J., Cheng, Z., Wen, T., & Song, T. (2016). Harbin: A rust belt city revival from its strategic position. *Cities*, 58, 26–38.

Xu, G. (1999). Socio-economic impacts of domestic tourism in China: Case studies in Guilin, Suzhou and Beidaihe. *Tourism Geographies*, 1(2), 204–218.

Xu, J., & Yeh, A. G. (2013). Interjurisdictional cooperation through bargaining: The case of the Guangzhou–Zhuhai railway in the Pearl River Delta, China. *The China Quarterly*, 213, 130–151.

Xu, Z., & Zhang, J. (2016). Antecedents and consequences of place attachment: A comparison of Chinese and Western urban tourists in Hangzhou, China. *Journal of Destination Marketing & Management*, 5(2), 86–96.

Yearbook of China Tourism Statistics (2017). China Tourism Press, Beijing.

Yin, K., Li, X., Zhang, G., & Xiao, L. (2010). Analysis of socio-economic driving forces on built-up area expansion in Xiamen. *International Journal of Sustainable Development & World Ecology*, 17(4), 279–284.

Yuan, F., Gao, J., & Wu, J. (2016). Nanjing-an ancient city rising in transitional China. *Cities*, 50, 82–92.

Yusuf, S., & Wu, W. (2002). Pathways to a world city: Shanghai rising in an era of globalisation. *Urban Studies, 39*(7), 1213–1240.

Zhang, D., Aunan, K., Seip, H. M., Larssen, S., Liu, J., & Zhang, D. (2010). The assessment of health damage caused by air pollution and its implication for policy making in Taiyuan, Shanxi, China. *Energy Policy, 38*(1), 491–502.

Zhang, L. C., Zhu, T. M., & Yao, S. M. (2005). Evolvement of urban spatial structure and main drives in Wuxi, China. *Chinese Geographical Science, 15*(4), 309–314.

Zhang, Y., Xu, J., & Zhuang, P. (2011). The spatial relationship of tourist distribution in Chinese cities. *Tourism Geographies, 13*(1), 75–90.

Zhou, G. (2001). The international and internal experience of regional economic integration and its enlightenment to the economic integration of Changsha-Zhuzhou-Xiangtan. *World Regional Studies, 1.*

PART III

Sustainable tourism development policies in cities

12 Overtourism – identifying the underlying causes and tensions in European tourism destinations

Ko Koens and Jeroen Klijs

Introduction

Tourism in cities is booming[1] both with regard to leisure and to business travel. Not only are more and more people travelling anyway, but urban tourism is growing even faster than other types of tourism destinations (UNWTO, 2018). The relatively uncontrolled growth does come with a price though, and 'overtourism' is now a commonly used term both in practice and among academics. After years of relative neglect – the topic was discussed extensively over 40 years ago (see, for example, Butler, 1980; Canestrelli and Costa, 1991; Doxey, 1975) – since 2018 a large number of individual case studies and multiple books on the topic have now been published (see, for example, Milano et al., 2019a; Pechlaner et al., 2019). Indeed, it has even been argued that the emphasis on overtourism in academia has been so all-encompassing in recent years that other highly important debates, such as the ways in which cities need to prepare for the impact of climate change, have remained rather neglected (Aall and Koens, 2019).

Besides academic work, several practice-oriented reports have been produced that focus on the ways in which overtourism can be managed (UNWTO, 2018, 2019; WTTC, 2017). Such work has proven valuable in that it has highlighted different aspects of overtourism but has been criticized for being focused on mitigating the direct, and often short-term, effects of overtourism, rather than taking a more long-term perspective and dealing with underlying causes and issues (Aall et al., 2015; Peeters et al., 2018). In addition, they pay only limited attention to the idea that overtourism differs by locality and that what works in one city may not work in another. Managing the complex interactions of different groups of residents and tourists, whose interests do not necessarily align, is highly challenging and context-dependent (Ashworth and Page, 2011).

This includes not just elements related to tourism (e.g. the number of visitors, the types of visitors, the number of offerings), but also the characteristics of the host city and the issues outside of tourism that a city is facing (Koens et al., 2018).

Rather than focusing on creating a list of management solutions, it may be more useful to try to better understand different tensions that underlie tourism in different localities. In this chapter, which is based on practice-oriented work in European cities, we compare and contrast tensions that can be observed in relation to tourism development in these cities. In doing so, we provide insights into the complexity of tourism as well as the differing impacts of different tourism activities between and within cites. It is argued that to fully understand the impacts of tourism and to achieve sustainable urban development, it is necessary to better delineate the different ways in which tourism interacts with local developments, be it economically, socially or environmentally.

How does tourism interact with the local environment?

Cites are highly dynamic, complex, multifunctional environments where different stakeholders come together to live, work and spend their leisure time. The fact that cities have been designed to facilitate a great number of different users has made them increasingly attractive for tourists in recent years. Not only do cities offer a wide range of tourism-specific activities (e.g. sites and attractions), but they are well-suited to allow visitors to enjoy what may be tentatively called tourism of everyday life, where urban everyday life can "turn into a matter of tourist interest" and residents can enjoy tourist experiences (Stors et al., 2019, pp. 1–2). Such developments have led to increased contact between residents and visitors, as they share urban facilities, infrastructure and services and visit the same festivals and events. The increased contact between residents and visitors and the additional strain that tourism puts on facilities that were initially developed mainly for local use have been argued to be potential reasons for the rise of the overtourism phenomenon (Koens et al., 2018). Indeed, negative perceptions with regard to tourism are particularly prominent in spaces where the primary function used to be domestic use, but where now tourism activities are starting to compete with such use (McKercher et al., 2015).

Whilst the discussion on overtourism has largely been dominated by the negative social impacts, it is important to realize that tourism development also impacts on the quality of the natural and built environment in cities.

Regarding the former, in cities tourism, mobility itself leads to air pollution, but tourists also contribute to energy use and waste. In areas where drought is an issue, excessive water usage is a potential problem, particularly when tourism increases water use excessively, either because of direct use by tourists, or because of evaporation of water through outdoor pools (Becken, 2014; Yoon et al., 2018). On a global level, the contribution of city tourism should not be underestimated and requires attention (Aall and Koens, 2019; Peeters et al., 2018). Turning to the impact of tourism on the built environment, it was already noted in the 1990s that tourism can endanger a city's built and cultural heritage and this continues to be an issue in various European cites (García-Hernández et al., 2017; Van den Berg et al., 1995; Van Der Borg, 1992).

Even the contribution to local economic development, which is often used as an argument in favour of tourism growth, is not clear cut. Whilst it is true that tourism often provides economic benefits on a city level, these benefits are not necessarily shared equitably among different groups of residents (Colomb et al., 2016; Koens and Thomas, 2016; Richter, 2010). A clear example of this can be observed within the context of online short-term rental services (e.g. Airbnb, Homeaway). These benefit existing house-owners and real-estate investors, whilst other groups are faced with rising rents and potentially even displacement (Barron et al., 2019; Cócola-Gant and Gago, 2019). Such perceived injustice with regard to the sharing of benefits is one of the drivers behind the social movements that criticize excessive tourism development (Milano et al., 2019b).

In trying to prevent overtourism and develop tourism more sustainably, two strands of thought have started to gain interest. One deals with the use of Smart technology to manage overtourism. Currently such solutions focus mainly on monitoring tourist behaviour (e.g. using apps and city cards) and using this information to redistribute tourists to less crowded areas (Pinke-Sziva et al., 2019; Skeli and Schmid, 2019). Smart solutions represent a challenge though, in that they require cooperation and exchange between a variety of sources (Fontanari and Berger-Risthaus, 2019). Also, getting people to use smart solutions is not easy, as city governments already report being overloaded with smart apps and tools that they need to promote. Given that the issue is so complex, smart technology alone will not solve overtourism (Koens et al., 2018). This leads to the second strand of thought, which argues that to solve overtourism it is important to create a common strategic vision for destinations, which stakeholders can rally behind (Chettiparamb and Thomas, 2012). Cities have started to experiment with more open and participatory planning of tourism. Examples of this include dialogues with residents and other stakeholders as to what type of tourism they are most comfortable with and which type of tourism they would like to avoid (Lammers et al., 2019; UNWTO, 2018). An issue here is that it has proven to be highly difficult to bring together different stakeholders, who often do not know each other and who may have different interests and/or opposing perspectives on the causes of and solutions for overtourism. To prevent the overtourism debate from developing into a binary pro–against debate, it is necessary to frame the debate on tourism impacts in different ways, which may include looking at context-specific solutions for this highly complex issue (Boom et al., 2021).

Using a smart city hospitality framework for analysing (over)tourism

A way to deal with the complexity is to utilize the Smart City Hospitality Framework, which was developed to support a meaningful discussion and develop a context-specific strategy towards a type of tourism that contributes to a city-wide sustainability transition (Koens et al., 2019). The framework seeks to provide an integral perspective on tourism development, city planning and sustainable development. It is set up to link the tourism system with wider issues and developments and interprets sustainable urban tourism as "tourism that supports a transition of the city as a whole towards being more sustainable in every sense of the word" (Melissen and Koens, 2019, p. 9). As interventions need to go beyond addressing the short-term impacts (Aall et al., 2015), the emphasis is on working towards the long-term ability of the city as a whole to become more resilient and successful in reacting and adapting to future developments (Koens et al., 2019).

To provide a well-rounded perspective, the framework merges the concepts of sustainable development and city hospitality. Sustainable development is conceptualized using an adapted version of the triple bottom line (Wise, 2016): natural viability, equitability and economic wealth. Natural viability relates to the quality of the natural environment, but also to longer term issues such as climate change. Economic wealth is about the financial benefits earned via tourism while equitability concerns the distribution of benefits and costs of tourism among stakeholders. City hospitality relates to the city acting as a good "host" to all of its "guests", be they residents, tourists, businesses and entrepreneurs or NGOs, etc. It consists of liveability, experience quality and smart hospitality. Liveability is the extent to which the city provides residents *and* all other stakeholders (including commuters, local business owners and tourists) with a good place to live and work. Experience quality deals with the extent to which the city helps fulfil the experience needs and wishes from

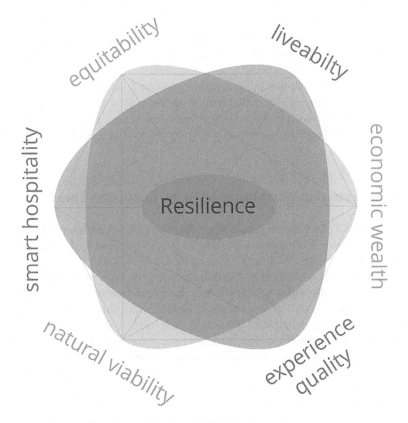

Figure 12.1   The Smart City Hospitality framework

a leisure perspective for visitors *and* other stakeholders, including residents. Both concepts are founded on the idea that city users are diverse and their roles are interchangeable (i.e. a resident may act as a tourist at some point and vice versa). To develop tourism that contributes to a city becoming (more) sustainable, it needs to account for the perspectives and interests of the stakeholders that shape the city *together*. Thus, smart hospitality is defined as the extent to which stakeholders take on their joint responsibility in shaping the tourism system in the city. This means that the term "smart" is not necessarily related to investments in IT infrastructure supporting data collection, but rather to the extent to which stakeholders achieve ownership and impact on the development of tourism. Technology can help with this, but it is a means, rather than a goal itself (Koens et al., 2019; Melissen and Koens, 2019).

A key element of the framework is the relations between these individual elements. More specifically, it is argued that there are potential tensions between the different elements. Whilst it is possible that actions help strengthen multiple elements of the framework in an integral way (e.g. reducing waste is likely to improve both liveability and experience quality), often this is not the case (e.g. reducing air pollution by limiting car and coach access can hinder liveability and experience quality). The framework provides a diversity of lenses to frame specific tensions that fit within a local context and, as a result, support a contextualized analysis of impacts and intervention strategies of city tourism.

Tensions and opportunities in three European cities

The empirical part of this research brings together insights from several studies on (over)tourism in European cities that have been performed over the course of the last five years. Within the studies, desk research into the situation of tourism in cities was combined with qualitative research among key stakeholders (e.g. policymakers, politicians, industry, residents, NGOs). For this chapter we succinctly introduce the role of tourism in three cities in Europe (Gothenburg, Darmstadt and Warsaw), each with a different relation to tourism. A deliberate choice was made here not to focus on the major tourism cities that are commonly associated with overtourism, to highlight how overtourism, or elements thereof, can also be observed in other city destinations. For a future research agenda on city tourism, it is important to also take note of such cities, as visitor pressure in these cities is likely to rise as well due to the growth of global tourism numbers.

Gothenburg

Gothenburg is the second-largest city in Sweden with 580,000 inhabitants. Its port is the largest in the Nordic countries and, as such, the city is seen as one of the gateways to Scandinavia and the Baltic states. The city has a respectable leisure/tourism industry, but is also an important business tourism destination with multiple conferences being organized in the city each year. In addition, the city regularly hosts international events (e.g. Women's Handball World Cup). Annually, the city provides around 5 million commercial overnight stays, of which about 23% are for international visitors. The city seeks to grow tourism strongly in the next ten years. What is particularly interesting in Gothenburg is that the city has seats on the board of commercial entities such as the harbour (e.g. boards of directors), which makes it easier for them to engage with business stakeholders.

Looking at the experience of tourism in the city, overtourism is not (yet) seen as a key issue, even when interviewees do note that it is getting busier in the city and some worry about the expected strong growth in the coming years. However, by using the Smart City Hospitality framework, a more precise indication can be given with regards to the perceived issues in the city. In particular, the focus in Gothenburg was on the ways in which tourists contributed to greater inequality in the city and the emphasis on economic wealth. With regard to the former, multiple interviewees noticed that the city is becoming less hospitable for economically weaker groups in society. This included refugees, who came to the city in recent years, but also other groups who live in poorer neighbourhoods on the outskirts of the city. These issues are not directly related to tourism and were already perceived as problematic long before the overtourism debate. However, it has meant that tourism developments that could contribute to greater inequality (e.g. Airbnb), but also renewal of the city centre, were singled out as problematic. Also, in spite of the government's presence and the well-developed Swedish social-democratic system, interviewees remained critical of the growth imperative that was seen as underlying tourism development and the impact it could have on citizen engagement (smart hospitality). As one civil servant in the city mentioned:

> [I]n every city, you say that 'we have to be successful compared to Amsterdam, compared to Valencia'. Therefore, we must do this because otherwise we cannot attract the tourists, and the tourists are not the poor people, they are the people with money and they like this. And, therefore, we must sort of construct, design the central city of Gothenburg so that it fits their needs and demands. [...] That means that you have transferred democratic power away from the people towards plutocratic money interests. (Interview G3)

Besides these issues, there is a worry about air travel and the impact it has on the environment. Interviewees noted that they believe it is inevitable that most international travellers come by plane, due to their geographical location. However, as a harbour city, there is an awareness, at least among some, that, in the long run, rising water levels can threaten the city and that excessive growth of air travel is undesirable but unavoidable unless wider city policies, also beyond tourism, drastically change.

Darmstadt

The historic city of Darmstadt, located in the Southwest of Germany, is relatively small with 150,000 residents. In 2019, the city received around 350,000 visitors, most of whom were day-visitors. The city is currently seeking to gain UNESCO world heritage status for the Mathildenhöhe area, which features a large number of Jugendstil buildings and used to house the Darmstadt artists' colony. The city prides itself on being a "city of science" and the influence of the local university is visible in that a relatively large number of international students can be found in the city. If we look at the role of tourism in the city, on the whole stakeholders do not see it suffering from overtourism. Indeed, hardly any issues were mentioned when it comes to disturbances to local life or nature. Short-term rental services were seen more as a positive opportunity for residents and the world heritage bid has increased the pride that residents felt. In addition, the presence of tourists was said to increase liveliness in the city. There is a perception of overcrowding near places of touristic interest, which is particularly visible during busy days in the weekend, but, fitting with its self-perception of having an image of science and technology, it was argued that "technological" solutions will help solve this.

Whilst this suggests there are hardly any issues, tensions could be observed when it comes to liveability and experience quality. Residents are critical of the dominance of the UNESCO World Heritage when it comes to tourism, as well as the positive spin that is generated related to this. They argue that the World Heritage status has become a prestige project and attention should also be given to other important economic aspects of life (e.g. the university as a big employer and contributor of internationalization). It was also argued that the bid may lead to more tourism-specific infrastructure at the expense of infrastructure that is required by residents and other local stakeholders. When trying to engage, some feel their interests will never be considered. As one hotel owner argued: "The aim is to involve the stakeholder groups not in order to give them decision making power, but to implement politicians' interests and needs in decision making" (Interview D8). It is important to realize that this critical view of citizen engagement did not arise out of the world heritage discussion, but instead this discussion provided a focal point for such a perspective. With this, the Darmstadt case serves to show how tourism can make underlying issues visible. At the same time, it can act as a warning that even when tourism is perceived as very positive, there is always the danger of (groups of) stakeholders feeling excluded.

Warsaw

After World War II, a meticulous restoration and reconstruction of Warsaw's old town led to the inclusion of its historical centre in the World Heritage Sites (UNESCO World Heritage Centre, 2018). The historical centre, with its traditional architecture, monuments, churches and narrow streets with colourful townhouses, represents the main tourist offer and the most frequent reason for visiting (Warsaw Tourist Office, 2017). In the last decades, Warsaw has attracted an increasing number of tourists (Coffey, 2017) whereby, unlike other eastern EU destinations, domestic tourism outweighs international tourism.

Tourism in Warsaw is mainly concentrated in the April–October period and in the historical centre. Despite the important residential function of the old town, more than 80% of the service facilities are tourism-related (Derek, 2018). Even though no hotel accommodation is offered in the old town, over 100 private apartments are now available for tourism rental. The majority of listings are from commercial enterprises rather than home sharing (Gyódi, 2019). The growing presence of online rentals increases accommodation prices, causing negative sentiments towards tourism among residents (Derek, 2018). Such feelings were reinforced by the progressive displacements of local-oriented shops and facilities (Pawlikowska-Piechotka & Ostrowska-Tryzno, 2015). Tourism has also led to "visible signs of the physical damage at historic properties: wear and tear, litter and pollution, vandalism" and "throngs of people filling the narrow streets and their sometimes antisocial behaviour, or noise they make until the early hours" (Pawlikowska-Piechotka & Ostrowska-Tryzno, 2015).

The local community would like to see tourism development controlled. Nevertheless, there is a low level of confidence in the real intention of the local government in involving residents (Pawlikowska-Piechotka & Ostrowska-Tryzno, 2015). For example, in 2010, the Warsaw City Council Office held a series of consulting meetings with the local community regarding the management of the old town, but very few people participated (Pawlikowska-Piechotka & Ostrowska-Tryzno, 2015). This mistrust might be related to the ineffectiveness of the local authorities' tourism management system, with overlapping competences among different units and insufficient coordination, which has resulted in generalist policies rather than specific actionable plans (Best Place Institute, 2017).

The case of Warsaw highlights how tensions between liveability, natural viability and experience quality appear to have been heightened by the short-term rental sector, indicating that technological advancements can heighten existing tensions rather than support sustainable tourism development. In addition, it provides an example of the difficulties that municipalities may face when trying to find "smart hospitality" solutions to overcome the sentiment of people not being taken seriously in policy design. Simply organizing consulting meetings is insufficient to stimulate citizen engagement, particularly when there is a level of distrust towards government. Instead, mobilizing stakeholders is a complex process that requires trust, as well as context-specific solutions (Healey, 2002), which, at the moment, may be lacking in Warsaw.

Conclusion and discussion

Overtourism is increasingly used as a catch-all word to highlight a wide range of issues ascribed to excessive tourism development. This has made the term less suitable for analysing what are the most important issues in individual cities, or parts thereof. By using the Smart City Hospitality framework, we have been able to look more specifically at individual issues in three cities, which are not commonly associated with the overtourism debate. Doing so has helped explicate the difficulties of achieving sustainable tourism. More specifically, it has made clear how the problematic relationship between tourism and the live-ability of cities for local stakeholders, as well as the lack of equality with regard to the distribution of benefits and disadvantages, harm the sustainability of urban tourism development.

Looking at individual cities, it is striking that even in cities not (yet) seen as suffering from overtourism, in certain aspects disturbance is already visible, and that issues are context-specific and differ by city, and even between different parts of the city. The differences between perceived issues in different localities suggest a need for more specific guidance than general lists of possible policy measures. More elaborate descriptions of policy measures and the ways in which they work are already more useful, but this work often remains limited to single case studies, which makes it more difficult to appreciate why certain measures work in one locality and not elsewhere. There is a need to identify the conditions under which measures are or are not likely to be successful.

With regard to this, on a theoretical perspective, the current research also demonstrates that in all three cities an underlying problem is the difficulty for stakeholders to engage with each other. Results highlight the disillusionment of people with the extent to which their voice is heard and taken seriously as well as a lack of trust between stakeholders, both of which may hinder effective strategic measures to cope with the negative impacts of tourism that go beyond "sticking plasters" on the current tourism system. Whilst this is not a new finding (see, for example, Ashley and Wolmer, 2003; Boom et al., 2021; Jordan et al., 2013; Pforr and Brueckner, 2016), it is one that continues to warrant further critical investigation.

A framework like the one put forward in the current research can be used to investigate tensions between different elements that determine the hospitality of a city to its users, or identify different ways of framing the (over)tourism debate (Boom et al., 2021). However, in itself, it does little to support stakeholders to align their thinking on these issues. To do so requires work on a smaller scale, which investigates more closely what are the specific underlying causes of tensions, including the different perspectives of stakeholders. Concepts such as community-participation and co-creation were used regularly in the cities, but did not always result in bringing stakeholders together successfully. While cities are experimenting with new forms of engagement, such as serious gaming (see, for example, Koens et al., in revision), more experimentation is needed.

To truly allow tourism to transition into becoming more sustainable, it may be necessary to stimulate transformations of the wider socio-spatial systems that tourism operates in. In the urban planning and innovation studies there is a burgeoning literature on this matter (e.g. Grin et al., 2010; Loorbach and Shiroyama, 2016), but this work is only slowly developing within the tourism literature (Gössling et al., 2012; Koens et al., 2019). A potentially useful avenue for future research on this matter lies with the development of tourism living labs, which are being set up and developed as places of co-creation and knowledge sharing (Gerritsma, 2019). Also interesting as a future avenue for research is the debate on degrowth in tourism, which engages with the fundamental principles of tourism and the seemingly inevitable drive towards increasing visitor numbers (Fletcher et al., 2019; Milano et al., 2019b).

Note

1 Or this was at least the case before the COVID-19 pandemic, when this article was written.

References

Aall, C., Dodds, R., Sælensminde, I., and Brendehaug, E., 2015. Introducing the concept of environmental policy integration into the discourse on sustainable tourism: A way to improve policymaking and implementation? *Journal of Sustainable Tourism*, 23, 977–989. https://doi.org/10.1080/09669582.2015.1032300

Aall, C., and Koens, K., 2019. The discourse on sustainable urban tourism: The need for discussing more than overtourism. *Sustainability*, 11, 4228. https://doi.org/10.3390/su11154228

Ashley, C., and Wolmer, W., 2003. Transforming or tinkering? New forms of engagement between communities and the private sector in tourism and forestry in southern Africa; sustainable livelihoods in Southern Africa. Research Paper 18. Institute of Development Studies, Brighton.

Ashworth, G.J., and Page, S.J., 2011. Urban tourism research: Recent progress and current paradoxes. *Tourism Management*, 32, 1–15. https://doi.org/10.1016/j .tourman.2010.02.002

Barron, K., Kung, E., and Proserpio, D., 2019. Research: When Airbnb listings in a city increase, so do rent prices. *Harvard Business Review*, April.

Becken, S., 2014. Water equity – Contrasting tourism water use with that of the local community. *Water Resources and Industry*, 7–8, 9–22. https://doi.org/10.1016/j.wri .2014.09.002

Best Place Institute, 2017. Diagnosis of the tourism status in the City of Warsaw in 2017. Retrieved from http://warsawtour.pl/wp-content/uploads/2018/04/Diagnosis-of-the -tourism-status-in-the-City-of-Warsaw.-Summary.pdf

Boom, S., Weijschede, J., Melissen, F., Koens, K., and Mayer, I., 2021. Identifying stakeholder perspectives and worldviews on sustainable urban tourism development using a Q-sort methodology. *Current Issues in Tourism*, 24(4), 520–535. https://doi .org/10.1080/13683500.2020.1722076

Butler, R., 1980. The concept of a tourist area cycle of evolution: Implications for management of resources. *Canadian Geographer/Géographe Canadien*, 24, 5–12.

Canestrelli, E., and Costa, P., 1991. Tourist carrying capacity: A fuzzy approach. *Annals of Tourism Research*, 18, 295–311. https://doi.org/10.1016/0160-7383(91)90010-9

Chettiparamb, A., and Thomas, H., 2012. Tourism and spatial planning. *Journal of Policy Research in Tourism, Leisure and Events*, 4, 215–220.

Cócola-Gant, A., and Gago, A., 2019. Airbnb, buy-to-let investment and tourism-driven displacement: A case study in Lisbon. *Environmental Planning A: Economy and Space* 0308518X19869012. https://doi.org/10.1177/0308518X19869012

Coffey, H., 2017. The most overcrowded tourist destinations. Retrieved July 23, 2018, from https://www.independent.co.uk/travel/news-and-advice/most-overcrowded -tourist-destinations-amsterdam-rome-venice-warsaw-dubrovnik-a8108096.html

Colomb, C., Novy, J., and Novy, J., 2016. *Protest and Resistance in the Tourist City*. Routledge. https://doi.org/10.4324/9781315719306

Derek M., 2018, Spatial structure of tourism in a city after transition: The case of Warsaw, Poland. In: D.K. Müller and M. Więckowski (Eds.), *Tourism in Transitions. Recovering Decline, Managing Change*. Springer, pp. 157–171.

Doxey, G.V., 1975. A causation theory of visitor-resident irritants: methodology and research inference. In: *Travel and Tourism Research Associations Sixth Annual Conference Proceedings*. San Diego, pp. 195–198.

Fletcher, R., Mas, I.M., Blanco-Romero, A., and Blázquez-Salom, M., 2019. Tourism and degrowth: an emerging agenda for research and praxis. *Journal of Sustainable Tourism*, 27, 1745–1763. https://doi.org/10.1080/09669582.2019.1679822

Fontanari, M., and Berger-Risthaus, B., 2019. Problem and solution awareness in overtourism: A delphi study. In: H. Pechlaner, E. Innerhofer, and G. Erschbamer (Eds.), *Overtourism, Tourism Management and Solutions*. London: Routledge.

García-Hernández, M., de la Calle-Vaquero, M., Yubero, C., García-Hernández, M., de la Calle-Vaquero, M., and Yubero, C., 2017. Cultural heritage and urban tourism: Historic City centres under pressure. *Sustainability*, 9, 1346. https://doi.org/10.3390/ su9081346

Gerritsma, R., 2019. Overcrowded Amsterdam: Striving for a balance between trade, tolerance and tourism. In: C. Milano, J.M. Cheer, and M. Novelli (Eds.), *Overtourism: Excesses, Discontents and Measures in Travel and Tourism*. Wallingford: CABI, pp. 125–147. https://doi.org/10.1079/9781786399823.0125

Gössling, S., Hall, C.M., Ekström, F., Engeset, A.B., and Aall, C., 2012. Transition management: A tool for implementing sustainable tourism scenarios? *Journal of Sustainable Tourism*, 20, 899–916. https://doi.org/10.1080/09669582.2012.699062

Grin, J., Rotmans, J., and Schot, J., 2010. *Transitions to Sustainable Development: New Directions in the Study of Long Term Transformative Change*. Routledge.

Gyódi, K., 2019. Airbnb in European cities: Business as usual or true sharing economy? *Journal of Cleaner Production*, 221, 536–551. https://doi.org/10.1016/j.jclepro.2019.02.221

Healey, P., 2002. On creating the "city" as a collective resource. *Urban Studies*, 39, 1777–1792. https://doi.org/10.1080/0042098022000002957

Jordan, E.J., Vogt, C.A., Kruger, L.E., and Grewe, N., 2013. The interplay of governance, power and citizen participation in community tourism planning. *Journal of Policy Research in Tourism, Leisure and Events*, 5, 270–288.

Koens, K., Klijs, J., Weber-Sabil, J., Melissen, F., Lalicic, L., Hutchinson, K., Mayer, I., Önder, I., and Aall, C., In revision. Serious gaming to stimulate participatory urban tourism planning. *Journal of Sustainable Tourism*.

Koens, K., Melissen, F., Mayer, I., and Aall, C., 2019. The Smart City Hospitality framework: Creating a foundation for collaborative reflections on overtourism that support destination design. *Journal of Destination Marketing & Management*, 100376. https://doi.org/10.1016/j.jdmm.2019.100376

Koens, K., Postma, A., and Papp, B., 2018. Is overtourism overused? Understanding the impact of tourism in a city context. *Sustainability*, 10, 4384. https://doi.org/10.3390/su10124384

Koens, K., and Thomas, R., 2016. "You know that's a rip-off": Policies and practices surrounding micro-enterprises and poverty alleviation in South African township tourism. *Journal Sustainable Tourism*, 24, 1641–1654. https://doi.org/10.1080/09669582.2016.1145230

Lammers, M., Schapmans, M., Laure Leger, A., Bouwen, G., de Groote, E., Standaert, F., and Lataire, K. (Eds.), 2019. *Reizen Naar Morgen; Op Weg Naar Een Florerende Bestemming*. Brussels: Toerisme Vlaanderen.

Loorbach, D., and Shiroyama, H., 2016. The challenge of sustainable urban development and transforming cities. In: D. Loorbach, J.M. Wittmayer, H. Shiroyama, J. Fujino, and S. Mizuguchi (Eds.), *Governance of Urban Sustainability Transitions, Theory and Practice of Urban Sustainability Transitions*. Springer Japan, pp. 3–12. https://doi.org/10.1007/978-4-431-55426-4_1

McKercher, B., Wang, D., and Park, E., 2015. Social impacts as a function of place change. *Annals of Tourism Research*, 50, 52–66. https://doi.org/10.1016/j.annals.2014.11.002

Melissen, F., and Koens, K., 2019. The Smart City Hospitality (SCITHOS) project: Background and main outcomes. Breda University; MODUL University; Worldline; Western Norway Research Institute; CELTH, Breda.

Milano, C., Cheer, J.M., and Novelli, M. (Eds.), 2019a. *Overtourism: Excesses, Discontents and Measures in Travel and Tourism*. Wallingford: CABI. https://doi.org/10.1079/9781786399823.0000

Milano, C., Novelli, M., Cheer, J.M., 2019b. Overtourism and degrowth: a social movements perspective. *Journal of Sustainable Tourism*, 0, 1–19. https://doi.org/10.1080/09669582.2019.1650054

Pawlikowska-Piechotka, A., and Ostrowska-Tryzno, A., 2015. Innovative Local Community Partnership and Sustainable Urban Development - The Old Town in

Warsaw. *Economic Problems of Tourism*, 3(31), 139–158. https://doi.org/10.18276/ ept.2015.3.31-08

Pechlaner, H., Innerhofer, E., and Erschbamer, G. (Eds.), 2019. *Management Strategies for Overtourism – From Adaptation to System Change*. London: Routledge.

Peeters, P., Gössling, S., Klijs, J., Milano, C., Novelli, M., Dijkmans, C., Eijgelaa, E., Hartman, S., Heslinga, J., Isaac, R., Mitas, O., Moretti, S., Nawijn, J., Papp, B., and Postma, A., 2018. Study on Overtourism in Europe for the TRAN Committee of the European Parliament (No. IP/B/TRAN/IC/2018-058.). European Parliament, Policy Department for Structural and Cohesion Policies, Brussels.

Pforr, C., and Brueckner, M., 2016. The Quagmire of Stakeholder Engagement in Tourism Planning: A Case Example from Australia [WWW Document]. https://doi .org/info:doi/10.3727/108354216X14537459508892

Pinke-Sziva, I., Smith, M., Olt, G., and Berezvai, Z., 2019. Overtourism and the night-time economy: a case study of Budapest. *International Journal of Tourism Cities*, 5, 1–16. https://doi.org/10.1108/IJTC-04-2018-0028

Richter, A., 2010. Exploiting an 'army of friendly faces': Volunteering and social policy implications. *Journal of Policy Research in Tourism, Leisure and Events*, 2, 184–188. https://doi.org/10.1080/19407963.2010.482278

Skeli, S., and Schmid, M., 2019. Mitigating overtourism with the help of smart technology - a situation analysis of European city destinations. In: C. Maurer and H. Siller (Eds.), *ISCONTOUR 2019 Tourism Research Perspectives: Proceedings of the International Student Conference in Tourism Research*. Norderstedt: BoD – Books on Demand.

Stors, N., Stoltenberg, L., Sommer, C., and Frisch, T., 2019. Tourism and everyday life in the contemporary city: An introduction, In: T. Frisch, C. Sommer, L. Stoltenberg, N. Stors (Eds.), *Tourism and Everyday Life in the Contemporary City*. Abingdon, Oxon; New York, NY: Routledge, pp. 1–23.

UNESCO World Heritage Centre, 2018. Historic Centre of Warsaw – UNESCO World Heritage Centre. Retrieved 23 July 2018, from http://whc.unesco.org/en/list/30/

UNWTO, 2018. *Overtourism? Understanding and Managing Urban Tourism Growth Beyond Perceptions*. Madrid: UNWTO.

UNWTO, 2019. *Overtourism? Understanding and Managing Urban Tourism Growth Beyond Perceptions. Volume 2: Case Studies*. Madrid: UNWTO.

Van den Berg, L., Van der Borg, J., and Van der Meer, J., 1995. *Urban Tourism: Performance and Strategies in Eight European Cities*. Aldershot: Avebury.

Van Der Borg, J., 1992. Tourism and urban development: The case of Venice, Italy. *Tourism Recreation Research*, 17, 46–56. https://doi.org/10.1080/02508281.1992 .11014649

Wise, N., 2016. Outlining triple bottom line contexts in urban tourism regeneration. *Cities*, 53, 30–34. https://doi.org/10.1016/j.cities.2016.01.003

WTTC, 2017. *Coping with Success - Managing Overcrowding in Tourism Destinations*. London: WTTC (World Travel and Tourism Council).

Yoon, H., Sauri, D., and Rico Amorós, A.M., 2018. Shifting scarcities? The energy intensity of water supply alternatives in the mass tourist resort of Benidorm, Spain. *Sustainability*, 10, 824. https://doi.org/10.3390/su10030824

Warsaw Tourist Office, 2017. *Tourism in Warsaw – Report 2016*. Retrieved from http:// warsawtour.pl/wp-content/uploads/2018/03/Tourism_in_Warsaw_Report_2016 .pdf

13 Is another tourism possible? Shifting discourses in Barcelona's tourism politics

Antonio Paolo Russo, Elsa Soro and Alessandro Scarnato

Introduction

A little revolution seems to have taken place in Barcelona, one of the world's top urban destinations, and it has to do with the posture of the city (administration, public opinion and part of the business community) in regard to its tourism. Until recently, tourism was considered a staple of the city's success (Smith, 2005; Degen and García, 2012). Administrations of different political colour have promoted tourism development during the last three decades within the broader programme of transition to a post-industrial economy (García and Claver, 2003; Blanco, 2013). The tourism industry has been a last-instance job generator even when the financial meltdown of the late 2000s made all other sectors of the regional economy shrink (López Palomeque et al., 2016).

It is no wonder then that public opinion has been enduringly benign with tourism development, awarding it a very high approval rate in official surveys.[1] Widespread social and political support has characterized, and made possible, Barcelona's renaissance in the last decades, supported by intense public–private collaboration – the so-called "Barcelona Model" (Monclús, 2003; Capel, 2007). Though sectors of civic society and the academy have criticized this model as "neoliberal" in nature (Balibrea, 2001), they have never managed to substantially block such consensus.

In recent years, however, the relentless growth of visitors, now estimated at around 30 million,[2] has started to face contestation by wider sectors of society. Barcelona is not the only celebrated destination where this turn against tourism seems to be taking place in public opinion – see the breakthrough article by Becker (2015), followed by substantial media scrutiny and academic engagements with "overtourism" (Goodwin, 2017). Yet it is arguably one of the very few where it has prompted political change: the 2015 municipal elections were won by the *Barcelona en Comú* (BeC) platform. Their programme, reclaiming a radical turn in the city's socio-economic agenda, apparently clicked with sizeable sectors of the community, and especially with an impoverished middle class struggling to defend its quality of life in a city that they came to share with more and more visitors.

The new municipal government, led by Mayor Ada Colau, has introduced a new vocabulary and an altogether new approach to the policing of tourism, focusing on controlled de-growth, a fight against illegal practices, stricter regulation of public space and employment conditions in the tourism sector. Although having a very narrow majority in the Barcelona City Council (BCC), great polarization of opinions and strong pressure from various tourism-related lobbying groups, the BeC government has managed to carry out important reforms in a strongly participatory framework.

An important object of the analysis and critique of neoliberal urbanism – of which tourism-led regeneration projects have had an important role, as clarified among others by Judd and Fainstein (1999) – has indeed been its discursive dimension. Especially since the 1990s, when faced with the shortcomings of hard-core liberalism, neoliberal power structures have come to embrace forms of governance and regulation stretching to the purely discursive field (Peck and Tickell, 2002), ratifying "boosterish" storylines of community pride, partnership and interurban competition (Hall, 2006). In this sense, growth coalitions operate through the construction of a storyline which is "seen as 'the discursive cement' that keeps a coalition together" (Hajer, 1995, p. 65), bringing about "unique thought" (Swyngedouw, 2004) about the inevitability of neoliberal politics, yet widening social breaches and dispossessing communities from democratic control over their own destinies (Arantes et al., 2000; Colomb and Novy, 2016).

Consensus-building is seen to rely on the discursive power of text, which transforms strategic documents into norms (Vaara et al., 2010), and on the pervasiveness of media communication, which articulates and channels these norms to society. McCombs (1997) in this respect notes how by filtering the salience of problems affecting public opinion, the media inherently shape the community agenda and reduce the visibility of contrasting visions and differences. Thus, for McCann (2004) the media legitimize hegemonic ideas about what is "good" in local (economic) development politics, and their normative role should be central to political economy approaches to urban studies. On the other hand, as noted by Peck and Tickell (2002, 401), "progressive local alternatives are persistently vulnerable, in this turbulent and marketized environment, to social undercutting, institutional overloading, and regulatory dumping", and doomed to be marginalized and reified by hegemonic power structures (Miraftab, 2004).

While few academic works address urban regimes in tourist cities (i.e. Hall, 1994, and specifically discuss the case of Barcelona, Smith, 2005; Casellas, 2006; Blanco, 2013), what is generally not investigated, as noted by Conti and Perelli (2007), is what kind of alliances and discourses sustain "tourism first" growth strategies. Conversely, we also lack evidence of discursive shifts which may unearth alternative alliances and legitimize turns in tourist policy towards a "lower-class opportunity expansion regime" (Mossberger and Stoker, 2001). This is a relevant question at a moment when the phenomenon of "overtourism" seems to have been picked up by the mainstream media globally. Recent works invite examining how – if place disruption from excess tourism is not exactly news (Dredge, 2017) – "overtourism" may well connote a shift in social sensibility over this issue in the context of less affordable cities (Martín Martín et al., 2018; Milano, 2018) and its "politicization" within the broader backdrop of rising struggles and protests in and about urban space (Novy, 2018).

The case of Barcelona is, in this sense, exceptional as it hints at the possibility that to some extent, and under certain conditions, discourses from the opposition can become hegemonic, configuring favourable preconditions for an urban regime transition in the framework of Stone (1993) and McGovern (2009). Put simply, Barcelona may well be the first documented case (and probably not the last) of a large city in which the public perception of tourism has shifted to such an extent that it came to legitimize a radical alternative in urban politics.

This chapter focuses specifically on the discursive practices that might have fostered such a political turn. To accomplish this, we have analysed the range of discourses on – and representations of – tourism channelled by different printed media on the occasion of four successive electoral campaigns in Barcelona (from 2003 to 2015), underlining the elements of discontinuity between these periods. This analysis is framed in socio-semiotics, an approach that studies social phenomena and practices through their textual and narrative representations (Greimas, 1976; Landowski, 1989; Marrone, 2001).

The chapter is structured as follows: in the next section we introduce the analytical framework of our research. In the third section we develop our analysis of the case of Barcelona, evaluating the diffusion of tourism-related discourses and the positioning of key urban actors, as well as making sense of the shifts noted throughout the four electoral periods in the light of contextual information from a plurality of primary and secondary sources. In the fourth section we conclude, reflecting on the weight that shifting sensibilities around the policing of tourism could have as a catalyst for regime transitions, and questioning whether, in the light of the Barcelona case, political change under the drive of "the revolt against tourism" is to be expected in other places.

Analytical framework

Semiotics approaches in tourism studies

Tourism – practices, development processes, politics and the operations of the marketplace – is intimately associated with meaning and representation. It could thus be considered a field of interest *par excellence* of semiotics, the study of meaning-making, signs and meaningful communication. Although different sociological and anthropological perspectives have engaged with the study of tourism politics, semiotics would focus on tourism as a system of producing signs and meanings (Echtner, 1999). Semiotics may clarify how tourism practices and the agencies involved "make" tourist places, attributing to them distinct qualities such as "worth visiting", and also which of these representations become hegemonic, while others are shielded off, or how different meanings are assumed over time, contributing to a better understanding of the politics of place development.

Jaworski and Thurlow (2010), inspired by a socio-linguistic approach, conceive tourism as a "semiotics landscape" and assume texts as the main analytic object, including spoken, written and visual representations that fathom tourism as a global cultural industry (e.g. Cohen, 1989). This epistemology is then operationalized in many different methodological approaches, such as Critical Discourse Analysis, which examines the role played by language in the construction of power relationships and the reproduction of domination (Fairclough, 1995; van Dijk, 2001). An example of CDA in tourism research is given by Vaara et al. (2010), who examine how the style and vocabulary of the strategic text reproduce corporate rhetoric in tourism development, and by so doing reveal the societal, political and economic entrenchments of policymaking. While CDA relies on the assumption that any interpretation of discourse should be based on the lexical and grammatical features of the text, more recent semiotics perspectives (e.g. Volli, 2003; Brucculeri and Giannitrapani, 2009) focus on the cultural values enfolded in travel and holidaymaking, redirecting and rescaling the analytical focus from lexical occurrences to the broader field of representations and practices (Hunter, 2013).

For the sake of this paper, *socio-semiotics* is the particular approach we chose to scrutinize the deep structure of meanings circulating in a society. Socio-semiotics is a branch of semiotics that studies social phenomena and practices through their textual and narrative representation within a given social context (Greimas, 1976; Landowsky, 1989; Marrone, 2001). By clarifying how value systems and power relations are constructed, recognized or legitimated by different social discourses – defined by Landowsky (1989) as the representations that a given society produces of itself over time through different and heterogeneous media forms, thus a socio-cultural construct that only exists in relation to the meaning that individuals and groups assign to it within a given social context – this theoretical perspective seeks to understand how certain ideas become hegemonic in society while others are marginalized. The theoretical starting point of structural semiotics, on which socio-semiotics is based, relies on an axiological opposition between values prior to the manifestation of discourse (Greimas and Courtés, 1979). The way in which the discourse is articulated translates such values into narrative and populates it with themes, figures and actors. Hence, the texts and discourses that circulate in society, for instance through mass media, reveal how new or dominant visions of the world emerge, and how social meaning changes through time; the analysis of their narrative forms is apt to illustrate the confrontations and negotiations between different values and how such values are embodied in social practices by different actors.

The analysis in this paper thus looks into the structural elements articulating discourses on tourism as the reproductive (or disruptive) tool of urban regimes. The empirical object of our analysis is the discourses that circulate in the media during a crucial period of time for the characterization of political stances in Barcelona, such as electoral periods. Following our conceptual entry points, our focus on public discourses is meant to offer a more nuanced view of the socio-political construction of a policy programme and of the related conflicts and positioning, beyond what eventually surfaces in the formal policy text, which is likely to efface such complexity.

Sources

Even though in recent years the influence of traditional media on public opinion-forming has been yielding to new media and social networks, the printed press is still of great use to track the evolution of social discourse over time in Catalonia. In that regard, our analysis uses a selection of articles published in four sources: two Catalan newspapers with national circulation (*La Vanguardia, El Periódico*, leaning respectively towards a conservative and a more progressive readership), a well-respected grassroots magazine (*La*

Table 13.1   Newspaper articles consulted in the analysis

Source	2003 (10/5-7/6)	2007 (12/5-19/6)	2011 (7/5-4/6)	2015 (9/5-19/6)	Total by source
La Vanguardia	47	45	39	45	176
El Periodico	35	22	20	58	135
La Veu del Carrer	6	8	10	16	40
The Guardian	0	2	3	14	19
Total by period	88	77	72	133	370

Veu del Carrer), a media format that has a long tradition in Barcelona, and an international newspaper that gives ample coverage to Barcelona's issues (*The Guardian*).

These four sources cover reasonably well the range of political and societal sensibilities on urban issues and the different readerships which are called to form an opinion on Barcelona's tourism. The articles analysed cover extensively the period of the electoral campaigns for municipal elections and the first month in charge of elected administrations, over the last four electoral periods (2003, 2007, 2011 and 2015), and namely the 2–3 weeks preceding the election day and the couple of weeks following it, when a municipal government is formed based on the electoral results.

Methods

The objective of our analysis is the detection and characterization of the main themes and figures that have been publicly associated with tourism in Barcelona over the last 15 years and the positioning of different actors in that respect. The methodological framework was thus organized as follows.

First, we selected all the articles in the media sources illustrated above (370 articles – see Table 13.1) that directly or indirectly mention the word "tourism" and other tourism-related terms such as "hotel", "visitors", "season", and registered the specific topic tackled in the article. A direct mention would for instance be reflected in an article on a tourism-related issue as a campaign topic; an indirect mention could emerge in an article discussing urban projects or the economic climate of the city.

Second, we noted, for each of those entries, the actor delivering a statement or positioning him/herself on that topic (again, directly, as in an interview, or indirectly as in an opinion or review piece on that topic), classifying them into social actors (citizens' associations, civic movements and unions), experts and academics, political actors and the business community. Among political actors we distinguish between four major political orientations: the radical left (including the red–green coalition *Iniciativa per Catalunya-Verds* ICV, converged in the BeC), the moderate left (including the Catalan Socialist Party PSC, which held the city mayoralty until 2011), the moderate liberal right (including the *Convergència i Unió* CiU coalition, which held the mayoralty from 2011 to 2015) and the conservative right (including the main Spanish government party, Popular Party – PP). We have also included the Catalan government, until 2010 held by the PSC or in coalition with other parties of the left, then by the CiU). Among business actors we included the hospitality and tourism industry and their professional bodies, the cultural and events industry, and the real estate sector, especially including the so-called peer-to-peer apartment rental platforms.

Third, we registered how such actors positioned themselves on the different topics registered. In order to track such positioning, we used the semiotics categories of "euphoria" and "dysphoria", which in Greimas and Courtés (1979) represent the basic structure from which any value attributed by actors to objects derives. In this respect, we attributed each entry/actor a certain score in terms of euphoria/dysphoria based on the authors' subjective evaluation (from –6 to +6), and we clustered "neutral" opinions or narrations of a topic as a "challenge" around the 0.

A main challenge of this study was to organize these elements graphically so as to facilitate their visualization and analysis. The "mapping" of each entry involved three dimensions: the topic, the actor and the positioning. We thus recurred to a boxplot as shown in Figure 13.1 to map the entries analysed in each period, charting each entry along the euphoria/dysphoria scale (y-axis), attributing it to an actor and including a short definition of the topic. It must be noted that the position of the actors along the x-axis is not an ordinal sequence, although we tried to keep social and business actors separated and the political actors in the middle to visually simplify the analysis of how political forces align with a pro-community or pro-business imperative. A same topic can (and generally is) mentioned and valued by more than one actor throughout the media sample in each period, thus a further step in the analysis was to identify topics on which there is consensus (either "euphoric" or "dysphoric").

The initial array of tourism-related topics detected in the analysis was so extended that the mapping itself hampered visual comprehensibility. Hence they were reclassified into five broader "themes": "tourism and business" (employment, economic vitality and competitiveness), "tourism and local identity" (the affirmation of the Barcelona brand of specific idiosyncratic features of the city's cultural and social landscape), "tourism and mobility" (transport and accessibility), "tourism and public space" (issues of quality of life, safety, amiability, etc.) and "tourism and housing & population" (concerns about social change and resilience, diversity, integration, affordability, etc.).

While software-based content analysis (see for instance Stepchenkova et al., 2009) would have identified the specific semantic and lexical occurrences related to each macro-theme, the semiotics approach seeks to sort out how these macro-themes are manifested at a surface-level of the text, through concrete figures and topics on which the different actors position themselves.

The contextualization and interpretation of results from the analysis fleshed out in the next section also relied on a number of in-depth, open-ended interviews with key actors of the four periods examined, carried out in different periods of time between 2015 and 2017. These interviews helped us clarify the context of the "topics" emerging from the media analysis in the years in which the events investigated took place, and make sense of the positioning, confrontations and alliances tracked. In total we interviewed 14 people, including a former mayor, four former or current elected counsellors in charge of aspects treated in our study, three municipal planners, two leading architects, one journalist with a long track record of covering the transformation of post-Olympic Barcelona, two scholars and a civic activist.

Empirical findings

Barcelona has been at the forefront of strategic planning for various decades, enjoying international recognition for having successfully accomplished the transition from declining industrial city to a major hub of the post-industrial economy and one of Europe's top urban destinations. The Olympics boosted the visibility of the city in the media beyond expectation, with the effect of "putting Barcelona on the world map" (Maragall, 1986).

After the 1992 event, Barcelona started its race to become one of Europe's top destinations through different stages. In the 1986–2000 period, the strategic collaboration between the administration and the private sector (the so-called "Barcelona Model"), established the bases for its physical and symbolic regeneration into an attractive Mediterranean city. The following years saw a progressive shift towards the establishment of an urban brand, with tourism increasingly being valued as an employment generator and a crucial tool for the global positioning of the city (Casellas, 2006; Degen and García, 2012). The BCC portrayed urbanism as an appealing tool for global investors and elites (Ajuntament de Barcelona, 2008), and continued to do so when in the 2008–2014 period the global financial crisis swept over Spain and considerably affected the Barcelona economy. In 2015, the electoral success of the BeC marked a turning point, since its government was openly critical of the neoliberal course of the previous decades, pointing the finger at the extractive nature of tourism development projects and advocating a radical turn in urban politics founded on defence of the "right to the city".

For the scope of this paper, we will now more clearly focus on four distinct periods within this transition, bookended by municipal elections, illustrating for each of them the key tourism-related events and the more general urban context. For each period we will then order and analyse the discursive representations of tourism as an "issue" for debate according to the framework introduced in the previous section.

1999–2003: the post-Olympic period

A decade after the celebration of the Olympics, Barcelona was still surfing optimistically on its wave, channelling its efforts to the reconstruction of the physical and symbolic landscape of the city. The "Barcelona model" was furthered with private sector investment (mainly national). The construction sector is a pillar of the Spanish economy, and Barcelona profited from this dynamism to renovate its housing stock and provide adequate infrastructure needed to accompany its transition to the advanced service economy. In these years the "22@" project was launched: the transformation of a former industrial area into a new knowledge-economy cluster, through a finely-grained scheme of investment and risk-sharing between public and private partners. At this time, the leadership of the city by the *Partit dels Socialistes Catalans* (PSC) reached its apogee (the PSC came first in all the municipal elections from 1979 to 2011). For the first time since the restoration of democracy, it was also accompanied by a Socialist Catalan government chaired by Pasqual Maragall, who as Barcelona's mayor had been the political brain behind the Olympics, leading to a unity of intents that also reformulated the position of the city in its regional and metropolitan neighbourhood.

Another ambitious plan launched in this period was the revival of the Olympic urban planning model. Taking advantage of the possibility of hosting the "Universal Forum of Cultures" (hereafter: Forum), an otherwise minor UNESCO-sponsored international event to be celebrated in 2004, the municipality saw an opportunity to complete the regeneration at the northern municipal border, with a project that included upgraded meeting and cultural venues, luxury housing, business estates and hotels. The PSC, also with this impulse, won the 2003 elections, although the lack of a clear majority required the incumbent mayor Joan Clos to form a coalition government with the red–green ICV party.

The range of topics aired by the media sources in this electoral period is represented in Figure 13.1. The discourses around tourism were mostly related to the success of Barcelona's internationalisation strategy and the optimistic tones were transversal to most political, business and social actors. The main challenge shared by most actors concerned the role that tourism success could play in the attraction of foreign investment and the necessity to stabilize tourism growth and job creation through a wider range of attractions. The role played by urban planning in this vision is pointed out by members of the BCC, intellectuals and outstanding professionals, who consistently depict the relentless quest for the modernization of Barcelona as its main attraction, embodied in the development of iconic public space and architectural landmarks (Delgado, 2005; Pizza, 2007; Scarnato, 2016).

In order to enhance the readability of these results, we offer a schematic resume (Figure 13.2) of how the themes introduced in the previous section developed over the four periods. In this image, the centroids of the four areas represent the balance between conformity and disconformity (we use the opposite terms "euphoria" vs "dysphoria", since they are more typical of semiotic analysis) registered in the various articles on a scale from –6 to +6; their dimension is approximately proportional to the number of topics/cites that the theme includes; and their shape covers the actors taking on such topics. In other words, the wider the shape, the more sources mention the related topic, while the position is referred to the level of euphoria about the topic.

Unsurprisingly, there is little divergence among political actors about the benefits of tourism especially for leveraging the city's status, international visibility and business opportunities (Figure 13.2(a)). The divisive themes (illustrated by dotted lines) mainly regard the planning of the Forum, and the rising concerns about the standardization of the urban landscape and the insecurity of tourist areas, heralded especially by civic groups and the conservative opposition. More fundamental critiques to tourism development are hardly represented by the media and are mostly voiced by academics and independent experts. This representation graphically clarifies the general and transversal positive view about tourism as an economic engine and an element structuring and diffusing the local identity values; disconformity on the issues generated by tourism in

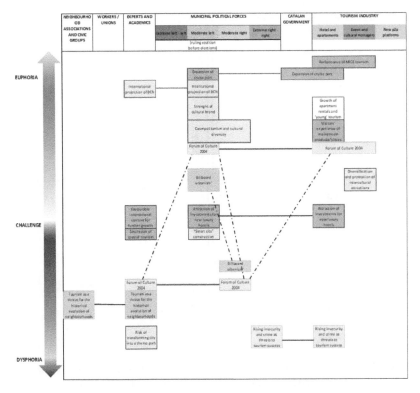

Figure 13.1 Topics, actors and discourse characterization from media sources, 2003 electoral period

the realm of public space is limited and relegated to a niche of actors, while mobility is seen as a challenge for the new government.

2003–2007: constructing a cultural capital

Barcelona began to be enormously popular for a new generation of international tourists attracted by the coexistence of a sophisticated and dynamic urban landscape and a Mediterranean essence sculpted in its historical neighbourhoods, waterfront and street life. Barcelona claims to be the "tourist capital of the Mediterranean", extending efforts to offer first-class infrastructure and events, as well as architectural landmarks and "designed" public spaces.

The institutional cultural policies led by Ferran Mascarell did not explicitly target visitors, but Barcelonans, seen as a community and still not enamoured

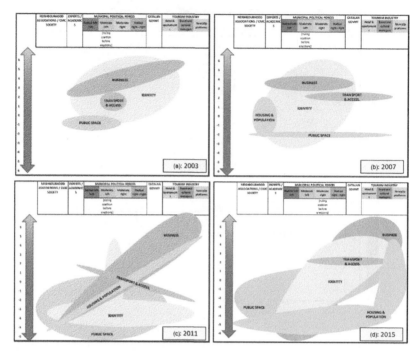

Figure 13.2   Representation of tourism-related themes in four electoral periods; (a): 2003; (b): 2007; (c): 2011; (d): 2015

of their own city. At that moment, tourism was still perceived as a welcome side-effect of the broader morphological and functional reshaping of the city. Also, for cultural initiatives such as the international Gaudí Year 2002 or the Year of Design 2003, huge visitor attendance was a secondary goal compared with the activation of local interest and the promotion of Barcelona as a reference in the international cultural scene, considered (in the words of Mayor Clos) "an essential asset in order to attract foreign investments" (Ajuntament de Barcelona, 2004).

Nevertheless, the momentum of the Olympic scheme for urban regeneration was starting to wane. A symptom of this was the controversy generated by the Forum. Not only did it underperform in terms of assistance, but the development generated around the event also attracted social opposition for the negligible regenerative impacts on surrounding areas and its legacy of empty luxury housing and office space. The social returns of private investments in the city became a matter of concern for the academy and sectors of the society (e.g. Trallero and Reboredo, 2004), although this critique hardly extended to the increasingly hegemonic role of tourism in the city's economy, noted instead by Delgado (2005). The PSC won the 2007 elections in a climate of increasing confrontation, losing votes to the conservative opposition; the new mayor Jordi Hereu – who replaced Joan Clos, appointed Minister of Industry and Tourism in the Spanish central government – had to form the "Tripartite", a coalition of the PSC, the ICV and the Catalan nationalist party *Esquerra Republicana de Catalunya* (ERC).

In a period when the Spanish economy was in full swing, Barcelona did so well that it is not surprising that tourism did not gain a central place in the political debate (note in Table 13.1 the substantial diminution of references to tourism in the media considered in our study). As illustrated in Figure 13.2(b), the economic leverage provided by tourism remained basically undisputed, although slightly less talked about, while a certain divergence of opinions emerged with respect to the position of tourism in the broader realm of public life and place identity, with government forces entrenched in praise of the increasing diversification of tourism activities and markets attracted. Tourism-driven gentrification and the compatibility between tourist and residential uses emerged as a new topic for concern, attracting moderate concerns by social forces and academics. The proliferation of apartment rentals was first noted as a problem mainly by the hotel industry, while political forces took pride in the local transit system for a more sustainable tourism mobility.

2007-2011: the Barcelona Brand and the global crisis

The government of the "Tripartite" was marred by the crash of the global financial crisis over Spain, with the direst effects experienced after 2009. The construction sector collapsed, leading to a standstill of the large infrastructure works that characterized the previous periods, progressively substituted by precise interventions focusing on public space design and the renewal of commercial spaces. The crisis also left important scars in the socio-economic fabric of the city, with thousands expelled from employment (320,000 jobs lost in the metropolitan area of Barcelona between 2008 and 2012) while it tried to show a happy face to its tourist consumers.

Although charged with good intentions, especially in enhancing the civic infrastructure of the city and its mobility system, the Tripartite had a hard time keeping hold of the socio-economic situation, and when Mayor Hereu proposed reviving the Olympic successes through a candidature of Barcelona and the Pyrenees for the 2022 winter games, this was met with a cold reception by most social and institutional actors. This period saw a notable inflow of global companies, lured by the many city amenities, the excellent education and research sector and, not marginally, by the cheap cost of human resources. Yet the only thing that seemed to be going at full swing was tourism, and the wealth and jobs of Barcelonans were increasingly dependent on the visitor economy.

Possibly as a consequence, the agenda-setting role of the municipal government started to yield to the private sector and especially the tourism and hospitality industry, which had exclusive control of the main promotional body of the city sector, *Turisme de Barcelona*. This body took the leadership in enhancing the appeal of the city for tourists, concentrating decidedly on culture and sports events, heritage rehabilitation and a new wave of hotel supply expansion, while the reform of the commercial and public space use of the Ramblas promoted by the Tripartite was eventually stopped.

The CiU candidate Xavier Trias obtained a landslide success at the 2011 elections and formed a majority government at the worst moment of the economic decline. The new government, though not disputing the successes of the Barcelona Model, was less tuned to strong planning visions, and insisted instead on the "brandification" of the city with the promise of putting things back on track for Barcelona through an attraction strategy that would boost the city's role as a global hub and recover employment.

While different sectors of academia and civic society were questioning that the "Barcelona Model" had turned from social project to machinery mainly oriented towards rent extraction (Pizza, 2007), Trias declared that rather than a planning model he would promote Barcelona as a "seductive cocktail of primary colours" (Degen, 2008), offering to the world a prime example of a proper Smart City, completely interconnected and fit for the new cosmopolitan lifestyles of new and old residents.

The representation of the themes brought to public attention in the 2011 campaign is shown in Figure 13.2(c). The picture is quite different from that of the two previous periods; the economic meltdown occupied centre stage in the campaign, yet, remarkably, was seen as unrelated to tourism. Almost all five tourism-related themes tended to be brought into the debate by almost any actor, and were quite divisive in opinions, except for the general concern on the increasingly problematic effects of tourism on public space.

The business climate of tourism was positively evaluated by private actors, while public actors became moderately concerned; the identification of the city image and identity with tourism practices and representations was also generally contested, with the exception of the governing coalition, and the first symptoms of over-saturation of the city started to be noted by social actors. The optimistic discourses on tourism of the incumbent left-wing government coalition were remarkably divorced from the increasing concerns of the public opinion and experts, a fact that seemed to be capitalized especially by the conservative opposition, advocating less grand plans and more "money in the pocket" for a middle-class constituency impoverished by the crisis, and emphasizing the need to "sell the city" and keep it secure and clean as a way to boost tourist competitiveness.

2011–2015: the end of the Barcelona Model and the rise of the new resistance

One of the first measures of the Trias government was to shelve the Strategic Plan for Tourism 2010–2015, which confronted the emerging issues produced by "overtourism" in the city centre. Meanwhile, licensing procedures for the opening of new hotels and apartment rentals were simplified by the Catalan Government – again held from 2010 by the CiU – as a measure to recover employment and household income. While the new players in the sharing economy, such as Airbnb, promised to bring back a bit of money to families affected by the crisis, the combined effects of failing household income and tourism-driven gentrification were overwhelming. Evictions were the city's new social emergency: in total, between 2010 and 2014, 28,500 families lost their homes for failing to pay the mortgage (Delgado and Escorihuela, 2017), and a fair share of them in central neighbourhoods (Gutiérrez and Delclòs, 2016). International investment funds and real estate companies purchased whole buildings, evicted or mobbed out the insolvent tenants, renovated them and put them back on the market as short-term rental apartments (Quaglieri Domínguez and Scarnato, 2017).

The success of the Trias government was notable in the field of professional events: the World Mobile Congress, the world's most important trade fair for the portable technology sector, is anchored to Barcelona with a multi-year contract, bringing more than 100,000 delegates and becoming a springboard for many other initiatives in the technology field. Yet, in this period, tourism started to be publicly recognized as a force of dispossession and disruption of residents' livelihoods. Residents in areas with a high concentration of tourist activity especially perceived tourism as a major problem, and Barcelonans "against further tourism development" for the first time exceeded those in favour (Mumbrú, 2017).

Two important political events marked this period. In 2010, the Constitutional Tribunal of Spain invalidated large sections of the reformed Statute of

Autonomy of Catalonia, previously approved by a popular referendum and then sanctioned in the Spanish parliament. This event triggered a resurgence of the Catalan nationalist movement, now openly secessionist, which gained increasing force until the recent (2017) botched attempt to declare independence.

The other event had to do with a new rise in radical activism. While grassroots movements have a long tradition in Barcelona, a new period of social engagement and protest in Spain and elsewhere in the world (the "Occupy" movement) materialized in multitudinous "campings" in the heart of the main cities. It came to be known as 15M from the date, 15 May 2011, when the first tents were set up in the squares of Porta del Sol in Madrid and Plaça Catalunya in Barcelona. Even in a context of nuanced economic recovery, the widened income and opportunity gaps, the increasing instability of employment and the increasing reliance on public budget cuts and privatizations as the escape route from the crisis became the main issues of contestation. Such movements started building a new national coalition, which eventually became *Podemos* ("we can").

One of the grassroots entities born in this period was the *Plataforma de Afectados por la Hipoteca* (Platform of the Affected by the Mortgage – PAH). This group advocated against the Spanish law that obliges evicted tenants to continue to pay their debt to the bank even after they lose their house. The young leader of the PAH, Ada Colau, managed to bring the issue of evictions to public debate, with memorable speeches given at the Spanish and European parliaments. Her reputation was such that, when the new movements connected with neighbourhood associations and critical sectors of the academic world, she was the natural choice for leading the new coalition project for a municipal candidature.

On 24 May 2015, the BeC was the most voted party at the municipal elections and Colau was the first woman to be elected mayor of Barcelona. Her electoral programme was openly critical of the business-friendly politics of the incumbent administration in the field of tourism, and urged radical reforms based on social inclusion, controlled development and protection of the city commons from processes of dispossession. Soon after the elections, the BeC launched an ambitious zoning plan that capped the proliferation of hotels and apartments in central neighbourhoods, and engages in tough negotiations with Airbnb and similar platforms to stop them promoting unlicensed rentals; then it started a Strategic Plan for Tourism 2020 based on ample citizen participation and aiming at an overall restructuring of the city's tourism governance.

In Figure 13.2(d) we track the representation of tourism-related themes in the crucial 2015 electoral campaign. The first thing to note is the appearance of tourism as a central topic in the campaign, with quotes in the consulted media almost doubling compared with the previous periods (and tripling in *El Periodico*, the progressive-leaning newspaper in our collection – see Table 13.1). Almost every social, institutional and economic actor had something to say on tourism, and the number of topics brought into the public debate was decidedly larger than in the past, knitting tightly with other issues such as welfare, labour, housing and the environment.

The opinions on the five themes were also greatly divisive. It can be noted that positive opinions on tourism remained firm among private parties, though the traditional hospitality sector in particular manifested a certain apprehension about the rise of p2p rentals. The traditional political establishment (from centre-left to right) mostly aligned with the understanding that tourism is good for the city economy and society, while the far more critical opinions of social and academic actors – attributing to unbridled tourism development the most problematic regressions in the welfare and quality of life of citizens, especially in the most "touristified" areas – only resonated in the discourse of the radical left, the BeC and the pro-independence coalition *Candidatura d'Unitat Popular* (CUP). The harshest critiques focused on the effects of tourism on public space and the quotidian life of residents, on the impacts of tourism growth on housing affordability and speculative practices, but also remarkably on tourism-related employment, badly paid and precarious, reproducing and widening social breaches. It is important to note that even a liberal newspaper such as *La Vanguardia*, with a middle to high-class readership, opened the electoral debate to topics such as the advisability of "de-growing" tourism, the questionable benefits of cruise tourism and the defence of affordable housing for residents.

Discussion

In the last part of this section we will analyse how the five themes have shifted in salience, representation and divisiveness along the four periods under examination. This is illustrated in Figure 13.3, where the five themes are represented with different geometric symbols, their salience (number of quotes in the sample of articles examined) is proportional to the size of each symbol, and the shades (lighter to darker) stand for higher disconformity of opinions amongst the actors considered (measured as the variance of the scores received along the euphoria/dysphoria scale).

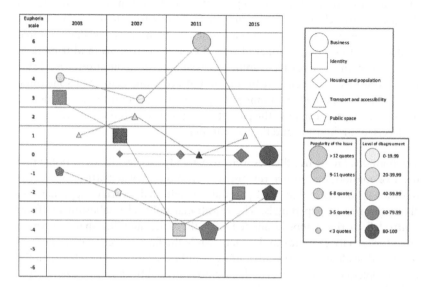

Figure 13.3 Development of tourism-related themes over the 2003–2007 to 2011–2015 periods

Figure 13.3 illustrates how tourism-related themes generally gained in salience throughout the four periods, increasing their exposure in the media; the business-related and housing-related themes above the rest. More remarkably, all the themes (except for transport and accessibility) became far more divisive throughout the years, reaching the highest scores in the last period. As for their representation, on average the economy-related topics are characterized more negatively in the last period with a sharp decline after the 2011 period. The theme of local identity, which in the first two periods received a globally positive characterization, became negatively represented in the third and fourth, with a slight reprise in the latter. The housing and population-related theme maintained a score around zero, polarizing opinions. The characterization of public space also worsened over the years with a generally negative representation, which only improved slightly in the last period.

The interpretation of these results needs framing in the contexts of the different periods, and so does their relationship with the electoral events they are associated with. In particular, it could be proposed that the critiques levied by the candidature of the BeC to the tourist model of Barcelona in the 2015 campaign focused on the material conditions produced by tourism growth in the city, and not so much on the representational issues (identity, decor, image, etc.). In previous periods, pro-growth discourses had resonated with a thriving middle class (in 2003 and 2007), and "recovery" discourses in 2011 had been seconded by a public opinion in severe straits from the loss of jobs. Yet, in 2015, the political force that proposed a structural critique of the dominant economic model – a derivative of the "Barcelona Model" with weaker public-sector guidance – started representing tourism as something that could be given up, or at least put on a leash, in favour of more resilient alternatives. This discourse was perceived as radical and genuinely "different" by those large sectors of society that, after being hit by the effects of the crisis, were facing the growing unaffordability of the city, worsened employment conditions and rising impediments to quotidian practices. When tourism-related themes increased in divisiveness, the coalitions that were in charge of municipal politics in the first three periods examined did not align with the majority of social actors; this position was instead occupied by the BeC, turning an emerging critical positioning in society into the new approach in Barcelona's tourism policy. The range of themes elicited in this positioning also suggests that the political shift extended to related areas of government such as city marketing, housing and public space policy, socio-economic priorities and mobility politics.

Conclusions

Our analysis of representations of tourism and tourism politics in Barcelona allowed a discursive shift to be detected, from enthusiastic boosterism, when tourism was nested in the urban regeneration programmes led by the socialist mayoralties in the 1990s and 2000s, to the less ambitious idea of the "city as brand" in the early 2010s under the leadership of the moderate CiU coalition, and eventually the critical and "reductionist" approach currently sustained by the BeC administration and its organized constituency. This shift may hint at an urban regime change extending to the city's global political orientation.

The first mandate of Mayor Colar ended in 2019 and was renewed after the elections of the same year. Nevertheless, the BeC did not win the polls, and only after establishing an alliance with the PSC (and receiving the unexpected one-time support of former French Prime Minister Manuel Valls, now involved in Barcelona's political life leading a moderate-right movement) was Colau able to be reconfirmed as mayor. It is certainly remarkable that during the electoral period, characterized by a harsh confrontation often affected by the situation of the surrounding political instability (both at a regional level in Catalonia and in the whole Spanish scenario), the general discourse on tourism was fairly aligned among most political forces. None of these vehemently opposed Colau's reformist agenda in that respect, something unimaginable only four years before, when the activist candidate was labelled as "dangerous" for her critical vision about the benefits of this industry.

However, the first steps of this second term reflected the difficulties related to the political instability in Catalonia, with the BeC caught in an uncomfortable "midway" position in the confrontation between independentists and "union-ists", climaxing in the contested referendum for independence and the subsequent incarceration of the main political leaders of the regional government. Leading the City Council far from a comfortable position of clear majority, the BeC faced a day-to-day struggle to advance its political agenda through negotiation with other political forces (in alliance or opposition), inevitably diminishing its impact and scope. The "touristification" of housing has not ceased to significantly contribute to pushing up rents despite the stricter controls and regulations enforced by the municipal government, reaching a historic peak in the first months of 2018. While investments in social housing and area plans may eventually ease off this pressure, the incompletion of the "paradigm change" in tourism politics is fleshed out by the ongoing struggle over the city's promotion, still a (contested) prerogative of the Turisme de Barcelona private body and its business allies.

Yet there is little doubt that the tide has turned in relation to the public perception of tourism: few political forces today defend a return to a boosterish and deregulatory agenda, and most of the criticism of the BeC's political action regards the short-term ineffectiveness of its measures. On another level though, Colau's administration is in tune with many other city governments, in Spain and elsewhere, which recognize "overtourism" as a key social challenge, and join forces to advocate common regulatory frameworks, for instance in regard to p2p hospitality and housing regulations, the taxation of tourist activity, mobility management and labour standards; stances that are currently under scrutiny at the European Commission. In this sense it may be proposed that, despite its local weakness, the BeC government has managed to scale up its tourism politics and turn a critical approach into a possibly hegemonic one.

Our research has hopefully helped unpack the details of the transition to this new playing field, bridging social perception, discourse and agency, and analysing the shifts observed throughout the last 15 years against the evolving context. Beyond this approach there is the idea that in the "age of mobilities", where tourism increasingly blurs into the quotidian, discourses on tourism are increasingly embedded in the plethora of other positioning, converging and overlapping in the urban context. It is the combination of all these discourses that helps influence the views of public opinion on tourism and at the same time reflects and influences tourism politics.

The research on which this chapter is based is open to refinements and extensions – for instance the deployment of computerized techniques to track, systematically, social positioning in a variety of texts, printed and visual, and the consideration of TV and social media as sources. Indeed, we hope that our approach will prompt other scholars to make use of the socio-semiotics toolbox and engage in more fine-grained analyses of tourism politics.

Notes

1 All recent yearly surveys on citizens' concerns are available at: https://ajuntament
  .barcelona.cat/turisme/es/estadistiques_enquestes
2 Estimate included in the working documents of the Barcelona Tourism Strategic
  Plan 2020 (see https://ajuntament.barcelona.cat/turisme/ca/pla-estrategic)

References

Ajuntament de Barcelona (2004) *Barcelona [in]progré[s]*. (Catalogue of the exhibition, Fòrum building, 9 May–26 September 2004). Barcelona: AJMT BCN.

Ajuntament de Barcelona (2008) *Barcelona transformació, Plans i projectes*. Barcelona: AJMT BCN.

Arantes OBF, Vainer CB and Maricato E (2000) *A cidade do pensamento único: desmanchando consensos*. Petropolis: Vozes.

Balibrea MP (2001) Urbanism, culture and the post-industrial city: Challenging the "Barcelona model". *Journal of Spanish Cultural Studies* 2(2), 187–210.

Becker E (2015) The revolt against tourism. *New York Times*, 17 July. Available at: http://www.nytimes.com/2015/07/19/opinion/sunday/the-revolt-against-tourism.html?_r=0 (accessed 10 February 2018).

Blanco I (2013) Analysing urban governance networks: Bringing regime theory back in. *Environment and Planning C: Government and Policy* 31(2), 276–291.

Brucculeri MC and Giannitrapani A (2009) Turismo ed effetto città. In: M Leone (ed), *La città come testo. Scritture e riscritture urbane*. Roma: Arcane, pp. 171–186.

Capel H (2007) El debate sobre la construcción de la ciudad y el modelo Barcelona. *Scripta Nova* 11, 229–255. Available at: http://revistes.ub.edu/index.php/ScriptaNova/article/view/1307 (accessed 10 February 2018).

Casellas A (2006) Las limitaciones del «modelo Barcelona». Una lectura desde Urban Regime Analysis. *Documents d'anàlisi Geogràfica* 48, 61–81.

Cohen E (1989) Primitive and remote: Hill tribe trekking in Thailand. *Annals of Tourism Research* 16(1), 30–61.

Colomb C and Novy J (eds) (2016) *Protest and Resistance in the Tourist City.* London: Routledge.

Conti G and Perelli C (2007) Governing tourism monoculture: Mediterranean mass tourism destinations and governance networks. In: P Burns and M Novelli (eds), *Tourism and Politics. Global Frameworks and Local Realities.* Amsterdam: Elsevier, pp. 235–261.

Degen M (2008) *Sensing Cities: Regenerating Public Life in Barcelona and Manchester.* London: Routledge.

Degen M and García M (2012) The transformation of the "Barcelona model": An analysis of culture, urban regeneration and governance. *International Journal of Urban and Regional Research* 36(5), 1022–1038.

Delgado L and Escorihuela I (eds) (2017) *Exclusió residencial al món local, Informe de la crisi hipotecària a Barcelona (2013–2016).* Barcelona: Observatori DESC-PAH.

Delgado M (2005) *Elogi del vianant, Del "model Barcelona" a la Barcelona real.* Barcelona: Edicions de 1984.

Dredge D (2017) "Overtourism": Old wine in new bottles? Retrieved from https://www.linkedin.com/pulse/overtourism-old-wine-new-bottles-dianne-dredge.

Echtner C (1999) The semiotic paradigm: Implications for tourism research. *Tourism Management* 20(1), 47–57.

Fairclough N (1995) *Critical Discourse Analysis. The Critical Study of Language.* London: Longman.

García M and Claver N (2003) Barcelona: Governing coalitions, visitors and the changing city center. In: LM Hoffman, S Fainstein and DR Judd (eds), *Cities and Visitors: Regulating People, Markets, and City Space.* John Wiley & Sons, pp. 113–125.

Goodwin H (2017) The challenge of overtourism. Responsible Tourism Partnership Working Paper 4. Available at: http://haroldgoodwin.info/pubs/RTP'WP4Overtourism01'2017.pdf (accessed 25 May 2018).

Greimas AJ (1976) *Semiotique et Sciences Sociales.* Paris: Seuil.

Greimas AJ and Courtès J (1979) *Sémiotique.* Paris: Editions Hachette.

Gutiérrez A and Delclòs X (2016) The uneven distribution of evictions as new evidence of urban inequality: A spatial analysis approach in two Catalan cities. *Cities* 56, 101–108.

Hajer M (1995) *The Politics of Environmental Discourse: Ecological Modernization and the Policy Process.* Oxford: Oxford University Press.

Hall CM (1994) *Tourism and Politics: Policy, Power and Place.* Hoboken, NJ: John Wiley & Sons.

Hall CM (2006) Urban entrepreneurship, corporate interests and sports mega-events: The thin policies of competitiveness within the hard outcomes of neoliberalism. *Sociological Review* 54(2), 50–70.

Hunter WC (2013) China's Chairman Mao: A visual analysis of Hunan Province online destination image. *Tourism Management* 34, 101–111.

Jaworski A and Thurlow C (2010) Introducing semiotic landscapes. In: A Jaworski and C Thurlow (eds), *Semiotic Landscapes. Language, Image, Space.* London: Continuum, pp. 1–40.

Judd DR and Fainstein S (1999) *The Tourist City.* New Haven, CT: Yale University Press.

Landowski E (1989) *La Société Réfléchie. Essais de Sociosémiotique.* Paris: Seuil.

López Palomeque F, Torres Delgado A and Font X (2016). System of tourism indicators for the sustainable management of destinations in the province of Barcelona. In:

A Makua and R Ahedo (eds), *Improving Sustainable Tourism in XXIst Century*. Universidad de Deusto, pp. 57–69.

McCann EJ (2004) "Best places': Interurban competition, quality of life and popular media discourse. *Urban Studies* 41(10), 1909–1929.

McCombs M (1997) Building consensus: The news media's agenda-setting roles. *Political Communication* 14(4): 433–443.

McGovern SJ (2009) Mobilization on the waterfront: The ideological/cultural roots of potential regime change in Philadelphia. *Urban Affairs Review* 44(5), 663–694.

Maragall P (1986) *Refent Barcelona*. Barcelona: Planeta.

Marrone G (2001) *Corpi Sociali. Processi Comunicativi e Semiotica del Testo*. Torino: Einaudi.

Martín Martín J, Guaita Martínez J, and Salinas Fernández J (2018). An analysis of the factors behind the citizen's attitude of rejection towards tourism in a context of over-tourism and economic dependence on this activity. *Sustainability* 10(8), 2851–2869.

Milano C (2018). Overtourism, social unrest and tourismphobia. A controversial debate. *PASOS: Revista de Turismo y Patrimonio Cultural* 16(3), 551–564.

Miraftab F (2004) Making neo-liberal governance: The disempowering work of empowerment. *International Planning Studies* 9(4), 239–259.

Monclús FJ (2003) The Barcelona model: and an original formula? From "reconstruction" to strategic urban projects (1979–2004). *Planning Perspectives* 18(4), 399–421.

Mossberger K and Stoker G (2001) The evolution of urban regime theory the challenge of conceptualization. *Urban Affairs Review* 36(6), 810–835.

Mumbrú J (2017) Els Barcelonins que no volen més turistes són majoria per primer cop. *Ara*, 15 April. Available at: http://www.ara.cat/societat/barcelonins-que-volen -turistes-majoria_0_1778822129.html (accessed 10 February 2018).

Novy J (2018) Urban tourism as a bone of contention: Four explanatory hypotheses and a caveat. *International Journal of Tourism Cities*. DOI: 10.1108/IJTC-01-2018-0011

Peck J, and Tickell A (2002) Neoliberalizing space. *Antipode* 34(3), 380–404.

Pizza A (2007) Barcellona "critica": gli scenari dell'attualità. *Area* 90, 4–13.

Quaglieri Domínguez A and Scarnato A (2017) The Barrio Chino as last frontier. In: M Gravari-Barbas and S Guinand (eds), *Tourism and Gentrification in Contemporary Metropolises: International Perspectives*. Oxford: Taylor & Francis, pp. 107–133.

Scarnato A (2016) *Barcelona Supermodelo. La Complejidad de una Transformación Social y Urbana, 1979–2011*. Barcelona: Comanegra.

Smith A (2005) Conceptualizing city image change: The "re-imaging" of Barcelona. *Tourism Geographies* 7(4), 398–423.

Stepchenkova S, Kirilenko AP and Morrison AM (2009) Facilitating content analysis in tourism research. *Journal of Travel Research* 47(4), 454–469.

Stone CN (1993) Urban regimes and the capacity to govern: A political economy approach. *Journal of Urban Affairs* 15(1), 1–28.

Swyngedouw E (2004) Globalisation or "glocalisation"? Networks, territories and rescaling. *Cambridge Review of International Affairs* 17(1), 25–48.

Trallero M and Reboredo S (2004) *Barcelona 2004 Como mentira!* Barcelona: Belacqua.

Vaara E, Sorsa V and Pälli P (2010) On the force potential of strategy texts: A critical discourse analysis of a strategic plan and its power effects in a city organization. *Organization* 17(6), 685–702.

Van Dijk T (2001) Discourse, ideology and context. *Folia Linguistica* 1–2, 11–40.

Volli U (2003) Svago, sguardo, iper-esperienze. In: R Bonadei and U Volli (eds), *Lo Sguardo del Turista e il Racconto dei Luoghi*. Milano: Franco Angeli.

14 Post-COVID-19 urban tourism research

Sebastian Zenker

Introduction

The COVID-19 pandemic is unquestionably one of the most impactful events of the twenty-first century – including for the tourism industry. With borders closed, air fleets grounded, cruise vessels docked and hotels, restaurants and touristic sights in shutdown for months, the tourism industry took a heavy blow (Karabulut et al., 2020). Some estimations see 75 million jobs in tourism at immediate risk, while the industry could lose more than 2.1 trillion US$ in turnover (WTTC, 2020). Other forecasts anticipate a drop in tourism of between 30.8 and 76.3% in 2021 (compared with 2019), suggesting that the recovery will not be immediate (Fotiadis et al., 2021).

Understandably, this immense shock to the global systems that underlie tourism has created a flood of research in this area (Bausch et al., 2020). Urban tourism, in particular, is facing a reckoning about the attractiveness of such travel: since urban tourism is often associated with crowding and multiple shorter trips, it is especially vulnerable to health risks and is thus logically less attractive than more social-distance-friendly rural or coastal tourism.

More broadly, this pandemic has forced some questions about our basic assumptions regarding travel – indeed, what "was previously taken for granted may not hold anymore in the COVID-19 era" (Kock et al., 2020, p. 2). In the aftermath of the crisis, "some aspects of our behaviour might be affected by true paradigm-shifts" (Zenker & Kock, 2020, p. 2) and will involve permanent changes. However, this does not mean that all tourism research is now obsolete – far from it.

The desire for travel will remain a human need, as evidenced by previous research indicating that tourism regularly recovers from crises and disasters (e.g., Cró & Martins, 2017). While no prior crisis has served as a real transition event, crises do tend to hasten changes and improvements that were already underway (Hall et al., 2020). Therefore, this chapter intends to discuss some areas of potential change that have been illuminated by the current pandemic, as well as offer some suggestions for an urban tourism research agenda in a post-COVID-19 world.

COVID-19 pandemic's impact on urban tourism

While the pandemic has broadly impacted the general tourism domain, urban tourism has endured some distinct setbacks (e.g., as stated, urban tourism seems less suited to a social-distancing-friendly type of travel). In this sense, there is research value in differentiating between different travel types (e.g., rural vs. urban tourism) or among target groups that attribute high importance to urban tourism (e.g., the specifics of post-COVID-19 business travel). However, the field should resist the urge to simply present "the obvious and purely descriptive" (Zenker & Kock, 2020, p. 3); it is important to understand *what* has changed, but we must also evaluate *why* the changes happened in the first place.

First, we need to acknowledge that crises and disasters are generally well-researched phenomena. Tourism studies on Ebola (Novelli et al., 2018), influenza pandemics (Page et al., 2006), SARS (Zeng et al., 2005), and bird-flu (Rittichainuwat & Chakraborty, 2009) show comparable patterns on smaller scales – thus, not all aspects of COVID-19 are novel enough to justify further research. To avoid simply repeating previous studies as part of an explosion of "COVID-19 related research", we need to adopt inter-disciplinary, multi-disciplinary, or even anti-disciplinary research. The goal should be "to enable out-of-the-box, creative and flexible thinking that challenges and goes beyond existing pre-assumptions and mindsets" (Sigala, 2020, p. 313).

At the time of writing this chapter, there were already some interesting (theoretical and empirical) COVID-19 tourism papers that could be reframed with the urban tourism lens. To name just a few: Sigala (2020) discussed the general implications of resetting the tourism industry and outlined several research endeavours, most of which would be applicable to urban tourism.

Farzanegan et al. (2020) examined the direct impact of tourism on the spreading of the Coronavirus. Differentiating between different travel types and travel groups in this way could be helpful for assessing the risk factors of different tourism types for future pandemics.

Buckley and Westaway (2020) focused on the mental and social health outcomes of outdoor tourism for women. Their main argument is that outdoor tourism has a positive impact on mental and social health, but it remains unclear whether urban tourism exerts a similar effect.

Zenker et al. (2021) showed that anxiety about COVID-19 leads to a lower intention to visit a place. Further, this anxiety is theoretically and empirically distinct from the concept of xenophobia, which is a general need to avoid unknown or foreign experiences (Kock et al., 2019a). By adapting the authors' Pandemic Anxiety Travel Scale (PATS), this relationship could be tested in several moderating settings (e.g., urban vs. rural tourism).

Urban tourism researchers might also turn to tourist behaviour studies on crises for inspiration. For instance, Hajibaba et al. (2015) conceptualized a segment of crisis-resistant tourists that might explain why some tourists keep travelling, while Seabra et al. (2013) examined the safety perceptions of international tourists. Diving deeper into the travel preferences of such crisis-resistant tourists could be valuable.

The political aspect of the COVID-19 pandemic shares similarities (and thus, theoretical foundations) with tourism research conducted during the Arab Spring uprising (Avraham, 2015) or the refugee-crisis (Zenker et al., 2019), which grapple with how a country's image is affected by political conflicts (e.g., Alvarez & Campo, 2014). Likewise, the economic crisis activated by COVID-19 overlaps with papers on the 2008 economic crisis (Papatheodorou et al., 2010) and others that address how tourists' economizing strategies shift their travel behaviours (Campos-Soria et al., 2015). Again, none of these papers have specifically explored urban tourism and compared it with different travel types.

Looking at the management of disasters and crises, Okuyama (2018) analysed the optimal timing of recovery policies, Ritchie (2004) provided a strategic approach to crisis management and Wang and Ritchie (2012) researched managers' crisis management. On the meta-level, three recent literature reviews summarize the most relevant findings (Jiang et al., 2017; Mair et al., 2016; Ritchie & Jiang, 2019) that could be applied to urban tourism.

To dive deeper, let us focus on the specifics of the COVID-19 pandemic for the three main tourism stakeholders (i.e., tourism demand, tourism supply, governments and policies) within the urban tourism field.

Urban tourism demand

The COVID-19 pandemic might galvanize general changes to tourism behaviour. Existing evolutionary psychology research provides comprehensive evidence that a pathogen threat shapes behaviour in important ways, which will almost certainly extend to the Coronavirus (Kock et al., 2020): we can already see how the COVID-19 health risk perception plays a significant role in affecting people's mental well-being and perceived uncertainty (Chua et al., 2020). Both factors ultimately lower the attractiveness of international travel and increase both short- and long-term travel avoidance (Zheng et al., 2021). Neuburger and Egger (2020) similarly showed that COVID-19-induced travel risk perceptions changed the travel behaviour of certain target groups, while others seemed to worry less and did not alter their behaviour dramatically.

In general, research shows that people become more collectivistic when exposed to a disease threat (Cashdan & Steel, 2013). As a result, tourists may increasingly select domestic over foreign destinations in an attempt to support their local economy – a behaviour that existing research has coined tourism ethnocentrism (Kock et al., 2019b). This reaction may constitute a shift in tourist behaviour away from far-flung urban destinations to regional ones.

Furthermore, research has found that pathogen threats make people more aware of and cautious about crowdedness (Wang & Ackerman, 2019). This propensity could initiate a mental shift in tourists' travel behaviour, leading them to avoid overcrowded and mass-tourism urban destinations in favour of more remote, less popular rural or costal destinations.

Finally, a pathogen threat triggers a behavioural immune system, which motivates people to avoid unknown things (i.e., xenophobia). Thus, tourists could also show more xenophobic behaviour (Kock et al., 2019a), resulting in less foreign travel, the avoidance of foreign food, more group travel and more travel insurance purchases.

These general changes to travellers' psyche (Zheng et al., 2021) could ultimately reshape the demand for urban tourism. Industry players would need to quickly adapt their offers in order to accommodate the desire for more space and exclusivity, while minimizing crowding. Practitioners are also challenged to restore trust and lower travellers' uncertainty. That said, more research is needed to increase the effectiveness of such communication strategies and crisis management more generally (Ritchie, 2004; Wang & Ritchie, 2012).

We must also acknowledge the financial hardships imposed by the current pandemic. Economic crises do have a significant short-term impact on travel behaviour (Campos-Soria et al., 2015; Papatheodorou et al., 2010), which might lead to a difference in price sensitivity and perception (Zhang et al., 2020).

For urban tourism, the business travel sector might be even more of a concern (Ashworth & Page, 2011). This sector is expecting a huge estimated drop in demand (McKinsey, 2020) that will probably culminate in long-term changes to business travel. The pandemic taught many companies that not all business travel is necessary and that video-conferencing can be a more cost- and time-efficient solution. For instance, Microsoft co-founder Bill Gates predicted that business travel will decrease by more than 50% in the pandemic's aftermath (CNBC, 2020, November 17). Again, this will have a dramatic impact on the supply side of tourism, as many tourism and hospitality business models rely on high-level business travel.

Urban tourism supply

The pandemic's impact on the tourism and hospitality industry has been a prominent topic in the media. Obviously, many tourism companies are in direct risk of bankruptcy due to losing months' worth of revenue. Many countries have created special programmes to save some of their national tourism and hospitality companies (e.g., airlines). However, not all tourism businesses were negatively affected – for instance, short-term vacation rentals increased their market share (Forbes, 2020, October 22). Similarly, the real estate market for holiday homes had a very successful year (Globetrender, 2020, September 24).

Against this backdrop, one of the most heavily discussed urban tourism cases involves Airbnb (Stors, 2020). Previously seen as "new urban tourism", boosting travel to urban destinations and enabling travel for new target groups, it has encountered heavy criticism for its negative impact on over-tourism, gentrification and putting pressure on the rental market (Zach et al., 2020). How (and if) Airbnb and similar platforms will be affected by the pandemic in the long-run remains unclear. Dolnicar and Zare (2020, p. 1), for instance, postulated that "the proportion of investor-hosted listings will drop, and trading of space on Airbnb and similar platforms will not recover to its pre-COVID-19 levels".

In other areas, the pandemic is working to hasten the digital revolution. Airports, hotels and restaurants, for instance, have re-engineered their servicescapes to make them safer and contact-free. Many companies rapidly installed mobile apps, self-service and e-shopping, even if they were previously resistant. The "new operating environment enforced by COVID-19 measures requires firms to adopt new technologies and applications to ensure management of crowds [...], human disinfectors and hand sanitiser equipment, applications identifying and managing people's health identity and profiles" (Sigala, 2020, p. 319). With so many companies leveraging the pandemic as a transformative moment of change, there is a need for more e-tourism research (Gretzel et al., 2020) with a specific focus on urban tourism.

At this moment, it is important to consider the long-term picture. Most research on crises has focused on the immediate effects, but the full impact of the COVID-19 pandemic will not be known until we can account for the long-term and indirect effects as well.

The issue of sustainability is an illustrative example (e.g., Garay et al., 2017). Before the pandemic this was a high priority for many tourism stakeholders, but we can now envision two different long-term scenarios. On the one hand, governments and businesses may seek to preserve the existing economic system through financial support and deregulations (Masco, 2017). Companies will need to divert financial resources away from intended sustainability investments in order to simply stay afloat. Meanwhile, the recession may incline consumers to look for the lowest price rather than the most sustainable option. Because sustainability behaviour in the tourism industry has largely been driven by internal stakeholder consent and industry best practices (Garay et al., 2017), there is a risk of a vicious cycle where sustainability efforts are undercut by too many businesses moving in a different direction.

Another scenario might be a real paradigm shift (Ioannides & Gyimóthy, 2020). Due to the external shock, many tourism companies will close down and create an opportunity for new business models to develop. Given the positive correlation between sustainability initiatives and financial performance in the tourism industry (Singal, 2014), it is likely that these new businesses will invest in sustainability and might be more open to change and innovation. Urged by this development, other businesses might follow suit (Garay et al., 2017). Customers might also see the pandemic as a reason to behave more sustainably. These changes could create a virtuous cycle in support of sustainable development. However, given the difficulty of predicting long-term and indirect effects, urban tourism research needs more long-term and carefully constructed projects.

The cruise tourism industry offers a useful focus as well (Choquet & Sam-Lefebvre, 2021; Pan et al., 2021). With ships docked for months, many older vessels have been sent in to be decommissioned (Reuters, 2020, October 3) – much earlier than previously planned. At the same time, five new cruise ships were put into service in 2020 and eight are planned for 2021 (CruiseCritic, 2020). Since these new vessels will have a much better ecological footprint than the old ones, they will contribute to a more ecologically sustainable industry. At the same time, this development (and the government subsidies for big cruise companies) prevents the industry from collapsing and forcing a real re-start (or a more critical rethinking of the current state of cruise tourism in a larger context). This is partly why the cruise industry has been highly scrutinized as of late, especially in the lens of urban tourism; the current development can only be seen as a minor improvement.

Finally, the fundamental changes to business travel are disrupting the business model of many tourism and hospitality companies for urban tourism. Airlines often rely on business travellers to subsidize other customers and thus make them special deals. For instance, the typical weekend visits of urban tourism rely on the fast and direct connections of a dense network of flights. If that is not economically sustainable for the airlines, urban destinations will lose connections that make them so attractive for all types of travellers. The same goes for the business models of many high- and middle-class hotels and restaurants, which will become less profitable with a lower percentage of business travellers.

A post-COVID-19 urban tourism research agenda should aim to advance our knowledge about recovery processes and how to build a more crisis-resistant tourism business ecosystem, especially in partnership with another important stakeholder: the governmental institutions and destination management organizations (DMOs).

Urban tourism policies

Urban tourism is a highly political field. Due to COVID-19, governmental bodies and DMOs have gained strength in urban tourism by implementing stronger (health-related) tourism policies and taking a more protective role over the tourism and hospitality industry (e.g., through tax relief, subsidies and payment deferrals; Sigala, 2020).

At the beginning of the pandemic, many practitioners and researchers hoped that governments would use this crisis as an opportunity to rethink a more sustainable tourism industry (e.g., Ioannides & Gyimóthy, 2020) – but reality has proven us wrong so far. Similar to previous crises, governments appear to be preserving the status quo rather than leveraging the crisis as a real transition event (Hall et al., 2020; Masco, 2017) for rethinking (urban) tourism as such. However, we expect that that effort will meet with more failures than success.

Despite the reverberations of the pandemic, we expect that governments and DMOs will continue to face many of the same problems. While they must currently grapple with the problem of under-tourism, it may not be long before they are once again staring down the issues of overtourism – such as crowding, allocating resources, prioritizing interests, and achieving ecological, economic and social sustainability. The COVID-19 pandemic simply "pressed pause" on these challenges; urban tourism policymakers still need to find answers.

Governments will also have to navigate new issues spurred by the pandemic. For instance, the economic impact of the pandemic is heavily skewed towards low-salary jobs (e.g., waiters, hotel staff) and self-employed tourism workers (e.g., artists working in the cultural service industry). While most governments subsidized the larger "system-relevant" tourism companies and will probably save them, their actions raise a question about social fairness (Sigala, 2020). In this vein, research might focus on evaluating the impact and effectiveness of such policies for urban tourism and society as a whole.

Another focus in this regard might be the "infodemic" and "(mis)infodemic" that accompanied the COVID-19 pandemic (Williams et al., 2020). The pure flood of constantly changing information during the pandemic (e.g., death tolls, infection indices, health regulations) might have led people to differently perceive and process information. Worse still, the deluge of misinformation that occurred (the (mis)infodemic) "can change risk perceptions of travel, resulting in travel patterns based on technological, regulatory, and perceived behavioral homophily" (Williams et al., 2020, p. 1). Here governments need to better understand the underlying mechanisms and develop counter-strategies for future crises.

Tourism destination organizations often spend a large amount of their resources on the management and improvement of a destination image (Zenker et al., 2017), which exerts significant influence over tourists' destination choice. Existing research indicates that images can change across time (e.g., Kock et al., 2016); hence, there is a need to examine how the COVID-19 pandemic has altered the images of particular urban destinations. Specifically, some destinations (e.g., New York) are suffering from high infection rates, which could have altered the images that potential tourists attribute to them. Two potential outcomes are discernible: first, the destinations exposed to

COVID-19 may face a liability in future attempts to attract tourists because of their worsened image, particularly among those tourists who are risk-sensitive and vulnerable. Second, and in contrast, these urban destinations may benefit from future tourists' willingness to economically support those places shaken by COVID-19.

Drawing on the same theory, residents may also become less welcoming of incoming tourists and less supportive of tourism development (i.e., resident xenophobia). Indeed, the pandemic might shift the perceived costs of tourism for residents (Qui et al., 2020). This could potentially lead to in-group/out-group biases among both residents and tourists – a phenomenon that remains under-researched (Chien & Ritchie, 2018). Such knowledge could have a strong impact on tourism policies and how politicians prioritize interests in relation to urban tourism.

Some preliminary conclusions and consequences for an urban research agenda

In the aftermath of crises there is often a sentiment that "things will never be the same again" – but, with time, most people return to their normal routines. It is still too early to say if this will also hold true for the current COVID-19 pandemic.

Nevertheless, this crisis represents an important change in urban tourism research that carries with it exciting research possibilities. The field thereby has a real opportunity to not simply carry the old flame of urban tourism, but to challenge the growth paradigms and habits that led to the current situation (Ioannides & Gyimóthy, 2020; Sigala, 2020; Zenker & Kock, 2020). Obviously not all of our knowledge and foci will become obsolete, but we should be prepared to constantly question our assumptions and address the evolving realities of the urban landscape.

References

Alvarez, M. D., & Campo, S. (2014). The influence of political conflicts on country image and intention to visit: A study of Israel's image. *Tourism Management, 40*, 70–78.

Ashworth, G., & Page, S. J. (2011). Urban tourism research: Recent progress and current paradoxes. *Tourism Management, 32*(1), 1–15.

Avraham, E. (2015). Destination image repair during crisis: Attracting tourism during the Arab Spring uprisings. *Tourism Management, 47,* 224–232.

Bausch, T., Gartner, W. C., & Ortanderl, F. (2020). How to avoid a COVID-19 research paper tsunami? A tourism system approach. *Journal of Travel Research,* 0047287520972805.

Buckley, R., & Westaway, D. (2020). Mental health rescue effects of women's outdoor tourism: A role in COVID-19 recovery. *Annals of Tourism Research, 85,* 103041.

Campos-Soria, J. A., Inchausti-Sintes, F., & Eugenio-Martin, J. L. (2015). Understanding tourists' economizing strategies during the global economic crisis. *Tourism Management, 48,* 164–173.

Cashdan, E., & Steele, M. (2013). Pathogen prevalence, group bias, and collectivism in the standard cross-cultural sample. *Human Nature, 24*(1), 59–75.

Chien, P. M., & Ritchie, B. W. (2018). Understanding intergroup conflicts in tourism. *Annals of Tourism Research, 72*(September), 177–179.

Choquet, A., & Sam-Lefebvre, A. (2021). Ports closed to cruise ships in the context of COVID-19: What choices are there for coastal states? *Annals of Tourism Research, 86,* 103066.

Chua, B. L., Al-Ansi, A., Lee, M. J., & Han, H. (2020). Impact of health risk perception on avoidance of international travel in the wake of a pandemic. *Current Issues in Tourism,* 1–18.

CNBC (2020, November 17). Bill Gates says more than 50% of business travel will disappear in post-coronavirus world. Video. Accessed 9 January 2021 from https://www.cnbc.com/2020/11/17/coronavirus-bill-gates-says-more-than-50percent-of-business-travel-will-disappear-long-term.html

Cró, S., & Martins, A. M. (2017). Structural breaks in international tourism demand: Are they caused by crises or disasters? *Tourism Management, 63,* 3–9.

CruiseCritic (2020). New cruise ships on order. Accessed 10 January 2021 from https://www.cruisecritic.com/articles.cfm?ID=167.

Dolnicar, S., & Zare, S. (2020). COVID19 and Airbnb – Disrupting the disruptor. *Annals of Tourism Research, 83,* 102961.

Farzanegan, M. R., Gholipour, H. F., Feizi, M., Nunkoo, R., & Andargoli, A. E. (2020). International tourism and outbreak of coronavirus (COVID-19): A cross-country analysis. *Journal of Travel Research,* 0047287520931593.

Forbes (2020, October 22). Temporary changes in travel result in increased demand for short-term rentals. *Forbes.* Accessed 10 January 2021 from https://www.forbes.com/sites/forbesrealestatecouncil/2020/10/22/temporary-changes-in-travel-result-in-increased-demand-for-short-term-rentals/?sh=52af86cb70fe.

Fotiadis, A., Polyzos, S., & Huan, T. C. T. (2021). The good, the bad and the ugly on COVID-19 tourism recovery. *Annals of Tourism Research, 87,* 103117.

Garay, L., Font, X., & Pereira-Moliner, J. (2017). Understanding sustainability behaviour: The relationship between information acquisition, proactivity and performance. *Tourism Management, 60,* 418–429.

Globetrender (2020, September 24). Pandemic restrictions fuel demand for buying holiday homes. *Globetrender.* Accessed 10 January 2021 from https://globetrender.com/2020/09/24/pandemic-increase-demand-holiday-homes/.

Gretzel, U., Fuchs, M., Baggio, R., Hoepken, W., Law, R., Neidhardt, J., Peson, J., Zanker, M., & Xiang, Z. (2020). E-tourism beyond COVID-19: A call for transformative research. *Information Technology & Tourism, 22,* 187–203.

Hajibaba, H., Gretzel, U., Leisch, F., & Dolnicar, S. (2015). Crisis-resistant tourists. *Annals of Tourism Research, 53*, 46–60.

Hall, C. M., Scott, D., & Gössling, S. (2020). Pandemics, transformations and tourism: Be careful what you wish for. *Tourism Geographies, 22*(3), 577–598.

Ioannides, D. & Gyimóthy, S. (2020). The COVID-19 crisis as an opportunity for escaping the unsustainable global tourism path. *Tourism Geographies, 22*(3), 624–632.

Jiang, Y., Ritchie, B. W., & Benckendorff, P. (2017). Bibliometric visualisation: An application in tourism crisis and disaster management research. *Current Issues in Tourism, 22*(16), 1–33.

Karabulut, G., Bilgin, M. H., Demir, E., & Doker, A. C. (2020). How pandemics affect tourism: International evidence. *Annals of Tourism Research, 84*, 102991.

Kock, F., Josiassen, A., & Assaf, A. G. (2016). Advancing destination image: The destination content model. *Annals of Tourism Research, 61*, 28–44.

Kock, F., Josiassen, A., & Assaf, A. G. (2019a). The xenophobic tourist. *Annals of Tourism Research, 74*, 155–166.

Kock, F., Josiassen, A., Assaf, A. G., Karpen, I., & Farrelly, F. (2019b). Tourism ethnocentrism and its effects on tourist and resident behavior. *Journal of Travel Research, 58*(3), 427–439.

Kock, F., Nørfelt, A., Josiassen, A., Assaf, A. G., & Tsionas, M. G. (2020). Understanding the COVID-19 tourist psyche: The evolutionary tourism paradigm. *Annals of Tourism Research, 85*, 103053.

Mair, J., Ritchie, B. W., & Walters, G. (2016). Towards a research agenda for post-disaster and post-crisis recovery strategies for tourist destinations: A narrative review. *Current Issues in Tourism, 19*(1), 1–26.

Masco, J. (2017). The crisis in crisis. *Current Anthropology, 58*(S15), S65–S76.

McKinsey (2020). *For corporate travel, a long recovery ahead.* Report McKinsey & Company. Accessed 9 January 2021 from https://www.mckinsey.com/industries/travel-logistics-and-transport-infrastructure/our-insights/for-corporate-travel-a-long-recovery-ahead#

Neuburger, L., & Egger, R. (2020). Travel risk perception and travel behaviour during the COVID-19 pandemic 2020: A case study of the DACH region. *Current Issues in Tourism*, 1–14. DOI: 10.1080/13683500.2020.1803807

Novelli, M., Burgess, L. G., Jones, A., & Ritchie, B. W. (2018). "No Ebola... still doomed"–The Ebola-induced tourism crisis. *Annals of Tourism Research, 70*, 76–87.

Okuyama, T. (2018). Analysis of optimal timing of tourism demand recovery policies from natural disaster using the contingent behavior method. *Tourism Management, 64*, 37–54.

Page, S., Yeoman, I., Munro, C., Connell, J., & Walker, L. (2006). A case study of best practice—Visit Scotland's prepared response to an influenza pandemic. *Tourism Management, 27*(3), 361–393.

Pan, T., Shu, F., Kitterlin-Lynch, M., & Beckman, E. (2021). Perceptions of cruise travel during the COVID-19 pandemic: Market recovery strategies for cruise businesses in North America. *Tourism Management, 85*, 104275.

Papatheodorou, A., Rosselló, J., & Xiao, H. (2010). Global economic crisis and tourism: Consequences and perspectives. *Journal of Travel Research, 49*(1), 39–45.

Qui, R. T., Park, J., Li, S., & Song, H. (2020). Social costs of tourism during the COVID-19 pandemic. *Annals of Tourism Research, 84*, 102994.

Reuters (2020, October 3). Cruise ship dismantling booms in Turkey after pandemic scuttles sector. *Reuters.* Accessed 10 January 2021 from https://www.reuters.com/

article/health-coronavirus-turkey-ships/cruise-ship-dismantling-booms-in-turkey
-after-pandemic-scuttles-sector-idUSL8N2GT33H.

Ritchie, B. W. (2004). Chaos, crises and disasters: A strategic approach to crisis management in the tourism industry. *Tourism Management, 25*(6), 669–683.

Ritchie, B. W., & Jiang, Y. (2019). A review of research on tourism risk, crisis and
disaster management: Launching the annals of tourism research curated collection
on tourism risk, crisis and disaster management. *Annals of Tourism Research,
79*(November), 102812.

Rittichainuwat, B. N., & Chakraborty, G. (2009). Perceived travel risks regarding terror-
ism and disease: The case of Thailand. *Tourism Management, 30*(3), 410–418.

Seabra, C., Dolnicar, S., Abrantes, J. L., & Kastenholz, E. (2013). Heterogeneity in risk
and safety perceptions of international tourists. *Tourism Management, 36*, 502–510.

Sigala, M. (2020). Tourism and COVID-19: Impacts and implications for advancing
and resetting industry and research. *Journal of Business Research, 117*, 312–321.

Singal, M. (2014). The link between firm financial performance and investment in
sustainability initiatives. *Cornell Hospitality Quarterly, 55*(1), 19–30.

Stors, N. (2020). Constructing new urban tourism space through Airbnb. *Tourism
Geographies*, online first, 1–24. DOI: https://doi.org/10.1080/14616688.2020
.1750683.

Wang, I. M., & Ackerman, J. M. (2019). The infectiousness of crowds: crowding experiences are amplified by pathogen threats. *Personality and Social Psychology Bulletin,
45*(1), 120–132.

Wang, J., & Ritchie, B. W. (2012). Understanding accommodation managers' crisis
planning intention: An application of the theory of planned behaviour. *Tourism
Management, 33*(5), 1057–1067.

Williams, N. L., Wassler, P., & Ferdinand, N. (2020). Tourism and the COVID-(Mis)
infodemic. *Journal of Travel Research*, 0047287520981135.

WTTC (2020). *Latest research from WTTC*. World Travel & Tourism Council (WTTC).
Retrieved 8 April 2020, from https://www.wttc.org/about/media-centre/press
-releases/press-releases/2020/latest-research-from-wttc-shows-an-increase-in-jobs
-at-risk-in-travel-and-tourism/.

Zach, F. J., Nicolau, J. L., & Sharma, A. (2020). Disruptive innovation, innovation adoption and incumbent market value: The case of Airbnb. *Annals of Tourism Research,
80*, 102818.

Zeng, B., Carter, R. W., & De Lacy, T. (2005). Short-term perturbations and tourism
effects: The case of SARS in China. *Current Issues in Tourism, 8*(4), 306–322

Zenker, S., Braun, E., & Gyimóthy, S. (2021). Too afraid to travel? Development of
a Pandemic (COVID-19) Anxiety Travel Scale (PATS). *Tourism Management, 84*,
104286.

Zenker, S., Braun, E., & Petersen, S. (2017). Branding the destination versus the place:
The effects of brand complexity and identification for residents and visitors. *Tourism
Management, 58*, 15–27.

Zenker, S., & Kock, F. (2020). The coronavirus pandemic – A critical discussion of
a tourism research agenda. *Tourism Management, 81*, 104164.

Zenker, S., von Wallpach, S., Braun, E., & Vallaster, C. (2019). How the refugee crisis
impacts the decision structure of tourists: A cross-country scenario study. *Tourism
Management, 71*, 197–212.

Zhang, K., Hou, Y., & Li, G. (2020). Threat of infectious disease during an outbreak:
Influence on tourists' emotional responses to disadvantaged price inequality. *Annals
of Tourism Research, 84*, 102993.

Zheng, D., Luo, Q., & Ritchie, B. W. (2021). Afraid to travel after COVID-19? Self-protection, coping and resilience against pandemic 'travel fear'. *Tourism Management*, *83*, 104261.

15 Towards *A Research Agenda for Urban Tourism*. A synthesis

Jan van der Borg

Introduction

At the end of 2019, there seemed to be no cloud in the sky for tourism in general and for urban tourism in particular. The United Nations World Tourism Organization (UNWTO) predictions of a doubling of international travelers between 2015 and 2030 appeared on the pessimistic rather than the optimistic side. With the continuous growth in the number of travelers worldwide, the economic importance of the industry would also steadily increase. A study by the World Travel & Tourism Council (WTTC), in collaboration with Oxford Economics, showed at the beginning of 2020 that the travel and tourism industry experienced a growth of no less than 3.5% in 2019, driving global economic growth of 2.5% for the ninth consecutive year. Between 2015 and 2019, one in four new jobs were created within the sector. And in 2019 alone, the total impact of the travel and tourism industry worldwide accounted for a gross product of $8.9 trillion, 10.3% of the total gross product. The industry and its supply companies created approximately 330 million jobs in 2019, which equates to one in ten jobs worldwide. According to the experts, the tourism industry had grown into the most important industry in the world economy.

The coronavirus, which spread rapidly across the world at the beginning of 2020 thanks to our travel behavior, brought all this to an abrupt end. From a booming and leading industry, the tourism industry, along with the cultural sector, became the worst affected industry in the world economy. Destinations for urban tourism were particularly hurt by the pandemic. The UNWTO estimates that, despite the short-lived upswing during the summer months, the number of travelers in 2020 will have fallen between 60 and 80% and that about 100 million jobs have been lost in the tourism industry. This blow was especially hard in those parts of the world that are very dependent on tourism economically. In countries such as Greece, Italy and Croatia, and in cities such as Amsterdam, Bruges, Prague and Venice, the socio-economic misery generated by the COVID-19 crisis is still incalculable.

From a tourist point of view, the COVID-19 crisis certainly also has a number of important advantages. Biodiversity has increased significantly in many places. Especially in the first half of 2020, the airlines saw their carbon footprint, together with the number of flight movements, reduced to almost zero. And the aforementioned tourist art cities were no longer overrun with hordes of mass tourists from one day to the next, but their inhabitants found some well-deserved rest. The inhabitants took possession of their cities again in record time. At the same time, researchers, policymakers and residents' organizations saw the overtouristic storyline, to which they had paid so much attention before the crisis, melt from one day to the next like snow in the sun.

On balance, the desire to return to business as usual seems to be very strong. The summer of 2020 was just a preview of what is likely to be in store for tourism if the world is liberated from the virus and a general rethink is left out. When the European borders reopened on 15 June 2020, many southern European beaches immediately filled up and it immediately became busy again in the main art cities. This is of course not surprising. After more than a year of strict and less strict restrictions on freedom of movement, the urge to travel again is stronger than ever before. In addition, the tourism industry (especially smaller family businesses with very little financial reserves and which are certainly not in the front row in obtaining state aid), which has seen its revenues and profits almost completely evaporate, is eagerly looking forward to a return to business as usual.

Although hardly surprising, this would be a missed opportunity. Because it is precisely at this dramatic moment of relative calm that the aforementioned moment of reconsideration seems more appropriate than ever. And because it is unlikely that, for reasons discussed above, the tourist or the tourist entrepreneur will take the lead here, it will mainly depend on the clarity of the vision and the persuasiveness of the policymakers whether the tourism industry expects to exchange the mass tourism business model from before the pandemic for a business model that is profitable as well as sustainable and safe. That is, a business model where quality takes precedence over quantity, and all stakeholders – but above all residents and local entrepreneurs – can benefit from the attractiveness of the destination. A business model in which luxury is not necessarily identical to "expensive," but rather to unique and therefore often priceless experiences of which interaction with the inhabitants is an essential ingredient. Finally, a revenue model that not only explicitly looks at the turnover of the tourism industry and the gross product of the destination, but also at the collective costs that tourism development entails.

Traveling will never be the way it used to be. In the future, for example, travelers will never be as thoughtless as before the pandemic. Tourism companies will therefore continue to pay more attention to hygiene and safety standards. Many tourists will feel much more uncomfortable in a crowded plane, in a long queue in front of a museum, or in a crowded amusement park, than before. The inhabitants themselves also seem more sensitive to the crowds that are partly caused by visitors, whether it concerns their park, their town square, their city bus or their beach. Some form of social distancing will undoubtedly remain an integral part of our behavior in general and our tourism behavior in particular.

All this makes the discussion of how the scarce public space and the scarce facilities can be optimally used, which was so typical in iconic European urban tourism destinations, and which seemed to have disappeared completely with the pandemic, more relevant than ever. It also means that the tools developed to reduce the nuisance caused by tourism in a number of these destinations will continue to be of strategic importance in the future. This includes, for example, determining the so-called tourist carrying capacity of destinations and concrete protocols for controlling visitor flows, in order to spread the tourist pressure as much as possible in time and space, for example by booking the visit to a beach resort or an art city.

It will be quite a challenge to rebuild urban tourism after months of misery. We must not lose this momentum and it is very important that policymakers at all levels realize that they can and must play a key role here. Hopefully, the reconstruction will take into account the lessons we learned, both before and during the coronavirus crisis. A more viable, sustainable and safer business model will eventually prove to be in the interest of all those involved in the urban tourism development processes: the resident, the (tourist) entrepreneur, and of course also the traveler him or herself.

These introductory considerations are the foundations for defining the priorities that ought to be addressed in the research agenda for urban tourism as soon as the global COVID-19 crisis is under control. However, before outlining this agenda, let us first have a general look at the sustainability of tourism development in cities.

Understanding the issue of sustainability in urban tourism

The red thread that runs through the various chapters of this research agenda for urban tourism is that of finding a synthesis between the two dominating discourses – tourism as a booster of social and economic development in cities and tourism as a force that suffocates the economy and that damages the social texture of a city – that can be found in the literature. One of the most important challenges for urban tourism research in the coming years is to find some sort of synthesis between these two discourses. The first discourse perceives urban tourism development to be an important opportunity for cities to strengthen their economic base and to generate jobs, in particular for lower-skilled workers that risk being excluded from other recent urban development trajectories, for example the move to knowledge hubs. Publications by Ashworth, Law, Page and Van der Borg in the 1990s laid the foundations for this discourse, a discourse that has recently been taken up by many authors, for example in those of the papers collected by Wise and Jimura (2020) that look into the urban regenerative power of urban (cultural) tourism, and by Bellina and Pasquinelli (2017) that argue in their book, *Tourism and the City*, that the excessive focus in urban tourism research on the negativities that tourism provokes should be countered by research on the positive role tourism is playing in many cities. In fact, this second discourse, which has led for example to the introduction and the overwhelming popularity of the overtourism concept, focused very much on the flipside of the success of cities in developing themselves as attractions able to capture an important share of the tourism market.

By simply applying the business model of mass tourism to urban tourism, it has grown out to become a devastating force that was suffocating inhabitants and local entrepreneurs, and in the end was even hurting the interests of visitors and local tourism firms. This particular discourse can already be found in studies that investigated tourism in smaller South-European heritage cities such as Granada, Coimbra and Venice (see for example, Quinn, 2007 and Troitiño and Troitiño, 2010). Twenty-seven experts on urban tourism development from all over the world have contributed to this book, embracing different disciplines and looking into urban tourism developments in destinations in different geographic and economic contexts. The book thus provides readers with an overview of the issues that have proven to be essential for research in the debate on the role tourism can play in urban development processes. The resulting discourse will be relevant to discussing tourism in cities over the coming years, both from an academic and a policy point of view. The various chapters in this research agenda for urban tourism have been trying to find whether sustainable tourism development paths exist that are neither undertouristic nor overtouristic. The research agenda that derives from this quest reflects the recent insights that have been gathered about tourism in urban environments, helping cities to turn tourism into a force that makes them smarter, more inclusive, more sustainable and much safer.

Urban tourism became an important segment of the tourism market. Ashworth and Voogd (1990), Law (1993), Van den Berg et al. (1995), Jansen-Verbeke (1998), and Judd and Fainstein (1999) contributed to a better understanding of the opportunities that tourism offers for the economic and social development of (especially former industrial) cities. In these publications the predominant discourse was that urban tourism is able to help urban economies and societies compensate for the loss of the manufacturing sector, which was relocating to more peripheral areas in search of cheap land or to countries where labor was still cheap, in order to retain competitiveness in a global economy; and that of the population, which was moving towards the suburbs and secondary cities in search of bigger homes and amenities that could not be found in the cities, such as a cleaner environment, and where they could start reinventing themselves (see for example Cheshire and Hay, 1989). Cities such as Baltimore, Lyon, Manchester and Rotterdam were examples for other industrial and port cities to use tourism as a means of diversifying their economic base.

A much less popular discourse in those early studies on urban tourism was that of concentrating on what can be seen as the flipside of the success of cities in developing themselves as attractions able to capture an important share of the tourism market: overtourism. By simply applying the business model of mass tourism to urban tourism, it has become clear that tourism in cities has the potential to become a sometimes devastating force that could suffocate urban economies and societies. This particular discourse can be found in studies by, among others, Van der Borg (1991), Troitiño (1995), and Costa et al. (1996). Most of the cases studied in this context were smaller South-European heritage cities such as Granada, Coimbra and Venice, which served as cases studied to analyze the mechanisms that led to diseconomies and discontent among inhabitants. The idea that some form of sustainable development path exists for urban destinations as much as for destinations that depend on natural wealth has now finally become mainstream in research. It seems, though, that the current and rather trendy academic attention on overtourism in cities such as Barcelona, Bruges, Stockholm and Venice is dominating the urban research agenda, while the original idea that tourism might still be a powerful engine of economic and social development for cities – dominating in cities such as Addis Ababa, Rotterdam, Shanghai, all cases treated in the previous chapters – tends to be neglected. Much of this apparent disequilibrium stems from the way tourism has been developing over time. In fact, the development of the tourism phenomenon at large knows a number of very distinct phases and in each phase of development a particular business model has been embraced.

The first phase of this development process is widely known as the period of the so-called Grand Tour, the phenomenon that lies at the very basis of the word 'tourism'. People belonging to what now is known as the creative class (mostly academics, artists and clerics) and youngsters from wealthy families, travelled Europe to meet their peers, to study textbooks in important libraries, to gaze at works of art and architecture, and to admire particular landscapes. Collecting significant experiences and gathering knowledge were important motivations for travelling, sometimes in rather difficult conditions given the fact that the hospitality and the transportation sector were hardly developed.

After the Second World War things changed completely. In many parts of especially the industrialized countries, the average income per person, the number of paid vacation days, and car possession, among others, rose quickly and, from a rather exclusive activity, tourism rapidly became a mass phenomenon. Not only did the number of people travelling, especially through Europe and the USA, rise exponentially and in less than a decade, but also these travelers happened to go to exactly the same places in the same periods of the year: e.g. coastal areas during the summer months. Mass tourism was born and with it the mass tourism business model, based on the mere replication of successful formulas, on the search for economies of scale, and on price competition. Although the tourism market has diversified incredibly over the past decades, this particular business model continues to be the dominant one, both for other forms of tourism such as cultural tourism or urban tourism, as well as for particular branches such as the cruise industry or the airline industry. In such a business model, emphasis continues to be laid on the economic impact of tourism, as has become evident following the narratives that organizations representing the tourism industry, such as the WTTC and the UNWTO, were bringing forward in their reports in the 1990s and in the beginning of this millennium.

Yet, because of the exponential growth of tourism demand, and of the tourism industry facilitating this growth, and of the strong concentration of tourism in specific periods of the year, the high season, and in particular places, the so-called vacation hotspots, the first criticism on this model appeared, in particular with respect to tourism in natural areas. In the 1990s, a number of authors argued that other types of destinations might also suffer from an excessive touristic pressure, pressure related to the mass touristic business model the destinations were embracing. Today, cities such as Venice (as illustrated in Chapter 6 of this book), Stockholm (see the Chapter 8) and Barcelona (see Chapter 13) suffer from what has been frequently called 'overtourism' (UNWTO, 2019), and this has been considered specifically for urban tourism destinations in Chapter 12, written by Koens and Klijs.

Although overtourism has become a fashionable issue to write about, it is undeniable that these concerns remain very much something for policymakers to worry about. In fact, the various stakeholders that have traditionally been involved in the development processes of tourism, in particular policymakers and the tourism industry, still very much foster the traditional business model of quantity over quality and the economy over the other facets of life in destinations. The success of a destination is still very much measured in the number of overnight stays and the total expenditure of visitors and this is reflected in the statistical information that is systematically gathered for tourism in countries, regions and places.

This development, as Van der Borg (2017) has argued, is partly related to the very nature of the tourism product's core. The primary tourism products or the attractions are unique, not reproducible and, therefore, extremely scarce on the one hand, and on the other are often public goods, for which a market is either non-existing or far from efficient. The combination of extreme scarcity, which makes the search for an optimal allocation so important, and of being a public good, often leads almost automatically to the overutilization of tourism assets, whether they are natural or cultural assets, touristic facilities, infrastructure, or plain public spaces. Improvisation (or the market) does not induce a destination (automatically) to optimize the allocation of such assets but rather to maximize their utilization in pursuing economic gain. This is, as we will see later, what might be called the 'tragedy of tourism commons', paraphrasing Hardin (1968). It has proven to be very difficult to keep or to get popular destinations to form a similar, devastating development path and to embrace a radically different business model.

On the other hand, overtourism is not the only form of non-optimal allocation of tourism assets. Underutilization, the opposite direction in which the earlier-described market inefficiency might go, is socially and economically undesirable. In this case, the absence of market prices, and hence value, demotivates entrepreneurs or local policymakers to invest in tourism and to valorize the assets the destination possesses. Obviously, not using the potential for tourism development is, in essence, as undesirable for destinations as is overtourism. This is not only for destinations as a whole, but also for the often-noted unequal distribution of tourism in cities, with crowded city centers that contrast with (almost) tourist-free suburbs. One could also ask the question of whether this is a function of misallocation (see for example

Russo, 2002, or Jansen-Vebeke, 1998), or simply the spatial variability of the distribution of resources that is seen in almost every social and economic field.

It is not difficult to see that these two families of the misallocation of tourism assets fit the framework Butler presented in the *Canadian Geographer* in 1980, namely that of the tourism area life cycle (or TALC). Indeed, a situation of underutilization corresponds to the initial stages of Butler's life cycle, labelled either 'Exploration' or 'Involvement', creating a situation in which many attractions are already in place, but when demand and the subsequent income generated is not yet sufficient to cover the costs, for example to promote the destination or to render the destination and its attractions accessible, then attempts need to be made to valorize these attractions adequately.

The situation of overtourism is reflected in the life cycle's 'stagnation' stage. In fact, in his original article, Butler indicates that a 'critical range of elements of capacity' exists and, hence, he suggests that, above a certain threshold, tourism becomes what now is called overtourism. Surpassing this critical range of elements of capacity, or the tourist carrying capacity (see for example Van der Borg, 2017 or Bertocchi et al., 2020), provokes the appearance and growth of a whole range of economical, logistical, social and environmental externalities that cause the balance between collective benefits and collective costs to turn negative. This not only hurts the pertinent interests of the locals and of the firms that are not part of the tourism industry, but eventually also hurts the destination's visitors and, therefore, in the end also the tourism industry.

These considerations seem to lend themselves to another interpretation. Following Raworth (2017), a destination might be represented as a doughnut. The tourism doughnut has two boundaries, very similar to the "critical range of elements of capacity" of Butler's TALC model. In addition, the various, rather concrete and – at a destination level – easy to identify dimensions of the impacts that tourism generates (see for example Mathieson and Wall, 1982) are very similar to the different variables or dimensions Raworth presents in her model of the economy. The first boundary, the inner one, is the social boundary. The second boundary is the environmental or biophysical one. Paraphrasing O'Neil and Nalbandian (2018), pursuing a doughnut-type development for a tourism destination means, on one hand, using tourism in "meeting the people's basic needs" (the earlier-mentioned social, inner boundary), but not so intensive "as to transgress planetary boundaries" (the ecological, outer boundary).

In the doughnut model, the level and type of development of the economy that remains stuck below the social boundary is not able to satisfy the basic needs of the people (Raworth, 2017, calls this a *shortfall*), a situation that looks very much like the one that reigns in Butler's first stage of tourism development, of the underutilization of tourism assets, which was described in the previous paragraphs. And overshooting the ecological boundary has similarities with that of the violation of the already mentioned tourism-carrying capacity. The violation of the carrying capacity involves, as was already argued, the emergence of negative (environmental) damage that is incompatible with the destination's sustainability. Overtourism is therefore reconcilable with Raworth's overshooting of the outer boundary of the (tourism) doughnut. Representing a tourism system using the doughnut paradigm helps to understand the two dilemmas of tourism development, that is developing tourism to such a level that the needs of the stakeholders are served, while avoiding overshooting of the tourist carrying capacity so that the negative impact does not explode.

Obviously, Raworth's model seems better suited for the national or even the global level. Nevertheless, a number of important cities that are also looking for a sustainable tourism development path, such as Amsterdam (Van den Bosch, 2020), have embraced doughnut thinking to update their urban development strategy.

The core of the destination's tourism offer consists of primary tourism products. These are not only unique and hardly reproducible, but they also belong to what economists call public goods or common goods, and they are therefore non-exclusive and non-excludable. This, obviously, is not only true for many natural resources (beaches, forests, lakes, wildlife, and so on), but also, and maybe even more frequently so, for many cultural-historic resources (such as churches, palaces, gardens, and town squares). Some cities of art, and Venice is a very good example, are monuments in their totality.

This gives rise to the risk that destinations fall victim to what is called the *tragedy of the commons* (Hardin, 1968). In Hardin's article in *Science*, he describes a pasture that is "open to all." He asks us to imagine the grazing of animals on a common ground. Individuals that aim to increase their wealth are pushed to add to their flocks. Yet, every animal added to the total helps to degrade the commons marginally but significantly. Although the degradation for each additional animal is small relative to the gain in wealth for the owner, if all owners follow this pattern the commons will ultimately be destroyed. And, assuming that all actors maximize their wealth, each owner continuous to add to their flock:

> Therein is the tragedy. Each man is locked into a system that compels him to increase his herd without limit – in a world that is limited. Ruin is the destination

toward which all men rush, each pursuing his own interest in a society that believes in the freedom of the commons. (Hardin, 1968)

In many of these situations, the problem lies in the fact that perfectly reasonable individual behavior causes long-term damage to the common good, to others and, eventually, to oneself. The discussion regarding urban commons has recently gained momentum (see for instance Borch and Kornberger, 2015). The problems regarding the tourist destination are even more complicated. Not only are local inhabitants, local tourism firms and individual visitors competing for the unlimited use of the destination's amenities, but multinational tourism firms are also directly or indirectly using them without a corresponding fee that expresses the intrinsic value the amenities possess. And because tourism development immediately introduces external users and producers, the problem of the commons is even more profound in the case of tourism.

In effect, while urban tourism assets are, because of their uniqueness and non-reproducibility, extremely scarce, the fee that the visitors in particular are paying for using them is surprisingly often equal to zero, or in any case not at all in line with their use-values or the costs linked to their conservation. The absence of some kind of a market (or pricing) mechanism as an implicit and automatic instrument of regulating the use of heritage makes it that tourism development tends to become unsustainable in the end: since visitors are not paying (enough) for using the cultural-historic assets or, as indeed is the case for Venice, for the city of art as a whole, they will never perceive the scarcity of these assets and the demand for those assets will tend to infinity. Once total effective tourism demand has reached the destination's capacity to absorb these visitors, negative externalities, such as wear-and-tear, congestion, pollution, and gentrification of inhabitants and economic activities, will rapidly emerge and make the destination unattractive for inhabitants, commuters, residential tourists and, in the end, even visitors themselves (Van der Borg, 2017).

There is a strong connection between the sustainability of tourism development and the different stages of tourism development. Van der Borg (1991) shows that during the *first stage* of tourism development of the destination, which is characterized by a relatively strong, yet almost unused, primary tourism product being used by mostly day-trippers, and also because the secondary product is fairly underdeveloped, tourism hardly contributes to the local economy. On the contrary, in this stage the first investments are being made, especially those that render the destination accessible, and only after this crucial infrastructure has been put in place will people start to come en masse.

The net effect of tourism for the local economy is certainly positive in the *second stage* and the first part of the third stage of the cycle. The destination is now complete, its reputation very strong, and residential tourists are thus eager to visit it, spending their conspicuous holiday budgets on everything the tourism industry offers them during their stay that, per definition, lasts more than 24 hours. Tourism is now one of the pillars of the local economy, contributing strongly to the income that locals earn, to the number of jobs, as well as to some essential facilities (airports, cultural facilities, exhibition centers, stations, and so on) that are used by visitors and locals alike. Inhabitants and all local firms perceive tourism as beneficial for, respectively, their wellbeing and their profits.

The situation changes somewhere in the *third stage*. Although demand continues to rise, albeit much more slowly than before, the number of residential tourists is already diminishing, a decline compensated by a rise in day-trippers. This means that the benefits generated by the visitors might very well decline, notwithstanding the continuous expansion of total tourism demand. Moreover, since it is probably in that precise moment that the tourist carrying capacity is reached and surpassed, the already mentioned negative externalities will rise exponentially. The net impact of tourism for the local economy is now most likely to be negative.

The negative externalities will have a devastating effect on the non-reproducible touristic 'commons' and quality tourism will shift its focus away from the destination in question to more attractive alternatives, leaving the destination with an increasingly poorer and, in the *fourth stage*, even declining number of day tourists. Again, the balance between benefits and costs that are generated by tourism are *per saldo* negative.

Understanding the mechanisms that are responsible for keeping urban tourism unsustainable or that push urban tourism development to violating the outer boundaries of sustainability will help us to design the research agenda for urban tourism and, eventually, create and implement proper urban tourism policies.

Towards a research agenda for urban tourism

After having presented the nature of and the mechanisms that determine urban tourism development and its sustainability, it now become possible to identify the various focal points of a research agenda for the coming years.

On the basis of the chapters of the book and the discussion above, a research agenda for urban tourism might be formulated, referring to three important pillars: (1) research into the specificity of urban tourism and of urban tourists; (2) research into the sustainability of urban tourism; (3) research into the policies that make and keep urban tourism sustainable. These three pillars will be discussed further in the next sections.

Research into the specificity of urban tourism and of urban tourists

The first important issue that ought to be addressed by research is the conceptualization of urban tourism itself. Notwithstanding the importance that the urban segment of the tourism market seems to represent, further studies on what urban tourism actually is are urgently needed. In his chapter of this book, Richards has already paid explicit attention to the importance of the question of what urban tourism actually is for analysis and for policy. In addition. Edwards et al. (2008) in their article pay quite some attention to this question.

Generally speaking, two important and fundamentally different approaches can be found in literature.

The *first approach* is that of understanding the peculiarities of urban tourism from a motivational point of view, putting the "urbanness" of the traveler central in the discussion.

This demand side approach has taken two directions. Some authors (see for example Bellini and Pasquinelli, 2017) have argued that the origin of the visitors, that is the place they travel from, is an important element in defining urban tourism. Since a majority of the world population lives in cities and has a high propensity to travel, it is supposed that this fact alone makes them 'urban' during their vacations.

Others (see Edwards et al., 2008, for a review of the literature on this theme) have successfully shown that visitors of cities have a number of important characteristics in common, like a distinct interest in the cultural offer of the places they visit. In fact, Richards suggests in this book that an urban tourist might very well be a specific type of cultural tourist, as motivations related to culture provide the best explanation for people to travel to cities. In fact, a broad spectrum of culture-centered, urban tourism niches seem to exist, all more or less belonging to the family of urban tourism, for example travel to visit friends and relatives (in fact, an important motive for visiting cities), slum tourism, industrial tourism, festival tourism, sports tourism, conference tourism, film-induced tourism, and so on. Obviously, the role of culture in each of these segments differs, but it is beyond discussion that culture in the broad sense is an important part of the drive of people to visit cities. Moreover, the growing importance of multipurpose holidaying makes it increasingly difficult to pin down a single motive that has moved the urban tourist.

It is obvious that much more research is needed here. More research efforts have to be put into fine-tuning the already existing consumer-oriented definitions of urban tourism, especially looking into the behavior of the visitors once they have reached the city, as the destination of their trip or their vacation.

However, not many destinations, in general, and urban destinations in particular, organize regular visitor surveys to reconstruct the profile of their visitors and understand their logistical and economical behavior. The icon of urban tourism, Venice, for example, surprisingly organized its most recent visitor survey in 2012. Traditional visitor surveys are indeed difficult to organize, time-consuming and expensive, which scares policymakers off. This makes reliable statistical information on a (sub)municipal level extremely scarce. In fact, most statistics on tourism are systematically gathered for countries rather than regions or municipalities. Information on a subnational level is often anecdotal, because it is principally based on targeted case studies, and incomparable with that of similar realities, urban or not. Moreover, since almost all available statistics are based on the registration of the clients of official tourism accommodation, the variables considered in a systematic and continuous way are mainly regarding the arrivals and overnight stays in these structures and a number of additional characteristics, such as the nationality of the clients and the period of the year the registrations were made.

This makes the analysis of tourism on a destination level especially difficult and often partial, whether dealing with issues regarding the competitiveness or the sustainability of tourism development. It remains, for example, unclear what exactly has triggered the visits to a destination in the first place, and hence not knowing what are the unique selling propositions, essential for evaluating a competitive position, makes it difficult to determine competitive positions of destinations. With the growth of day tourism, most destinations underestimate the number of visitors and with it the positive and negative impacts. Take for example the subject of Chapter 6, the City of Venice: although estimates differ because of methodological difference, roughly 75% of the visitors to Venice are day tourists that remain outside the reach of official statistics, but certainly not out of the reach of big data analysis. The same is true for the collective benefits and costs that they produce. Paradoxically, 50% of the day tourists are officially registered as residential tourists in places as far as 500 km distance from Venice. Venice is not the only destination with a so-called functional tourism region (Van der Borg, 1991) that is much bigger than the corresponding administrative region. This phenomenon can be observed for most popular cities of art: Barcelona, Bruges, Dubrovnik, Prague, to name but a few well-documented cases. Saving some money on accommodation is an important reason for not choosing a central location.

The absence of sufficiently detailed, more or less comparable and, moreover, systematically gathered statistical information on the motivation behind touristic consumption of urban environments and the behavior of city trippers, means there is understandably a major handicap for tourism research and also for urban tourism research. As suggested before, big data analysis might solve the basic profile data problem, but it does not address motivation.

This is probably the reason for the fact that many authors prefer the *second way of delimiting urban tourism*, focusing on supply rather than on demand: urban tourism is simply and rather tautologically defined as tourism that has cities as destinations, a definition that is driven from the characteristics of the supply rather than that of the demand. In other words, all visitors to cities are urban tourists, whatever their motivations, profile, or logistical or economical behavior once they are at their destinations. Given the importance of multipurpose holidaying that has been growing continuously until the COVID-19 crisis struck, this seemed to make some sense, as was explained before.

In reality, the touristic offer of many cities is variegated. Part of the offer is what many will consider as typically "urban": museums, monuments, historical neighborhoods, theatres, cinemas, conference venues, shopping malls, concert halls, iconic spots that feature in films and TV series, stadiums, and so forth. Furthermore, the offer increasingly consists of immaterial ingredients, of unique and authentic experiences (Pine and Gilmore, 1999). Richards and Wilson (2007) mention in this context the existence of creative tourism experiences, and since urban tourism is to a large extent cultural tourism, the idea of creative tourism that they launched has become extremely relevant for urban destinations as well (see also Chapter 3 by Richards in this book). On the other hand, many urban areas offer also numerous attractions that can be considered as typically 'non-urban': beaches, mountains, rural bubbles, deserts, forests, theme parks, and so on. Day tourists in particular might very well be attracted by such a non-urban attraction and be labelled as urban tourists for the simple fact that the attraction is located in an urban area. Moreover, with the increasing numbers of 'non-urban' elements the boundary between urban, suburban and rural becomes increasingly blurred.

Taking into account a number of the above-mentioned considerations, it seems absolutely necessary to direct future research efforts to defining urban tourism more precisely and trying to allow researchers, entrepreneurs and policymakers to distinguish urban tourism more precisely from other forms of tourism. This will help, for example, urban destinations to evaluate their competitiveness more effectively, to improve the quality of the statistical information they produce, and, therefore, to measure the impacts of tourism on the urban environment and, consequently, of the sustainability of tourism development, more precisely. Eventually, also urban tourism policies, which are founded on these measurements, will become more adequate because they are evidence-based rather than improvising.

Profiling visitors and keeping track of the hotspots that tourists visit, of their expenditure, and of their perception of the quality of the touristic offer, is getting easier. While Keul literally stalked visitors to respectively Salzburg, Austria (Keul and Kühberger, 1997), Shoval pioneered using new technologies to monitor visitors to Akko, Israel (Shoval, 2008). The rapid diffusion of new information and communication technologies allows researchers to gather detailed information on tourists and tourism. This is especially true for urban destinations that are rich in ICT facilities and visited by persons that have a relatively high propensity to use ICT not only during but also for their visit. Many different authors have discussed the opportunities that ICT, in combination with big and open data paradigms, offer to understanding tourism better (Mariani et al., 2014). Mobile phones allow researchers to track the movements of visitors almost in real time, the scraping of portals and the analysis of social media allow researchers to perform sentiment analysis, security cams allow researchers to measure phenomena such as congestion, while smart paying systems allow researchers to get a better grip on the expenditure of visitors. Future urban tourism research might contribute to improving still rudimentary ICT-based research methods and fine-tuning them.

Moreover, and this is going to be the most important challenge, the different traditional sources of information should be combined with the novel sources of information by creating an integrated information system, a sort of dashboard that supports research into urban tourism and helps policymakers devise innovative, ICT based, urban tourism policies. Bertocchi et al. (2020) have argued that only recently have tourism observatory tools and dashboards been considered relevant and strategic to monitor tourism growth, performance of the destination's tourism industry, the impacts generated, as well as trends in demand and supply and the appeal of territories and regions for visitors (Haldrup and Larsen, 2009; Benito et al., 2014). Destination managers are finally starting to adopt these tools more systematically, not only to collect and to store an entire dataset pertaining to a single destination in one digital location, but also to have a place where such data are translated into indicators and knowledge that is able to support decision-makers in developing sustainable (or smart) tourism strategies. In addition, observatories can help to uncover the interconnected economic relationships created by business networks and make tourism forecasts capable of monitoring and informing the number of visitors that cities can attract, thus allowing an analysis of how tourists interact with the local economy and society in urban destinations. While this is true in general, it is more so for such an important slice of the tourism market such as city tourism.

With these new tools, researchers, entrepreneurs and policymakers operating in cities will be able to monitor, often in real time, tourism activity in their territories, either locally or nationally, and provide timely and reliable insights on a destination's evolution, trends, dynamics and market position (Milheiro et al., 2011). As argued by Varra et al. (2012) the so-called *tourist destination observatories* are tools of innovation, they define new codified and shared processes for the development of a destination, and their design is based on the monitoring of phenomena linked to the competitiveness and sustainability of a destination and the active involvement of stakeholders. Moreover, observatories can become an important tool providing support and leadership among all stakeholders, helping to cultivate a constructive and positive energy. This eventually improves the quality of the governance and of the organizing capacity of the urban destination.

Fine-tuning definitions of urban tourism and city tripping, using these definitions to improve measuring the importance of urban tourism in all its dimensions is the first challenge here. On the basis of these measurements and also embracing big and open data analysis, urban tourism observatories or dashboards should be designed that help the different stakeholders that are involved in urban tourism development to make it more sustainable and safer. Very important here are not only the concrete and economic dimensions of sustainability, but also the immaterial (experiences) and social dimensions of sustainability. These challenges together form the first fundamental pillar of the future research agenda for urban tourism.

Research into the sustainability of urban tourism

After the turn of the millennium, much more attention has been paid to the concept of sustainable tourism development, especially when applied to urban environments, than in the past. As was discussed in the previous section and was illustrated by the various case studies presented in this book, much progress has been made since the first specific studies on urban tourism were published in the 1980s and 1990s. Nevertheless, there still remain a number of important gaps in our knowledge regarding the sustainability of urban tourism development. Studies that deal with sustainable urban tourism development should therefore continue to be an important second pillar of our research agenda for the coming years.

A lot has already been said about sustainable urban tourism in the various chapters of this book. In particular, the different cases that have been presented have shown that the sustainability of tourism development processes is far from automatic. On the contrary, following Hardy's idea of the tragedy of the commons, leaving tourism development merely to improvisation will almost always lead to some form of unsustainability, whether it is environmental, economic or social. This has always been evident for tourism development in delicate and sensitive natural environments. Thanks to the rather recent discussion about overtourism, however, have researchers have invested an increasing amount of energy in sustainable urban tourism development.

The terms under- and overtourism imply that two forms of unsustainable tourism exist, together with some optimal level of tourism development, which indeed is sustainable but which needs adequate and innovative tourism policies to achieve this level and to consolidate it. The contents of such policies will form the third pillar of the research agenda and will be discussed hereafter. The different cases that have been discussed in this book all deal with the way tourism development may contribute to the urban economy and the urban society. In both Addis Ababa and Rotterdam, but also in the North American and Chinese contexts, attention still seems to be focused first on the ability tourism has to boost economic and social development, even if the first warning signals have alarmed some policymakers (see for example the case of Rotterdam in Chapter 7 of this book) that the pressure tourism is exerting on the urban system has increased too fast. The other cases that are presented in this book, in particular the cases of Barcelona, Bruges, Stockholm and Venice, are a confirmation of the existence of the second form of unsustainability, namely that of tourism exerting an excessive pressure on the urban system.

In the various chapters in the book, a number of consolidated and widely used theoretical constructs were presented that might be used to find a synthesis between these two opposite, but equally undesirable, forms of unsustainability. The first is the destination development scenario. Empirical evidence of the existence of what may be called a tourism destination life cycle and the implications of the cycle for the sustainability of tourism development (see the previous section) has become widely available. This is especially true for urban destinations (see for example Chapter 11 by Feng, Derudder and Zhu). It is evident that more research is needed to extensively test the TALC model for urban destinations in different geographical and economical contexts and to understand the mechanisms that are supposed to underlie the transformations of urban destinations over the tourism life cycle.

It has already been argued (see for example Van der Borg, 1991) that the very idea of unsustainability can be expressed in terms of collective costs generated by tourism, of collective benefits generated by tourism, and of the balance between them. Moreover, it is assumed that the balance between these collective costs is negative in both forms of unsustainability. In the case of under-tourism benefits are marginal and the costs of creating the facilities needed to host visitors and to promote the destination are huge, while in the case of over-tourism, as was also made clear by the reports of the UNWTO on overtourism and the report on overtourism presented to the European Parliament, negative externalities such as crowding, the rise in the cost of living, gentrification, pollution and wear-and-tear, will outweigh the collective benefits, notably gross income, employment and the positive effects facilities for tourists have on the quality of life of the inhabitants. Although this discourse seems rather intuitive, not much systematic research has been done to measure or quantify the impact of tourism development on urban systems. First of all, many studies merely focus on the collective benefits of tourism development and simply forget about the collective costs. Second, since many of these impacts are hard to monetarize, most analyses of benefits and costs are inventories of impacts at best and fail to quantify both the single positive and negative impacts as well as their balance. Exploring ways to quantify benefits and costs related to urban tourism development is an important future challenge for research on urban tourism. Obviously, research into the impacts of urban tourism is closely linked to that into the profile and the behavior of urban tourists and that into the peculiarities of urban tourism that was described before (the first pillar of the research agenda).

This way of reasoning suggests that there are two critical thresholds to the sustainability of urban tourism development. A minimum threshold, below which tourism development is still too timid to make up for the energies that are invested in putting the destination on the map, and a maximum threshold, above which tourism development is excessive with respect to the destination's ability to accommodate visitors without the different subsystems the destination possesses being overwhelmed and the earlier-mentioned externalities starting to explode. This leads us to another theoretical construct, often criticized, namely that of the carrying capacity. This tourism carrying capacity has been discussed intensively in the literature. One of its most recent utilizations, as was mentioned before, is that of Bertocchi et al. (2020) for the case of Venice. This simple analysis of Venice's carrying capacity has always been very policy induced. Although the linear programming model that was used to reconstruct the carrying capacity of Venice, that is maximizing the benefits linked to tourism development subject to a number of linear restrictions that reflect the capacities of the principal subsystems that are used by inhabitants and visitors alike, seems intuitive enough, the criticism on the use of the concept of the carrying capacity is fundamental and widespread. This criticism ranges from the biased choice of the dimension that is maximized, e.g. income from tourism, to the fact that the capacity restrictions do not take into account the fact that these restrictions can be modified or that they do not model the conflict between inhabitants and visitors realistically enough. Further research into the tourist carrying capacity of urban destinations is required, and there is still much room to present innovative ways to model the tourist carrying capacity as well as to investigate the relationships between inhabitants and visitors more intensely. The work that has recently been done by Neuts and Nijs on the attitude of inhabitants with respect to tourism development, described in Chapter 5, is very promising in this respect.

A further element that deserves the attention of researchers is to find a model of urban tourism that is capable of wrapping the various ingredients of what can be called a model of sustainable tourism together. As was already suggested, the ideas of Raworth (2017) might offer an interesting opportunity in this respect. In fact, the doughnut economy envisages both the under- as well as the overutilization of the resources the world possesses. The doughnut as such has two boundaries, a lower one and an outer one. If economic development is not strong enough to reach the lower boundary, many of the socioeconomic goals that are functional to satisfying the needs of the economic agents can't be satisfied and, hence, development does not meet the sustainability goals that have been defined by the United Nations. If, however, the pace of economic development is exceeding the outer boundary, many economical goals are reached but in particular ecological goals are jeopardized. Since Raworth's model works in essence at a macroeconomic level, it seems to make sense to decline her ideas at the meso level, to the level of the destination. Complex urban tourism systems are perfect candidates for testing the concept of what may be called the *doughnut destination*.

Many studies exist on the issue of how to strengthen the reputation or a brand of a destination. The use of what may be called traditional instruments to enhance the reputation of an urban destination is usually discussed in cases of undertourism, in places where tourism needed a strong boost to offset the shrinking of the economic base due to deindustrialization: the organization of megaevents, the construction of iconic buildings, and other city marketing efforts. More recently, considerations regarding the possibility of using city marketing and branding techniques to counter situations of overtourism have gained importance – see for example Braun et al. (2013) and Zenker et al. (2017). The way (selective) city marketing policies can help destinations to become more sustainable and how they can be of support to visitor management strategies offers an interesting theme for urban tourism research.

Last but not least, as for example Ashworth and Page (2011) have argued, the urban tourism system does not find itself in some kind of bubble but is an integral part of the urban system. Tourism development is strongly linked, for better or worse, with urban development in general. Urban tourism researchers seem to be very much unaware of the existence of the dynamics of urban development at large and, at the same time, many urban researchers (economists, geographers as well as planners) seem to be underestimating the power that tourism has to change urban development trajectories. This is indeed a paradox, and any research agenda for urban tourism should try to anchor an urban tourism discourse in a more general study of urban systems and the way they seem to develop.

This leads us to the following challenges regarding the second pillar of the research agenda for urban tourism, which treats sustainability of urban tourism in detail:

1. Test the TALC model for urban destinations, using an increasing amount of empirical evidence, in different geographical and economical contexts to better understand the mechanisms that are supposed to underlie the transformations of urban destinations over the tourism life cycle;
2. Explore ways to quantify benefits and costs related to urban tourism development;
3. Perform research into the tourist carrying capacity of urban destinations;
4. Elaborate on Raworth's idea of sustainable development and design what might be called a *doughnut destination*;
5. See to what extent classical instruments that were used to boost urban tourism development (for example events and city branding) can also help, for example by being more selective and supporting visitor management strategies, urban destinations become and stay sustainable;
6. Explicitly embed an urban tourism discourse in a more general study of urban systems and the way they seem to develop.

Having understood sustainable urban tourism development in all its facets, the third pillar of the research agenda deals with urban tourism policy.

Research into the policies that make and that keep urban tourism sustainable

The third pillar of the research agenda for urban tourism ideally builds upon the first two. In effect, without a thorough knowledge of the urban tourist and urban tourism and without knowing what sustainable tourism development is and what its underlying mechanism are, it is impossible to design adequate and innovative urban tourism development policies. These policies should be aimed at making and keeping tourism development in cities sustainable, e.g. within the lower and outer boundary of the urban destination doughnut. A number of concrete examples of these policies were mentioned in the closing chapters of this book.

One of the first considerations that has emerged in the general debate about tourism policies after the COVID-19 crisis is that a new business model for urban tourism is urgently needed. The prevailing business model for city tourism was nothing more than a translation of the traditional sun-sand-and-sea business model that was applied to cultural and urban tourism without making fundamental changes. This business model system-atically chooses quantity over quality, economies of scale over economies of scope, and the fate of the tourism industry over that of the inhabitants. It has turned many smaller flourishing and highly diversified cities into touristic monocultures. The pandemic has shown first of all how extremely fragile such a business model is, both in terms of economic as well as social resilience. Moreover, it has strengthened the call for a more responsible, sustainable and safe way to travel. Generally speaking, as was also argued by Zenker in the pre-vious chapter, a research agenda for urban tourism should first of all address the question how a post-pandemic business model for tourism in general and for urban tourism in particular might actually look like.

More concretely, before tourism will return on its pre-COVID-19 trajectory, this new business model should lead to urban tourism policies – at least if we believe Butler's TALC is a useful representation of a destination's development process – that ought to be designed so that they are anticyclical, and, therefore, explicitly disruptive. In practice, this means that when a destination finds itself in the stages of exploration or involvement, tourism policies should be proac-tive and constructive. On the other hand, in the consolidation and saturation stage, tourism policies should be oriented towards consolidating the number of visitors, rather than looking for its continuous growth, and improving their quality in terms of their net impact on the urban economy and society, for example through innovative visitor management strategies that are supported by the implementation of new technologies. Much attention has been paid to using new technologies, for example smartphones, tablets and internet portals to make destinations smarter and, hence, more resilient to especially excessive tourism demand. In Chapter 12, Koens and Klijs provide a number of concrete examples of, as they have called them, smart city hospitality systems. In addition, Petrić and Mandić in their chapter offer many concrete examples of smart destination initiatives in Croatia. As was already mentioned, these policies should be supported by dashboards that provide crucial intel to inhabitants, visitors, entrepreneurs and policymakers, a DSS that uses big and open data paradigms to collect *and* supplies old and new types of information regarding the tourism system in real time.

But notwithstanding the level of sophistication of the technologies introduced to make tourism smarter, the management of public space and public facilities, with the objective of guaranteeing their accessibility for inhabitants and visitors and safeguarding an optimal level of utilization, might become even more important than it already was before 2020. Russo, Sora and Scarnato, in their chapter discussing the case of Barcelona, have paid explicit attention to the tensions between locals and visitors and how these tensions have entered the political agenda of the Mayor of Barcelona. Indeed, the question how exactly to efficiently and effectively allocate public space and public facilities in urban destinations, where conflicts between inhabitants, local firms and visitors are very likely to emerge, should be high on the research agenda for urban tourism.

Much has already been written about traditional tourism policies, such as tourism marketing and destination development. However, the awareness that tourism policy is strongly intertwined with other urban policy has always been present but has become even stronger recently due to the overtourism debate. Tourism is a transversal phenomenon that runs diagonally through all the sectors of the urban economy and all the spheres of urban life. The expansion of the so-called sharing economy has changed the urban tourism system radically. In particular, the accommodation sector and local transportation have been changing greatly because of the entrance of players in the market such as Airbnb and Uber. Sometimes, these social and technological innovations have been given too much blame for what has been going wrong in many urban destinations that are struggling with overtourism. Many of the negative consequences of the explosive expansion of the informal accommodation sector or of the peer-to-peer transportation services are principally a consequence of the 'wrong' tourism business model that cities have been pursuing rather than their cause. Probably, many of the social costs incurred by the sharing economy can easily be smoothened by implementing the correct housing policies or local public transportation policies. Moreover, research in Antwerp, Utrecht and Venice has shown that users of B&Bs are often quite interesting visitors to cities and surely preferable over day-trippers. Nevertheless, it makes sense to investigate the tourism edge in traditionally non touristic urban policies more intensively.

Obviously, the synchronization of the timing in which tourism policies are implemented with that of the different stages of tourism development is also essential for the success they will have. If a policy is not implemented in a timely fashion, the results obtained may be even more devastating than not implementing a policy at all. More research is needed to support the correct temporization of urban tourism policies.

As far as the concrete ingredients of adequate and innovative urban tourism strategies are concerned, a number of interesting fields of research are still offering a lot of opportunities for further exploration. Some additional suggestions can be found below.

The first regards the need for infrastructural interventions and investments in facilities that enhance safety and sustainability. A buffer of terminals should be created around historic centers or cities that succeed in intercepting the flows of visitors before they mix with the flows of commuters and arrive in the historic center. Splitting the inbound and outbound visitor flows from the commuter flows allows the local transport companies to avoid congestion, reducing capacity costs on public transport and, in addition, diversifying the city's access points and terminals which, especially in the peak period of the tourist season, often cannot withstand the flow. Communication is an important instrument in this respect. A revisitation of the city marketing literature might be worthwhile here. Additional research on the impact of these types of infrastructures and of facilities and in communication is urgently needed, especially in destinations that were prone to overtourism.

Visitor management interventions ought to be based on reservations and incentives. A reservation system could be put in place to regulate the visits to successful destinations. Such a system would make all visitors, and therefore day tourists in particular, aware of the scarcity of the primary tourism product the destination offers, forcing visitors to plan their visit rather than improvise it. Reserving a visit to a city may also be non-mandatory when the correct incentives are created that will push tourists to practice it anyway. It will be enough to make a destination "difficult" and very expensive for those who do not book, and "easy" and relatively cheap for those who announce their intention to come early. For those who are willing to reserve, however, fast lanes might be created, and a discount package made available, which includes not only benefits on public transport and museums, but also in private establishments such as hotels, restaurants and shops. Limited access to unique attractions could be the killer application that determines the success of such a system. A city card for tourists might be the system integrator that wraps the various possible incentives together. The City of Dubrovnik in Croatia has been implementing policies that go in this direction (see, for instance, Camatti et al., 2020). What seems unconstitutional, however, is to close a destination as such to visitors and ask for an entrance ticket. More research into the economic and logistic behavior of visitors (the first pillar of our agenda) and the impact of such a reservation system on the quality of the experience of both the visitors and the inhabitants as well as on the turnover of the local tourism firms is needed.

Finally, the desirability of fiscal policies should be high on the research agenda for urban tourism. As has been argued by Van der Borg (1991), disincentivizing price policies and tourism taxation are often useless in the struggle against unsustainable tourism development. In practice, the existing taxation schemes are neither raising enough resources to restore the balance between collective benefits and costs, nor are they having the effect Pigou foresaw when undesirable behavior is taxed. This can be easily explained. Both in the case of under- as well as overtourism, the share of day tourists in the overall number of visitors is high. Day tourists are hardly using any facilities nor are they consuming much during their visit to the destination. This is especially true for accommodation, since they either visit the destination of their excursion from their homes or from their holiday destination. Tourism taxes, however, are usually raised through the accommodation sector as a fixed mark-up of the price per person per night of a room. This thus exempts day tourists from paying this tax; worse, they may even pay tourism taxes in the places where they sleep rather than there where they generate most of the collective costs. It is for this reason that some destinations, among them Venice, are studying methods to explicitly tax all forms of day tourism rather than residential tourism. The study of efficient and effective ways to make visitors contribute to both the investments in facilities that are required to become a destination in the first place, as well as to the maintenance of the urban system in the case of overtourism, ought to be high on any research agenda for urban tourism.

A certainly non-exhaustive list of themes for a research agenda for urban tourism that address the issues related to the governance of an urban tourism system and urban tourism policies that result from the discussion above is the following.

1. Design the contours of a business model for tourism in general and for urban tourism in particular;

2. Find ways to efficiently and effectively allocate public space and public facilities in urban destinations among the different categories of city users;
3. Investigate the tourism edge in traditionally non-touristic urban policies much more intensively;
4. Study the correct timing of the implementation of the many possible urban tourism policies that have been proposed;
5. Understand the impact of important investments in fundamental infrastructures and facilities in destinations faced with under- and with overtourism;
6. Analyze the economic and logistic behavior of visitors and the impact of visitor management techniques (for example a reservation system) on this behavior, on the quality of the experience of both the visitors and the inhabitants as well as on the turnover of the local tourism firms;
7. Study efficient and effective ways to make visitors truly contribute, also financially, to the destination they visit.

Following the research themes that were formulated, in this book in general and this chapter in particular, an agenda for urban tourism research for the coming decade has thus been given shape.

Concluding remarks

Over the past few decades, tourism has grown to become one of the principal cornerstones of the global economy as well as part of the economic base of almost all cities in the world. The COVID-19 pandemic has not only shown how fundamental tourism is for the global economy, but also how vulnerable the tourism system is to disruptive events. This is especially true for cities that were hit particularly hard by the COVID-19 crisis. But sooner rather than later, tourism will recover and an adequate and innovative strategy – which is able to help urban destinations to recover, to consolidate and to flourish again – ought to be in place.

The current research agenda for urban tourism is a first, but important, step in a process that transforms urban tourism systems into something much more sustainable and safer. It thus supplies policymakers, tourism entrepreneurs and academics with a plausible trajectory for future research into various forms of urban tourism. This trajectory reflects the idea that tourism development might indeed be a powerful engine of development for cities and urban areas in general, and art cities, but only if the right balance is struck between appreciating and promoting urban tourism, on the one hand, and the conservation of the immaterial and material cultural goods uniquely possessed by them on the other.

By embracing a development strategy that focuses on sustainable urban tourism, the assets that are the fundament of urban tourism development will be used optimally. Only then will the various stakeholders involved, that is the local population, local entrepreneurs and visitors, truly benefit from the opportunities that tourism offers them, especially in the longer run. The current COVID-19 pandemic might very well accelerate the process towards a new business model for urban tourism, in which quality is preferred to quality and in which the local population and local entrepreneurs play a central role. Hopefully, this research agenda will contribute to constructing a sound foundation for such a new business model and support an innovative and visionary development strategy for urban tourism that might help eliminate a number of the paradoxes in research and in policy that have persisted for decades.

References

Ashworth, G. and Page, S. (2011) Urban tourism research: Recent progress and current paradoxes. *Tourism Management*, 32(1), 1–15.

Ashworth, G. and Voogd, H. (1990) *Selling the City*. London: Belhaven Press.

Bellini, N. and Pasquinelli, C. (Eds) (2017) *Tourism in the City. Towards an Integrative Agenda on Urban Touri*sm. Heidelberg: Springer.

Benito, B., Solana, J., and López, P. (2014) Determinants of Spanish regions' tourism performance: A two-stage, double-bootstrap data envelopment analysis. *Tourism Economics*, 20(5), 987–1012.

Bertocchi, D., Camatti, N., and Van der Borg, J. (2020) Tourism observatories for monitoring MED destinations performance. The case of ShapeTourism project. *Turizam*, 68, 466–481.

Borch, C. and Kornberger, M. (2015) *Urban Commons. Rethinking the City*. London: Routledge.

Braun, E., Kavaratzis, M. and Zenker, S. (2013) My city – my brand: The different roles of residents in place branding *Journal of Place Management and Development*, 6(1), 18–28.

Butler, R. (1980) The concept of a tourist area cycle of evolution: Implications for management of resource. *Canadian Geographer*, 24(1), 5–12.

Camatti, N., Bertocchi, D., Caric, H., and Van der Borg, J. (2020) A digital response system to mitigate overtourism. The case of Dubrovnik. *Journal of Travel and Tourism Marketing*, 37, 887–901.

Cheshire, P.C. and Hay, D.G. (1989) *Urban Problems in Western Europe, An Economic Analysis*. London: Unwin Hyman.

Costa, P., Gotti, G., and Van der Borg, J. (1996) Tourism in European heritage cities. *Annals of Tourism Research*,), 306–321.23(2), 306–321.

Edwards, D., Griffin, T. and Hayllart, B. (2008) Urban tourism research: Developing an agenda. *Annals of Tourism Research*, 34(4), 1032–1052.

Haldrup, M. and Larsen, J. (2009) *Tourism, Performance and the Everyday*. London: Routledge.

Hardin, G. (1968) The tragedy of the commons. *Science*, 162(3859), 1243–1248.

Jansen-Verbeke, M. (1998) Tourismification of historical cities. *Annals of Tourism Research*, 25(3), 739–742.

Judd, D. and Fainstein, S. (1999) *The Tourist City*. New Haven: Yale University Press.

Keul, A. and Kühberger, A. (1997) Tracking the Salzburg tourist. *Annals of Tourism Research*, 24(4), 1008–1012.

Law, C. (1993) *Urban Tourism Mansell*. London: Mansell Publishing..

Mariani, M., Baggio, R., Buhalis, D., and Longhi, C. (Eds.) (2014) *Tourism Management, Marketing, and Development*. London: Palgrave Macmillan.

Mathieson, A. and Wall, G. (1982) *Tourism: Economic, Physical, and Social Impacts*. London, New York: Longman.

Milheiro, E., Dinis, G., and Elsa Correia, E. (2011) Strategic tools for decision support: The regional tourism observatory of Alentejo. *Tourism & Management Studies*, 143–150.

O'Neil, R. and Nalbandian, J, (2018) Change, complexity, and leadership challenges. *Public Administration Review*, 78(2), 311–314.

Pine, J. and Gilmore, J. (1999) *The Experience Economy: Work is Theatre & Every Business a Stage*. Boston: Harvard Business Review.

Quinn, B. (2007) Performing tourism Venetian residents in focus. *Annals of Tourism Research*, 34, 458–476.

Raworth, K. (2017) *Doughnut Economics: Seven Ways to Think Like a 21st-Century Economist*. London: Random House Business.

Richards, G. and Wilson, J. (2007) Developing creativity in tourist experiences: A solution to the serial reproduction of culture? *Tourism Management*, 27(6), 1209–1223.

Russo, A.P. (2002) The "vicious circle" of tourism development in heritage cities. *Annals of Tourism Research*, 29(1), 165–182.

Shoval, N. (2008) Tracking technologies and urban analysis. *Cities*, 25, 21–28.

Troitiño, Vinuesa M.A. (1995) El Turismo en las Ciudades Históricas. i, 49–66.

Troitiño, Vinuesa M. and Troitiño, Torralba L. (2010) Historic cities and tourism: Functional dynamics and urban policy. *The Open Urban Studies Journal*, 3, 47–57.

UNWTO (2019) *Overtourism? Understanding and Managing Urban Tourism Growth beyond Perceptions. Volume 2: Case Studies*. Madrid: UNWTO.

Van den Berg, L., Van der Borg, J., and Van der Meer, J. (1995) *Urban Tourism*. Aldershot: Ashgate.

Van den Bosch, H. (2020) Humane by choice, smart by default: 39 building blocks for cities of the future. *Smart Cities*, 2(3), 111–121.

Van der Borg, J. (1991) *Tourism and Urban Development*. Amsterdam: Thesis Publishers.

Van der Borg, J. (2017) Sustainable tourism in Venice: What lessons for other fragile cities on water. In S. Caroli and S. Soriani (Eds.), *Fragile and Resilient Cities on Water*. Cambridge Scholars Publishing, 15–32.

Varra, L., Buzzigoli, C., and Loro, R. (2012) Innovation in destination management: Social dialogue, knowledge management processes and servant leadership in the tourism destination observatories. *Procedia–Social and Behavioral Sciences*, 41, 375–385.

Wise, N. and Jimura, T. (Eds.) (2020) *Tourism, Cultural Heritage and Urban Regeneration. Changing Spaces in Historical Places*. Heidelberg: Springer.

Zenker, S., Braun, E., and Petersen, S. (2017) Branding the destination versus the place: The effects of brand complexity and identification for residents and visitors. *Tourism Management*, 58, 15–27.

Index

Printed and bound by CPI Group (UK) Ltd, Croydon, CR0 4YY

16/04/2025

14658490-0005